THURGOOD MARSHALL

Praise for *Thurgood Marshall*

"I highly recommend *Thurgood Marshall* by Mike Davis and Hunter Clark. This impressive book captures the sweeping drama and courageous struggles that have filled Thurgood Marshall's life and career. The story of Justice Marshall is that of one of the greatest Americans in the twentieth century. Davis and Clark provide a compelling portrait of Marshall's immense humanity and integrity in this fine biography." —Congressman John Lewis of Atlanta.

"Thurgood Marshall is a giant of a man at a time when giants are scarce and desperately needed. This wonderful biography takes his measure." —(Rev.) Theodore M. Hesburgh, C.S.C., President Emeritus, University of Notre Dame

"Davis and Clark have given us an engagingly written and conscientiously researched biography of a twentieth-century icon. It should be widely read and much discussed by all who care about the large, principled issues Justice Marshalls' life embodies." —David Levering Lewis, author of *W. E. B. Dubois: Biography of a Race*

THURGOOD MARSHALL

Warrior at the Bar, Rebel on the Bench

Updated and Revised Edition

Michael D. Davis and Hunter R. Clark

093549

A Citadel Press Book
Published by Carol Publishing Group

To the memories of our fathers,
John Preston Davis, 1905–1973,
and Hunter Clark, 1911–1991

A Citadel Press Book
Published by Carol Publishing Group
Citadel Press is a registered trademark of Carol
Communications, Inc.
Editorial Offices: 600 Madison Avenue, New York, N.Y. 10022
Sales and Distribution Offices: 120 Enterprise Avenue, Secaucus,
N.J. 07094
In Canada: Canadian Manda Group, P.O. Box 920, Station U,
Toronto, Ontario M8Z 5P9
Queries regarding rights and permissions should be addressed to
Carol Publishing Group, 600 Madison Avenue, New York, N.Y. 10022

Carol Publishing Group books are available at special discounts
for bulk purchases, for sales promotion, fund-raising, or
educational purposes. Special editions can be created to
specifications. For details, contact: Special Sales Department,
Carol Publishing Group, 120 Enterprise Avenue, Secaucus, N.J.
07094

Manufactured in the United States of America
10 9 8 7 6 5 4 3 2 1

Library of Congress Cataloging-in-Publication Data

Davis, Michael D., 1939–
    Thurgood Marshall : warrior at the bar, rebel on the bench /
Michael D. Davis and Hunter R. Clark.
      p. cm.
    "A Citadel Press book."
    ISBN 0–8065–1494–9 (pbk.)
    1. Marshall, Thurgood, 1908–1993. 2. United States, Supreme
Court—Biography. 3. Judges—United States—Biography. 4. Civil
rights—United States. I. Clark, Hunter R. II. Title.
KF8745.M34D38 1994
347.73'2634—dc20
[B]
[347.3073534]   93–44236
[B]   CIP

Contents

Acknowledgments

The authors would like to exercise their prerogative of thanking a few of the people who made important contributions to *Thurgood Marshall: Warrior at the Bar, Rebel on the Bench.*

Esme Bhan, of Howard University's Moorland-Springarn Research Center, for valuable assistance in locating long-forgotten documents and serving as a sounding board as the manuscript was developing.

The research staff of the New York Public Library's Schomberg Center for Black Culture, for its assistance.

The Baltimore Sunpapers, and especially Ernest Imhoff, for allowing us to use the paper's library.

Hillel Black, our editor, for the dedicated concern and attention of a loving literary father.

Edward A. Novak III, our literary agent, for inspiring us with the remark "I want this to be the book my daughters Anna and Kate read one day to learn about race relations in America." We hope we have met Ed's high expectation.

William L. Robinson, dean of the District of Columbia School of Law, and Brian Baker, research assistant at Catholic University of America's White Law Library, for giving us access to their schools' libraries and research facilities.

Historian and author Arthur Davis, for his constant availability and for offering suggestions, at his insistence, from his hospital bed at George Washington Hospital Center, as we completed the manuscript's final draft.

Attorney Rozan Cater, for her review of the manuscript.

Former *Washington Star* reporter Toni House, Ersa Poston, Federal Judge Constance Baker Motley, Leigh Dingerson, Jon Waterman and Carol Joy Smith for their encouragement and contributions.

The family of Juanita Jackson Mitchell, for allowing us to have precious moments with her in the months before her death.

We are indebted to our publisher, Steven Schragis, whose vision made this book possible.

THURGOOD MARSHALL

ONE

A Rumpled Bear of a Man

> Don't worry, I am going to outlive those bastards.
>
> —Thurgood Marshall

The day after the U. S. Senate confirmed Thurgood Marshall's lifetime appointment to the Supreme Court in 1967, he told his old friend Harvard Law School graduate John P. Davis, "The only thing I have to do now, Johnny, is stay alive." Marshall, questioned frequently about the possibility of retirement years later, each time scoffed at the idea. "I was appointed to a life term, and I intend to serve it," he said in a typical response. But now, on June 28, 1991, after twenty-four years as the only Afro-American ever to sit on the Supreme Court, the time had come for him to go.

He was just four days away from his eighty-third birthday, and in less than six weeks doctors at Bethesda Naval Hospital would put a pacemaker in his chest to stabilize an irregular heartbeat. The years of chain-smoking three packs of Winston cigarettes a day, his fondness for bourbon, fried chicken, and pigs' feet, and the burden of the nation's legal conscience he had carried since he was a fledgling lawyer in his native Baltimore had finally taken their toll. The day before, in a brief note to President George Bush,

3

Thurgood Marshall told him and the nation he was retiring because of his "advancing age and medical condition."

Supreme Court press secretary Toni House had prepared the Court's ornate East Conference Room. The Washington press corps snaked its microphones to the lectern atop the red-carpeted dais. Photographers elbowed their way into advantageous positions, ready to capture on tape and film the parting words of the Supreme Court's most liberal justice.

Marshall, whose intimate friends nicknamed him "Turkey" years ago because of his proud, head-high, defiant strut, entered the room walking slowly, with a cane, but would have none of the thronelike chair House had provided for him. Instead, he sat, facing reporters at eye level, on an antique mahogany chair under an oil portrait of John Jay, the nation's first chief justice. His tie, loosely knotted, was pulled to one side, and his pants were hitched up over his spreading belly, displaying the white surgical socks he wore to prevent a recurrence of the blood clot that had formed in his right leg several years earlier.

His wife, Cecilia "Cissy" Marshall, was there with his law clerks and staff, his son Thurgood, who was a member of Massachusetts senator Edward M. Kennedy's staff, and his daughter-in-law Colleen Mahoney, a lawyer at the Securities and Exchange Commission. They took turns holding their two-year-old son, Thurgood William Marshall, given his middle name in honor of Marshall's closest personal and ideological friend on the Court, retired justice William J. Brennan Jr.

"How do you feel?" a reporter asked.

"With my hands," Marshall replied, displaying his gnarled hands flecked with the brown liver spots of old age. It was vintage Thurgood Marshall. For the next thirty minutes this curmudgeon parried with reporters, punctuating his remarks with his cane and displaying all his legendary fieriness.

The reporter who asked the first question rephrased it, attempting to regain credibility among his smiling colleagues. "What's wrong with you, sir?"

"What's wrong with me?" Marshall barked incredulously in his baritone voice, implying the answer was plainly visible in his sagging shoulders and the deep wrinkles of his eighty-two-year-old face. "I'm old. I'm getting old and coming apart."

Marshall's health had been a subject of Capitol Hill gossip for more than a decade, as both liberals and conservatives speculated about how long the ailing justice could hold on to his seat on the nation's highest court. Marshall had had a heart attack in 1976 and since then had been treated for recurrent bouts of pneumonia and viral bronchitis. In October 1979 he had fallen down the marble steps of the Capitol after an appointment with the Capitol's attending physician, Dr. Freeman H. Carey, fracturing his right wrist and left elbow and sustaining a nasty laceration on his forehead. In August 1990 he had fallen in the lobby of Chicago's Hyatt Regency Hotel, where he was attending the American Bar Association's annual convention. He wore a hearing aid, and for several years his vision had been clouded by glaucoma.

Even earlier, in July 1970, during Marshall's hospitalization for bronchitis at Bethesda Naval Hospital, aides to President Richard M. Nixon quietly inquired about his prognosis. Marshall's attending physician, Captain C. F. Lambdin, would not release the information without his patient's permission. When Lambdin told Marshall about the White House inquiry, Marshall grabbed a red felt-tipped marker from the doctor's pocket and scrawled on his medical folder in bold capital letters NOT YET! He was not about to give President Nixon a conservative appointment to the Court by dying.

Later, in a 1987 interview with columnist Carl Rowan, Marshall made no attempt to hide his displeasure with another president, describing Ronald W. Reagan as the "worst president in my lifetime." He said President Reagan "has done zero for civil rights" and noted that "on the racial issue you can't be a little bit wrong any more than you can be a little bit pregnant or a little bit dead."

In 1988, similarly determined, he told a group of judges and lawyers who questioned him about the Supreme Court's increasingly conservative composition, "Don't worry, I am going to outlive those bastards."

At the final press conference, he was asked, "Do you have any plans for your retirement?"

"Yep."

"What are they?"

"Sit on my rear end."

Pointing his cane at another reporter, who referred to his departure as a "resignation," Marshall quickly corrected him. "It's a retirement," he said.

When a reporter asked him to comment on the status of "black people," he said, "In the first place I am not a 'black people,' I am an Afro-American," making clear his recent personal decision to use that term to describe his race. "Now, you want to talk about an Afro-American?" he asked the reporter. "No, I am not free, certainly I am not free."

And then he began one of his characteristic reminiscences, telling the story of a Pullman porter he knew as a child, one of his father's Baltimore friends who worked on the Baltimore & Ohio Railroad. "He had been in every city in this country, he was sure, and he had never been in any city in the United States where he had to put his hand in front of his face to find out he was a Negro. I agree with him," Marshall said. "No, I am not free."

On the day Marshall announced his retirement, the Supreme Court issued its final opinions for the 1990–91 term. As he had done increasingly in recent years, Marshall found himself on the dissenting side of decisions that struck at the heart of issues vital to him during more than fifty years—as chief counsel for the National Association for the Advancement of Colored People (NAACP), a U.S. appeals court judge, the nation's solicitor general, and a Supreme Court justice.

Several reporters suggested Marshall was leaving in anger and frustration after watching the liberal Court of Chief Justice Earl Warren, which he joined in 1967, move gradually to the right as four Republican presidents—Richard M. Nixon, Gerald R. Ford, Ronald W. Reagan, and George W. Bush—replaced retiring liberal justices with conservatives. Marshall had found a comfortable seat on the Warren Court, which saw its role as protecting individual rights, the poor, women, minorities, criminal defendants, and political dissidents. He replaced centrist Justice Tom C. Clark, whose vote at times created a five-to-four conservative majority. Though Marshall's votes at times swung the Court's posture to liberal positions during his early tenure, the judicial pendulum soon began to swing again to the conservative right.

Chief Justice Warren E. Burger and Justice William H. Rehnquist, Burger's eventual successor as Chief Justice, were appointed by Nixon. Two other Nixon appointments, one by Ford, and three by Reagan placed the Court firmly in the hands of conservatives. By the end of the 1980s the only justices with decidedly liberal records were Marshall and his aging friend Justice Brennan, appointed by President Dwight D. Eisenhower.

The solid conservative majority quickly set about the task of dismantling much of what Marshall, Brennan, and their former liberal colleagues had accomplished. As one of the last Supreme Court justices to believe that Americans could depend on the government and the Court to resolve social problems, Marshall increasingly found himself dissenting from majority opinions. By temperament and experience he was suited to the outsider's role. In fact, many Court observers believe Marshall's best opinions were issued in dissent.

Marshall himself said dissenting opinions were important to him and made that clear when he interviewed candidates for clerkships. "For the past four or five years, whenever I interviewed prospective law clerks I always asked them if they liked writing dissenting opinions," he said in 1975. "If they said no, they didn't get the job."

"If there was a leitmotif to Marshall's dissents," said A. E. Dick Howard, professor of law at the University of Virginia, "it was his concern for the unempowered, the poor, minorities, those outside the mainstream."

At the last press conference, Marshall was asked, "Your retirement has been characterized as leaving in anger or frustration, finding yourself on the dissenting side. Is that true? Is that an accurate characterization?" a reporter asked.

"Who said that?" Marshall snapped.

"It's on the front page of the *New York Times* this morning."

"The front page of the *New York Times* said that I was frustrated?"

"And angry at finding yourself in dissent."

"That's a double-barreled lie. My doctor and my wife and I have been discussing this for the past six months or more. And we all eventually agreed, all three of us, that this was it, and this *is* it."

When asked what major tasks the Supreme Court faced in the years ahead, he said, "To get along without me."

A reporter asked Marshall if the president should replace him with a black judge. "I don't think race should be used as an excuse one way or the other.... I mean for picking the wrong Negro and saying, 'I'm picking him because he is a Negro.' I am opposed to that. My father told me long ago, 'There is no difference between a white snake and a black snake. They both bite.'"

The humor Marshall displayed at his parting press conference was characteristic of the folksy style he embraced all his life. Marshall said early in his career he intended to "wear life like a loose garment." He delighted in using subtle, often off-color humor and his penchant for earthiness to challenge those who took a more traditional approach to their existence. Marshall's background, of course, was much different from those of his Supreme Court brethren, for, after all, he was the only Supreme Court justice who experienced segregation from the back of the bus, the only justice to be chased from rural southern towns by the Ku Klux Klan, and the only justice who had defended a black man accused of murder.

He was fond of putting Chief Justice Warren Burger ill at ease with black street-corner colloquialisms. "What's shaking, Chiefy baby?" was his customary greeting when he encountered Burger in the court's staid halls. Burger would return Marshall's salutation with a puzzled glare. The two men later developed a cordial relationship.

On one occasion Marshall found great pleasure in allowing several white tourists, who mistakenly entered an automated elevator reserved for the justices, to assume he was the operator. They stepped to the rear and called their floor. Marshall, in his best Uncle Tom voice, said, "Yassah, yassah," and pushed the button. When the car arrived at their floor he stepped back and ushered them out, glowing in triumphant delight as he watched them walk down the hallway, slowly realizing who he was.

"He was earthy and bright," said Jack Greenberg, his successor at the Legal Defense and Educational Fund. "He related to people, not abstract theories."

During his years on the Supreme Court, Marshall turned from a quick-witted verbal combatant to a philosophical joker whose wit and humor became legendary. His working habits were a part of the legend. Clerks often commented that Marshall and Justice Potter Stewart met in the halls each day at noon—Stewart on his way to work and Marshall on his way home.

Though his body was now aged, his pants gone baggy and his face in seams, there was no doubt on the day of his retirement he still possessed the feisty humor, combativeness, and sharpness of his younger days, when he won landmark civil rights cases before the Supreme Court and breached the wall of legal segregation in the United States.

Marshall changed with the years. A 1950 story in *Afro-American* newspapers pictured him as "handsome" and "the amazing type of man who is liked by other men and probably adored by women. He carries himself with an inoffensive self-confidence....He wears and looks especially well in tweed suits." In 1955 *Time* magazine called him "a big, quick-footed man, with a voice that can be soft and raucous, and an emotional pattern that swings like a pendulum from the serious to the absurd." In 1956 the *New Yorker* saw "a tall, vigorous man with a long face, a long, hooked nose above a black mustache and heavy-lidded, but very watchful eyes." In 1959, *Newsweek* magazine, noting his tweed suits were now rumpled and dusted with cigarette ashes, described him as "a rumpled bear of a man."

If the *New York Times* wrongly suggested that Marshall was leaving the court in "frustration and anger," his dissenting opinions delivered on the day of his retirement certainly made clear his displeasure with the current Court and most of his colleagues. On that day the Court closed its 1990–91 term by overturning one of its own precedents. It reversed a decision prohibiting prosecutors in death penalty cases from giving jurors, during the sentencing phase of a trial, evidence about a victim's character and the impact of the homicide on the victim's family.

Marshall, who remained adamantly opposed to capital punishment, was on the dissenting side of the six-to-three decision, written by Chief Justice Rehnquist. The opinion—*Payne v. Tennessee*—upheld the death sentence of a Tennessee man convicted of murder. Thurgood Marshall did not like the decision issued just ninety minutes before he announced his intention to retire, and he used his final dissenting opinion to speak his mind plainly about the Court's composition and its future. He took issue with the Court's reversal of precedent, suggesting it was a portent of more ominous things to come, including the reversal of *Roe v. Wade,* the controversial and emotionally charged 1973 decision upholding women's constitutionals rights to safe abortions. Marshall wrote:

"Power, not reason, is the new currency of this court's decision making....

"Neither the law nor the facts supporting Booth and Gathers [plaintiffs in an earlier case that halted executions] underwent any change in the last four years. Only the personnel of this court did. In dispatching Booth and Gathers to their graves, today's majority ominously suggest that an even more extensive upheaval of this court's precedents may be in store.

"Cast aside today are those condemned to face society's ultimate penalty. Tomorrow's victims may be minorities, women, or the indigent. Inevitably this campaign to resurrect yesterday's 'spirited dissents' will squander the authority and the legitimacy of this court as a protector of the powerless.

"Today's decision charts an unmistakable course. If the majority's radical reconstruction of the rules for overturning the court's decisions is to be taken at face value—and the majority offers us no reason why it should not—then their over-ruling of Booth and Gathers is but a preview of an even broader and more far-reaching assault upon this court's precedents."

Marshall's defense of precedents in his final dissent was in ironic contrast to the many Supreme Court decisions he won as the NAACP's civil rights lawyer, where his victories resulted from his ability to persuade the Court to reverse precedents of long standing. It was in contradistinction, too, to liberal Justice William O. Douglas, who in 1949 told the Bar of the City of New York he wanted nothing more from past decisions than "a sense of continuity...a feel for the durability of a doctrine....Even for the experts, law is only a prediction of what judges will do under a given set of facts. We have experience that they [former Courts] never knew. Our vision may be shorter or longer. But it is ours. It is better that we make our own history than be governed by the dead."

Thurgood Marshall began his lifelong pursuit of equal rights as an undergraduate at Pennsylvania's Lincoln University, when, with a group of students, he sat in the whites-only orchestra section of an Oxford, Pennsylvania, movie theater. As a student at Howard University Law School in Washington, D.C., he worked with lawyers from the NAACP on important early civil rights cases.

In 1933, after graduating from law school, he opened a one-man civil and criminal law practice in Baltimore, but his increasing involvement in local civil rights activities soon became the major focus of his early career. He traveled through Maryland's Eastern Shore counties for the NAACP investigating lynchings, won salary equalization for Maryland's black teachers, and staged boycotts forcing Baltimore's A & P stores to hire black clerks.

His first major civil rights victory was a case of "sweet revenge." In 1935, with his Howard professor and mentor, Charles Hamilton Houston, he won a suit to integrate the University of Maryland's law school—the same school that had rejected his application because of his race.

In 1936 Marshall became the NAACP's assistant special counsel in New York City. Four years later he was appointed director-counsel in charge of planning the legal strategy for the organization's Legal Defense and Educational Fund.

In 1944 Marshall won voting rights for thousands of disfranchised black southerners when he successfully argued *Smith v. Allwright,* the Supreme Court suit overthrowing the South's Democratic "white primary." After he won that case, just ten years out of law school, the trustees of Howard University awarded Marshall a prophetic citation of recognition:

"Within the short span of the first ten years of your professional career you have fully justified the exceptional promise of your student days.

"You are winning significant and enduring victories for a disadvantaged people. Your unceasing labors are opening the way for the achievement of an even greater measure of justice and equality under the law. Your star still rises, and though it is not yet at its zenith the brilliance of your accomplishment and the value of your service to your fellow man already marked you as an advocate, a legal scholar and humanitarian of the first magnitude."

As NAACP counsel Marshall implemented a legal strategy to integrate graduate schools, where there was less resistance to black and white students attending the same schools than there was at the public school level. Marshall said: "Those racial supremacy boys somehow think that little kids of six or seven are going to get funny ideas about sex and marriage just from going to school together, but for some equally funny reason, youngsters in law school aren't supposed to feel that way. We didn't get it, but we decided if that was what the South believed, then the best thing for the moment was to go along."

Two years later, in 1946, the NAACP gave Marshall the Spingarn Medal, its highest award. In 1948 he argued and won *Shelly v. Kraemer,* a Supreme Court decision striking down the legality of racially restrictive residential housing covenants, and in 1950 he won Supreme Court victories in two graduate school cases—*Sweatt v. Painter* and *McLaurin v. Oklahoma State Regents*—laying the foundation for broader victories.

In 1951 Marshall went to Japan and South Korea for six weeks to investigate charges of mistreatment of black soldiers under the command of southern white officers. And then, in 1954, Marshall and a team of NAACP lawyers won *Brown v. Board of Education of Topeka,* the case that struck down segregation in public education in America. The Warren court ruled unanimously that "separate educational facilities are inherently unequal," overturning the separate-but-equal doctrine established in *Plessy v. Ferguson* in 1896.

His crowning legal achievement was the celebrated victory in *Brown. Brown* became the wedge that Marshall and other civil rights lawyers used to dislodge most legalized segregation in America.

On September 23, 1961, eight months after taking office, President John F. Kennedy appointed Marshall to the U.S. Court of Appeals for the Second Circuit, serving New York, Vermont, and Connecticut. Though the judgeship doubled his NAACP salary, the decision to step down as the NAACP's chief legal advisor was a difficult one. "I had to fight it out with myself," he told a *New York Times* reporter. "By then I had built up a staff—a damned good staff—an excellent board, and the backing that would let them go ahead. And when one has the opportunity to serve his government, he should think twice before passing it up." Later Marshall told the *Washington Post,* "I've always felt the assault troops never occupy the town. I figured after the school decisions, the assault was over for me. It was time to let newer minds take over."

During his tenure as a federal appellate judge he wrote more than 150 opinions—including opinions declaring loyalty oaths required of New York teachers unconstitutional and limiting the authority of immigration officials to deport aliens summarily— and issued decisions enforcing the Fourth and Fifth Amendments in cases of illegal search and seizure and double jeopardy. None of his ninety-eight majority decisions was reversed by the Supreme Court.

In July 1965 President Lyndon B. Johnson appointed Marshall to the office of U.S. solicitor general, the nation's highest-ranking lawyer. Marshall, the great-grandson of a slave and the grandson of a Union soldier, was the first Afro-American to hold that post. Between 1965 and 1967 he won fourteen of the nineteen cases he argued for the United States, many of them mandating compliance with the Civil Rights Act of 1964. As solicitor general Marshall pleaded the government's position on civil rights and privacy cases, two issues important to him.

On June 13, 1967, standing in the White House Rose Garden with Marshall at his side, President Johnson announced his nomination of Thurgood Marshall to the U.S. Supreme Court. "I believe it is the right thing to do, the right time to do it, the right man and the right place. I believe he has already earned his place in history, but I think it will be greatly enhanced by his service on the court." The president's nomination spread a tidal wave of joy across black and liberal America.

Marshall became the first Marylander to sit on the Court since Chief Justice Roger B. Taney, who had ruled in the Dred Scott decision, 110 years earlier, that black Americans had no rights protected by the Constitution.

President Johnson had a dream of building what he called "the Great Society" in America. His appointments of Thurgood Marshall as solicitor general and later to the U.S. Supreme Court were integral components of that dream.

Justice William J. Brennan Jr., writing in the November 1991

issue of the *Harvard Law Review,* spoke of Marshall, his closest
friend on the Court:

> Indeed, he leaves behind an enviable record of opinions
> supporting the rights of the less powerful and less fortunate.
> One can add that, for more than twenty-five years before he
> joined the judiciary, Thurgood Marshall was probably the
> most important advocate in America, one who used his
> formidable legal skills to end the ills of discrimination.
> Thurgood Marshall is simply unsurpassed as a raconteur.
> On many occasions, some fact or event will remind him of an
> earlier episode in his richly varied life. When that moment
> arrives, a flicker of recollected amusement passes over his
> face, the magic words 'You *know...*' signal the onset of
> another tale, and soon Thurgood has plunged his audience
> into a different world. The locales are varied—from dusty
> courtrooms in the Deep South, to a confrontation with
> General MacArthur in the Far East, to the drafting sessions
> for the Kenyan Constitution. They are brought to life by all
> the tricks of the storyteller's art: the fluid voice, the mobile
> eyebrows, the sidelong glance, the pregnant pause and the
> wry smile.

The last day Marshall sat on the Supreme Court, retired Justice
Brennan came to watch the proceedings. Brennan, now eighty-five
and frail, was one of the first people Marshall told about his
intention to retire. An architect of some of the Warren Court's
most liberal opinions, Brennan was described as the "intellectual
leader" of its liberal majority. Until his retirement in 1990, the
Court's dwindling liberals could at times sway the vote of conservative justices Sandra Day O'Connor and Byron R. White. But
after Justice David Souter replaced Brennan, the conservatives
held a solid and commanding five-vote majority.

As news of Marshall's retirement spread across the nation's
capital, official reaction came swiftly. In an obligatory White
House statement President Bush said Marshall rendered "extraordinary and distinguished service to his country as a civil rights
lawyer, a judge on the U.S. court of appeals and in his tenure on
the Supreme Court. His career is an inspiring example for all
Americans." But less than an hour after the president's comments

on Marshall's retirement, Washington radio station WTOP was broadcasting a report that President Bush had already narrowed his Supreme Court nomination A-list to several candidates, including a black conservative U.S. appeals court judge named Clarence Thomas.

In a tribute to Marshall, Senator Orrin G. Hatch said, "I don't know of anyone on the bench who has had a more profound effect on American jurisprudence. No other person in the court's history has done more from a legal standpoint, or any other standpoint." Delaware Democrat Senator Joseph D. Biden, chairman of the Senate Judiciary Committee, said, "The Supreme Court has lost an historic justice—a hero for all America and for all times." The chairman of the Democratic party, Ronald H. Brown, characterized Marshall's retirement as "truly a loss for all America and a tragedy for this country. His resignation leaves a tremendous void that George Bush will never understand."

Voices chimed in from outside Washington as well. "Whether you agree with his opinions or not, he is one of the greatest Americans our legal system has ever produced. He dismantled the American apartheid," said University of Chicago law professor Cass Sunstein, a former Marshall clerk. And in Cambridge, Massachusetts, Harvard Law School professor Lawrence H. Tribe said Marshall's departure meant that "there is no one there who has the slightest idea of what it's like to be seriously oppressed, segregated, the victim of relentless prejudice and who has not led a life of privilege."

Not all the comments pouring into the city's newsrooms that day were complimentary. Richard A. Viguerie, chairman of the United Conservatives of America, rejoiced at the news of Marshall's retirement. "Hallelujah," he said, adding that the vacancy created by Marshall's departure would give President Bush the opportunity to "remake the American judiciary and change the face of the country." "Marshall is the most activist jurist of this century, and his resignation is good news for the country and the pro-life movement," said Douglas R. Scott, vice-president of the Christian Action Council, a group that opposes abortion.

Reactions from others did not make the front pages of the next day's *Washington Post* or *New York Times*. Retired Washington,

D.C., schoolteacher Evon Stevens sat sipping a glass of white wine at Faces, a popular Georgia Avenue tavern not far from Howard University. "I remember when colored people couldn't try on a dress or a pair of shoes in a downtown department store unless they were going to buy them," she said. "Thurgood had a lot to do with changing all that, and now he's gone."

T W O

A Cunning and Powerful
Strategist

I didn't undertake this job for money, but to
help redress an evil and errors that go back far
beyond our lifetime.

—Howard Jay Graham

Marshall leaned forward on his elbows at the conference table in the Overseas Press Club and inhaled slowly on a Winston cigarette. It was the fall of 1953. The conference he had called as director-counsel of the NAACP Legal Defense and Educational Fund was drawing to a close. For five days, more than a hundred people had been gathered in New York City to answer five questions posed by the justices of the U.S. Supreme Court at the end of the first round of oral arguments in *Brown v. Board of Education*. The conferees included many of the nation's leading educators, historians, legal experts, political scientists, and thinkers of every stripe: historians Howard K. Beale, C. Vann Woodward, and John Hope Franklin; professors John Frank and Walter Gellhorn of Yale and Columbia Law Schools, respectively; Robert K. Carr, a professor of law and political science at

Dartmouth College who became president of Oberlin College; and civil rights expert Milton Konvitz, to name but a few.

As the lawyer for black schoolchildren and their parents in *Brown*, Marshall asked the Court to end, once and for all, segregation in public education. He claimed segregation was detrimental to black children, adversely affecting their hearts and minds in a way that denied them the equal educational opportunity to which they were entitled under the Fourteenth Amendment to the U.S. Constitution. Opposing lawyers for the states of Kansas, South Carolina, Virginia, and Delaware and the District of Columbia asked the Court to uphold segregation as a time-honored practice, approved by the Supreme Court in *Plessy v. Ferguson* in 1896 and sanctioned by the Court a number of times since.

The Court listened to both sides argue their cases over the course of three days in December 1952. After the arguments were presented, the justices decided to reserve judgment. Integration was a divisive and potentially explosive issue. The blacks demanded nothing less than that the Court compel America to live up to its creed that all men are created equal. A ruling that upheld segregation was sure to be viewed as a denial of the inalienable rights promised at that nation's founding by Thomas Jefferson.

At the same time, the justices were aware that school desegregation would likely be resisted violently throughout the South. A number of southern leaders had already expressed their fear that integration in public education would lead to a breakdown of racial barriers in other aspects of American life. Some contended that putting blacks and whites side by side in the classroom at an early age would lead to miscegenation, interracial sex and marriage, the disappearance of the white race.

Whichever way the justices ruled, opponents of the decision were likely to challenge whether the Court legitimately had the power even to address the issue. For this reason the justices decided they must hear each side's answers to five basic questions concerning the Court's power before rendering what was certain to be one of the most momentous decisions in American history. At the heart of what the Court wanted to know was this: Did the men who wrote the Fourteenth Amendment intend to abolish school segregation?

From the Court's central question, four others followed. If the framers themselves did not intend to end segregation, did they at least intend to give Congress or the courts the power to abolish it at some future time, in light of changed social circumstances? If not, how was it now within the Supreme Court's power to abolish segregation in the public schools? If the Court did have the power to end segregation and chose to do so, should it do so gradually or order it done all at once? And how should the Court handle the particular situations presented in the five cases that were combined into *Brown*—with specific, detailed decrees or with sweeping, general directions to be followed by lower courts?

Adopted in the wake of the Civil War, the Fourteenth Amendment was designed to ensure former slaves and their descendants the equal protection of the laws. The language of the amendment did not squarely address segregation. The crux of the amendment is the equal protection clause, which states simply, "No State shall...deny to any person within its jurisdiction the equal protection of the laws." In *Plessy v. Ferguson* the Supreme Court ruled that the Fourteenth Amendment did *not* prohibit states from separating people by race as long as blacks and whites were treated equally. This became known as the separate-but-equal doctrine.

Marshall called the conference primarily for the purpose of hearing the views of two men: Alfred H. Kelly, chairman of the History Department at Wayne State University, and Howard Jay Graham, a bibliographer at the Los Angeles County Law Library. Both were white. Each was preeminent in his field. Kelly, a lanky, blond-haired, blue-eyed midwesterner, was the coauthor of a widely acclaimed book, *The American Constitution: Its Origins and Development*. Graham was stone deaf, but his hearing impairment did not keep him from becoming one of the foremost published authorities on the Fourteenth Amendment. Both graciously accepted Marshall's invitation to participate in formulating the NAACP's response, agreeing to contribute their time and effort over the summer in return for payment of their expenses.

Kelly said the chance to work with Marshall "struck a certain point of idealism in me about the role of the Negro in American life." He recalled, "It just seemed to me that the constitutional and statutory impediments to Negro equality were an outrage—almost as bad as slavery in their own way."

Graham felt the same way. He told Marshall, "I didn't undertake this job for money, but to help redress an evil and errors that go back far beyond our lifetime. It promises to be one of the most satisfying experiences of my life."

Marshall crushed his Winston in an ashtray teeming with mashed cigarette butts. He sipped from a glass of milk his secretary brought him. Milk was recommended by his doctor for his stomach ulcers. He preferred sipping bourbon.

He looked out over the conferees—tall, short, angular, stout, women and men, blacks and whites of all ages, together, the way it should be. He tried to focus on what the historians were trying to say. It was not what he wanted to hear. Research of the Fourteenth Amendment's history revealed, among other things, that when the amendment took effect in 1868, twenty-four of the nation's thirty-seven states had segregated schools. This, together with the fact that segregation was barely discussed in the debates over the amendment's ratification, showed that state legislators of the day did not regard the amendment as having an impact on segregation in public education.

Moreover, public schools in the District of Columbia, controlled by Congress under Article I of the Constitution, had been segregated since 1864, before the end of the war that was fought to free the slaves. And Congress refused to abolish school segregation in the District after the Fourteenth Amendment was adopted, although the question was debated thoroughly during the early 1870s. If Congress had intended for the Fourteenth Amendment to outlaw segregation, then why had Congress itself not abolished school segregation in the District after the amendment was passed?

Marshall had only five lawyers on staff at the NAACP's New York headquarters. Robert L. Carter, his top assistant, specialized in cases involving discrimination in interstate and intrastate transportation. He is now a district court judge for the Southern

District of New York, as is Constance Baker Motley, who specialized in housing discrimination. Jack Greenberg, at twenty-eight the youngest staffer, went on to become the NAACP Legal Defense and Educational Fund's director, succeeding Marshall. He handled military courts-martial, labor law, and criminal cases. David Pinsky and Elwood Chisholm were research attorneys. The six lawyers were supported by seven secretaries, seven paralegals, and two bookkeepers.

It was an effective but bare-bones operation. *Brown* was but one of six Supreme Court appeals the office was handling. The legwork, the research, the interviewing of witnesses and review of court records from any number of states, were monumental undertakings. And the Supreme Court appeals were not the only business of the office. Marshall himself handled as many as fifty lower court litigations at any given time in addition to the Supreme Court work, and he also oversaw the operations of the office. He logged on average sixty thousand miles a year traveling from courthouse to courthouse across the country. The volume of his responsibilities was three to four times beyond that normally demanded of a lawyer.

The NAACP's legal staff had achieved a number of impressive victories in the Supreme Court in recent years. These achievements were, of course, a positive reflection on Marshall, the boss. But he was characteristically modest about the success of his operation. He once told a reporter, "The only reason I look good is that I get expert advice and take it."

Fortunately the New York staff was reinforced by the NAACP Legal Committee, composed of fifty-one attorneys from around the nation, appointed by the NAACP board of directors. These lawyers contributed their services free of charge in the interest of advancing what was known at that time as the "Negro cause." Without their help Marshall would not have had the resources to undertake the rigorous and in-depth research called for by the Court's five questions. Even with the Legal Committee's assistance, however, he felt he needed more help in the form of an interdisciplinary assault on the Fourteenth Amendment's history. For this reason he called together the assembled experts from diverse fields.

William Robert Ming Jr., a black law professor at the University of Chicago, wrote a brief that tried to argue around the historians' discoveries. He took the position that, despite the specifics, the Radical Republican abolitionists who developed and sponsored the Fourteenth Amendment were motivated by humanitarian aims. Achieving an egalitarian society, Ming argued, was their underlying objective. To this extent, he contended, the specific practices of the era should be given secondary consideration. Of primary importance was achieving the overriding goal of full black equality. Compromises may have been forced by political realities or the need to bind sectional wounds that followed the Civil War. Nonetheless, Ming argued, the amendment's broader purpose should be interpreted to include segregation's abolishment. Kelly, who collaborated on the brief, later explained, "Ming had proceeded on the theory that it would not do to get too far involved in specific historical detail with respect to framer intent and that the [NAACP's] case might best be cast in very generalized terms with a deliberate avoidance of the particular."

Kelly and Ming had worked tirelessly on the brief over the course of three days, cloistered with a stenographer in a suite of offices at the NAACP's main headquarters on West 40th Street. Kelly recalled, "The brief drafting was mostly Ming and comparatively little Kelly; in the first place, Ming knew how to draft a brief and I didn't; moreover, I found he had very positive ideas about what he wanted to say. My role, it appeared, was to challenge him repeatedly; to fight and quarrel with him, attack his history and constitutional law as unsound, and so on." Kelly went on, "Since being unpleasant comes naturally both to lawyers and academicians, we got on famously. Evenings, we went back to the general sessions, which invariably lasted until long after midnight. At the end of three days we had a brief which Ming said would do."

Thurgood Marshall was disappointed. The approach was not persuasive; there was nothing concrete in it. Ming's brief hedged; it did not confront the questions. Marshall knew he could not win with it. A week after the conference closed, he asked Kelly to return for a second attempt at composing a brief.

"In the curiously winning manner so characteristic of the man," Kelly said, "he informed me that since I wasn't doing anything anyhow, I might as well come down to New York for four or five days and waste my time there. My help, he said with careful flattery, was needed very badly on the brief. My vanity thus touched to the quick, I came."

"I gotta argue these cases," Thurgood complained to Kelly, "and if I try this approach, these fellows [on the Court] will shoot me down in flames."

With Kelly back on board, the staff began a week-long review of the historical evidence. Marshall urged those involved in the effort to see the bigger picture rather than to focus on or emphasize the uncovering of some "objective" or "empirical" truth. The practice of law, Marshall explained, is *advocacy.* "I am very much afraid that...I ceased to function as an historian and instead took up the practice of law without a license," Kelly recalled. He went on, "The problem we faced was not the historian's discovery of the truth; the problem instead was the formulation of an adequate gloss on the fateful events...sufficient to convince the Court that we had something of a historical case....It is not that we were engaged in formulating lies; there was nothing as crude and naive as that. But we were using facts, emphasizing facts, bearing down on facts, sliding off facts in a way to do what Marshall said we had to do—'get by those boys down there.'"

Marshall drove his staff relentlessly but asked nothing of them that he did not demand of himself. "I have *never* seen a man work so long and so hard," recalls historian John Hope Franklin. "It was nothing for him to say at 1:00 A.M., 'How about a fifteen-minute break?' I never worked for harder taskmasters."

William Coleman was a black graduate of Harvard Law School who clerked for Justice Frankfurter. Marshall put him in charge of organizing the research efforts of the contributing historians from across the country. Coleman remembers, "There were no prima donnas in that room."

Kelly was inspired by what he saw as Marshall's "profoundly moving sense of identity with the Negro's tragic role in America, and his tremendous moral commitment to the work in which he was engaged." He wrote, "I came to understand why Thurgood Marshall was such a cunning and powerful strategist in the campaign for Negro rights in America."

Kelly said years later that another thing he came to understand in those autumn conferences was this: "Thurgood Marshall was...an America patriot. He truly believed in the United States and the Constitution, but that the whole system was tragically flawed by the segregation laws. Wipe away those laws and the whole picture would change." He added, "Marshall and his colleagues were no rebels. They felt the social order was fundamentally good. What they wanted was the chance to share in it like men."

Bringing that about, Marshall's first wife, Vivian, realized, was a daunting task. It was during this period that she really began to worry about him. She commented to friends about how her husband had changed physically during the past five years, how he had aged, that he was nervous where he used to be calm. "The work is taking its toll of him," she once said. "You know, it's a discouraging job he's set himself."

At times Marshall wondered exactly what that job was. Was it saving the Negro? Or was it saving the white man's soul? He thought of Clarendon County, South Carolina, where Negro children ran around with bloody, bare feet from walking on the jagged shards of tin roofs blown off their ramshackle lean-tos. He was only forty-five. But how could a young man see that and not be old?

He knew that the Court was ready to end segregation. He believed in the judicial system, that it worked, and was confident that the groundwork for segregation's demise had been laid by him and his mentor, Charles Hamilton Houston, during the years leading up to the *Brown* litigation. Case by case they had chipped away at *Plessy*'s separate-but-equal doctrine, persuading the Court—in *Gaines, Sipuel, McLaurin, Sweatt,* and other cases—to narrow *Plessy*'s holding here, limit its application there, affirming or extending black rights in certain circumstances, implying their extension to others. Two years earlier, in the *Annals of the American Academy of Political and Social Science,* he had written:

"As a direct or indirect result of these decisions, Negroes are now attending graduate and professional state schools in

Arkansas, Texas, Maryland, Delaware, Kentucky, Oklahoma, Virginia, West Virginia, and Louisiana....Thus a major modification in the pattern of American life is in the making....Although its approach has been undeniably cautious, the Court seems to be making a real effort to deal effectively with our most disturbing problem with practical wisdom and insight. If it continues along the path blazed by its recent decisions, the Constitution's mandate of equal protection of the laws will eventually accomplish the objective its framers intended—that of prohibiting all forms of community discriminatory action based upon race or color."

Call it a gut feeling, intangible, but throughout the three days of oral argument that past December something ineffable, an air of inevitability, had hung over events. What the Court now wanted, Marshall believed, was the chance to redeem itself for what it had done a half century earlier, when, by adopting the separate-but-equal doctrine, it had consigned African Americans to lives of indignity and second-class citizenship. That was the reason for the five questions. Marshall was sure of it. What the court was looking for was some credible, some legitimate, basis for doing what he was sure it wanted to do, anyway.

Sometimes he wondered what it was like to be a white man. He took it as a given that the average white man did not lose as much sleep worrying about the evils of the segregation systems as Marshall lost trying to correct them. He could not help resenting white apathy.

If Kelly was taken aback by Marshall's resentment, at first he was also puzzled by Marshall's liberal use of the word *nigger,* which Kelly naturally regarded as derogatory. The word made Kelly uncomfortable. Later, however, he arrived at an understanding of how Marshall used it. "That word seemed to epitomize for him the entire tragedy of the black man's situation, but he wasn't somber about it. He could invest the word with as much humor as sadness."

In feigned Negro dialect, Marshall once reminded his secretary sternly "who's the H.N. around here," meaning "Head Nigger." Another time, Marshall came upon a story in a newspaper of Civil War vintage about a black railroad worker who had fallen into a hole. The headline read "Nigger in a Pit!" Marshall rambled around the office yelling, "Nigger in a pit! Nigger in a pit!"

Of course, Thurgood Marshall was no racist. He knew that all white men were not alike. Some—like Kelly and Graham, for instance—were committed to the Negro cause. Others, like his young assistant Charles Black, went so far as to *become* Negroes.

Born in eastern Texas, Black finished near the top of his class at Yale Law School. He went on to become a professor of law at Columbia University in New York City but never really became a part of faculty life there. Instead, he indulged in his eclectic interests: studying the trumpet and frequenting Harlem night-spots; writing poetry and haunting the coffeehouses and bars in Greenwich Village. Eventually Black joined the faculty of his alma mater and became one of the nation's foremost authorities on admiralty law.

He offered his services to Marshall that summer and fall of 1953. "There was a fair sense of social injustice gnawing at him," recalls an associate of Black's at Columbia. When Marshall asked him why he was interested in working for the NAACP, Black made no effort to ingratiate himself with his new boss. Instead, he drawled: "I come from deep, deep in Texas. I'd heard of this really terrible organization way up North called the N-A-A-C-P. It was an awful place with a great big office all the way up there in New York, they said. And the worst thing of all about it was that right in that big office there was this room, this special secret room....And inside that room, they said, there was nothing but hooks on the walls—hundreds and hundreds of hooks—and do you know what was hanging on each and every one of those hooks? Why, they said that on each of those hooks was a key to the bedroom of a southern white woman. And so I figured *that's* an organization I wanna get involved in!"

Black's efforts were valued greatly, for he was a superb writer. He demonstrated his skill as well as his compassion in the work he did on the five questions. His contribution to the final brief related to the fourth of the five questions: he urged the Court to act swiftly, rather than gradually, and abolish segregation all at once. He wrote:

"These infant appellants are asserting the most important secular claims that can be put forward by children, the claim to their full measure of the chance to learn and grow, and the inseparably connected but even more important claim to be treated as entire citizens of the society into which they have been born. We have discovered no case in which such rights, once established, have been postponed by a cautious calculation of conveniences. The nuisance cases, the sewage cases, the cases of the overhanging cornices, need not be distinguished. They distinguish themselves."

After he read the passage, Marshall was moved to tell Black, paternally, "You are a Negro."

After three days of round-the-clock effort, as if there were a force in the universe that responds to hard work and good intentions, Marshall, Kelly, and company made their hoped-for discovery. It came in the form of a speech delivered by Ohio congressman Thaddeus Stevens in 1866. Stevens, an ardent abolitionist, was the leader of the Radical Republicans and the most powerful man in the U.S. House of Representatives after the Civil War. When the Fourteenth Amendment was introduced by its author, Radical Ohio congressman John A. Bingham, Stevens rose to stamp upon Bingham's proposal the Radicals' interpretation of its meaning. "Where any State makes a distinction in the same law between different classes of individuals," he declared, "Congress shall have the power to correct such discriminations and inequality." He vowed that "no distinction would be tolerated in this purified Republic but what arose from merit and conduct." The term *purified,* connoting absolution from sin, meant "with slavery removed."

Jay Graham then suggested strengthening the brief by adding remarks made by Bingham himself concerning the difference between writing statutes and writing constitutional provisions. Statutes, according to Bingham, should be drafted narrowly and with great specificity. Constitutional provisions, by contrast, should be "writ broad for ages yet unborn." As Kelly put it, "In our minds' eye, Bingham almost seemed to be speaking for our purposes, saying to the Court in the twentieth century that if your age, far beyond our span of time, sees in this amendment a new birth of liberty, it will be altogether legitimate for you to use it for that purpose."

There it was: concrete support for the proposition that the original proponents of the Fourteenth Amendment intended it to be used flexibly to address discriminatory situations as they arose and to correct any distinction imposed by law that was not based exclusively on "merit and conduct."

"Hot damn!" exclaimed Marshall. "Here's something finally that we can use that isn't manipulating the facts."

Next, Thurgood applied a crafty lawyer's inverse reasoning. After all, there were two ways to approach the Court's questions. Either the Court was looking for something that said, "Yes, you have the power to end segregation," or the Court was just making sure that nothing said, "No, you do *not* have the power to end it."

Marshall had found nothing that specifically gave the Court the power to end segregation. But he had come across nothing that explicitly denied the Court that power, either. He decided to tell the justices that the Court had the power to end segregation unless his opponents could point to something that explicitly said the Court did not. He assured his staff, "A nothin' to nothin' score means we win the ball game."

Marshall ordered a rewrite of Ming's brief. He assigned the task to his best writer, Spottswood W. Robinson III, another protégé of Charles Houston's, from Virginia. Robinson hammered out a masterful product, soaring in its eloquence and anchored firmly in historical fact. It attacked the half-century-old separate-but-equal doctrine:

"When the Court employed the old usages, customs and traditions as the basis for determining the reasonableness of the segregation statutes designed to resubjugate the Negro to an inferior status, it nullified the acknowledged intent of the framers of the [Fourteenth] Amendment, and made a travesty of the equal protection clause."

In his conclusion Robinson cried out for justice:

"Segregation was designed to ensure inequality—to discriminate on account of race and color—and the separate-but-equal doctrine accommodated the Constitution to that purpose. Separate but equal is a legal fiction. There never was and never will be any separate equality. Our Constitution cannot be used to sustain ideologies and practices which we as a people abhor."

Now Marshall was satisfied, comfortable in the knowledge that he was giving the Court what it wanted, something to which the Court could peg its redemption. Time would prove him right. In the spring of the following year, when it rendered its final decision in *Brown*, the Court chose to interpret the Fourteenth Amendment in light of modern-day circumstances rather than to be guided by whatever practices were in place at the time of the amendment's ratification. Writing for a unanimous Court in *Brown*, Chief Justice Earl Warren concluded with regard to the amendment's legislative history:

"This discussion and our own investigation convince us that, although these [historical] sources cast some light, it is not enough to resolve the problem with which we are faced. At best, they are inconclusive. The most avid proponents of the post-War Amendments undoubtedly intended them to remove all legal distinctions among 'all persons born or naturalized in the United States.' Their opponents, just as certainly, were antagonistic to both the letter and the spirit of the Amendments and wished them to have the most limited effect. What others in Congress and the state legislatures had in mind cannot be determined with any degree of certainty."

Years later, summarizing the historians' role in *Brown*, Kelly wrote, "The historians had produced at least the 'draw' that Marshall and his colleagues had asked for. It was all they needed in order to win. So we historians can assure ourselves, I think, that we had something to do with the victory." Marshall certainly agreed. Kelly recalled that Marshall thanked the historians who assisted in the research, "assuring us that enlisting the history profession on his side had been the NAACP's smartest move in the whole complicated case."

History, as well as the historians, had proved to be on Marshall's side, assisted by his own cunning and perseverance. But the forces that produced the ultimate victory over segregation were set in motion long before Kelly and the other historians came on the scene. The catalyst for Marshall's success was American society itself, particularly the injustices that steeled his determination to break down racial barriers. He had lived with them all his life.

THREE

Growing Up in Baltimore

Anyone calls you "nigger" you not only got my
permission to fight him—you got my orders to
fight him."

—William Canfield Marshall

T hurgood Marshall was born July 2, 1908, in Baltimore, Maryland, in the Chesapeake Bay region that proclaims itself "The
Land of Pleasant Living." It was a city where many white people
remained proud of being south of the Mason-Dixon Line.

His maternal great-grandfather, a slave whose name the family
never knew, was brought to America by slave traders during the
1840s and sold to a plantation owner on Maryland's Eastern
Shore. Marshall said his great-grandfather came from the Congo,
known as the Republic of Zaire since 1971: "His more polite
descendants like to think he came from the cultured tribes in
Sierra Leone, but we all know that he really came from the
toughest part of the Congo."

In a *Time* magazine interview, Marshall described his great-
grandfather as "one mean man." Elsewhere he characterized him
proudly as the "baddest nigger" in Maryland. "One day his owner
came up to him and said, 'Look, I brought you here so I guess I

can't very well shoot you—as you deserve. On the other hand, I can't with a clear conscience sell anyone as vicious as you to another slaveholder, and I can't give you away. So, I am going to set you free—on one condition. Get the hell out of this county and never come back.'

"That was the only time Massuh didn't get an argument from the old boy," Marshall added. Still defiant, his great-grandfather married a white woman and raised his family just a few miles from his former owner's plantation, living there until he died.

Thurgood Marshall speaks fondly of his forebears, often using the word *nigger* because he understands the expression is spoken affectionately in black social circles, especially among groups of light-skinned middle-class blacks. The words *colored, Negro,* and *black* were equally respectable terms for more than half a century. Then, in the mid-1980s, black Americans sought a linguistic mechanism for identifying with their African heritage by calling themselves "Afro-Americans or African Americans." In his formal writings and speeches, Marshall settled for a while on *African American.* Finally, in 1991, he declared he would no longer employ *black* or *Negro:* "I use the term *Afro-American* because the term is a more respectful reflection of the contributions that descendants from diverse and culturally rich African traditions have made to the mosaic of American society."

Thurgood Marshall traced his family's history and name to Africa. The only name many slaves had was their owner's. Thurgood's paternal grandfather was a freedman—a former slave—known as Marshall. During the Civil War he joined a black regiment, one of 186,000 former slaves to fight with Union troops. Soldiers were required to have first and last names, so he took the first name Thoroughgood to comply with that regulation. "I was named after him," Marshall told an interviewer, "but by the time I was in second grade, I got tired of spelling all that and shortened it."

At the end of the Civil War, Thoroughgood Marshall joined the U.S. Merchant Marine. When his tour ended he settled in Baltimore, the home of his merchant marine vessel, and married Annie, a mulatto from Virginia who was uncertain of her heritage. She had been raised in Virginia by family members whose complexions were much darker than hers. Most likely her father had been a white Virginia slave owner and her mother a slave.

Maryland census takers did not know whether to classify Annie Marshall as black or white. "She never knew her real name, her age, her parents, or her race," Thurgood Marshall recalled. "All she knew was that she was raised by a Negro family in Virginia— and she never changed her story, no matter what the census takers threatened.

Thoroughgood Marshall had saved several hundred dollars while working as a merchant marine and received a military pension. He opened a grocery and produce store at the corner of Dolphin and Green streets in west Baltimore. He used a second name, Thornygood, which allowed him to receive a second pension check from his merchant marine service. Whether he did this deliberately is a matter of dispute. Thurgood Marshall speculates the duplicity of names and the double pension checks may have resulted more from Thoroughgood Marshall's "poor penmanship" than an attempt to defraud the government.

Thoroughgood and Annie Marshall took pride in their home, their neighborhood, and their grocery store. When workmen from the Baltimore Gas and Electric Company arrived to erect a light pole in front of the store, Annie Marshall became furious. She told them the sidewalk in front of the store belonged to her and she did not want a light pole there. The utility company obtained a court order and sent a work crew to raise the pole.

The workmen arrived the next morning and found Annie Marshall sitting firmly in a cane-backed kitchen chair directly over the place where the utility company planned to raise the light pole. The men returned for three days and each day found a determined Annie Marshall sitting in her kitchen chair. The company finally gave up and found another location to erect its pole. In 1965 Marshall told an *Ebony* magazine writer, "Grandma Annie emerged as the victor of what may have been the first successful sitdown strike in Maryland."

Thoroughgood and Annie raised a family at 1838 Druid Hill Avenue in west Baltimore, a racially mixed neighborhood where whites and blacks, Jews, Episcopalians, and Catholics lived side by side. It was a proud neighborhood of three-story brick and brownstone houses with arched doorways and Baltimore's fabled white marble steps, which homeowners scrubbed religiously each Saturday. It was a good house and a good neighborhood, especially for a black family, shortly before the turn of the century, with upwardly mobile ambitions.

Many affluent black families—the Ridleys, the Murphys, the Rhettas, and the Kogers—resided side by side with white families. "If you were a black person and owned a house on Druid Hill Avenue in those days, you had arrived," said Betty Murphy Moss, a member of the black fourth-generation Baltimore family who published the *Afro-American* newspapers.

In other sections of Baltimore, black families of lesser means lived in squalid, cobblestoned back alleys and ramshackle dwellings that were once slave quarters, carriage houses, or stables. Biddle Alley, a short distance from the Marshall house, was known as "lung block" because so many of the people there had tuberculosis. The death rate from tuberculosis in the area was 958 per 100,000 people, compared with 131.9 for the rest of the city. A 1907 housing survey by the Association for the Condition of the Poor found only one outdoor toilet for every two alley houses.

Elite white families who traced their heritage to the revolutionary war lived only four blocks away, in an area now called Bolton Hill. White flight to the surrounding Maryland suburbs would not begin for another forty years.

Today the Marshall family house on Druid Hill Avenue, the birthplace of Thurgood Marshall's father, William Canfield Marshall, stands vacant, its windows and doors covered with half-inch sheets of plywood. Broken liquor bottles, empty beer cans, and spent condoms clutter a yard overgrown with weeds. Druid Hill Avenue has become a black working-class area that suffers the agony of many of America's inner-city neighborhoods—crime, hard-core unemployment, poverty, and drugs.

Synagogues, where the neighborhood's Jewish population worshiped in the early 1900s, have been converted to Christian churches with black congregations or convenience stores where clerks serve customers from behind thick sheets of bulletproof glass. Six-pointed Stars of David remain carved in their stone façades. Only the few remaining wrought-iron boot scrapers at the foot of the marble steps and the chipped marble carriage-mount blocks bespeak the once-proud neighborhood. Few would imagine they are passing through the neighborhood where a former Supreme Court justice spent his childhood.

Thurgood Marshall's maternal grandfather was a sailor who loved opera. Isaiah Olive Branch Williams, like Thoroughgood Marshall, served in the merchant marine, after completing a three-year tour of duty in the Union army during the Civil War. Williams, who lived in Maryland's Washington County, joined the Seventh Regiment U.S. Colored Troops in October 1863. He was nineteen years old. A year earlier, the Maryland General Assembly had passed a bill providing a three-hundred-dollar payment for the state's white men who enlisted. Black men, however, received only fifty dollars on enlistment and fifty dollars on discharge. Williams's enlistment is recorded on the Bounty Rolls of Colored Troops in the Maryland State Archives in Annapolis.

Williams received a commendation for "coolness and bravery in action" from his commanding officer, Maj. Edelman M. Lockwood. His citation said: "On October 28, 1864, he advanced beyond the skirmish line to a very conspicuous place for the purpose of ascertaining the position of the enemy's artillery."

Black troops of the Seventh Regiment were housed in the Birney Barracks on Holliday Street in east Baltimore. It was there, on November 1, 1864, that Williams and other black soldiers stood in review as General D. B. Birney announced that Maryland's General Assembly, four hours earlier, had adopted a constitutional amendment abolishing slavery in the state.

Williams's name appears on a list of black Civil War soldiers who deposited their military pay at the Baltimore branch of the Freedmen's Savings and Trust Company. His account, number 240, had a balance of fifty dollars in December 1864 when he married Mary Eliza, settled in Baltimore, and—opened a grocery store. Thurgood Marshall said Williams spoke often about one of his ports of call, Arica, Chile, where he had attended a performance of Vincenzo Bellini's 1831 opera *Norma*. When the couple had a daughter—Thurgood's mother—they named her Norma

Arica. He had also become enamored with the works of William Shakespeare. They named two of their other children Avonia Delicia and Avon—a girl and a boy—after the river near the Shakespeare home. They named their other children Cyrus Mentor and Ravine. Denmedia Marketa was the name they chose for the grocery store.

After the war Williams bought a house in west Baltimore, next door to a white man who attended the integrated St. James Episcopal Church with the Williams family. He did not particularly like living next door to a black family, but when the fence between their houses needed repair, he reluctantly sought Williams's help. "After all," he explained, "we belong to the same church and are going to the same heaven."

Williams told his neighbor, "I'd rather go to hell."

Isaiah Williams was active in public protests to improve conditions for his fellow black citizens. In the 1870s he organized a mass meeting to protest the beatings of several black citizens by the Baltimore police officers. It was the first time the city's usually passive black community demonstrated that it could unite in a common cause. During the post-Civil War era, when the Ku Klux Klan and other groups were making strident efforts to establish their racial supremacy in Maryland, an act of black defiance was unusual.

Norma Arica Marshall attended Baltimore's segregated schools and, like her mother, became an elementary school teacher. She graduated from Maryland's black Coppin Normal College and later earned graduate credits at Columbia University's Teachers College in New York City. Like her father, she had a passion for music. She sang and played the piano in local opera and theater productions.

Norma and William Canfield Marshall had gone to school together, and though their families operated competing grocery stores in the same neighborhood, they became friends. They married in 1904, when she was seventeen and he was twenty-one, and had Aubrey that same year and Thurgood four years later.

In 1909 the Marshalls moved temporarily to New York City and took a small apartment in Harlem while Norma Marshall pursued graduate studies in education at Columbia. They returned to Baltimore frequently to visit family and friends and moved back there after five years, when Thurgood Marshall had turned six.

Both of Thurgood Marshall's parents were light-skinned. This set them apart in color-conscious Baltimore, where lighter-skinned black people were treated better by white people than those with less white blood in their veins and more black pigmentation in their skin. Black color consciousness and its political ramifications would surface repeatedly throughout Thurgood Marshall's life. But the Marshalls were strong race people, proudly aware of their black heritage as well as the limitations placed on all black Americans, even those like William Canfield Marshall, who had straight hair and blue eyes.

At the time of Thurgood's birth his father worked for the Baltimore & Ohio Railroad as a Pullman dining-car waiter on the Washington-to-New York run. Though a good job for a black man without a college education, it often required him to be away from home. With two infant sons who needed his love and attention, Will Marshall left the railroad and became a waiter at the whites-only Gibson Island Club, located on a peninsula that juts into the Chesapeake Bay, twenty miles southeast of Baltimore.

Thurgood Marshall's relatives described him as a baby with big, dark eyes and curly hair, a description confirmed by his childhood pictures. His aunt Media Dodson said he was a "timid" child. She told a *Time* magazine writer: "One day—he must have been around five—he stopped crying and became a pretty tough guy. Now, I don't know what caused the change. Maybe the boys slapped his head."

His aunt Elizabeth Marshall told an interviewer, "He wasn't any Mama-dress-me-and-send-me-to-Sunday-School sort of boy. He was always a smart, alert little fella, full of life and laughter."

A friend of the Marshall family, Odell Payne, told *Ebony* magazine Thurgood was "a jolly boy who always had something to say." But she added that he appeared to be harboring serious thoughts at an early age. "I can still see Thurgood coming down Division Street every Sunday afternoon about one o'clock. He'd be wearing knee pants with both hands dug way into his pockets and be kicking a stone in front of him as he crossed Dolphin Street to visit his grandparents at their big grocery store on the corner. He was in a deep study, that boy, and it was plain something was going on inside of him."

Thurgood was high-spirited and rambunctious, traits that often got him into trouble. A *New York Times Magazine* story quotes Thurgood Marshall as saying, "We lived on a respectable street, but behind us were back alleys where roughnecks and the tough kids hung out. When it was time for dinner, my mother used to go to the front door to call my older brother. Then she'd go to the back door and call me."

His elementary school principal would send recalcitrant students to the school's basement with a copy of the Constitution and orders to memorize a passage before returning to the classroom. Thurgood spent many hours in the basement. "Before I left that school," he later told a reporter, "I knew the entire Constitution by heart."

It was in the school basement that he first became concerned about certain provisions of the Constitution, especially the Fourteenth Amendment's guarantee of equal rights. He knew that Baltimore's white children—his neighbors—attended newer schools, while the city's black children went to schools like his own on Pennsylvania Avenue, which needed repair, had no playground, and used outdated, worn books passed down from the white school system.

Thurgood thought the Constitution had special meaning for black Americans, especially the Thirteenth, Fourteenth, and Fifteenth Amendments, passed by the Reconstruction Congresses to protect the rights of newly freed slaves. In 1921 thirteen-year-old Thurgood asked his father why white citizens had more rights than black ones.

William Marshall did not have a formal education, but he possessed an analytic mind and kept abreast of current events, and he, too, had read the Constitution. He studied criminal and civil court cases as a hobby, reading newspaper accounts of trials in the *Baltimore Sun* and spending many of his free hours, frequently accompanied by young Thurgood, as a spectator in Baltimore's courtrooms. When he served on a grand jury—the first black man to do so in Baltimore—he became angry because jurors always asked whether the person under investigation was white or black and blacks were far more likely to be indicted than whites. On his third day of service he suggested the panel abandon the practice of determining an individual's race before deciding whether or not to return an indictment. To Marshall's surprise the white jury foreman agreed with him, and the race question was never again raised by that jury.

William Marshall told his thirteen-year-old son the Constitution was the Founding Fathers' blueprint for the way things should be, not a description of the way things were. He explained that, shortly after the Civil War, Congress passed bills designed to safeguard the rights of black Americans. But the Supreme Court soon retrenched, handing down decisions sharply restricting the scope and intent of the post–Civil War legislation. These crippling decisions returned control of civil rights to the states, and black Americans lost much of what they had gained.

At its inception, he explained, the Constitution included provisions that recognized slavery in states where it existed, and when questions on the status of blacks came increasingly before the Court, slavery was upheld. He described the separate-but-equal doctrine enunciated by the Court in *Plessy v. Ferguson,* which reinforced emerging practices of segregation and precipitated a flood of state laws putting it firmly and legally in place. At the end of Reconstruction, white political rule in the South was restored. Slavery was no longer the nation's prime racial issue. It had been replaced by the practices of segregation and discrimination.

Thurgood Marshall told a *U.S. News & World Report* writer that it was his father who steered him toward a legal career. "He never told me to become a lawyer, but he turned me into one. In a way, he was the most insidious of my family rebels. He taught me how to argue, challenged my logic on every point, by making me prove every statement I made, even if we were discussing the weather." Though it would make an appealing footnote, Marshall has never claimed that reading the Constitution in the school basement was a catalyst for his legal career.

As Thurgood Marshall grew up, political developments further encroached on the rights of black citizens. Maryland, Oklahoma, and several other states began passing Jim Crow legislation designed to disfranchise black voters and mandating separate facilities for blacks and whites in public accommodations. Many southern states instituted laws providing that only citizens whose ancestors had been entitled to vote before the Civil War could cast ballots in current elections without taking literacy tests. Prospective black voters who could not satisfy the criterion had to take examinations that were designed to make them fail. The result was a severe restriction of black voting rights.

Norma Marshall hoped Thurgood would become a dentist, filling cavities instead of filing briefs. As a second-generation teacher she believed education was important. She challenged her sons intellectually and followed their progress in school closely. It was an easy task. Her brother and her colleagues were her sons' teachers. Thurgood Marshall's uncle "Fearless" Cyrus Williams taught mathematics at the elementary school Thurgood attended and monitored his nephew's schoolwork closely. He gave him an A in algebra and said it was earned. Despite his rambunctious behavior, Thurgood earned good grades in his other subjects, too.

Norma Marshall also exercised other controls over the playful Thurgood. "Mama taught me a lot," Thurgood remembered. "She used to say, 'Boy, you may be tall, but if you get mean, I can always reach you with a chair.'"

Despite the high expectations his parents held for his future, Mary Eliza Williams, his maternal grandmother, adopted a practical approach guided by her realization of discrimination and segregation in America. She took her grandson into her kitchen one day and told him she was going to teach him to cook. "I am with your parents in wanting you to be a professional man," she said, "but I want to make sure you can always earn a dollar. You can pick up all that other stuff later, but I bet you never saw a jobless Negro cook." Though he never had to earn his living as a cook, Grandma Mary's lessons were not lost on her grandson. Cooking—especially she-crab soup, a state delicacy made from Maryland's famous blue-claw crabs—became a lifelong hobby.

William and Norma Marshall sheltered their sons in a home filled with love, the necessities of life, and protection from the brutality and violence spawned by racism. But there came a time when young Thurgood discovered that the world outside was

much different from the protected and nurtured existence he
enjoyed.

Years later he told a *Time* magazine reporter about the incident
that brought this awakening, "I heard a kid call a Jewish boy I
knew a 'kike' to his face," Marshall explained. "I was about seven.
I asked him why he didn't fight the kid. He asked me what would I
do if someone called me 'nigger'—would I fight? That was a new
one on me. I knew 'kike' was a dirty word, but I hadn't known
about 'nigger.' I went home and wanted to know right that minute
what all this meant. That's not easy for a parent to explain so it
makes any sense to a kid, you know."

Will Marshall indeed had difficulty defining the racial slur, but
he had no problem telling young Thurgood how he should
respond when anyone called him "nigger." "Anyone calls you
'nigger,' you not only got my permission to fight him—you got my
orders to fight him." It was an order Thurgood Marshall would
follow physically and legally for the rest of his life.

The first occasion that inspired Thurgood to carry out his
father's command took place in 1922, when Thurgood was a
fourteen-year-old high school student with an after-school job
delivering supplies for a Baltimore hat company. It was the first
time he met racial hostility face-to-face. One Saturday, the day
before Easter, he was carrying a tall stack of hatboxes and could
barely see over them. While he waited for the streetcar he chatted
with one of his father's friends, a black man named Truesdale.
When the streetcar arrived, Thurgood juggled the hatboxes as best
he could and stepped up the platform. A white man grabbed his
arm and yanked him backward. "Nigger, don't you push in front
of no white lady again," the man said.

"I hadn't seen any white lady," Marshall recalled. "I tore into
him." The hatboxes fell to the pavement as Thurgood and the
white man went at each other. Truesdale tried in vain to separate
them.

Several minutes later, policeman Army Matthews arrived and
broke up the fight. His handling of the incident was far different
from what another officer's might have been. In the early twentieth century, especially in the South, a black man striking a white
man was almost certain to be arrested and might well be beaten by

white onlookers or even the police. Few white policemen would have been willing to listen to a black person's side of a racial dispute. But Matthews, a white policeman with a neighborhood reputation for racial tolerance, asked Truesdale to describe the events that precipitated the fight. He then took Marshall and the white man to the police station and released them a short time later without filing charges.

The second event that made Marshall painfully aware of segregation took place one Saturday shortly after that hatbox incident. He discovered there were no public restrooms for black people, not even in the department stores where their patronage and dollars were welcomed. He hopped aboard the trolley, hoping it would carry him quickly to his home. He made it as far as the front door. It was an indignity he would never forget.

Though he had become a defender of his rights, dignity, and self-worth, Marshall soon learned that pragmatism pays. His father helped him obtain a summer job as a waiter where he once worked, on the Baltimore & Ohio Railroad. Thurgood would use the money to help pay his college expenses. On his first day at work the dining-car steward gave him a pair of waiter's pants. The tall, lanky teenager found the pants too short and asked for another pair. "Boy," said the steward, "we can get a man to fit the pants a lot easier than we can get pants to fit the man. Why don't you scrunch down a little more?" Years later Marshall, with a laugh, recalled, "I scrunched."

One of the qualities that endeared Thurgood to his friends and colleagues over the years was a pragmatic tendency not to take himself too seriously. As a young man of twenty-one, in 1929, he worked as a waiter at the posh Gibson Island Club in the Chesapeake Bay, which is separated by a narrow causeway from the mansion-strewn Maryland mainland near Annapolis.

The club, in its grandeur, was a haven of exclusivity for the white power elite that came thirty-five miles from Washington to dine on the finest crab dishes and oysters in the world while politicking under portraits of Confederate generals. Marshall's father had been working there for a number of years as the head steward, and he hired Thurgood that summer so he could earn money for his law school tuition.

One evening a U.S. senator from a western state entered the dining room escorting two attractive young women. "Nigger, I want service at this table!" he announced, summoning young Thurgood. Throughout the evening, and on other nights that followed, Marshall served the senator and his coterie adroitly, despite the senator's prodigious use of the word *nigger* while Marshall attended to him.

Disturbed by the man's incivility, one of the club members, Senator "Cotton Ed" Smith of South Carolina, finally called Marshall aside and asked, "Thurgood, what's that senator callin' you?" Marshall replied that the senator was merely calling him "boy," racially derogatory but acceptable in civilized white society.

Thurgood could not lie to his father, however, who from the doorway heard the abuse to which his son submitted sheepishly. It was too much to take for a man who taught his son early to fight anyone who called him "nigger." The elder Marshall scolded him: "Thurgood, you are a disgrace to the colored people!"

That prompted a confession from Thurgood. Each night when the offending senator left, he tipped Thurgood twenty dollars. As Marshall confided to a friend many years later, "In a few days, I got myself almost enough money to pay off all my bills." So he told his pal in a jocular, folksy drawl, "Anytime you wanna call me 'nigger,' you just put your twenty dollahs down on this table. And you can keep doing it all day. But the second you run outta them twenties I'm gonna bust you in the nose."

Thurgood completed high school in 1925, at the age of sixteen, and worked that summer to earn money for tuition and books at Lincoln University. At the end of the season he had not earned enough, so Norma Marshall pawned her wedding and engagement rings and gave him the money. She never redeemed them.

Thurgood's brother, William Aubrey Marshall, had completed his undergraduate education and was now attending medical school at Howard University in Washington, D.C., on his way to becoming an eminent chest surgeon. Norma Marshall held fast to her desire for Thurgood to become a dentist, for she was convinced the medical profession would be a safe harbor for her sons and ensure their economic success.

During the 1920s the choice of black students destined for college was limited. White southern colleges did not accept them. That was the law. Very few black students attended integrated schools in other parts of the United States. Thurgood applied to Lincoln University in Chester, Pennsylvania, the nation's oldest black college and his brother's alma mater. It had been founded in 1854 by a Presbyterian minister and his wife. Lincoln's charter called for "the scientific, classical and theological education of colored youth of the male sex." Though it now accepts male and female students of all races, it was all black and all male and had an all-white faculty at the time Marshall attended. Known as the "black Princeton" because most of its faculty had been educated at that Ivy League institution, Lincoln attracted students from America's black middle class and from African and Asian countries.

More than half of the school's alumni went on to graduate work and professional careers. Marshall's classmates included educators William V. Fontaine, Therman B. O'Neal, Fannin Belcher, and W. Edward Farrison. Toye Davis would become a noted physician with degrees from Harvard University. Kwame Nkrumah was a future president of Ghana, and Benjamin Nnamdi Azikiwe became the first African governor general of Nigeria. Cabell Calloway, Marshall's childhood friend from Baltimore, attended Lincoln with him for two years before dropping out to become internationally renowned as bandleader Cab Calloway. Langston Hughes, who had already started his literary career, was another classmate and one of Marshall's closest friends. He would become the poet laureate of Harlem's Black Renaissance and black America's strongest literary voice.

During his first semester at Lincoln, the seventeen-year-old Marshall, no longer under the guidance of his parents, continued his pranks. He was a founding member of the school's Weekend Club, a group of happy-go-lucky, party-going students who proudly boasted they never opened a book or could be found studying on the Lincoln campus on weekends. He played pinochle and poker frequently and later confided to friends that he played well enough to keep himself in spending money.

In his sophomore year, Thurgood and several fellow students delighted in hazing freshmen. One night they descended upon the

freshman dormitory and shaved the heads of most of the un-
derclassmen. The school's administration did not look kindly
upon their tonsorial zeal and charged twenty-six sophomores,
including Marshall and Hughes, with the deed. Hughes drafted a
statement acknowledging collective guilt, which was signed by
each member of the group. They were collectively fined $125, and
Marshall, Hughes, and several others were suspended for two
weeks. "I got the horsin' around out of my system," Marshall
recalled.

Despite his antics and his assertion that he "never cracked a
book," Marshall obtained good grades. He maintained a B
average and read prolifically. He was impressed with the writing
of educator W. E. B. Du Bois, a founding member of the NAACP
and author of *The Souls of Black Folk,* a pointed collection of
essays on black life in America. Du Bois was also editor of the
NAACP's *Crisis,* and his searing editorials in the magazine struck
right at the heart of America's racial inequities. During his final
two years in college, Marshall became interested in the emerging
literature of the Harlem Renaissance, an era that produced a
prolific outpouring of contemporary black writers, including
Countee Cullen, Claude McKay, Jean Toomer, and Hughes. His
exposure to these "race writers" stimulated his intellectual curiosity about the role of black people in America.

"Lincoln was a school of all Negroes with one or two excep-
tions," Marshall told the *American Bar Association Journal.* "And
an all-white faculty. We argued over general principles. And we
were brainwashed. We discussed it [discrimination]," he recalled.
"What we discussed was, why did we have to take it? Why
shouldn't we do something about it?"

One night Marshall went with a group of six fellow students to
a movie theater in nearby Oxford. After they purchased their
tickets, an usher reminded them that black patrons were restricted
to the balcony, commonly referred to as the "nosebleed section"
or "nigger heaven." The students ignored the usher's admonition
and took seats in the theater's whites-only orchestra. When the
usher ordered them to move, they kept their seats, seemingly
engrossed with the western movie. Thurgood recalled hearing a
bitter voice in the theater's darkness saying, "Nigger, why don't
you just get out of here and sit where you belong?"

Marshall told the man that he had paid for his ticket and did not intend to move from his comfortable orchestra seat. Recalling the incident in a letter to his parents, he wrote, "You can't really tell what a person like that looks like because it's just an ugly feeling that's looking at you, not a real face. We found out that they only had one fat cop in the whole town and they wouldn't have the nerve or the room in the jail to arrest all of us. But the amazing thing was that when we were leaving, we just walked out with all those other people and they didn't do anything, didn't say anything, didn't even look at us—at least, not as far as I know. I'm not sure I like being invisible, but maybe it's better than being put to shame and not able to respect yourself."

Thurgood said the Oxford movie theater incident started his civil rights career. "The leader of that group at Lincoln was a guy named U. S. Tate. "He was the leader who said we ought to do something about it. We desegregated the theater in the little town of Oxford. I guess that's what started the whole thing in my life."

As a religion-based institution, Lincoln encouraged students to attend church services, and Marshall and several of his friends frequently went to Philadelphia's Cherry Street Memorial Church. Years later Marshall provided an explanation for their becoming churchgoers: "We went there [Cherry Street Memorial Church] because we learned that's where all the cute chicks went."

Vivian Burey, a University of Pennsylvania undergraduate, was the "cute chick" who quickly caught Marshall's eye. They dated on weekends, sometimes attending the Oxford movie theater he had integrated with his classmates, and they soon fell in love. "First we decided to get married five years after I graduated, then three, then one, and we finally did, just before I started my last semester," he recalled. They were both twenty-one years old when they married on September 4, 1929. It was a childless marriage, with four miscarriages, that was to last for twenty-five years, until Vivian's death from cancer in February 1955.

Thurgood and Vivian, who had already received her degree, moved into a small apartment in Oxford, not far from the Lincoln University campus. Vivian "Buster" Marshall, who had a reputation for being a smart and levelheaded woman, had a stabilizing influence on her husband's life. His days of campus carousing and drinking with classmates came to an abrupt end. It was time to get down to the hard and serious business of supporting a wife and paving the financial path for his continuing education. He took part-time jobs as waiter and bellhop to meet the rent on the small apartment, pay tuition, and buy textbooks for his last semester at Lincoln. Vivian worked full-time as a secretary.

Marshall, who had honed his forensic skills in combative discussions with his father, joined the college's debating club his sophomore year. He was the star of Lincoln's debating team and led the squad to a long string of impressive victories against white schools, including Bates, Bowdoin, and Colby. His oratorical skills and fiery delivery earned him the nickname "the Wrathful Marshall." "If I were taking debate for credit I would be the biggest honor student they ever had around here," he wrote in a 1929 letter to his father.

That year, while Lincoln's debating club flourished, its football team suffered a series of crushing defeats. At a pep rally the night before the homecoming game, Marshall leaped to the stage and delivered an enthusiastic twenty-minute-speech. The next day Lincoln's football team played its finest game of the season. The result was a scoreless tie, but Marshall took credit for it, saying that the team had put an end to its long string of defeats and at least had not lost the important game.

In June 1930 Marshall marched to receive his bachelor's degree with honors as his proud parents and wife sat in the first row. He had majored in American literature and philosophy. As Norma Marshall watched her son receive his diploma, she knew he was not going to be a dentist.

William and Norma Marshall offered their son and daughter-in-law a home in their Baltimore row house. It was a graduation present, for the elder Marshalls understood the young couple would need to save every dollar they could for Thurgood's law school expenses. Buster and Thurgood accepted. Norma Marshall liked Buster and believed she would be a settling, stabilizing influence on her son. The two women were kindred spirits with a common interest—Thurgood Marshall. Buster redecorated Thurgood's old third-floor bedroom, and the couple settled in, ready to take on the challenge of law school.

FOUR

Howard Law School and the Social Engineers

Build a law school and train men to get the constitutional rights of [your] people. Once you train lawyers to do this, the Supreme Court will have to hand your people their civil and constitutional rights.

—Louis Dembitz Brandeis

Thurgood applied to the University of Maryland's Law School in 1930. It was a logical choice. The law school was located in downtown Baltimore, on Redwood Street, a ten-minute trolley ride from the Marshall family home. As a Maryland resident, Marshall would pay less tuition than he would at an out-of-state law school. After graduating, he would be well steeped in Maryland law and ready to begin his Baltimore law practice.

But as *Baltimore Sun* columnist H. L. Mencken later observed, there had never been an "Ethiop among the Aryan, larval Blackstones" at the state law school, and the University of Maryland was not about to make an exception for this black native son. Thurgood Marshall would avenge that decision later. In the meantime he applied for, and was quickly admitted to, Howard University's law school in Washington, D.C.

Howard University was founded in 1867 in an old red-brick dance hall on a Georgia Avenue hill two miles north of the nation's Capitol. It opened as a school for freed slaves, but its charter did not specifically mandate the race of prospective students. Federally funded, Howard produced most of the nation's black lawyers, scientists, doctors—including Aubrey Marshall—dentists, nurses, pharmacists, educators, engineers, and architects. It was the citadel of graduate and professional education for America's black students.

Marshall committed himself to the study of law and the twice-a-day forty-mile rides in segregated rail cars, reading law books all the way. It was a grueling schedule. During his first year in law school, Thurgood left Baltimore every weekday at 5:30 A.M., attended classes until 3:00 P.M., then returned to one of his part-time jobs as a waiter, a bellhop, and a baker at Preece's Bakery on Pennsylvania Avenue. Then he studied until midnight. "I heard law books were to dig in," he said, "so I dug deep. I got through simply by overwhelming the job, and I was at it twenty hours a day, seven days a week."

Despite the rigorous routine, during which time the weight on his six-foot frame dropped from 170 to 130 pounds, law school proved a rewarding and challenging experience. Remembering his first week at Howard, he said, "This is what I wanted to do for as long as I lived." Thurgood said that he enjoyed the forensic debates and the verbal sparring that went along with his studies and that he believed his oratorical skills would be an asset in the practice of law.

In 1929, the year before Marshall arrived at Howard, Charles Hamilton Houston was appointed the law school's vice dean. This was one of the most significant events in Thurgood Marshall's legal career and in the lives of hundreds of other black law students who earned their degrees at the "school on the hill." Houston was the man who transformed Howard's law school into a fully accredited institution and then used it as the NAACP's "legal laboratory" to plan strategies for important civil rights cases. Houston became Marshall's teacher, his mentor, his colleague, and his friend.

Howard's law school opened on January 6, 1869. The part-time evening program was coeducational, interracial, and non-denominational, but it received little recognition in legal academic circles because it lacked accreditations from the American Bar Association (ABA) and the Association of American Law Schools (AALS), the professional organizations that set standards for legal education. Their approval was essential for the important professional recognition a law school's students needed if they were to become successful lawyers. The ABA and the AALS did not look favorably upon Howard's part-time evening program, with its understaffed faculty, its inadequate law library, and its small physical plant, at 420 Fifth Street NW. Even Washington's black bourgeois community jokingly called it "Dummies' Retreat."

A 1922 Carnegie Foundation study of legal education in America concluded that the nation's part-time afternoon and evening law schools were incapable of providing quality legal educations because they operated under lower educational standards than full-time day schools. Despite these allegations of inadequacy, Howard University Law School had already produced an impressive number of black and white graduates who had distinguished themselves professionally. Its alumni included William H. Hart, LL.B., 1887, who, while a law school professor at Howard, successfully litigated *Hart v. State (of Maryland)*, a Jim Crow rail transportation case in which the state court held that forced separation of the races was unconstitutional in interstate travel. George W. Atkinson, a white graduate of the class of 1891, represented West Virginia in the U.S. House of Representatives while a Howard Law School student and, in 1896, became governor of his state.

Another of Howard's white graduates, Emma M. Gillett, became a founder of the Washington College of Law, now part of the American University in Washington, D.C. Ironically, the coeducational law school that Gillett helped found did not accept blacks. In fact, most of the nation's law schools not only did not admit blacks; they did not accept women of any race. In the 1920s other graduates included a U.S. registrar of the treasury, several municipal judges, and Charlotte Ray, a black woman who became the first American woman to graduate from a university-affiliated law school when she received her Howard degree in 1872. (The 1870

census had reported only five female lawyers in the United States.)
She was also the first woman admitted to practice law in the
District of Columbia.

In 1926 Dr. Mordecai W. Johnson was appointed Howard
University's first black president. A thirty-six-year-old Baptist
minister, Johnson earned degrees at the Atlanta Baptist College
(now Morehouse College), the University of Chicago, Harvard
University, and Rochester Theological Seminary. He came from
Tennessee and served briefly as pastor of a church in Charleston,
West Virginia, before coming to Washington. Johnson, a light-
skinned man with thin lips, a sharp nose, straight hair, and heavy,
dark eyebrows, might easily have crossed the color line and passed
for a white man. Instead, he fiercely reminded friends that his
Caucasian features did not result from the "sexual aggressiveness"
of his female slave forebears, because many slave owners had
fathered mulatto children.

Only two of Howard University's ten graduate schools—the
dental and medical schools—were accredited at their inception,
and in 1925, the year before Johnson arrived, the university's
federal appropriation totaled a meager $217,000. White southern
professional and graduate schools did not accept black students,
and only a few black high school graduates had the money and
backgrounds to attend a few of the mostly white northern or
western colleges. Mordecai Johnson inherited a university charged
with the awesome responsibility of educating a large number of
America's black students who might not otherwise have an
opportunity for advanced educations. But the university needed
drastic improvements if it was to fulfill this mission.

Johnson brought a brash vigor and strict academic discipline to
the task. He fired teachers he described as "deadwood," faculty
members who did not meet his high academic standards. He
became a frequent visitor to Capitol Hill, where he lobbied
Congress to increase the university's appropriation. As president
of a black university dependent on federal funds, he understood
the importance of having access to and maintaining relationships
with white people in positions of power, congressmen and senators who controlled the money he needed to build a first-rate
university. Johnson did not go humbly before congressional com-

mittees seeking support for Howard. More than once he critically reminded legislators who controlled Howard's appropriations how little they were doing to make Howard University an excellent institution.

He recruited some of the nation's finest black scholars, among them E. Franklin Frazier in sociology, Ralph Bunche in political science, Charles R. Drew and Montague Cobb in medicine, Charles Burch and Sterling Brown in literature, Alain Locke in philosophy, E. E. Just in natural sciences, and John Hope Franklin and Rayford Logan in history. These were men who had already established themselves in distinguished academic careers. Leon A. Ransom, a black student first in his class at Ohio State University's law school, and a young black lawyer from Texas, James Madison Nabrit Jr., a graduate of Northwestern Law School, also joined the faculty.

Amherst College graduate William Henry Hastie, who earned a degree from Harvard Law School, where he was an editor of the prestigious *Harvard Law Review,* also came to Howard to teach. Charles Houston's second cousin by marriage, Hastie became the nation's first black federal judge in 1949. Raised in a rural suburb of Knoxville, Tennessee, Hastie came to Washington, D.C., to work in the Bureau of Veterans Affairs. In 1930 he joined the law firm of Houston & Houston and began teaching at Howard. Houston and Hastie shared the compelling urgency to build a first-rate law school and to train quickly a group of superlative black lawyers.

Johnson maintained that Howard University as "an institution of learning, while it protect[s] the good and valuable in older traditions, must at the same time encourage that 'higher individualism' that constantly makes for new and greater values." He knew he had to expand and increase the quality of the faculty, improve the physical plant, and broaden the curriculum. He also knew that the night law school, which still operated without ABA and AALS accreditations from the small brick row house on Fifth Street, was in serious trouble.

Johnson cultivated relationships with benevolent white friends in positions of power who contributed their time and talent toward his mission. One of Johnson's closest friends was Supreme

Court Justice Louis Dembitz Brandeis, a liberal, legal iconoclast much different from his staid brethren on the High Court. The first Jew to sit on the Supreme Court, he knew what it meant to be a member of a minority group. He took a paternal interest in Howard's law school.

Brandeis and Johnson socialized frequently, even in segregated Washington, where white and black people did not eat in public together and seldom met as guests in private homes. They spent many evenings at each other's homes discussing the Constitution's unfulfilled promises to black America. One evening Justice Brandeis gave his friend some advice. "[Brandeis] told me that the one thing I should do was to build a law school and train men to get the constitutional rights of our people," Johnson recalled, "He said, 'Once you train lawyers to do this, the Supreme Court will have to hand your people their civil and constitutional rights."

Brandeis said to him frankly, "I can tell you most of the time when I am reading a brief by a Negro attorney. You've got to get yourself a real faculty out there or you're always going to have a fifth-rate law school. And it's got to be full-time and a day school."

In 1929 there were twelve million black Americans, and only eleven hundred of them were lawyers. Fewer than one hundred of them held degrees from accredited law schools. An aging white lawyer, Moorfield Story, had served as the NAACP's appellate warrior in five civil rights cases before the Supreme Court. He died in 1929 at the age of eighty-four. Brandeis told Johnson that African Americans could no longer depend on the charity of white lawyers like Story to win important civil rights cases for them. This was a task they would have to prepare for and take on themselves.

Johnson took his friend's advice and began making plans to upgrade the law school. He looked to Charles Hamilton Houston, a black Phi Beta Kappa graduate and class valedictorian from Amherst College, for help. Houston also held LL.B. and S.J.D. degrees from Harvard Law School and had graduated in the top 5 percent of his law school class. Since 1924 he had taught part-time at Howard Law School and worked in his father's Washington law firm.

After Harvard, Houston spent a memorable year studying at the University of Madrid and traveling in Spain and Italy, where he saw a world much different from his native Washington, D.C. It was a world in which he could eat in any restaurant when he had the money to pay the bill, sit where he wished on public transportation, and enjoy the opera from the orchestra section at Madrid's opera house. It was a world in which the color of a person's skin had little to do with the rights he or she enjoyed.

Houston was the only son of a prominent Washington couple, William and Mary Houston. He was born on September 3, 1895. His father worked as a clerk in the Record and Pension Office of the War Department while earning his degree at Howard University's night law school. He opened a small legal practice in Washington that did well, even as the nation was entering the Great Depression.

While Charles Houston labored on wills, civil suits, and property transfers for his father's law firm, he harbored a desire not just to practice law but to teach it. He arrived at that decision during his days at Harvard Law School, even though he once confided to a friend, poet Sterling Brown, that he agreed that "those who can, do, and those who cannot do, teach."

Like Justice Brandeis and Mordecai Johnson, Houston was concerned about the quality of legal education for African Americans. Houston studied under some of the nation's greatest legal minds, and they convinced him it was necessary to develop a cadre of competent black lawyers to fight for the rights of black Americans. Houston's mentors included Professors Felix Frankfurter and Joseph H. Beale and Harvard Law School dean Roscoe Pound. Houston believed teachers and legal scholars were the foundation of any law school that wanted to produce competent lawyers, especially lawyers with the commitment to win equal rights for millions of Americans.

Frankfurter had taken a special interest in Houston while he was a Harvard student, inviting him to his Cambridge home for dinners prepared by his wife, Marion. Frankfurter was born in Vienna and was the only Jew on the Harvard Law School faculty. He was a founder of the American Civil Liberties Union (ACLU) and served on the Legal Advisory committee of the NAACP. He argued with Harvard president Abbott Lawrence Lowell over the school's quota on the number of Jewish students admitted to Harvard. He was a guiding influence in Houston's legal education and helped Houston win the eighteen-hundred-dollar Sheldon Traveling Fellowship in 1923 that made it possible for him to study at the University of Madrid, where he met Roscoe Pound.

In December 1923 Roscoe Pound and Felix Frankfurter sent letters of recommendation to Howard dean Fenton W. Booth in support of Houston's application for a part-time faculty position. Frankfurter wrote that Houston was one of his best doctoral students at Harvard Law School. In 1924 Houston accepted Fenton's offer to teach at Howard.

The improvement of Howard Law School was a task that might have taken people of lesser talent, vision, and vigor years to achieve, but Johnson and Houston were impatient pragmatists and understood the importance of a first-rate legal school for black students. They wanted it quickly.

James Madison Nabrit Jr., another law school professor, who would later succeed Johnson as the university's president, warned Houston that the task of educating black lawyers was not an easy one. Nabrit explained, "The real problem in those days was that we didn't have the facilities to argue moot cases. We didn't have the law books, we didn't have the [earlier] cases.... We couldn't use the facilities or contacts of the bar associations, since they wouldn't let us belong."

In fact, black lawyers were not admitted to local bar associations. The District of Columbia Bar Association excluded non-whites, maintaining that it was a private, professional organization with the right to maintain a selective membership. In 1932, Felix Frankfurter petitioned it to admit black lawyers, and, while the association denied his request, it did allow black law students to use its extensive law library.

In 1925 Houston and Washington lawyers George E. C. Hayes, Louis R. Mehlinger, and J. Franklin Wilson incorporated the Washington Bar Association for the "improvement or enhancement of professional skills as well as professional and citizenship responsibilities of the members." Black lawyers now had their own professional association.

Houston welcomed the challenge of building a first-rate law school and he brought more than a keen, analytic legal mind and the desire to produce excellent lawyers to the job. He brought his friends. Frankfurter and Pound became frequent guest lecturers at the school, and in 1931 Clarence Darrow, the eminent trial attorney of the Scopes "monkey" trial and advocate of civil rights and civil liberties, gave a series of lectures. It was an academic luxury few law schools, even those affiliated with large state universities, could provide.

Endowed with a tremendous capacity for hard work, academic honesty, and scholarship, Houston demanded nothing less from his students. Thurgood Marshall remembered Houston as "hard-crust" when he came there as a student in 1930. "First off, you thought he was a mean so-and-so," Marshall recalled. "He used to tell us that doctors could bury their mistakes, but lawyers couldn't. And he'd drive home to us that we would be competing not only with white lawyers but really well trained white lawyers, so there just wasn't any point in crying in our beer about being Negroes. And I'll tell you—the going was rough. There must have been thirty of us in that class when we started, and no more than eight or ten of us finished up. He was so tough we used to call him 'Iron Shoes' and 'Cement Pants' and a few other names that don't bear repeating. But he was a sweet man once you saw what he was up to. He was absolutely fair, and the door to his office was always open. He made it clear to all of us that when we were done, we were expected to go out and do something with our lives."

In a speech to Howard law students many years later, Marshall said, "[What] Charlie beat into our heads was excellence." He said that Houston told his students, "When you get in a courtroom, you can't just say, 'Please, Mr. Court, have mercy on me because I'm a Negro.' You are in competition with a well-trained white lawyer, and you better be at least as good as he is; and if you expect to win, you better be better. If I give you five cases to read overnight, you better read eight. And when I say eight, you read ten. You go that step further, and you might make it."

Hastie later wrote of Houston, "He had a soldier's faith that winning the fight is all that matters, that every battle must be fought until it is won and without pause to take account of those stricken in the fray. He reflected that conviction in a slogan which he gave to his students: 'No tea for the feeble, no crape for the dead.'"

"Harvard was training people to join big law firms," Thurgood Marshall remembered. "Howard was teaching lawyers to go to court. The emphasis was not on theory, the emphasis in this school was on practice, on how to get it done."

Houston taught his students how to use the law to win civil rights and how to employ existing laws to fight racial injustice, constantly reminding them that upon graduation they would be not just lawyers but "social engineers." Houston believed the school's immediate objective was "to make itself a more efficient training school and to produce capable and socially alert Negro lawyers." His term "social engineer" described his philosophy that good lawyers could use the law as "tools to construct a legal machinery that provides and protects the equal rights of all Americans."

In early June 1928 Houston's doctor, Edward Mazique, told him the lingering cold he thought he had actually was tuberculosis. The District of Columbia's health codes prohibited tuberculosis patients from entering schools, so Houston reluctantly took a leave of absence during the 1929 academic year. But much to the dissatisfaction of his wife, Gladys, and his physician, he took his work to bed with him. He studied the Carnegie report and wrote a paper redefining his plan to win accreditation for Howard's law school. He worked on the NAACP's legal strategy to integrate education, and he kept in touch with his father's law firm. From his sickroom came a flood of memos to Howard University president Mordecai Johnson, the law school faculty, and NAACP officials in New York City.

In one memorandum, "Personal Observations on the Summary of Studies in Legal Education as Applied to the Howard University School of Law," he wrote: "Every group must justify and interpret itself in terms of the general welfare; the only justification for the Howard University school of law, in a city having seven white law schools, is that it is doing a distinct, necessary work for the social good,...the indispensable social function of eliminating legal racial discrimination in America."

He went on to describe the mission and the responsibility of black lawyers. "The Negro lawyer must be trained as a social engineer and group interpreter, due to the Negro's social and political condition. The Negro lawyer must be prepared to anticipate, guide and interpret his group's advancement.... Moreover, he must act as a business adviser... for the protection of the sacred resources possessed or controlled by the group.... He must provide more ways and means for holding within the group the income now flowing through it."

By the end of the 1928 academic year, Howard Law School was operating full-time, but it still needed the important American Bar Association and Association of American Law Schools credentials. On February 4, 1930, the law school's board of trustees gave Houston something he had wanted for a long time: It voted to move full speed ahead with Houston's plan to secure the accreditations and to close the night law school the following June.

The twenty-two night law school students vehemently protested the closing and took their argument to President Johnson. Critics of the decision to abolish the night school accused Johnson and Houston of attempting to "Harvardize" Howard. They argued that Houston's father, now a successful Washington lawyer, was a night-school graduate. A night school, they said, allowed students to earn a law degree while working full-time day jobs in order to pay for their evening classes. Houston and Johnson worked out an agreement that permitted night-school students to matriculate at the new day school and work at night. By December 1931 Howard Law School had earned the crucial ABA and AALS approvals.

Marshall finished first in his class his freshman year and earned the coveted job as assistant in the school's law library. The job lengthened his law school day to 8:00 P.M. and sometimes later, but it paid his tuition, bought his books, and meant he would no longer have to rush back to Baltimore and his part-time jobs. And the library assistant's job brought collateral benefits. It put Marshall in closer contact with Houston, Nabrit, and other NAACP lawyers who met in the school's library late at night preparing cases and planning strategy for the NAACP's legal attack on segregation. Marshall looked over their shoulders, and it was not long before the second-year law student was given meaningful research assignments that were to become integral parts of important civil rights cases.

NAACP executive secretary Walter White frequently attended the library sessions and was impressed with Marshall: "There was a lanky, brash young senior law student who was always present," White said. "I used to wonder at his presence and sometimes was amazed at his assertiveness in positions [taken] by Charlie [Houston] and the other lawyers. But I soon learned of his great value to the case in doing everything he was asked, from research on obscure legal opinions to foraging for coffee and sandwiches.

Professor William Hastie remembered the preparation of an appellate brief and a moot-court argument in class by Marshall and another student, Oliver Hill. "Their brief was better than many I've seen by practicing lawyers," he said. "I would have been willing to say unequivocally then and there that they were going to turn out to be darned fine lawyers."

FIVE

A Racist Capital

Wheel about, turn about,
   do just so.
Every time I wheel about
   I jump Jim Crow.

                —Minstrel song

During his last year in law school Marshall continued to work late at night, long after the last class had ended, with Hastie and Houston in the library and in private homes in the middle-class black neighborhood called Brookland, plotting strategies for their current NAACP cases. Marshall's personal association with Houston and other NAACP lawyers gained him entry into Washington's closed society of educated black people who were trying to articulate the plight of all black Americans.

It was a world that few of Washington's white people knew existed. Washington's black citizens could attend performances by Duke Ellington, Lena Horne, and other black entertainers at the black Howard and Lincoln theaters, but they were not allowed at the National Theatre or in Constitution Hall. Washington's large downtown nightclubs did not admit blacks, and most of the black-owned clubs along U Street and Florida Avenue catered to a black clientele that was socially and economically different from the city's black professionals.

The exclusion from first-class downtown entertainment created an interesting social phenomenon. Most Brookland residents socialized among themselves in the paneled basements and club cellars of their homes, and this created a close-knit group of networking black people interested in creating better lives for their children. Today many black Washington social organizations still exist, continuing their clannish tradition of restricting membership to those who have achieved professional status.

The Brookland network of black professionals in the 1940s included educators Herman Branson, Albert DeMond, and Ralph Bunche, poet Sterling Brown, and attorneys John P. Davis and Bernard Jefferson. They had an informal club they named the Brookland Rod and Gun Club but boasted that they never went hunting or fishing. They worked closely with the NAACP and other civil rights groups in lobbying key members of the Roosevelt administration, such as Harold L. Ickes, to ensure that the rising tide of New Deal programs would improve the lives of black Americans, as the Age of Jackson had done for white Americans a century earlier.

It was law school student Thurgood Marshall who made an amazing discovery one night in a Brookland basement. He found that in codifying the laws of the District of Columbia, the city's civil rights codes had been omitted. "Since it didn't apply to anyone but us, they left it out," Marshall remembered. "We eventually got to the court and got that straightened out."

In 1932 Hastie asked Marshall—then a second-year law student—to help prepare an appeals brief in the North Carolina desegregation case of Thomas Hocutt, a black student who had been refused admission to the University of North Carolina's law school. Hocutt claimed the refusal violated his constitutional right to equal-protection guarantees. Hocutt sued the university and lost. Hastie was asked to handle the appeal. Despite the argument devised by Hastie and Marshall, they lost the case in the North Carolina appeals court.

The court held that the University of North Carolina, though financed with public funds, was "not of a public character," and lawyers for the state contended Hocutt was "a reluctant colored man, poorly prepared and disqualified," and that he was "the instrument of outside agitators trying to force the university to admit Negroes." The appeals court said the school could legally be considered a private institution and had no obligation to extend equal rights to all applicants. Marshall met the defeat with dejection. He knew how it felt to be denied admission to his state's university.

Howard University's law school was quietly becoming the major advocate of the legal rights of black people. Houston, Hastie, and Walter White used it as a clearinghouse for the nation's civil rights litigation. Lawyers from small towns throughout the South sought counsel with the law school faculty before bringing cases to their local courts. And Houston took a special interest in selectively picking the best plaintiff for each NAACP case.

In 1933 Marshall graduated first in his class, magna cum laude. He had not only earned a law degree; he had gained early recognition as a promising, bright attorney with the potential to make important contributions in the struggle for human rights.

And he had forged an alliance with a law school that was becoming the national data bank for civil rights legislation and a crucial legal resource for lawyers across the nation who were waging the civil rights war on the front lines as the NAACP came of age. It is important to understand the changes that were taking place in the American civil rights movements and in the NAACP during the years before Thurgood Marshall completed law school, because it was the NAACP that was to become the vehicle responsible for his success.

Before Marshall graduated, the NAACP leadership decided that the time had come to implement a new, comprehensive strategy for combating racial discrimination. Since the organization's founding in 1909, and in large part due to its efforts, blacks had made undeniable progress toward entering the mainstream of American life. Some, like Marshall, were earning professional degrees at black educational institutions, and a small minority of them were attending integrated colleges and universities in the East. In many American cities—Washington, D.C., New York, Baltimore, Boston, Philadelphia, and Richmond—there was a thriving and self-contained, if small, black middle class. Well-credentialed African-American men and women of letters attested to some degree of black success at entering into and succeeding in top universities or the professions.

Moreover, blacks had acquired a sense of racial pride and self-worth, defying the stereotyping imprint of racial inferiority. For example, during the first quarter of the twentieth century, black nationalist Marcus Garvey, calling upon blacks to take pride in their skin color and ancient heritage, won over 1.5 million adherents to his Universal Negro Improvement Association's back-to-Africa crusade. Meanwhile, black painters, sculptors, actors, musicians, and athletes gained recognition both at home and abroad—for the insights they offered into black life certainly, but also for giving expression to the many facets and complexities of human existence and experience. They deepened and enlivened American culture to the delight of millions of whites and blacks in America and around the world. For the overwhelming majority of blacks, however, life in America was cruel, short, brutal, and impoverished. Inequality in every aspect of life—from jobs to housing to education—became the defining characteristic of their existence.

The 1910s and 1920s saw a rising tide of racism in its most virulent forms. In 1917 and 1918 nearly one hundred blacks were lynched in the South. In 1917 more than three thousand Tennessee citizens turned out to witness the burning of a "live Negro" in response to an invitation from a local newspaper. In the same year East St. Louis, Illinois, experienced race riots that left at least forty blacks dead. Then, in 1919, following the end of World War I, the nation experienced "Red Summer," a period of racial strife and violence unprecedented in American history that lasted from June until December. There were more than twenty-five major race riots during that time, from Chicago, Illinois, to Longview, Texas; Omaha, Nebraska; Elaine, Arkansas; and elsewhere. In 1921 violence broke out between blacks and whites in Tulsa, Oklahoma. The killing and destruction ended only after an angry mob of whites went on a week-long rampage, akin to the pogroms unleashed by the Cossacks against the Jews in czarist Russia at the turn of the century. The mob burned to the ground the entire black commercial and residential district located along Green Street. The once-thriving shops and commercial enterprises were eventually replaced with a huge oil refinery that refused to hire blacks. Scores of blacks were killed, and hundreds were dispersed from the city.

Not even the nation's capital, where blacks had managed to carve an unusually secure and comfortable niche since Reconstruction, was spared the turmoil. During Red Summer, false newspaper reports of white women being attacked by black men triggered three days of rioting in Washington by angry white soldiers, sailors, and marines who marauded through the streets attempting to enter and burn black residential neighborhoods. They were finally repulsed by armed black resistance. Six years later, in 1925, a Ku Klux Klan rally in Washington, D.C., drew thirty-five thousand robed Klan members to the Washington Monument grounds.

In addition, promoting racism in its more petty and demoralizing forms became the official policy of the federal government. Under the administration of "liberal" Democrat Woodrow Wilson, federal civil servants were officially segregated by race for the first time. During the Harding administration that followed, blacks were excluded from recreational facilities in Washington. Even at the dedication of the Lincoln Memorial, on Decoration Day in 1922, blacks were rigidly segregated from whites in what was, after all, supposed to be a tribute to Abraham Lincoln, the Great Emancipator.

What inspired the NAACP's decision to formulate a new battle plan, however, had less to do with any particular political or social development than with a change in the organization's financial fortunes. In 1922 Charles Garland, a wealthy Bostonian and Harvard graduate, refused to accept his share of the banking and investment fortune bequeathed him by his father. Instead, Garland used the money to establish the American Fund for Public Service, Inc., often called the Garland Fund, a foundation for the support of liberal and progressive causes, one of which became the NAACP.

The NAACP received a hundred thousand dollars that year to carry out a campaign "to secure for Negroes in this country a fuller and more practical enjoyment of the rights, privileges and immunities theoretically guaranteed them by the Constitution of the United States." For the first time in its history, the NAACP had in the bank funds sufficient to conduct a long-range, comprehensive strategy. With the Garland Fund grant in hand, NAACP leaders made their plans.

At first, the nation's black leadership differed over how best to achieve the desired goals. Leftist organizations, including the League of Struggle for Negro Rights and the International Labor Defense (ILD), argued that unorganized black workers represented an opportunity for direct political action. Both organizations were founded with support from the Communist Party USA. The ILD's purpose was to organize "a mass political and legal defense in...cases of...the class struggle" and to fight "legal and extralegal attacks against Negroes by KKK elements, acting either as outright lynch mobs or as lynchers clothed with the garb of legal authority." Among other things, the ILD undertook the defense of the Scottsboro boys, nine blacks between the ages of thirteen and twenty, framed for allegedly raping two white women in a railroad boxcar in Alabama in 1931. All but one of the defendants, a thirteen-year-old, were sentenced to death. The ILD used the trial to publicize and promote its political agenda by attracting national and international attention to the case. Eventually, two of the defendants' death sentences were commuted on appeal to the U.S. Supreme Court based on the fact that blacks had been excluded from both the grand and petit juries that heard the case.

Moderate thinkers, such as Roger Baldwin, a founder of the ACLU and one of the Garland Fund's administrators, and Ralph Bunche, who decades later would win a Nobel Peace Prize for settling an Arab-Israeli dispute on behalf of the United Nations, shared the views that direct mass political action was the most effective means to get results.

Ultimately, those who favored a legalistic approach prevailed. Among them were Felix Frankfurter of Harvard Law School, Arthur Spingarn, the NAACP's chief lawyer at the time, and Charles Houston, newly appointed dean of Howard Law School. The man selected in 1930 to head the NAACP's legal effort was Nathan Ross Margold, a Romanian-born Jew and protégé of Frankfurter's who had known Houston at Harvard.

Margold's research convinced him that the best way to attack and begin to eliminate racial discrimination in America was by suing to end discrimination in public education. After all, education was a proven key to success and advancement in America. It was therefore crucial that the public schools be opened to blacks on a genuinely equal basis. Margold saw good prospects for success on the legal merits of his position. His research of relevant U.S. Supreme Court and lower court decisions led him to conclude that while the Court had upheld the constitutionality of segregation as practiced in particular situations, the weight of judicial precedent did not give the practice an unqualified stamp of approval.

For example, in the landmark 1896 case of *Plessy*, the Court established the separate-but-equal doctrine. Basically, this doctrine meant that a state could satisfy the Fourteenth Amendment's requirement that all citizens be accorded the equal protection of the laws by providing people of different races with facilities that were substantially equal, even if separate.

The facts of the case were simple enough. In 1890, the Louisiana legislature passed a law requiring that "all railway companies carrying passengers in their coaches in the State shall provide equal but separate accommodations for the white and colored races by providing two or more passenger coaches for each passenger train, or by dividing the passenger coaches by a partition so as to secure separate accommodations." Two years after the law was passed, a light-skinned black Louisianian named Homer Adolph Plessy decided to challenge it. Plessy boarded a whites-only railway coach outside New Orleans and refused to leave his seat and move to the black coach when asked to do so. He was arrested by Detective Christopher Cain, charged with violating the separate-car law, convicted, and fined twenty-five dollars. His appeal was eventually taken up by the U.S. Supreme Court, which heard the case in 1896.

In a ruling that would stand for more than a half century, until Thurgood Marshall's victory in *Brown*, the Court upheld the Louisiana law in a seven-to-one decision. One justice, David Brewer, did not take part in the case. Writing for the Court's majority, Associate Justice Henry Billings Brown concluded:

"Laws permitting, or even requiring, [racial] separation in

places where [the races] are liable to be brought into contact do not necessarily imply the inferiority of either race by the other, and have been generally, if not universally, recognized as within the competency of the state legislatures in the exercise of their police power."

For those who desired to share fully in the American dream, the Court's ruling represented the root of the country's discriminatory evils. Despite Justice Brown's assertion that segregation did "not necessarily imply the inferiority of either race by the other," *Plessy* sanctioned the practice of separating blacks from whites by consigning blacks to the backs of buses, to the rear of trains, to the partitioned-off "colored" sections of waiting rooms and government offices, to the use of separate water fountains and toilet facilities designated "colored," and the like. The separate-but-equal doctrine became the foundation of social mores and practices whereby the lot to which people were consigned in life was determined solely on the basis of race, effectively relegating blacks to second-class citizenship.

Such policies were commonly referred to as "Jim Crow" by their black victims. The term originated with a song of that name sung by Thomas Rice in a minstrel show before the Civil War. Rice was a white actor who played the buffoon part of Jim Crow in blackface. He sang: "Wheel about, turn about, do just so. Every time I wheel about I jump Jim Crow." Jim Crow eventually came to symbolize white dominance over blacks and the laws of segregation that legally maintained it. Throughout his career Thurgood Marshall was fond of "ajumping Jim Crow" in portrayals of slaphappy, kowtowing plantation slaves. But he did it with humor and the implied understanding that he was really poking fun at those who believed the stereotype was an accurate representation of southern rural black life.

Margold's investigations also revealed a pattern of underfunding of black schools throughout the South. He hoped that in states where a historic, systematic pattern of underfunding black educational institutions could be demonstrated, the courts would be compelled under the equal-protection clause to outlaw segregation altogether. But in those states where less egregious disparities existed, simply applying the law as it then stood and demanding equal facilities, without challenging segregation in principle, might be enough.

The basis for this view was Margold's conviction that the cost of maintaining dual school systems that were substantially equal, as *Plessy* required, would prove prohibitive. Few states would be willing to assume the financial burden of upgrading their schools for blacks to a level on a par with those for whites in the middle of the Depression. It would be more cost-effective simply to desegregate the schools. Segregation would prove economically untenable and could be made to collapse of its own weight.

Years later Marshall suggested, in a humorous moment, that he would bring one suit for one student in each state that maintained segregated school systems and then force the states to construct institutions equal to white schools for that one student. "They would quickly get the point," he said.

Margold took a conservative approach, which the NAACP leadership considered with caution. At one end of the spectrum were those who feared that even the slightest failure would produce a legal precedent that would set the clock back decades, fortifying, not weakening, the hand of the segregationists. At the other were those who continued to press for direct, organized political action. They thought progress through the courts would be too slow.

A growing sentiment for black leadership began to cut across the entire spectrum of the NAACP's ranks. This was the view that Brandeis and Mordecai Johnson shared—namely, that it was time for black lawyers to take this struggle for equality into their own hands. The more prominent liberal, Jewish advocates, it was felt, should now step aside in favor of committed black attorneys for whom the efforts of men such as Spingarn, Brandeis, Frankfurter, and Margold had paved the way.

Three years after his appointment, in 1933, Nathan Margold left the NAACP to become solicitor for the Department of the Interior in Franklin D. Roosevelt's New Deal administration. Two years passed before he was replaced at the NAACP's legal helm. His successor was Howard Law School dean Charles Hamilton Houston, who took the job for which he had recommended Margold five years earlier.

Houston proceeded carefully. He agreed that public education was probably the most crucial area in which to wage the fight, stating that "since education is a preparation for the competition of life" and "all elements of American people are in economic competition," blacks must have equal educational opportunities if they are to be competitive. Unlike Margold, however, Houston did not believe that the time was right to attack the doctrine of segregation directly. Instead, his desire was first to win a series of judicial precedents at the lower-court level that could be relied upon later in a U.S. Supreme Court challenge.

Moreover, Houston saw his incremental approach as one that would have the additional benefit of stirring black people into political consciousness at the grass-roots level. Until that time, blacks had quite simply been afraid to assert their rights because they feared reprisals at the workplace and even physical retaliation. In a 1934 memorandum to the Joint Committee of the NAACP and the Garland Fund, Houston stated the view that "to the end of arousing and strengthening the local will to struggle, the general policy of the NAACP should be to lend a hand in contests already undertaken by the local communities themselves, rather than to precipitate a struggle on a community that does not want it." He concluded, "the inspiration value of a struggle is always greater when it springs from the soil than when it is a foreign growth."

Houston's appointment was historically significant for a number of reasons. Certainly his acceptance of the post meant black lawyers would from then on play the prominent role in the desegregation battle. With Howard Law School graduating top-flight lawyers each year, Houston could draw on a talented pool of young blacks to join the fight.

SIX

Justice on a Shoestring

He said you was a freebie lawyer.
—An elderly black woman from South Carolina

Marshall passed the Maryland bar examination in 1933, but not as brilliantly as reported several years later in a profile in the *Baltimore Afro-American* newspapers. He sent a note of correction to publisher Carl Murphy shortly after the article appeared: "As I remember it, it was about one point above the passing mark of 210." Murphy dutifully published the correction.

Marshall, twenty-four, had turned down a Harvard University fellowship for advanced legal study. His wife and parents had sacrificed dearly to see him through college and law school, and it was now time for him to begin paying his own way. He was anxious to set about the business of practicing law, ready to become one of Charles Houston's social engineers.

Marshall rented a small office, suite 604, on the sixth floor of the Phoenix Building, located at 4 East Redwood Street on the fringe of downtown Baltimore, not far from the University of Maryland's law school. He had modest stationery printed, a letterhead that for some reason did not include an office telephone number. Buster came to arrange the sparse, secondhand office furniture, and his mother, who had pawned her engagement and wedding rings to help pay her son's law school tuition, now parted with another personal treasure. She went into her Druid Hill Avenue living room, rolled up the prized Oriental rug that her seafaring father had brought back from one of his trips abroad, and spread it on Thurgood Marshall's office floor.

There were few black lawyers in the United States in 1933—one for every two hundred thousand citizens—and they had difficulty getting paying clients. The Baltimore courts were white-dominated, and many prospective black clients felt they would do better with white lawyers to plead their cases before white judges and predominantly white juries. Some Baltimore blacks even subscribed to the cruel and untrue assertion "If you want to die, go to a black doctor; if you want to go to jail, go to a black lawyer."

Though some clients could not afford even his modest fees, Marshall turned no one away. The nation was deep in the depression, and blacks in Baltimore and across the nation—"last hired, first fired"—suffered economically while waiting patiently for the promises of President Franklin D. Roosevelt's New Deal economic recovery programs to be realized.

Marshall began earning a reputation as "the little man's" lawyer. He spent a lot of time in Baltimore courtrooms, not unfamiliar territory, because he had often been there as a child with his father. He honed his courtroom skills on everyday, mundane legal work, from traffic offenses to eviction cases and some minor criminal matters. He had very few paying clients the first year, and his expenses exceeded his income by a thousand dollars.

Years later he told a reporter, "One day I'd bring two lunches, and the next day my secretary would bring two lunches, and sometimes we'd be the only two people in that office for weeks at a time." He paid his secretary $7.50 a week.

Marshall is fond of recalling the story of an elderly black woman who arrived at his office in May 1934, shortly after he opened his practice. She had recently moved to Baltimore from rural South Carolina, where she was accustomed to receiving free legal advice from a white county judge, a standard practice in southern rural communities where white people in positions of authority practiced a paternal benevolence over local black people who knew their place and stayed in it. When she sought the same free legal advice from a white Baltimore judge, he sent her to Thurgood Marshall. "He said you was a freebie lawyer," she told Marshall.

He didn't turn her away. He called his practice "justice on a shoestring."

Marshall's practice began to boom as word quickly spread that he was a competent attorney with a passion for indigent clients. But his income did not rise with his reputation. His pro bono work and his concern for the "little people" of Baltimore did not go unnoticed by publisher Carl Murphy and Lillie M. Jackson, a Baltimore housewife who was a fierce civil rights activist.

Carl Murphy's father, John H. Murphy Sr., was a whitewasher who purchased a small flatbed printing press and began publishing a Sunday school newspaper in his Baltimore basement in the late 1890s. Several years later he bought the fledgling *Afro* and turned it into a weekly newspaper. Carl Murphy took over the paper after his father's death and nurtured it into a powerful voice for black Americans.

A Harvard University graduate, Murphy studied at the University of Jena in Austria and taught German at Howard University. When he applied to Baltimore's John Hopkins University to do further work, his application was denied because of his race. Physically Murphy was a small man, with a penchant for tweed sport jackets and corncob pipes, but he had big ideas about how to bring about racial justice for black Americans. He once sued the Baltimore & Ohio Railroad for segregating him on a ferry crossing.

Lillie M. Jackson was a Baltimore housewife filled with righteous indignation in her fight for equal rights. She used her booming voice to carry her message to the basements of Baltimore's churches, attempting to recruit members for the NAACP. A Maryland governor once said, "I'd rather have the devil after me than Mrs. Lillie Jackson."

Born May 25, 1889, she grew up on Druid Hill Avenue, like Thurgood Marshall. Her father, Charles Carroll of Maryland's Howard County, was the grandson of the Charles Carroll who signed the Declaration of Independence. Her mother, Amanda Bowen, from Montgomery County, was the granddaughter of an African tribal chief.

Jackson enlisted Carl Murphy's financial and editorial support in strengthening the Baltimore NAACP and in her campaigns for federal antilynching laws, integration of the University of Maryland, the equalization of teachers' pay, voter registration drives across the city, and desegregation of Baltimore's public swimming pools.

Indeed, Murphy used his newspapers, one of the nation's largest and most influential black newspaper chains, to champion civil rights throughout the 1930s. The *Afro* published weekly editions in Baltimore, Washington, Philadelphia, and North and South Carolina, as well as a national edition that was sold in most major cities. Murphy shopped at the Marshall family's west Baltimore grocery store and was fond of the young attorney, whom he had known since Thurgood was a boy in corduroy knickers, kicking stones down Division Street.

Murphy retained Marshall to handle the *Afro*'s legal work and helped him acquire a major Baltimore laundry as a client. But Carl Murphy and Lillie Jackson had big plans for the young Baltimore-born attorney, and they were soon to enlist him as the legal warrior in their civil rights battle.

Elizabeth Murphy Moss, Carl Murphy's daughter, remembers: "My father was a shrewd man, and he knew that Thurgood's law practice was not doing very well economically. Baltimore, like the rest of the nation, was in the grip of the depression, and Dr. Carl knew that if he could give Thurgood some legal work to help meet his office expenses, he could get his help in the civil rights campaign that he was waging with Ma Jackson." Moss said her father and Marshall were very close. "My father had five girls, and in many ways Thurgood was a surrogate for the son he never had. Thurgood was impressive and had a forceful bearing and an outgoing personality that quickly made you like and respect him."

Carl Murphy frequently called upon Marshall for legal interpretations and advice to help him formulate the attacks he was launching against segregation and discrimination on the editorial pages of his newspapers. In 1934, the *Afro* was crusading for innovative federal legislation that would empower Congress to define civil rights and invoke penalties for violations of those rights. Murphy called Marshall on November 16 and asked him for an opinion on the efficacy of the proposed legislation. In a letter hand-delivered the next day, Marshall wrote:

"Pursuant to our conversation yesterday I looked up the Civil Rights Cases. In these cases the Supreme Court laid down finally that it is not within the legislative power of Congress to define what are the civil rights of life, liberty and property of individuals and affix and enforce penalties for their denial by private persons. Under the Constitution of the United States the Supreme Court has the final word concerning the constitutionality of any statute, so it seems that the Civil Rights Bill is out.

"I am enclosing a short brief of the Civil Rights Cases as they were decided."

Marshall's response to Murphy's inquiry was an early indication of his belief that the fate of civil rights for black Americans rested with the judicial, not the legislative, branch of government. This reflected the view also held by his mentor, Charles Houston.

In 1991, fifty-seven years later, Marshall had apparently tempered his 1934 position on the relation between the judicial and legislative branches of government in assuring civil rights. In a public statement he said: "The Fourteenth Amendment gives government the final word. It says Congress shall do everything to implement the 14th Amendment guarantees of due process and equal protection. Congress will eventually do that, but Congress never does anything soon except go to the Persian Gulf. They did that soon."

When Lillie Jackson became president of the NAACP's Baltimore branch, in 1934, the organization was moribund. Membership had fallen to about 100 of the faithful, and the branch had little support, especially among the city's less affluent black working class. The NAACP's Washington branch had also become primarily an elitist social group comprised of affluent, fair-skinned black professionals, more concerned about their social lives and fraternity and sorority ties than with the struggle for equal rights. Marshall jokingly repeated over the years that the initials NAACP at that time actually stood for the "National

Association for the Advancement of *Certain* People." This internal racial phenomenon was one of the problems the NAACP faced as it attempted to widen its appeal to all black Americans, for many of the NAACP's members, especially its leaders like Walter White and Roy Wilkins, belonged to this closed social circle.

Many black people who were light enough "crossed over" or "passed," living their lives as white people in other parts of the country. "Gone on the other side" was the expression commonly used to describe them. Washington's segregated National Theatre employed a black doorman to expose black Washingtonians who were attempting to gain entrance to the Pennsylvania Avenue theater by passing for white.

Although it was often spoken in jest, there was some truth to the statement that frequently made the rounds of Baltimore's and Washington's black middle class: "If you are white, you are all right; if you are yellow, you are mellow; if you are brown, you can stick around; but if you are black, stay back!" Darker-skinned black people often felt that lighter-skinned blacks were treated better by white people, got better jobs, and lived in nicer neighborhoods.

In the early 1930s Marshall's friend and Lincoln University classmate Langston Hughes lashed out poetically at the system of black caste and color class in Washington, where he lived briefly. His poem "Black Gal" includes the line "I hate them rinney yaller gals." In an article published in the Urban League's *Opportunity* magazine, "Our Wonderful Society: Washington," Hughes criticized the black middle class for not paying enough attention to promising black writers of the day, such as Jean Toomer and Rudolph Fisher, because the main characters in their novels were "too black." Hughes's friend Charles S. Johnson saw the article before it appeared and wrote Hughes a note: "You may be sure that you cannot live there [Washington, D.C.] again after it is published."

Carl Murphy and Lillie Jackson knew this internal racial division was one of the obstacles the NAACP would have to overcome on both the local and national levels to broaden its appeal and encompass all blacks. They enlisted Thurgood Marshall's talents in their campaign to rebuild the NAACP's Baltimore branch and to fight segregation and discrimination, retaining him as the attorney for the local chapter.

Marshall carried the NAACP's message to Baltimore's blackest and poorest neighborhoods, championing the civil rights organization's cause to hundreds of complacent black citizens who accepted segregation as a way of life. It was not an easy task for a tall, good-looking, college-educated, light-skinned attorney with hair like a white man's. But despite his light complexion and impressive credentials, he was popular among the ranks of Baltimore's less privileged working-class black citizens. He had no aversion to playing a friendly game of poker or sharing a pint of bourbon with residents of east Baltimore's ghettos as he tried to win their support for the NAACP. Using the same fiery rhetoric he had employed to inspire Lincoln University's losing football team, he made significant progress in unifying Baltimore's black community across educational, economic, social, and skin-color lines. Marshall and Jackson knew, however, it would take more than flashy speechmaking to demonstrate that the Baltimore NAACP was earnestly concerned about the plight of all black Baltimoreans. This was crucial if they were to increase membership and cast off the old impression that the NAACP was nothing more than a social organization for the privileged few.

Thurgood was ready to challenge the old order, and his west Baltimore home neighborhood was a good place to start. Marshall and Jackson organized a boycott of stores on Pennsylvania Avenue, the black commercial district two blocks from Marshall's Druid Hill Avenue home. Though most of the stores' customers were black, the white owners did not hire black workers. Marshall and Jackson mustered a group of unemployed black high school graduates, gave them picket signs, and had them march in front of the Pennsylvania Avenue businesses. Black customers stayed away, but instead of meeting the NAACP's demand to employ black clerks, the stores' angry owners sued the NAACP in federal court for interfering with their businesses.

Now, in October 1934, Marshall's job was to defend the boycotters and the NAACP's protest, and he called upon his former teacher Charles Houston for help. Houston had successfully defended a similar suit in Washington, D.C., when the

New Negro Alliance, a local civil rights group, boycotted shop owners there, and he responded quickly. Marshall did the research and the legwork, and Houston presented the oral arguments in Baltimore's federal court. Houston told the court that blacks had a right to withhold their patronage from merchants who would not employ them. Before a packed courtroom, the judge agreed. It was a victory for Houston, Marshall, the Baltimore NAACP, and the score of black high school graduates who were hired by some of the stores.

With that victory the Baltimore branch of the NAACP set in motion an ambitious agenda. Marshall lobbied Maryland's congressional delegation to support a federal antilynching bill. He won a manslaughter conviction for a western Maryland client who had been charged with burglary and murder and for whom prosecutors sought the death penalty. He brought a successful suit in Baltimore's federal court on behalf of the Monumental Golfers Association—*Charles Law v. Park Board*—that opened golf courses to black golfers. He instituted a series of tutorial classes to help black citizens pass civil service examinations. No case of alleged police brutality went unnoticed by the Baltimore NAACP.

Lillie Jackson and Marshall then turned their attention to the plight of Maryland's black schoolteachers. Like black teachers in most southern states, Baltimore's teachers received lower salaries than their white counterparts. Marshall and Jackson devised a plan to attack this inequity in court. Most black teachers, afraid they would be dismissed if they participated in the protest, did not want to be part of suits against their school boards. Marshall raised a legal defense fund and earmarked money to pay the salaries of any teachers who were fired for taking part in the suits.

It took two years, but Marshall, Jackson, and the teachers prevailed. Maryland's black schoolteachers, who had been earning $612 annually, the same salary as janitors, received a salary increase to $1,475 as a result of the successful litigation. At one point during the proceedings Marshall suggested that if the state did not want to raise the salaries of black teachers to the level of white teachers, it should lower white teachers' pay to that of black teachers. "They quickly got the point," he said.

Marshall began spending more time on the NAACP's legal affairs than on his private law practice, but a fringe benefit of the NAACP work was that it brought him some paying clients from Baltimore's middle-class black community. Handling property transfers, wills, and estates meant better fees than those he received from minor civil and criminal cases, and it did not require as many lengthy courtroom appearances, which left more time for NAACP work. His legal practice brought in about three thousand dollars, and the NAACP was paying most of the expenses he incurred in his civil rights work.

However, the Baltimore NAACP still needed a major case, one that would attract national attention, if it were to increase its membership, and Thurgood Marshall had just the case in mind. In fact, he had thought about it for a long time, ever since he had been denied admission to the University of Maryland's law school because of his race.

SEVEN

An Ethiop Among the Aryans

Compliance with the Constitution cannot be
deferred at the will of the State. Whatever
system it adopts for legal education now must
furnish equality of treatment now.
      —*Donald G. Murray v. University
                          of Maryland* (1935)

Thurgood Marshall and Donald Gaines Murray had several
things in common. They were both native Marylanders, born and
raised in west Baltimore by parents who were a little better off
than most other black Baltimoreans. Each man had earned honor
grades in undergraduate school—Marshall at Lincoln University,
Murray at Amherst College. And both men had been rejected for
admission to the University of Maryland's law school because they
were black. In fact, nine African-American students had been
refused admission to the law school, although neither state laws,
the university's charter, nor its rules mandated segregation. Racial
discrimination was in effect nothing more than a custom, a
personal bias practiced by those who administered the university.

Marshall had held preliminary discussions with Houston about
a University of Maryland Law School desegregation case in the fall

of 1933, and they had discussed a tentative strategy based on Houston's refinement of the Margold paper.

In January 1934 Marshall once again called on Charles Hamilton Houston for help:

> Dear Charlie,
>   Trust you had a good Christmas etc. I hate to worry you so much about this University of Maryland case. When are we to get together on it? Things are very slow just now and I would like very much to get started as soon as possible.

Marshall's letter went unanswered, but it was not because Charles Houston was uninterested. Rather, he was preoccupied with getting ready to move to New York City and his new position as the NAACP's chief counsel. Only after several meetings with NAACP secretary Walter White had he decided to leave Howard's law school and his father's law practice and head north. Following the advice he gave his students, he was going to become a social engineer and employ his legal talents full-time toward the task of civil rights.

As Marshall impatiently waited for Houston's answer, Belford V. Lawson Jr. turned his attention to the University of Maryland. A black Washington attorney and an organizer of the New Negro Alliance, a group of black Washingtonians that lobbied for the employment of blacks in government, Lawson served as counsel to Alpha Phi Alpha fraternity. Many of the national fraternity's members, like members of the Washington and Baltimore branches of the NAACP, were light-skinned and held coveted government jobs or were professionals who came from privileged families. The fraternity had a reputation for using the "paper bag test" for admitting members, an unwritten rule that a prospective member whose skin shade was darker than a paper bag would not be allowed to pledge. The fraternity also had a reputation for holding some of the most popular and best-attended social affairs in black Washington.

But color consciousness among light-skinned black people— their reluctance to have much social contact with darker members of their race and their indifference to the plight and problems of those less fortunate—did not start in the 1930s. It began in the 1880s when abolitionist Frederick Douglass's son founded a summer resort at Maryland's Highland Beach, where the "high-yellow elites," commonly referred to as the "black bourgeoisie," from Washington and Baltimore maintained vacation cottages on the bay.

The lines of exclusivity within the high-yellow societies of Baltimore and Washington were as sharply drawn as those that existed between black and white society. Admittance to the black middle class of Washington and Baltimore required more than a good income. Light skin, family background, education, and a professional position were the requirements for entry into this clique. Parents encouraged their children to socialize and marry within this select group; when birthday parties were held, nearly all of the children who attended were fair-skinned.

In 1934 the Alphas' Washington, D.C., chapter, aware of its image as an elitist group concerned more about their social lives than their civic responsibilities, earmarked several hundred dollars to bring an integration suit against the University of Maryland. Though the University of Maryland's law school was in Baltimore, its liberal arts colleges were on the College Park, Maryland, campus, just across the line from Washington's Brookland neighborhood, where the majority of the city's educated and professional black people lived. The Alphas persuaded Lawson to begin preparing the suit. He enlisted the help of the New Negro Alliance and the Washington branch of the NAACP and then wrote to Thurgood Marshall and asked if he wanted to join in the legal battle.

Lawson's letter distressed Marshall for two reasons: First, Marshall felt Lawson was about to take a case that Marshall himself wanted very badly to try. After all, Marshall was a native Marylander, and his rejection by the University of Maryland Law School in 1930 still rankled. Second, Lawson's letter indicated he was going to sue the university's undergraduate school at the College Park campus, not the university's law school, and that decision was counter to the NAACP's secret plan to attack "the soft underbelly" of segregated education.

Marshall and Houston planned to concentrate the NAACP's energies on graduate schools. They believed it was easier to demonstrate systematic discrimination in graduate schools, where there were fewer students than in public or undergraduate schools. And Marshall believed the NAACP should present a united front and not let it be publicly known that there was dissension within the ranks on the legal strategy for attacking segregation at the University of Maryland. The Margold strategy was not to attack the constitutionality of segregation itself but to challenge its legality as practiced by showing that no remotely equal educational opportunities were offered black students in segregated states, which was unconstitutional. Marshall and Houston reasoned that judges, who were themselves lawyers and products of graduate schools, would be apt to understand their argument that "separate" law schools were not "equal" law schools, and they believed that a small number of victories at the graduate and professional school levels would establish a foundation of precedents upon which they could build a case against the separate-but-equal doctrine for all other educational opportunities.

Nine months later, in October 1934, Marshall wrote another, more urgent "Dear Charlie" letter: "What about the University of Maryland case? B. V. Lawson has been writing me and seems to think the fraternity is going to try the case along with the local branches of the NAACP. I am up a tree as to just what is going to be done."

Again, Marshall's letter went unanswered. Meanwhile, Belford Lawson moved ahead with his plans. He invited Marshall and another black Baltimore attorney, William I. Gosnell, to a planning meeting in Washington. Houston was defending a NAACP case in Augusta, Georgia, when Marshall received Lawson's invitation to the Washington conference. Marshall sent Houston a telegram telling him about the meeting and asking for advice. This time, Houston telegraphed a response: "Attend Lawson's meeting. Get facts but be careful about commitments."

Marshall did not attend Lawson's meeting but sent Gosnell in his place with instructions to "take good notes." Gosnell told those assembled that the Baltimore branch of the NAACP was anxious to take the case and explained the intricacies of the Margold strategy of first launching desegregation suits against graduate and professional schools. Gosnell also insisted it was logical for the Baltimore branch of the NAACP to bring the suit because the school was in Maryland.

Despite Gosnell's arguments, Lawson decided to move forward with the case against the university's undergraduate school. When Houston heard of Lawson's decision, he told Marshall to commence the case against the law school immediately. He added he would be there soon.

Marshall and Houston began with the assumption that any desegregation suit against the University of Maryland's law school would eventually be decided by the Supreme Court. But they first had to exhaust all available local remedies by bringing a suit at the state level. The Supreme Court had set no precedent that would lead them to believe that this tack would not be successful. But the Court's composition at the time was not encouraging.

Marshall and Gosnell's search for the ideal plaintiff produced Donald Gaines Murray, who had graduated with honors from Amherst College that June. The twenty-year-old Baltimorean came from a prominent family. His grandfather was a well-known African Methodist Episcopal (AME) bishop.

Murray wrote to University of Maryland president Raymond A. Pearson requesting information about the procedures for applying to the law school. He received a form letter in reply:

> Under the general rules of the State the University maintains the Princess Anne Academy as a separate institution of higher learning for the education of Negroes. In order to insure equality of opportunity the 1933 Legislature passed Chapter 234, creating partial scholarships at Morgan College or institutions outside the State for Negro students who may desire to take professional courses or other work not given at the Princess Anne Academy.
>
> Should you desire to make application for such scholarship, notify me, and I will see that such application is duly filed.

Murray, however, did not want a state scholarship to an out-of-state law school. He wanted to attend the law school at the University of Maryland. In early January he filed a formal application for admission, including the required two-dollar fee. On February 9 he received a letter from the school's registrar: "President Pearson has instructed me today to return to you the application form and the money order, as the University does not accept Negro students, except at the Princess Anne Academy."

Marshall, Houston, and Murray drafted a response and sent it by registered mail on March 5 to each member of the university's board of regents, enclosing copies of Murray's application and money order:

> I am a citizen of the State of Maryland and fully qualified to become a student at the University of Maryland Law School. No other State institution affords a legal education. The arbitrary action of the officials of the University of Maryland in returning my application was unjust and unreasonable and contrary to the Constitution and laws of the United States and the Constitution and laws of the State. I, therefore, appeal to you as the governing body of the University to accept the enclosed application and money order and to have my qualifications investigated within a reasonable time. I am ready, willing, and able to meet all requirements as a student, to pay whatever dues are required of residents of the State, and to apply myself diligently to my work.

The application and money order were again returned by Pearson, but this time with a letter that must have struck a chord of secret pride in Charles Houston's heart. After again referring Murray to the Princess Anne Academy, Pearson told him of "the exceptional facilities open to you for the study of law at Howard University in Washington," noting that Howard Law School was accredited by the American Bar Association and the Association of American Law Schools and that its tuition was less than that at the University of Maryland's law school.

Now Marshall and Houston were ready to take the university to court. The case, styled initially *Murray v. Pearson* and later

Murray v. the University of Maryland, was heard on June 18, 1935, in Baltimore City before Judge Eugene O'Dunne. Will and Norma Marshall and Thurgood's wife, Buster, came to hear Thurgood's first major case.

In opening arguments, Houston said Murray had been wrongfully refused admission to the state law school. He introduced into evidence documents verifying that Murray was a Maryland resident. He also introduced Murray's Amherst College transcript, which showed he had made the dean's list. He argued that the university's decision to reject Murray's application was capricious and arbitrary on the part of the school's administration, since there was no state law requiring segregation at the university.

The university was represented by Maryland assistant attorney general Charles T. LeViness III. Judge O'Dunne asked him pointedly if Murray's race was the only reason his application was denied. LeViness responded yes, that it was public policy not to accept black students. Under further questioning LeVinnes testified that Maryland's General Assembly had appropriated ten thousand dollars to provide fifty two-hundred-dollar out-of-state scholarships for black students and that these funds had been allocated only after Murray applied to the law school. He said the state currently had 380 applications for those scholarships.

Marshall argued that the state of Maryland could not "export its obligation" by paying the tuition at out-of-state schools for Maryland residents who had been denied admission to Maryland's white professional and graduate schools because of their color. This was a clear violation of the state's obligation to provide equal protection under the Constitution's Fourteenth Amendment. As for Charter 234, Marshall contended that it was nothing more than an empty promise. The Maryland General Assembly had put that statute in place but had not allocated the funds to execute it at the time Murray applied to the law school, and it also allowed Maryland to escape its responsibility to provide educational facilities for black students in the state.

Houston called University of Maryland president Raymond A. Pearson to the stand. Pearson conceded quickly that Princess Anne Academy did not have the faculty, physical plant, or resources of the University of Maryland's law school and that

Murray met all of the requirements for University of Maryland Law School admission. Pearson testified that the two-year course at the Princess Anne Academy was comparable to that at the University of Maryland "in some instances." But when Houston asked Pearson if it was true that only one member of the Princess Anne Academy had a master's degree and that there were no faculty members with doctorates, Pearson admitted that he didn't know. He said he was unaware that the title "doctor" used by the president of the Princess Anne Academy was an honorary, not an academically earned, title.

Pearson was asked if the university would admit Mexican, Indian, and Filipino students if they were Maryland residents. Pearson responded yes. Then Houston asked Pearson why the university did not admit black Marylanders. The university president said he held no personal bias against black students attending the state's university, that he was only following a long-standing public policy. Pearson further testified that even if Murray had applied for a stipend to attend an out-of-state law school, the funds were not available at the time of his request for admission to the University of Maryland.

Houston called Maryland University Law School dean Roger Howell to the stand. Howell told the court that the university's course of study was structured around Maryland's law and state codes. He said twelve of the school's eighteen faculty members were either Maryland judges or private attorneys. Then Marshall forced him to admit that any student who wanted to practice law in Maryland and could not go to the University of Maryland's law school was being deprived of valuable educational opportunities. When asked why Maryland's university system had not constructed and staffed a law school for black students equal in every respect to the one at the University of Maryland, Howell said there was not a sufficient demand to justify the construction and staffing of a separate law school for African Americans.

Judge O'Dunne asked Dean Howell if states with segregated railroad cars were obligated to provide cars of equal quality for black travelers even if only a few people traveled. "How would you let them ride, in an oxcart?" he asked.

Dean Howell's answer brought laughter throughout the courtroom. "Well, if the oxcarts were about as good as the cars, I think I would."

Years later Marshall said that during the first hours of the Murray case he sensed that Judge O'Dunne "had a good grasp of the issues." This feeling, encouraged by the kinds of questions O'Dunne asked witnesses, fortified Marshall's belief in the correctness of the decision he and Houston had made to bring the attack on segregation in education at the graduate school level.

The state superintendent of black schools, a white man, was called. After testifying that Maryland's educational opportunities were "substantially the same" for students of all races, he revealed that Maryland's school year for black students was shorter than for white students, that the state had more one-room schoolhouses for black students than for white students, and that black teachers did not receive salaries equal to those of their white counterparts with the same qualifications. When Marshall asked him about the disparities in teachers' pay, he testified that it was a "known fact" that the cost of living for black teachers was less than that for white ones.

In his closing argument, Thurgood Marshall attempted to assure Judge O'Dunne that he would be on solid legal ground if he ordered Murray admitted to the university. There had never been a court-ordered desegregation of a public school, so Marshall could offer no strong precedent to support his position. "But it had to start someplace, and this was as good a place as any," he later said.

Several years earlier, in *Gong Lum v. Rice*, the U.S. Supreme Court had upheld Mississippi's sending a Chinese-American student to a "colored" school. This seemed to affirm, at least in part, the separate-but-equal doctrine. What Marshall argued in *Murray*, however, was that while the "separate" portion of the separate-but-equal doctrine had been sanctioned by the Court on several occasions, instances in which educational facilities available to black students were definitely not equal—as in *Murray*, because there was no state law school for black students—had never come before the Court. Marshall was convinced that Chief Justice William Howard Taft's majority opinion in *Gong Lum* left a door open. Taft had written, "Had the petitioner alleged specifically that there was no colored school in Martha Lum's neighborhood, a different question would have been presented."

Marshall's argument intrigued Judge O'Dunne, and LeViness was poorly prepared to respond to it. LeViness cited *Cummings v. Richmond County Board of Education,* an 1899 U.S. Supreme Court case in which blacks lost a suit to close a white high school until a black one in their district was reopened. Marshall quickly countered that Murray was not asking the court to close the University of Maryland's law school until the state provided an equal facility for black students. He wanted to be admitted to the existing law school.

LeViness cited *Plessy v. Ferguson* in his defense of Maryland's segregated schools. Marshall told Judge O'Dunne that Murray was not challenging Maryland's right to operate separate black and white school systems. Instead, Murray's challenge was to the inequalities and inadequacies of a system that did not provide equal educational opportunities for all Marylanders. Marshall contended that even in the *Plessy* decision the Supreme Court had stressed the state's obligation to provide equal facilities in a dual school system.

Marshall's final arguments showed the depth of his understanding of constitutional law. He argued that the "separate" part of the separate-but-equal doctrine had been upheld as constitutional by the Supreme Court but that the "equal" requirement provision had never been challenged or come under review. Since Pearson had already conceded that the separate facilities offered Murray at the Princess Anne Academy were unequal, Marshall insisted, the court had no choice but to order Murray's admission to the state's law school. "What's at stake is more than just the rights of my client," he concluded. "It is the moral commitment stated in our country's creed."

Shortly before 5:00 P.M. on June 25, 1935, Judge O'Dunne issued a writ of mandamus ordering President Raymond Pearson to admit Donald Gaines Murray to the University of Maryland's law school immediately. A few minutes later Charles LeViness spoke: "I wish to be quoted as saying that I hope Mr. Murray leads the class in the law school."

Carl Murphy, publisher of the *Afro-American* newspapers, invited Marshall and his family, Houston, Murray, and officers of the Baltimore NAACP to a party in the inner sanctum of his private office on Eutaw Street. They sat around his large horseshoe-shaped desk celebrating the victory as Murphy's reporters and editors prepared a banner-headline edition. "We celebrated until early in the morning, until the first editions of the *Afro* hit the streets," recalled Juanita Jackson Mitchell, a Baltimore NAACP official and civil rights attorney.

Mitchell said Thurgood's victory in the *Murray* case "set the colored people in Baltimore on fire. They were euphoric with victory....We didn't know about the Constitution. He brought us the Constitution as a document like Moses brought the people the Ten Commandments."

Despite the gracious statement of concession from the state's attorney, Maryland appealed the decision to the Maryland Court of Appeals and asked that the case be heard in a special session before the court's normal return from recess in October, when Murray would already be enrolled and attending law school. A special session was denied, and Murray began classes at the law school in the fall.

The *Baltimore Sun's* vitriolic columnist H. L. Mencken wrote: "There will be an Ethiop among the Aryans when the larval Blackstones assemble Wednesday." He also commented that the students and faculty should not object to "the presence among them of a self-respecting and ambitious young Afro-American, well prepared for his studies by four years of hard work in a class A college."

Mencken concluded it would be "brutal and absurd" for the appeals court to reverse Judge O'Dunne's decision. As for the suggestion that Murray attend Howard University, he wrote, "The regents might just as well advise him to go to Addis Ababa or Timbuctoo. He wants to get his training, not in Washington, but here in Baltimore where the laws and procedures of Maryland are at the bottom of the teaching and where he plans to practice."

Mencken believed university officials feared admittance of a black student to the law school would open the doors of the undergraduate schools at the College Park campus. He backhandedly dismissed this concern. "The so-called college of arts," he wrote, "is a fifth-rate pedagogical dump patronized largely by the children of Washingtonians, and it would be easy to bring the

Princess Anne Academy, which is for colored students, up to equality with it."

In January 1936 the Maryland Court of Appeals upheld O'Dunne's decision: "Compliance with the Constitution cannot be deferred at the will of the State. Whatever system it adopts for legal education now must furnish equality of treatment now." The State of Maryland did not appeal the decision to the Supreme Court.

Shortly after the victory, Marshall's Lincoln University class-mate Langston Hughes described him as a man "who has moved a judge to search his conscience and come up with decisions he probably did not know he had in him."

Marshall viewed the *Murray* victory as an important case in which there were "sharply defined issues" supported by "demonstrable evidence." He believed this case would be the springboard for attacking segregated school systems on a larger front.

Charles Houston was less optimistic. Since the *Murray* case, qualified black students had been denied admission to graduate schools in Virginia, Tennessee, and Missouri. In an article in the NAACP's December 1935 *Crisis,* "Don't Shout Too Soon," he cautioned:

"Lawsuits mean little unless supported by public opinion. Nobody needs to explain to a Negro the difference between law in books and the law in action. In theory the cases are simple; the state cannot tax the entire population for the exclusive benefit of a single class. The really baffling problem is how to create the proper kind of public opinion. The truth is there are millions of white people who have no real knowledge of the Negro's problems who never give the Negro a serious thought. They take him for granted and spend their time and energy on their own affairs."

After the *Murray* decision, the Maryland General Assembly sharply increased funding for the education of black students at out-of-state institutions and appropriated additional funds for teachers' salaries and construction at Morgan and Bowie state colleges, in an effort to stop the walls of segregated education from crumbling any further. The neighboring state of Virginia, which had sent lawyers to monitor the *Murray* case, moved quickly to establish out-of-state scholarships for Virginia's black students.

The *Murray* case was the invigorating catalyst the NAACP's Baltimore branch needed. By 1936 its "faithful few" had increased to fifteen hundred.

Though historically Marshall has been viewed as the David who killed his personal Goliath, he was first to give credit where he believed it was due. "I worked the case out on the ground, and I drew the pleadings since there was some intricate old Maryland common law involved, but outside the legwork, I did very little. The court presentation was his [Houston's] doing. The fact is, I never was chief counsel in any case that Charlie took part in."

The battle for equal education opportunities did not end with the *Murray* victory. That case was only the opening shot. Still, it was a very meaningful victory for Marshall. During the 1991 press conference at which Marshall announced his retirement from the Supreme Court, a reporter asked him about the University of Maryland case. "It was sweet revenge, and I enjoyed it no end," he said.

Results were mixed on other fronts, however. In fact, while awaiting the Maryland Court of Appeals ruling on Judge O'Dunne's decision in *Murray,* Marshall suffered his first defeat in a civil rights litigation.

In late 1935, Marshall and the Baltimore branch of the NAACP turned their attention to the plight of black grade-school and secondary students in surrounding Baltimore County. The county had ten high schools for white students but none for blacks, although blacks comprised nearly 10 percent of the county's population. County officials contended that the black population was too widely dispersed geographically to open a centrally located high school for blacks. The county's black students who wanted to continue their education beyond the seventh grade were given an examination to determine if they were qualified for admittance to the black Frederick Douglass High School in Baltimore.

Only 50 percent of the blacks who took the entrance exams passed and were allowed to go to Frederick Douglass High. Moreover, while the county paid a stipend to the City of Baltimore for each black student who went to Douglass, it did not provide transportation despite the fact that most blacks enrolled at Douglass lived at least fifteen miles away. White students attended high schools near their homes and did not have to pass entrance exams.

At the primary level, Baltimore County's grade schools for blacks were nothing more than two-room schoolhouses on unpaved back roads that flooded in foul weather. Their roofs leaked. They were cold in the winter. They had no playgrounds, and they were understaffed.

Marshall chose as his plaintiff a black Baltimore County girl who had just completed the seventh grade. He carried a petition on her behalf to a meeting of Baltimore County's board of education in Towson, Maryland. It was rejected. He then appealed to the state board of education. There, too, he was turned down.

Marshall contemplated what he viewed as his legal options. He could sue the county in an attempt to make it equalize educational facilities for all students. Or he could sue to have the county close its white high schools until it constructed equal schools for blacks. Or he could sue to have his plaintiff admitted to the white school nearest her home.

He decided on the third option, and the case was heard in September 1936, in the state circuit court. The presiding judge ruled that the county's board of education had sole authority to determine the guidelines for admitting seventh-grade students to high school. Marshall immediately appealed the ruling to the Maryland Court of Appeals, confident that the courts would see the similarity between the *Murray* case and the plight of the young seventh-grader. In Marshall's mind the latter situation was even more urgent. *Murray* involved a gifted graduate student who in all probability would go on to be a successful lawyer even if denied admission to the state's law school. But the current case involved thousands of African-American children just starting to climb the academic ladder; their futures seemed to lie in the balance.

After reviewing the case for several months, the Maryland Court of Appeals ruled in June 1937 that Marshall had blundered by seeking the wrong legal remedy. He should have sued to have his client admitted to Frederick Douglass High School in Baltimore without having to take the entrance test, the court stated. Instead, he mistakenly sued to have her admitted to one of the white high schools in Baltimore County. The court did not even address the question of whether or not Baltimore County had an obligation to provide separate high schools for black students.

It was a daunting setback for Marshall. But it did not take Charles Houston long to capitalize on the ultimate victory in *Murray* once the case was won. Or, that is to say, it did not take him long to try to make *Murray* into the kind of victory that he and Marshall wanted. Actually, it was defeat, not victory, that they were after. *Murray* was, after all, an unconditional triumph at the appellate level; the enemy conceded without escalating the struggle to the higher ground that Marshall and Houston sought to command. What Marshall and Houston had wanted to do in *Murray* was to lose in order to have a case they could appeal to the U.S. Supreme Court and thereby win a ruling that would change the law of the land. By its capitulation the State of Maryland denied them their ultimate objective. But what Marshall and Houston could not get from Maryland, Houston found in Columbia, Missouri.

The University of Missouri was founded in 1839, the first state university west of the Mississippi River. Its law school was established in 1872. Today the law school's colorful admissions brochure that is sent to prospective applicants from across the country boasts the school's commitment to affirmative action and to increasing the representation of minority groups in the legal profession. Its modern catalog of courses includes a required course in race, gender, and the law for first-year students and an elective course in employment discrimination for upperclassmen. Glossy photos capture black faculty members of both sexes addressing comfortably integrated lecture halls or mock courtrooms.

But in 1935 the University of Missouri's law school did not admit African Americans, and when Lloyd Lionel Gaines, a twenty-five-year-old St. Louis resident, applied there, his application was rejected because of his color. Attorneys for the St. Louis branch of the NAACP engaged Houston's help in bringing suit against the university registrar and curators to compel Gaines's admission. At the trial level the case was heard by the Circuit

Court of Boone County in Columbia, home of the university, situated midway between St. Louis and Kansas City.

Houston argued that Gaines's rejection constituted a violation of the equal-protection clause of the Fourteenth Amendment to the U.S. Constitution. Gaines was a graduate of the state-supported Lincoln University for blacks in Jefferson City, the state capital. Lincoln did not, however, have a law school, and the practice of Missouri officials was to pay the out-of-state tuition for Missouri blacks who wished to attend law schools of neighboring states such as Kansas, Nebraska, Iowa, or Illinois, which were not segregated. Houston contended that the offer to pay out-of-state tuition did not satisfy the state's obligation under the Fourteenth Amendment to provide Gaines with a legal education that was substantially equal to that provided the state's white residents. Houston asked the court to order the state either to admit Gaines to the University of Missouri law school or open a separate law school for Gaines with facilities, faculty, and staff substantially equal to what he would have received at the university's law school in Columbia.

The Maryland appellate court's decision in *Murray* was not, of course, controlling precedent for another state's courts. Besides, as lawyers for Missouri University pointed out, the facts in Gaines's case differed from those in *Murray* in several significant and fundamental ways. First, Missouri's offer to pay out-of-state tuition for blacks to attend law school elsewhere was real. State funds were earmarked for that purpose, and a number of blacks had in fact received the scholarships. In *Murray*, by contrast, the State of Maryland's offer to do the same rang hollow, and funds were not even appropriated for the purpose at the time Murray filed his law school application.

Second, Gaines could not claim, as could Murray, that the curriculum and faculty at Missouri's law school would offer him unique and special preparation for practicing law in his home state. The Missouri law school's curriculum was broader based than the University of Maryland's, which was centered around Maryland state practice and codes.

Last, and perhaps most significant, Missouri was so committed to maintaining separate education systems for blacks and whites that the state was in fact willing to open a separate law school at

Lincoln University that would educate only blacks, perhaps would do so just for Gaines, and ensure that its facilities and faculty were substantially equal to those at the white law school.

The Missouri trial court weighed the evidence and dealt Houston the defeat he wanted. The trial court's ruling was upheld subsequently by Missouri's supreme court, also as Houston hoped, thereby setting up the long-sought-after confrontation at the U.S. Supreme Court level. Marshall, now NAACP assistant special counsel, assisted Houston in the preparation of the brief. Two and a half years passed. Finally, on November 9, 1938, the Court heard opening arguments in the case that was eventually styled *Missouri ex rel. Gaines v. Canada*.

In their briefs and at oral argument, Marshall and Houston applied the original Margold strategy for the first time in a school desegregation case heard by the high Court. No effort was made to attack or overturn *Plessy v. Ferguson*. To the contrary, Marshall and Houston urged the Court to enforce *Plessy*'s mandate. Lloyd Gaines, they argued, was denied his right to an equal, if separate, education. The State of Missouri, they contended, could not circumvent its obligation to Gaines by shipping him away to law school out of state. Nor could Missouri suspend or delay living up to its duty to Gaines until the unforeseen time when the state would build, staff, equip, and open a separate, accredited law school for blacks. Gaines's right could only be satisfied by his immediate admission to the University of Missouri's all-white law school.

The U.S. Supreme Court agreed. In a six-to-two ruling, with Chief Justice Charles Evans Hughes writing for the majority, the Court emphasized the "equal" requirement that was contained in the separate-but-equal doctrine:

> The admissibility of laws separating the race in the enjoyment of privileges afforded by the State rests wholly upon the equality of the privileges which the laws give to the separated groups within the State. The question here is not of a duty of the State to supply legal training, or of the quality of the training which it does supply, but of its duty when it provides such training to furnish it to the residents of the State upon the basis of an equality of right.

Hughes then turned to the particular facts of the case:

> By the operation of the laws of Missouri a privilege has been created for white law students which is denied to negroes by reason of their race. The white resident is afforded legal education within the State; the negro resident having the same qualifications is refused it there and must go outside the State to obtain it. That is a denial of the equality of legal right to the enjoyment of the privilege which the State has set up, and the provision for the payment of tuition fees in another State does not remove the discrimination.

As for Missouri's plans to open a separate law school for blacks at some future date, the Court concluded simply, "We cannot regard the discrimination as excused by what is called its temporary character." The Supreme Court ordered Gaines to be admitted to the University of Missouri Law School.

EIGHT

Thurgood Comes to Harlem

I never hesitated to pick other people's brains—
brains I didn't have.

—Thurgood Marshall

The NAACP was organized not by the black working class but by a small group of black and white liberal intellectuals. Its initial leadership was predominantly white, though several black humanists, including Ida B. Wells, Francis Grimké, Bishop Alexander Walters, James Weldon Johnson, and W. E. B. Du Bois, played pivotal roles. The NAACP's white benefactors supported the association with their money, political influence, and legal talent for many years.

During its first quarter century the NAACP focused attention on mob violence and lynching by appealing to the American conscience. In 1914 Arthur B. Spingarn, a white liberal, became the NAACP's chief lawyer and enlisted the help of several other prominent white attorneys. Moorfield Story from Boston, Louis Marshall from New York City, and Clarence Darrow from Chicago volunteered their services, and these men won some significant victories for the rights of black Americans.

Now, in 1935, NAACP executive secretary Walter White knew it was time for black lawyers to lead this fight as segregation and discrimination escalated. The ranks of black lawyers were increasing, and fewer white lawyers were volunteering their services to the NAACP. Howard University president Mordecai Johnson's old friend Supreme Court Justice Louis Brandeis had been correct. The time had come for black lawyers to take command of the struggle.

Nathan Margold, the white lawyer directing the association's legal efforts, resigned in 1933. Two years later, Walter White convinced Charles Houston to come to New York City and take charge of the association's legal campaign. Houston had accomplished his goal of turning Howard University's law school into a full-time, fully accredited institution and was now ready to work for the NAACP full-time. That summer Houston, who had separated from his wife, took a room at the YMCA on 135th Street in Harlem and went to work at the NAACP's national headquarters at 69 Fifth Avenue as chief counsel, with responsibility for organizing the NAACP's new and massive campaign against legalized racial discrimination. It was an awesome job for a man with an untreated hernia who was recovering from tuberculosis. The demands placed on Houston's fragile health by the NAACP's increasing civil rights drive were great.

As chief counsel to the Baltimore branch of the NAACP, Thurgood Marshall called for help in times of crisis to his former law school professor Charles Houston. When Baltimore's white merchants sued the branch for boycotting their businesses, Houston rushed to Baltimore and planned a successful defense. When Marshall brought an integration suit against the University of Maryland's law school, Houston was there. It was now his turn to call for help, and in 1935 he summoned Marshall:

"I went to New York to do the special job of the educational campaign. By the time I was there a week I was doing all the legal work of the Association. The Association needs another full-time lawyer in the national office. I am not only lawyer but evangelist and stump speaker. I think this work necessary in order to back up our legal efforts with the required public supports and social force. But it takes me out of the office for long stretches at a time, and slows down the legal work in New York...I will be glad to recommend to Walter [White] and Roy [Wilkins] that just as soon as possible they give you an opportunity to come to the national office at $200 per month for six months if that interests you. I don't know of anybody I would rather have in the office than you or anybody who can do a better job of research and preparation of cases... Two lawyers would always put one in the office, except in rare instances when both might be away for several days in actual trial.

"You have been more than faithful in giving of your time to the Association and I know this has meant a sacrifice of private practice, so you can be assured I will do everything in my power to try to make some provisions for you."

Thurgood Marshall answered Houston's call after deciding he would devote his efforts full time to the pursuit of equality. Marshall explained years later that he was already spending more of his professional time on NAACP activities than on his Baltimore law practice, traveling through Maryland winning salary equalization for black teachers, investigating lynchings on Maryland's Eastern Shore, and representing criminal defendants who had not received fair trials. But he was seldom paid more than expenses for his civil rights work, and because of that work his law practice failed to bring in much money. Marshall desperately needed the "provision" mentioned in Charles Houston's letter. He had written to Houston several months earlier saying that "things are getting worse and worse" and asking Houston to petition White to see if he "could be assured of enough to tide me over. Then, in return, I could do more on these cases." He was asking for more money to continue his civil rights work in Baltimore.

The offer to come to New York as a full-time NAACP attorney fit well with Marshall's precarious financial situation and his career plan of plunging himself, unencumbered, into civil rights work. He accepted the job at an annual salary of twenty-four hundred dollars, even though Houston warned him the work would be "hard, difficult and at times dangerous." Remembering his first years as assistant counsel at the NAACP's New York City headquarters, Marshall said: "Between 1936 and 1938, I commuted practically between Baltimore and New York, and there was considerable practice in that period...I was based in New York, but I maintained an office in my mother's home in Baltimore, and I would come back to take care of the clients that really needed me until they adjusted over to new lawyers."

Before Thurgood Marshall went to New York as assistant general counsel, the NAACP had taken ten cases to the Supreme Court and only lost one of them, a decision upholding the legality of restrictive covenants. These cases involved voting rights, residential segregation, restrictive covenants, and the denial of due process and equal protection of black criminal defendants. None of them challenged the nation's segregated school system.

Writing about the NAACP's earlier legal work, Marshall said:

"These decisions served as guide posts in a sustained fight for full citizenship for Negroes. They have broadened the scope of protection guaranteed by the Thirteenth, Fourteenth and Fifteenth Amendments...in the fields of the right to register to vote, equal justice before the law, Negroes on juries, [and] segregation...

"In addition, they broaden the interpretation of constitutional rights for all citizens and extend civil liberties for whites, as well as Negroes.

"The activity of lawyers acting for the NAACP has added to the body of law on civil rights for all Americans. The Association, by pressing these cases, has brought nearer to realization the ideal embodied in the quotation engraved over the Supreme Court building in Washington, D.C., 'Equal Justice Under Law.'"

But not all black Americans in the battle for equality were as impressed as Thurgood Marshall with the NAACP's track record. The NAACP had detractors in its own ranks. In 1932 W. E. B. Du Bois, then the NAACP's director of publicity, published an article in the *Crisis* charging that the NAACP had had little impact on tearing down the walls of segregation and discrimination.

NAACP executive secretary Walter White, fair-skinned with blue eyes and blond hair, was often at odds with the darker-complexioned Du Bois. Du Bois, whose politics were socialist, thought White's administration of the NAACP was too conservative and too conciliatory to the white power structure. White had friends in the white political establishment, and this added to Du Bois's distrust of him. In an article critical of White, who served the NAACP for twenty-three years, Du Bois characterized him as "absolutely self-centered and egotistical...one of the most selfish men I ever knew...often absolutely unscrupulous.

"There are clear and incontrovertible facts" that segregation and discrimination still prevailed, Du Bois wrote. Walter White was disturbed by Du Bois's charges and personal attack and defended the NAACP's record, citing the string of court cases it had won. Ultimately White won the struggle over the tactics the NAACP would use, and Du Bois resigned a short time later and returned to his former teaching position at black Atlanta University.

But Du Bois's charges were not ignored by the NAACP. As segregation and discrimination became more pervasive, White realized it was time for black Americans to carry more of the organization's weight on their own shoulders. In 1936 Thurgood Marshall, twenty-eight, and Charles Houston, forty-one, now firmly in control of the NAACP's legal apparatus, were ready to launch a full-scale assault on all segregation and discrimination and silence the critics who claimed the NAACP was not doing enough.

Thurgood and Vivian Marshall found a comfortable one-bedroom flat at 409 Edgecombe Avenue, a large, popular Harlem apartment building not far from the YMCA where Charles Houston had taken a room. Harlem, America's largest black ghetto, was known as the "Capital of Black America" in the 1930s and 1940s. A major part of the borough of Manhattan, Harlem is bounded by Central Park, Washington Heights, and the Harlem and Hudson Rivers. About 470,000 of New York's blacks called Harlem home when the Marshalls moved there. It was a throbbing and vital community of churches, streetcorner orators, nightclubs, theaters, and numbers runners and pimps driving Cadillacs. Thousands of southern blacks trekked north to Harlem in the 1930s and 1940s seeking better jobs and fewer restrictions on their personal freedom than they found in their native South.

Harlem was the birthplace of the Harlem Renaissance, a cultural awakening in black literature, music, and the arts. Langston Hughes was writing about Harlem's "Sugar Hill" in poems and short stories, and poet Countee Cullen lived not far from the Marshalls' apartment in a flat on Seventh Avenue. Novelist Richard Wright was there, too, putting the finishing touches on what was soon to be his widely acclaimed novel *Native Son*. And performers such as Duke Ellington, Katherine Dunham, Willie Bryant, Roy Minton, and Dinah Washington made Harlem the heart of the black entertainment world.

The Marshalls enjoyed Harlem's nightlife, with its supper clubs and cabarets. On weekends the Marshalls frequently joined Walter White, Roy Wilkins, and other NAACP officials at Arthur "Happy" Rhone's club, on the corner of 143rd Street and Lenox Avenue. Rhone's, the NAACP's unofficial "after-hours headquarters," was a popular nightclub with white linen tablecloths and fine English bone china. Winthrop Rockefeller, Wall Street banker Robert Lehman and his wife, Kitty, and other wealthy white liberals "tipped uptown" in gowns, tuxedos, and limousines to get a taste of black culture and ample helpings of Rhone's well-known chitterlings, spare ribs, and pigs' feet, served with champagne.

Among Rhone's patrons was white novelist Carl Van Vechten. In fact, his 1926 book, *Nigger Heaven*, a portrayal of Harlem nightlife, had been largely responsible for the influx of wealthy white visitors to Harlem. He took a personal interest in black writers and artists and was instrumental in helping many of them gain recognition among whites.

The Marshalls went to after-hours jazz clubs along 125th Street, where they heard singers Florence Mills and Alberta Hunter belt out risqué songs like "Meet Me With Your Black Drawers On" after they finished working in white nightclubs downtown. They watched Bill "Bojangles" Robinson dance to the music of Fletcher Henderson's band, and Peg Leg Bates dance better on one leg than most people could on two. They ate the famous after-hours breakfasts of fried chicken and waffles at Dickey Wells's Seventh Avenue nigthclub as the sun came up over the East River and Harlem went to sleep. Other spots visited by Thurgood, Buster, and their friends included Mom Frazier's, Jennie Lou's, Creole Pete's, and Frank's Restaurant, a 125th Street gathering place for the social elite, professionals, and show business people where beef stew was about as "down home" as the cooking got.

Thurgood and Vivian found social life in Harlem very different from what they were used to. Class and caste lines drawn by skin color and hair grade, family, education, and occupation, which separated the black bourgeoisie from the less fortunate in Baltimore and Washington, were less sharply defined. Coming from a family that had lived in the Washington area for generations was a valuable social credential there, but Harlem was a much more transient community, with many recent arrivals from the South.

Howard University, as well as the possibility of government jobs, drew established and aspiring middle-class blacks to Washington; in Harlem there was no entrenched black middle class, and New York was a magnet for working-class blacks from the South, who needed only a strong back to find a job on the waterfront. In Baltimore and Washington, members of the black middle class socialized with their peers in the cloistered environs of their own homes. Blacks in Harlem, regardless of social standing, could meet and enjoy each other's company in nightclubs and other public places, reserving the intimate surroundings of their homes for gatherings with close friends. And emerging black pride had become a dominant social force in Harlem, with dark- and light-skinned alike seeking a common identity in "Mother Africa."

Vivian Marshall was well liked by New Yorkers. Friends remember a sharp-featured woman whose complexion was as light as Thurgood's, a popular member of New York's black "smart set." She was a founding member of what was to become a national women's social club, the Girl Friends. Ersa Poston and Anna Murphy approached Thurgood Marshall in 1938 and asked him to write the club's charter. "He gladly agreed," remembered Murphy, a former Girl Friends president, "and he didn't charge us anything."

The Marshalls' Harlem social life was not without pain. Constance Baker Motley, who worked with Thurgood from 1945 to 1961, was also close to Buster. "Buster couldn't have children," she recalled. "During the Harlem years Buster was pregnant three times and miscarried three times." The Marshalls sought help from physicians, including Thurgood's brother Aubrey, but Buster still could not successfully complete a pregnancy.

New York life for Thurgood was also hard work. The association had won some minor victories protesting Jim Crow in public accommodations and the lack of employment of black workers on government projects, such as the Hoover Dam and the Mississippi Valley and Tennessee Valley Authority projects. But it had not yet developed a strategy to attack inequality on all fronts nationwide, and it still did not have broad-based support among blacks. Houston and Marshall began laying the foundation for a series of legal cases that would call on the Supreme Court to overrule the separate-but-equal doctrine, and they devised a plan to broaden the NAACP's base by carrying its message to the Deep South. The messenger was Thurgood Marshall.

Marshall traveled through the South building a network of black and white attorneys across the Black Belt who were willing to take on civil rights cases. Equally important to this plan was finding the "proper plaintiffs" to bring these cases. In 1936, driving his 1929 Model T Ford through Virginia, Georgia, Alabama, Mississippi, and the Carolinas, Thurgood visited Howard Law School graduates and convinced them they had an obligation to help by taking NAACP cases in their towns.

"You have to understand that we had absolutely no money in those days," Marshall recalled. When Marshall and Houston traveled together filing suits, the old Ford was turned into a legal office on wheels. "Charlie would sit in my car—I had a little old beat-up '29 Ford—and type out the briefs. And he could type up a storm—faster than any secretary—and not just with two fingers going. I mean he used 'em all. We'd stay at friends' homes in those days—for free, you understand. I think the whole budget for the legal office then was maybe $8,000—that was for two lawyers and a secretary."

As a team the younger Marshall and the older Houston complemented each other. Houston was low-key, well organized, formal in his demeanor, and a stickler for the most minute detail. Thurgood was the gregarious extrovert, a backslapper who quickly won friends. Houston was smart. Marshall was shrewd. Houston was the better writer, Marshall the better speaker, lacing his conversations with humor, logic, salty and streetwise language, and black dialect that appealed to less educated black people.

In October 1937 Marshall, then twenty-nine, traveled alone through Virginia and North Carolina, seeking plaintiffs for teacher salary equalization cases, assessing voting rights for blacks, and reporting on the status of public education. He was attempting to strengthen local NAACP branches, basically small, church-member-based units, and to find the most opportune places to bring civil rights suits.

He wrote to Charles Houston from Petersburg, Virginia: "There is no franchise question in the immediate vicinity. Negroes just do not vote."

From the Virginia tobacco region he reported: "The school situation is terrible. The principal of the elementary school is a gardener and janitor for the county superintendent of schools and is a typical Uncle Tom. The addition to the high school at Halifax is not equipped. The elementary school is terrible. The question of voting has not arisen because so few register."

In Winston-Salem, North Carolina, he found a promising NAACP branch. "Only those Negroes are permitted to register who are 'alright' Negroes," he wrote Houston. "Others are refused. No one will bring a case on the question. The president of the branch stressed the point to his executive committee that they should start a program to break this down. We will have to keep behind this branch. Winston-Salem Negroes have money. They all work in factories and make good money. They have a bus company on the street owned and operated by Negroes. The branch should be strong. Winston-Salem should be one of the main spots for the franchise fight."

Often, while Marshall traveled alone through the South as the NAACP's "backroads ambassador," Houston was in New York fighting a personal battle. He had detractors from the Left and the Right. From the Left came charges he was too conservative, too concerned with winning a string of limited and narrow victories that left many broader issues unresolved. Others thought he was too radical and questioned his representation of some Communist defendants in civil rights cases. Despite his detractors, Houston continued his methodical approach of assembling a string of smaller precedent-setting victories, such as *Gaines* in Missouri, that would become the building blocks for the NAACP's biggest Supreme Court triumph, *Brown v. Board of Education*.

Houston's case of arrested tuberculosis was now complicated by cardiac problems, and in 1938 he decided to leave the NAACP's New York office.

NINE

Mr. Civil Rights

Hi, you black son of a bitch.

—Dallas police chief

When thirty-year-old Thurgood Marshall replaced Charles Houston in 1938 as chief counsel of the NAACP, he found himself in charge of black America's legal battle for equality and a New York office much too formal to suit his casual, jocular manner. "It operated with the formality of an embassy," he told the *New York Times*. "It was just too formal and tush tush. It was Dr. Whoois and Mr. Whatis and all kinds of nonsense like that, bowing and scraping like an embassy scene. Well, I took a long look, and I figured I'd have to bust that stuff up pretty quick. Believe me, I had them talking first names in *nothing* time, and no more of that formality business." Marshall was fulfilling his pledge to "wear life like a loose garment," and that would now be the attire of the people who worked for him.

Soon after replacing Houston, Marshall went to Dallas to investigate a racial incident that brought the city to the verge of violence. The sixty-five-year-old president of a local junior college was called to jury duty, but when he arrived at the courthouse and clerks discovered he was black, they told him to go home because the jury summons had been sent in error. He refused to leave after telling a bailiff he was a citizen of Texas and intended to serve on the jury. Two white court employees dragged the frail man from the courtroom and threw him down the courthouse steps.

Relations between blacks and whites in Dallas were already strained, and this event prompted the local NAACP branch to call Thurgood Marshall. He flew to Dallas and immediately observed the flaring racial tensions, but this time there would be no long legal cases and Supreme Court appeals to win the rights of black Texans to serve on juries. Marshall made a telephone call to the office of Texas governor James Allred in Austin. Allred, considered moderate on racial issues, was interested in this handsome, Texas-tall NAACP lawyer who had come all the way from New York City to see about the black college president flung down the courthouse steps. He agreed to meet Marshall the next day.

After spending an hour in the governor's office—their conversation was never reported—Marshall left, telling waiting statehouse reporters "no comment." But he must have had a convincing argument, because several hours later the Dallas courthouse was ringed with Texas Rangers and the FBI began an investigation of the incident involving the college president. Governor Allred issued a statement that prospective black jurors would no longer be harassed and from that day forward would serve in Texas courtrooms. He said his proclamation and their safety would be enforced by the powerful Texas Rangers. Thurgood Marshall had won a major victory without writing a brief or appearing in a courtroom.

But the trip to Dallas was not without a threat to Thurgood's safety. Later he recalled the incident. Shortly before his arrival, he said, "The chief of police told his men a nigger lawyer named Marshall was coming from New York City to cause trouble in the town. He told his men he would 'personally kick the shit' out of me. I sort of considered the idea of having a bad cold or something and not going down there." Marshall said the state police provided a trooper to protect him. When he left the courthouse, he came face-to-face with the police chief. "And when he saw me he said, 'Hi, you black son of a bitch. I've got you.' And I ran. The state trooper pulled out his gun and said to the chief, 'You stay right there.'"

Marshall continued traveling through the South during the 1940s, investigating lynchings and filing suits challenging denial of voting rights, jury service, and fair trials to black Americans. Vivian remained in New York.

But not all of Marshall's travels took him to oppressed blacks in the Deep South. There were racial problems just a few miles from the NAACP's Fifth Avenue doorstep. From Freeport, Long Island, came complaints that blacks were being harassed by police officers who were members of the Ku Klux Klan.

Marshall asked his friend Ted Poston, a reporter on the *Amsterdam News,* a black newspaper, to accompany him to Freeport to investigate. "Ted went with Thurgood to Freeport to interview people who had been threatened by the Klan," said his widow, Ersa Poston, "and as they drove around Freeport taking affidavits from victims, they were followed by Klan members. There was a big Klan organization in Long Island in those days, and when Ted got home he was shaken. Ted said Thurgood was 'laughing and joking' about what might happen to them as the Klan followed them and that Thurgood was not a bit frightened." Marshall filed complaints with the state's attorney, and the harassment stopped.

But there were other attempts at intimidation on Marshall's travels, and he did not respond to all of them with the same jocularity he applied to the trip with Poston. Houston's warning that the work would be "dangerous" was true. His arrival was considered a threat by white southerners who believed the NAACP attorney was arousing a new militancy in southern blacks who had complacently accepted conditions as they were. In many towns he was protected by armed black citizens. He would stay in a different house each night, and the local black residents would swap automobiles with him, making it more difficult for him to be followed. When the call "Men are needed to sit up all night with a sick friend" went out, blacks knew armed guards were being called to protect the house where Marshall would spend the night.

In 1949 one of Marshall's staff lawyers, Constance Baker Motley, went with him to Alabama for a hearing in a case against the board of trustees of the University of Alabama. She recalled, "During the course of that hearing we stayed in the Birmingham home of local attorney Arthur Shores. His home had been bombed on at least fifteen occasions. At night we were guarded by African-American men with machine guns, and during the day others carrying handguns escorted us to and from court."

Sometimes his color alone provoked harassment. In 1943 Marshall was waiting for a train in a small Mississippi town where he had investigated a lynching. "I got hungry and I saw a restaurant, so I decided that I'd go over there and put my civil rights in my back pocket and go to the back door of the kitchen and see if I could buy a sandwich," he recalled. "And while I was kibitzing myself to do that, this white man came up beside me in plain clothes with a great big pistol on his hip. And he said, 'Nigger boy, what are you doing here?' And I said, 'Well, I'm waiting for the train to Shreveport.' And he said, 'There's only one more train that comes through here, and that's the four o'clock, and you'd better be on it because the sun is never going down on a live nigger in this town.' I wasn't hungry anymore."

In October 1939 Walter White created a new organization to handle the association's legal work, the Legal Defense and Educational Fund, Inc. The name was too long—especially for its folksy director, who had even shortened his own birth name—so it became known as the Legal Defense Fund, then the Inc. Fund, and finally the Fund. The Fund was established separately from the NAACP to take advantage of new federal laws granting tax-exempt status to nonprofit organizations that did not have lobbying as their principal function.

Its charter stated its purpose clearly:

> To render free legal aid to Negroes who suffer legal injustice because of their race or color and cannot afford to employ legal assistance. To seek and promote educational opportunities denied to Negroes because of their color. To conduct research and publish information on educational facilities and inequalities furnished for Negroes out of public funds and on the status of the Negro in American life.

But it was to achieve much more under the guidance of Thurgood Marshall, who Walter White asked to become the Fund's director-counsel. Marshall served in that capacity for twenty-one years, and during that time he and the other Fund lawyers handled most of the civil rights cases in America. *United States Reports*, the official publication of Supreme Court decisions, noted that Marshall argued thirty-two cases and assisted in eleven others during that period. But Marshall, who argued only six of those cases alone, always gave credit to the Fund's staff. "I never hesitated to pick other people's brains—brains I didn't have," he said. "After a while you got to know who was best at what kind of thing."

White's creation of the Fund and his appointment of Marshall to direct it appeared an act of self-preservation. Marshall's southern trips brought him popularity among rank-and-file NAACP members and bold front-page headlines in black newspapers across the nation. His ability to identify and relate to blacks in all walks of life won him respect and confidence from the "little people" that the more formal Walter White and Roy Wilkins did not have.

To NAACP branch members and thousands of other blacks in the South, Thurgood Marshall was their knight in shining armor who came to town to fight their legal battles. To them he *was* the NAACP. "Thurgood is coming" was whispered among people anxiously awaiting his arrival to hear their complaints and file civil rights cases. When he returned to his New York office from a 1939 trip to Memphis, Tennessee, there was a letter on his desk: "We want you to know that the Memphis Branch is 100 percent for you, and we welcome your return anytime it may be convenient for you to do so at our expense."

Because of his broad popularity and high visibility, some thought Marshall would eventually challenge Walter White's position as the NAACP's executive secretary, but Marshall was not threatening White. He did not want to direct the NAACP. He wanted to continue to use his legal talents to champion its causes.

The Fund, in effect, was the NAACP's law firm, and Marshall soon built a staff of formidable legal talent. He called on old friends from Howard University's Law School, among them Leon Ranson, William H. Hastie, S. D. McGill, Carter Wesley, and W. Robert Ming Jr., and enlisted a cadre of emerging bright, young Howard Law School graduates to help as the Fund's caseload burgeoned. He had a staff of six full-time lawyers and four lawyers on retainer in the District of Columbia, Dallas, Richmond, and Los Angeles. Donald Gaines Murray, the man admitted to the University of Maryland's law school after Marshall successfully sued the school in 1934, volunteered his services to the Fund.

Describing the Fund's operation, Marshall wrote:

"We get either a letter or a telephone call or telegram from either a person or a lawyer saying that they have got a problem involving discrimination on the part of race or color and it appears to be a legal problem. Then the question is as to whether or not we will help. If it is a worthwhile problem, we look into it....If the investigation conducted either from the New York office or through one of our local lawyers reveals that there is discrimination because of race or color and legal assistance is needed, we furnish that legal assistance in the form of either helping in payment of the costs or helping in the payment of lawyers' fees, and mostly it is legal research in the preparation of briefs and materials."

Marshall exercised great care in the selection of cases he took to the Supreme Court. Marshall confided to a colleague that he and other Fund lawyers "carefully selected the cases to appeal to the courts and the Supreme Court in those areas where the likelihood of success would appear the greatest."

One of Marshall's first cases as Fund director, in 1940, involved a long-standing interest—equality and fair trials in the courtroom. He sought to overturn the convictions of three black men accused of murdering a white man in Florida. The men had confessed to the murder after five days of nonstop questioning by Florida police, during which they were not allowed to see lawyers, friends, or family members. In an earlier decision the Supreme Court had ruled confessions extracted by force inadmissible, but Florida courts held that force had not been used in the current case and that therefore the confessions were admissible.

Marshall argued that "sunrise confessions" from isolated and terrified suspects constituted "force" and violated the Fourteenth Amendment's guarantee of due process. The Supreme Court agreed and reversed the convictions. The case, *Chambers v. Florida*, was an important victory in Marshall's quest to win fair trials for murder defendants.

In 1941 Marshall took another case involving involuntary confessions. In the small town of Hugo, Oklahoma, the bodies of a white man, Elmer Rogers, his wife, and two children were discovered in their burning home. A black handyman named Lyons was arrested and held in jail for eleven days with little sleep or food. During questioning police took a pan of the victims' charred bones and tossed them in Lyons's lap. He confessed twelve hours later and subsequently signed a written confession.

Several people in Hugo believed Lyons had been framed, and they called the NAACP. Once again Marshall found a town ready to explode in racial violence. The local NAACP branch provided bodyguards for him, and each night he slept in a different house. But one night a white man discovered where Marshall was staying and came to visit him. The visitor had no intention of harming Marshall or running him out of town. He identified himself as the dead woman's father and said he had important information for Marshall. He said he did not know if Lyons was guilty or innocent, but he did know Lyons had been treated unfairly and beaten by the police. The man said one of his friends, a local policeman, had showed him a "nigger beater," an iron pipe used to pummel a confession out of Lyons. The man volunteered to testify at Lyons's trial. Speaking about his late-night visitor, Marshall later said, "Even in the most prejudiced communities, the majority of the people have some respect for truth and some sense of justice, no matter how deeply hidden it is at times."

The judge threw out Lyons's first confession but allowed prosecutors to refer to it during the trial. Marshall got police witnesses to admit to their "bone tactic." A clerk at a downtown hotel testified he had heard policemen talking about the "nigger beater" and Lyons's treatment at the hands of police. Marshall produced a photograph of a smiling police officer standing over the battered Lyons, but the officer would not admit to the beating. He testified he could identify himself, but not Lyons, because to him all blacks looked alike.

Marshall then tried to win dismissal of Lyons's second confession, arguing it, too, had been coerced by force and intimidation. The Oklahoma court found Lyons guilty of murder and sentenced him to life in prison. Marshall considered it a victory of sorts, because he was convinced he had saved Lyons from the death penalty.

He appealed Lyons's conviction to the Supreme Court, and *Lyons v. Oklahoma* was heard two years later, in 1944. Marshall again argued that the conviction had resulted from inadmissible evidence and that therefore his client had been denied due process. By a six-to-three vote the Court ruled against Marshall, saying Lyons's second confession was not "brought about by the earlier mistreatments." Justices Hugo Black, Wiley Rutledge, and Frank Murphy dissented. It was Marshall's first defeat in a major case involving the civil rights of a black defendant, but he would go on to win twenty-seven cases before the Supreme Court and lose only five.

Marshall strongly believed that protecting constitutional rights of criminal defendants was important, but he also knew that without the right to vote thousands of black Americans were powerless to change the oppressive conditions under which they lived. He knew the ballot could be a forceful weapon in challenging a system that denied black people even the essentials of a decent life. Without the right to vote, black communities were denied their fair share of public services, health care, employment, police protection, and adequate schools.

The ratification of the Fifteenth Amendment, in 1870, gave black men voting rights. Neither black nor white women could vote until 1920. Despite the Fifteenth Amendment, and several laws passed to strengthen it, few southern blacks went to the polls because of threats of violence and legal devices put in place to discourage them. Fewer than 3 percent of eligible southern blacks voted during the 1930s, and by 1940 even that slim percentage had decreased.

Ralph Bunche, who as a UN undersecretary would win the 1950 Nobel Peace Prize for negotiating a Middle East peace agreement, was a Howard University government professor in 1940. During that year he produced a startling document on black voting rights. He reported only 2.5 percent of eligible blacks voted in the Carolinas, Georgia, Alabama, Florida, Mississippi, Louisiana, Arkansas, and Texas in the 1940 presidential election.

The lack of black southerners' participation in the election process did not stem from their lack of interest in political affairs but from the legal barriers their states had contrived to prohibit blacks from voting. One of these was the poll tax, which few southern blacks could afford to pay. Another was the literacy test, with different versions for blacks and whites. Whereas whites might be asked only to spell their names, blacks in Alabama, for instance, were required to "understand and explain any article of the Constitution of the United States to the satisfaction of the registrars." The few blacks who could pass the tests and pay the poll taxes were often intimidated with threats of violence when they attempted to vote.

Even the few blacks who satisfied state requirements could not count on voting. In 1940, Marshall presented the Justice Department with affidavits from twenty black southerners who had been denied that right after paying poll taxes. At the city level, Columbia, South Carolina, in 1939 passed a law effectively requiring blacks to be at least eighty-seven years old in order to vote. Outside the law there was always the threat of violence. In June 1940 blacks in Brownsville, Texas, attempted to organize a voter registration drive; after the body of one of the organizers, Elbert Williams, was found in a river, the president of the local NAACP branch and seven others left town because they believed they would also be killed.

In 1932, to strengthen the restrictive nature of the Texas primary after a court challenge raised questions about its legality, the Texas Democratic Convention adopted a resolution. "Be it resolved that all white citizens of the State of Texas who are qualified to vote under the constitution and laws of the state shall be eligible to membership in the Democratic party and as such are entitled to participate in its deliberations." The resolution was passed.

The white primary was perhaps the most effective device states used to deny black voting rights. The Democratic party's candidates were selected in primary elections months before the general election, and since Deep South states were solidly Democratic, the primary winner was sure to win the general election. Primary voters were required to be members of a political party, but the Democratic party did not accept black members, effectively excluding them from the election process.

In 1941 Marshall challenged the white primary on behalf of

black Texan Lonnie E. Smith. Election judge S. C. Allwright and his deputy James E. Liuzza had told Smith he could not vote in the 1940 Texas Democratic primary because he was not a member of the Democratic party. Smith sued the party, but his case was dismissed after the court ruled that the Democratic party was a "private institution" with the right to include or exclude anyone it wanted and that, furthermore, the party's status as a private institution had been upheld in a 1935 Supreme Court challenge, *Grovey v. Townsend*.

But in a later Supreme Court case, *United States v. Classic*, in 1941, Marshall saw a glimmer of hope. In 1941 a group of white Louisiana Democrats complained to the Justice Department that their ballots had not been counted by party officials in a 1940 federal election. The Justice Department quickly filed suit. Federal lawyers argued that "election officials who willfully alter or falsely count and certify ballots in a primary election" were acting under the authority of state law. The court agreed with U.S. assistant attorney general Herbert Wechsler and ruled: "The times, places and manner of holding elections for Senators and Representatives shall be prescribed in each state by the legislature thereof; but the Congress may at any time make or alter such regulations where the primary is by law made an integral part of the election machinery."

The Texas and Louisiana Democratic primary procedures were similar, and Marshall believed he had the legal precedent he needed to successfully challenge white primaries. But he wanted a few more.

Marshall asked the Justice Department to join in the case as an *amicus curiae*, friend of the court, knowing it would strengthen his position to have well-known and successful government lawyers standing by his side. He made the request specifically of Assistant Attorney General Wechsler, the victor in *Classic*.

Wechsler turned down Marshall's request that the Justice Department join the NAACP in the case. Writing in the 1959 *Harvard Law Review*, Wechsler later said he understood and sympathized with Marshall's desire to extend the *Classic* decision to *Smith v. Allright*, but his decision was, in part, a political one.

"We were a government agency and had to get along with the Senate Judiciary Committee, which was dominated by Southerners, and this seemed an unnecessary fight." He said he also believed at the time that the *Classic* decision was "a narrow one" because it addressed complaints of white plaintiffs who were already qualified members of the Democratic party, not black citizens who could not vote because they were not party members. This fact, he said, raised questions of the applicability of the *Classic* decision to the Texas primary case.

Marshall and the Fund lawyers would have to go it alone, but there were political events taking place that would soon help Marshall plead the case. The nation's political climate was changing, and so was the Supreme Court, as President Franklin D. Roosevelt replaced retiring justices with men more attuned to his progressive New Deal policies.

Roosevelt picked the liberal Harlan Stone to replace the conservative Charles Evans Hughes as chief justice in 1941 and then named Robert Houghwout Jackson, a former U.S. attorney general and FDR's Chesapeake Bay fishing buddy, to take Stone's associate seat on the bench. James Clark McReynolds had retired. He had been appointed by President Woodrow Wilson and served on the court since 1911. McReynolds never attempted to shroud his racist and anti-Semitic feelings. He was replaced by liberal midwestern Wiley Rutledge, the Kentucky-born son of a Baptist preacher, who was a former dean of Washington University's and Iowa State University's law schools.

Hugo Black was a former U.S. senator; although he had once been a member of Alabama's Ku Klux Klan, his liberal decisions in civil rights cases marked him as one of black America's best friends on the court.

Frank Murphy had been governor of Michigan and, as Roosevelt's attorney general, had established the first civil rights section in the Justice Department. Murphy was the Court's only Roman Catholic. William O. Douglas, who chewed gum and struck matches on the seat of his pants while on the bench, was one of the strongest advocates of civil rights ever to sit on the Court. Black had written the unanimous opinion in the 1939 case of *Pierce v.*

Louisiana, the latest in a growing number of decisions reversing convictions by all-white juries in cities where blacks were systematically excluded from jury duty.

William Hastie, who had taught at Howard University Law School and worked with Marshall and Charles Houston, was now a civilian aide to the Department of War in 1941 as the nation prepared to enter World War II. A. Philip Randolph, head of the Brotherhood of Sleeping Car Porters and Maids, petitioned President Roosevelt for equal employment opportunities for blacks in steel mills, aviation plants, and munitions factories, where they were being hired only for low-paying, menial jobs. The president responded with Executive Order 8022: "There shall be no discrimination in the employment of workers in defense industries and in government because of race, creed, color or national origin...And it is the duty of employers and labor organizations...to provide for full and equitable participation of all workers."

Roosevelt gave black Americans access to the White House and established an unofficial "black cabinet" of Afro-American leaders to meet with him frequently at the White House. So, on the eve of *Smith v. Allwright*, Marshall had good reason to believe that decisions of the Supreme Court might now reflect the liberal attitudes of President Roosevelt, who appeared concerned about and responsive to the problems of black Americans.

Louisiana's Democratic party, much to the surprise and delight of Marshall and Hastie, and perhaps even some of the justices, did not send anyone to Washington to defend its actions with oral arguments in *Smith v. Allwright*. Marshall methodically outlined the precedents of the *Classic* case and then skillfully wrapped them around *Smith*. He explained the similarities in the Louisiana and Texas primaries that buttressed his case, gingerly skirting the legally sensitive issue of race. Texas officials, like officials in Louisiana, acting with the sanction and authority of the state, had denied citizens the right to vote, which was protected by the Constitution, Marshall argued. He told the Court that the Texas primary "effectively controls the choice" of candidates in Texas elections and that S. E. Allwright, who as an election judge was a state official, had violated the Fifteenth Amendment.

On April 3, 1944, the Supreme Court issued its decision. Justice Stanley Reed, speaking for the eight-to-one majority, said:

> When primaries become a part of the machinery for choosing officials, state and national, as they have here, the same test to determine the character of discrimination or abridgement should be applied to the primary as are applied to the general election. If the state requires a certain electoral procedure, prescribes a general election ballot made up of party nominees so chosen, and limits the choice of the electorate in general elections for state offices, practically speaking, to those whose names appear on such a ballot, it endorses, adopts and enforces the discrimination against Negroes, practiced by a party entrusted by Texas law with the determination of the qualification of participants in the primary. This is state action within the meaning of the Fifteenth Amendment.

Marshall was in his New York office when he received the telephone call telling him about the Court's verdict. It was the last call he took that day. Secretaries held messages for Marshall and the other Fund lawyers as they celebrated the victory with an office party. As a result, Marshall missed a congratulatory call from Associate Justice Frank Murphy, who wanted to invite him to lunch. Marshall said later, "I apologized profusely, and Murphy agreed that a guy had a right to get drunk at a time like that."

Thurgood Marshall appeared triumphantly at the NAACP's 1944 convention in Chicago before eight hundred NAACP branch secretaries and members. He told them that blacks were registering to vote for that spring's election all over the South and that the Justice Department was aggressively investigating incidents where blacks were not allowed to register. In a speech that brought the audience to its feet, he said:

"We must not be delayed by people who say 'the time is not ripe,' nor should we proceed with caution for fear of destroying the status quo. Persons who deny to us our civil rights should be brought to justice now. Many people believe the time is always 'ripe' to discriminate against Negroes. All right then—the time is always 'ripe' to bring them to justice. The responsibility for the enforcement of these statutes rests with every American citizen regardless of race or color. However, the real job has to be done by the Negro population with whatever friends of the other race are willing to join in."

The Supreme Court victory did not bring attempts to stop blacks from voting to an abrupt halt, and Marshall realized getting the law enforced was just as important as getting the law in place. Texas and several other southern states quickly attempted to circumvent the *Smith* decision. In 1945, a year after the Texas primary case, the South Carolina legislature repealed its voting statutes to give local registrars, who did not operate under state authority, control of the voter registration process. In a case argued in a South Carolina federal district court, Marshall won a decision prohibiting local registrars from refusing to register black voters for Democratic primaries.

In many small southern towns, registrars still turned black citizens away. The Justice Department received affidavits in 1946 from blacks who said they still could not register to vote, and Marshall petitioned the attorney general to enforce the law. "There is no reason why a hundred clear cases of this sort should not be placed before the United States attorneys and the attorney general every year until the election officials discover that it is both wiser and safer to follow the United States laws than to violate them," Marshall said during a New York City press conference.

But as late as 1953, fourteen years after the *Smith* decision, Marshall and the Fund were still fighting to ensure compliance with the ruling. That year, in *Terry v. Adams*, the Court struck down the "private club" status of the Jaybird Democratic Association, which refused to register black voters in Democratic primaries in Fort Bend County, Texas.

In speeches across the nation to NAACP branches in 1944 and 1945, Marshall continued to assert his belief that the American court system was the most effective tool for protecting and expanding the rights of black Americans. He said the Fund would continue to seek enactment of new civil rights legislation as well as the vigorous enforcement of existing laws. "In its broadest sense," he declared, "the term 'civil rights' includes those rights which are the outgrowth of civilization, the existence and exercise of which necessarily follow from the rights that repose in the subjects of a country exercising self-government."

However, in his speeches at this time, Marshall seldom mentioned plans for launching a legal assault on segregated education. It was clear that Marshall, the NAACP, and the Fund had not yet agreed on a definitive plan for attacking educational segregation, as they had for securing voting rights and constitutional protection of criminal defendants. Marshall and his colleagues were still wrestling with the difficult problem of whether to challenge the "equal" provision in the separate-but-equal doctrine or to launch a broader assault on all segregated public education. Marshall's public silence on the issue did not mean it was not on his mind. A decision would be made very soon.

TEN

Tan Yanks in Korea

Now, General, just between you and me, goddammit, don't you tell me there's no Negro that can play a horn!

—Thurgood Marshall

Thurgood Marshall was in New York City when he received news that his teacher, colleague, and friend Charles Hamilton Houston had died of a heart attack at Howard University's Freedmen's Hospital on April 22, 1950, at the age of fifty-four. Marshall rushed to Washington to share the Houston family's grief and seek consolation among old friends for his own.

Marshall's friend Gardner Bishop said Thurgood was greatly affected by Houston's death: "Turkey grieved for Charlie as if he were a brother, and I think his grief was compounded by the fact that sitting there in Rankin Chapel, staring at Charlie's casket, Thurgood suddenly realized he had lost a man who had been as important in his life as his father had been."

Charles Houston's death came at a time when Marshall and the NAACP were moving toward the final assault on what they saw as their biggest and most important challenge, segregated education. In the days before he died, Houston spent his time in his hospital room drafting handwritten memorandums on yellow legal pads outlining school desegregation strategy for Thurgood Marshall, receiving visitors who were plaintiffs in civil rights cases, and writing what would be a final letter to his son, Bo. His physician, Dr. Edward Mazique, had attempted to discourage him from being so active during what was presumed to have been a successful convalescence. But the flurry of activity in Charles Houston's hospital room was the product, perhaps, of something Houston knew and Mazique did not. Thurgood Marshall would now have to direct the NAACP's legal work without the advice of his old friend, but Charles Houston's legacy would be a powerful weapon.

At the funeral Houston's cousin William Henry Hastie, by then a U.S. appeals court judge, spoke eloquently of Houston's "unremitting struggle to win for the Negro full status without discrimination." He described Houston's civil rights work, which "stopped only when his body could no longer keep pace with his will and his spirit." Marshall helped carry Houston's casket from Howard University's ivy-walled Andrew Rankin Memorial Chapel, where Justices Hugo Black and Tom Clark, Interior Secretary Oscar Chapman, and civil rights leaders Roy Wilkins, Walter White, Lester Granger, Clarence Mitchell II, and John P. Davis had come to pay their respects to their friend.

"As we grieve we cannot forget that he believed, perhaps above all else, in strength; strength to do and to bear what lesser men would regard as impossible or unbearable. He counted nothing, no physical weakness and not even death itself, as an obstacle to the onward sweep of strong men and women in the accomplishment of worthwhile deeds...I know he would wish all of us to carry on in that spirit."

Marshall, who had shortened his first name from Thoroughgood, now had a new name, one that appeared in the headlines of black newspapers and magazines such as the *Amsterdam News*, the *Chicago Defender*, the *Pittsburgh Courier*, the *Afro-American,* and *Our World Magazine*. They called him "Mr. Civil Rights."

His hometown paper, the *Baltimore Afro-American*, characterized Marshall as "the nation's biggest race man," noting wryly that he had added about thirty pounds to his lanky six-foot-two-inch frame since the last time his picture had appeared on its pages. The *Afro's* observation was accurate. Thurgood's Arrow Collar Man good looks were slowly giving way to a slight middle-age spread, and he was paying less attention to the maintenance of his double-breasted suits and highly polished Florsheim shoes. Despite his title and national recognition, his NAACP salary was just $8,748 annually.

By 1951 the NAACP had made notable progress in the struggle to obtain for all Americans equal rights under the Constitution. Ten years earlier no school south of the Potomac and Ohio rivers had a biracial student body, but in 1951 black students were attending state universities in Virginia, Kentucky, Oklahoma, Texas, and Arkansas, and their admission had been ordered in Tennessee and Louisiana. Speaking about the early victories in the fight to desegregate education, Marshall said, "The complete destruction of all enforced segregation looms into sight. Segregation no longer has the stamp of legality in any public education."

There was progress on other fronts, too. Black baseball players—among them Jackie Robinson, Roy Campanella, Larry Doby, Don Newcombe, and Luke Easter—were playing on formerly all-white major-league teams. For the first time Hollywood was portraying a more honest version of black life in America in movies such as *Home of the Brave, Lost Boundaries, Pinky, Intruder in the Dust,* and *No Way Out*. Politically, President Harry S. Truman was throwing the federal government's weight and the power of the presidency behind black America's drive for equality. It was an expedient move for the man who became president when Franklin D. Roosevelt died in office and was now seeking a full term at a time when many blacks would be casting their first ballots.

In 1947 Truman had appointed a biracial group of citizens to study America's racial problems. That October the President's Committee on Civil Rights delivered its report, *To Secure These Rights*, to the White House. The report called for an end to segregation and other limitations of opportunity and fairness imposed on black Americans. After reading the panel's findings, Truman asked Congress to make lynching a federal crime, to outlaw the poll tax, to eliminate segregated interstate transportation, and to establish a Fair Employment Practices Commission to stop discrimination in hiring.

A year later, Truman ordered an end to all discrimination in federal employment and all segregation in the nation's armed services. Executive Order 9981 "declared to be the policy of the President that there shall be equality of treatment and opportunity for all persons in the armed services without regard to race, color, religion or national origin" and that promotions would be made "solely on merit and fitness." It sent shock waves through the Defense Department and rankled southern legislators and a few northern ones on Capitol Hill. The order established the President's Committee on Equality of Treatment and Opportunity, chaired by Charles H. Fahey, to work with the secretary of defense and the armed services' branch secretaries on plans and procedures for integrating the armed forces.

The date Truman signed Executive Order 9981—July 26, 1948—was politically significant. It was two weeks before a sharply divided Democratic party would convene to select its presidential candidate. Southern Democrats on one side and western and northern Democrats on the other were pitched in a bitter struggle that was dividing the party on racial issues. Thurgood Marshall's fight against poll taxes and literacy tests had made it easier for some southern blacks to register and vote, and their political voice was beginning to gain strength and recognition for the first time since Reconstruction. Truman had met earlier in an unpublicized White House session with several black leaders—Roy Wilkins, Lester Granger, A. Philip Randolph, John P. Davis, and Ralph Bunche—and was convinced his political future rested in the hands of voters in the big industrial cities and southern black voters.

Recognizing the emerging strength of the black vote, Democratic party leaders asked a black minister to open the convention, but when he rose to pray, Senator Cotton Ed Smith of South Carolina walked out. In a speech on the convention floor Truman promised to call Congress into special session to pass bold civil rights legislation and said he would move vigorously on all fronts to strike down barriers of segregation and discrimination.

Education opened the doors to jobs for returning veterans, but the doors of state universities remained shut to most black students. Blacks without college educations still obtained only menial jobs in government and industry, and some labor unions would not take black workers into their ranks. The nation's 800,000 black veterans of World War II, many with medals for valor and heroism, wanted not only jobs and decent housing but also quality educations. The GI bill would pay for books and tuition, but the black veterans found educational opportunities scarce. In southern states there was one black medical school and forty white ones; one black school of pharmacy and twenty white ones; no black engineering schools but thirty-six for white students.

Thurgood Marshall was convinced education was the cornerstone for full realization of the American dream and that education was ultimately more important than where people sat on a bus or train, what restroom they used, or what water fountain they used to quench their thirst. Marshall often reminded friends that the battle to open restaurants and hotels to blacks was futile unless they had the money to use the facilities.

Many black soldiers elected to remain in the army after World War II. Even though there was segregation and discrimination in the armed forces, there were still more opportunities for blacks in the service than in civilian life. Black recruits were also enlisting in large numbers, and by the middle of 1950 one of every four army recruits was black. Their sheer numbers created a "forced integration" of service units; black training and combat units could no longer absorb all of the incoming soldiers, so white units were integrated.

However, a disproportionately high number of southern white officers commanded black troops. General Dwight David Eisenhower had testified before the Senate Armed Services Committee in 1948 that he believed racial segregation in the military should not be continued at the platoon level and below. General Douglas MacArthur, the Far East commander, had spoken often about the valor of black troops under fire but had done little to integrate fighting forces. Other military commanders, like MacArthur, were also slow or reluctant to follow the president's order to treat and promote black soldiers equally. But as America became increasingly involved in the Korean conflict, black soldiers once again went to war.

Troops of the People's Republic of Korea crossed the 38th parallel into South Korea on June 25, 1950. The battlefield reports were grim; Republic of Korea troops retreated from one strategic position to another, suffering heavy combat losses. On July 12 the 24th Infantry Regiment, an all-black unit that had been part of the U.S. Army for eighty-one years, landed in Korea from their base in Japan. The *New York Times* reported the recapture of Yech'on, a major railhead, on July 22, 1950, after a bloody fifteen-hour battle won by the 24th: "Communist propaganda took it on the chin today at Yech'on when the Korea reds were blasted by American Negro troops who believed not only in the United States as it is, but in the better nation it will become when intolerance is also defeated."

On September 11, 1950, Lieutenant Colonel J. T. Corley became commanding officer of the 24th Regiment at Haman, Korea, and issued this memorandum to "The Fighting 24th Infantry Regimental Combat Team":

> Upon assumption of command, I cannot help but express my opinion of the Fighting 24th United States Infantry. In the sixty days of continuous combat, you have withstood a "toughness of battle" which I have not seen in five campaigns in Africa, Sicily and Europe with the First Infantry Division. You have held ground against superior forces. You have lived up to the regimental motto "Semper Paratus." The first United States victory in Korea was your action at Yech'on. It has been noted in Congress. The people back home cover in detail your efforts on "Battle Hill" west of Haman, Korea. Other units have been unable to accomplish what depleted companies of the Fighting 24th have done. I am proud of the "Blockhousers."

Despite this glowing comment from a commanding officer, during the early months of the Korean War, Thurgood Marshall and the NAACP received letters from black enlisted men complaining about the treatment they received from white southern officers.

They wrote about the high rate of courts-martial, improper convictions, and disproportionately severe sentences on charges ranging from being lost from their units— "melting into the night"—to "disobedience" and "misbehavior" under fire.

"What has happened in Korea is an old, old story—as old as Jim Crow in the armed services," Marshall told NAACP board members in 1951. "It is a story of the sacrifice of Negro troops upon the altar of segregation."

Marshall went on: "The pattern is little varied from war to war. First come reports from the front of some heroic deed done by Negro soldiers, an achievement to indicate the courage with which these men are facing the enemy and their ability to take the toughest kind of fighting. And then suddenly the reports change as if in a concerted effort to discredit the record of Negro fighting men. The tales we are beginning to hear are of incompetency, failure and cowardice—accounts which would make it appear that Negroes are not capable of combat duty and should be restricted to labor battalions."

Marshall continued: "This pattern was glaringly apparent in World War I. Negro regiments and Negro troops received wide publicity for bravery and strategic victories in the early days of the war. Later came the stories that they couldn't take it, that they were cowards, that they ran under fire and had to be court-martialed for violation of the Seventy-fifth Article of War, misbehavior in front of the enemy.

"Again in Italy, during World War II, this series of events was repeated. The all-Negro 92nd Division was accused of being unable to stand up under fire. Once more there were courts-martial of men unjustly accused of running from the enemy."

Marshall noted that the 24th Infantry's black Third Battalion was winning battles while other American forces were losing them. "It began to look as if, of all the American troops overseas, only the 24th was fighting and winning." He added, "And then it happened again. Such popular applause could not be tolerated.

"Soon," Marshall said, "there began to appear reports of a large number of court-martial cases involving Negroes—cases in which Negroes were tried and convicted of cowardice, of misbehavior in the presence of the enemy, of failure to perform their assigned duties. Thirty-six of these convicted men had appealed to the NAACP for assistance, and on hearing their cases in Washington it was clear something was wrong. The heroes of yesterday were now cowards; the same men, the same outfits—brave one day and frightened the next." Marshall said the NAACP had assumed the responsibility of protecting the rights of all black Americans and believed it had a special obligation to defend those who were fighting for their country.

Toward the end of World War II, Marshall had gone to California to investigate the so-called Port Chicago mutiny at what became the Concord Naval Weapons Station near Oakland. In July 1944, in the biggest domestic military disaster of the war, 320 sailors, of whom 202 were black, were killed when ammunition they were loading for shipment to the South Pacific exploded. Subsequently, 258 black survivors of the blast refused to return to the unsafe working conditions and were charged with mutiny and cowardice. Threatened with death by firing squad, most went back to work. But fifty who held out were sentenced to prison for between eight and fifteen years after courts-martial that lasted only eighty minutes. Marshall managed to win the men's release in July 1946, but all were given "less than honorable" discharges and denied veterans' benefits.

Now Marshall was concerned about the high number of charges against black soldiers in Korea and the unusually severe sentences they were given on conviction. In September 1951 he received a complaint concerning the arrest and conviction by court-martial of Lieutenant Leon A. Gilbert, one of the few Negro officers of the 24th Infantry. He was charged with leaving his assigned post in a combat zone, a violation of the Seventy-fifth Article of War, "misbehavior in the presence of the enemy." Gilbert was found guilty and sentenced to death. After the NAACP intervened on his behalf at a hearing before the Judicial Council of the Judge Advocate General in Washington, President Truman commuted his sentence to twenty years' imprisonment.

The NAACP sent Marshall to investigate the courts-martial. Douglas MacArthur, General of the Army, rejected Marshall's initial request for permission to travel to Japan and Korea. Walter White appealed the rejection to MacArthur and President Truman. Marshall recalled: "The general rescinded his former action and granted permission for me to go to the Far East on what became the most important mission thus far of my career. I lost no time in taking off, departing as soon as transportation could be arranged. I left New York by air on January 11 [1951] and arrived in Tokyo on the fourteenth."

Marshall met with General MacArthur, General Doyle O. Hickey, chief of staff, General Edwin A. Zundell, the inspector general of the Far East Command, and Colonel Hickman, the judge advocate. "In this initial conference I told them frankly that I thought there was a good possibility that the men had been victims of racial bias and unfair trials based on conditions inherent in the army's segregation policies," Marshall said.

"General MacArthur insisted that I be given the fullest coopera- tion from everyone under his command,"Marshall wrote in a report to the NAACP's board of directors. But in private com- ments to close friends many years later, he said he believed MacArthur's decision to receive him in Japan resulted from a direct order President Truman sent the general.

Marshall said he was surprised to find, on his arrival in Japan, that MacArthur had no black officers on his command staff; there was not even a black musician playing in a military band he heard several days after he arrived in Tokyo.

Marshall questioned MacArthur about the absence of blacks on his staff and in other positions of responsibility. He told Mac- Arthur, "Well, I just talked to a Negro yesterday who has killed more people with a rifle than any person in history, and he's not qualified?" MacArthur's answer was no.

Marshall continued, "I said, 'Well now, General, remember yesterday you had that big band playing at the ceremony over there?'

"MacArthur said, 'Yes, wasn't that wonderful?'

"I said, 'Yes, it's beautiful. Now, General, just between you and me, goddammit, don't you tell me there's no Negro that can play a horn!'

"That's when he said for me to go," Marshall concluded.

In later years Marshall said he was convinced MacArthur was a racist. "What else can you say?" he asked. "Every branch of the service was desegregated, but he wouldn't budge. And when he left, the army desegregated, too. Right away."

Marshall explained the method he used for investigating the servicemen's grievances. "First on my list of tasks was to interview the imprisoned men personally," Marshall recalled. "I spent three weeks making daily trips to the stockade in which they were confined—just outside of Tokyo—and interviewed thirty-four of the thirty-six accused men who had written for our assistance prior to my leaving New York. The other two were hospitalized at the time. I also talked to many others who requested assistance while I was there."

Marshall said he also interviewed witnesses who belonged to the same units as the accused men. "In all I spoke with eighty men and discovered the facts that were missing from the records," he said. "Checking and rechecking these facts, I sifted hearsay from their statements, and a half-dozen or more talks with Lieutenant Leon A. Gilbert secured for me his full and complete story."

He continued, "In the course of my investigation, one unbelievable story after another came to my attention. Take the case of one young GI convicted of cowardice. Enlisting at the age of fifteen, he was stationed in Japan and sent to Korea when the fighting broke out. Because he knew he would have been returned to the United States as a youthful hero rather than permitted to get into the thick of the fighting, he did not reveal his true age. This lad stuck at the front until he was yanked out on a trumped-up court-martial charge. It was not until I talked to him that his real age became known. He did not reach his eighteenth birthday until eleven days after he had been convicted by court-martial."

From Japan, where he began his preliminary investigation, Marshall flew to Korea. Wearing military fatigues and a combat helmet, the forty-three-year-old lawyer visited black troops in front-line trenches. Marshall's investigation led him to conclude defendants had not received fair trials under the strict Uniform Code of Military Justice. In four cases in which black soldiers had received life sentences, Marshall found, the trials had lasted less than fifty minutes. "Even in Mississippi a Negro gets a trial longer than that if he is brought to trial," Marshall said.

One soldier charged with "misbehavior in front of the enemy" was sentenced to fifty years, even though he testified he had sprained his ankle and could not keep up with his combat unit.

One of the cases Marshall found "unbelievable" was that of Private J. P. Morgan, a member of the 24th Regiment who was court-martialed for alleged misbehavior in the presence of the enemy and sentenced to ten years at hard labor. Marshall reported,

"Although he was able to prove he was in an army hospital during the period he was charged with not being on duty, his conviction was upheld by headquarters of the 25th Division, of which the 24th is a constituent unit. When his case was taken to Washington by the NAACP, the conviction was reversed, and Private Morgan was returned to duty with his outfit.

"In another instance four men were convicted of misbehavior in the presence of the enemy, although they were stationed miles behind the battle line and assigned to mess duty. Given time off one evening, they took a jeep and started to town, and they were arrested, charged with violation of the Seventy-fifth Article of War, convicted and sentenced to ten years each. Again, these convictions were upheld by the 25th Division, only to be reversed on appeal by the NAACP to Washington. The men are now back n the army fighting."

In his report to the NAACP, Marshall said, he discovered thirty-two black soldiers convicted under the Seventy-fifth Article of War from August through October 1950. During the same period, only two white GIs were convicted. One of those white soldiers, assigned to a first-aid tent near the front lines, became drunk while on duty and left his post. He was discovered at a rear position several days later and arrested. After being tried and convicted of dereliction of duty, he was given a five-year sentence, which was later reduced to one year. The other convicted white GI was given three years for disobedience in front of the enemy. Marshall noted that another white soldier, court-martialed for falling asleep at his sentry post, was acquitted even though his commanding officer testified he had seen the soldier sleeping.

"Justice in Korea may have been blind, but not color-blind," Marshall said.

During interviews with black soldiers on the front lines, Marshall was told that white officers "sneered" at black troops. One white officer reportedly told his soldiers, "I despise nigger troops, and I don't want to command you, and the regiment is no good, and you are lousy. You don't know how to fight." Marshall reported that while this was not true of all white officers, it was a prevalent attitude and created lack of confidence between the men and their assigned leaders.

"As long as we have racial segregation in the army, we will have

the type of injustice of which these courts-martial are typical."
Marshall said. "Men who are daily exposing themselves to injury
and death at the hands of the enemy should not be subjected to
injustice, additional hardships, and unnecessary danger solely
because of race."

Marshall noted that in several cases accused soldiers had "air-
tight excuses and perfect alibis" but did not present this information in their defense. He said he asked several soldiers, "Why
didn't you tell your lawyer that? Why didn't you speak up in
court?"

Marshall said the answer was always the same. As one soldier
told him: "It wasn't worth it. We knew when we went to trial that
we would be convicted—and we were hoping and praying that we
would only get life. They gave the officer [Gilbert] death solely
because he was a Negro. What could we expect? We know the
score."

Marshall said he was especially disturbed by the case of a
soldier he identified as "Sergeant X":

"A typical instance was the case of Sergeant X, one of the finest
men I ever met, a soldier with an outstanding record. He had kept
his company together during the administration of three succes-
sive commanding officers, all of whom were killed within a two-
day period. In more than ninety days at the front, he had never lost
a single wounded man. He always brought the wounded out,
sometimes on his own back. With his buddies being killed one
after another, he kept fighting day after day, many times in
command because there was no officer around. This soldier was
charged with refusing to obey an order. He went through his trial
without mentioning either to his lawyer or to the court that at that
moment he had in his pocket a statement from a medical doctor in
charge, saying the sergeant was on the verge of battle fatigue and
should be returned to the rear.

"Not until I saw him in the stockade did he mention it to
anyone. I immediately called the captain of the guard to check his
story. His impounded uniform was searched, and there, in his
wallet, the guard found the unsubmitted evidence. 'Why didn't
you tell them?' I asked. 'It wasn't worth it,' he answered. 'It
wouldn't have helped me.'"

Marshall reported that black troops in Korea ignored propaganda attempts by the Communists to exploit the condition of black Americans. "Despite the difficulties they have encountered," he declared, "our Negro troops have remained staunchly loyal, turning a deaf ear to Communist propaganda. Our Negro troops in Korea have not been lured by the song the Communists sing."

Marshall returned to New York and sent copies of his report in October 1951 to President Truman and General MacArthur. At a New York City press conference, Marshall said racism was still highly prevalent in the army. A short time later the army reduced the sentences of twenty of the thirty-two convicted black soldiers whose cases Marshall had reviewed.

By the time an armistice brought an end to fighting in Korea, in June 1953, more than 90 percent of all blacks in the army were assigned to integrated units. The air force and the marines had eliminated their segregated units. Younger recruits soon found it difficult to believe that an all-black combat unit like the Fighting 24th had ever existed.

NAACP executive secretary Walter White said Marshall's trip to Japan and Korea "underscores the need for immediate elimination of segregation from the United States Army and for the full implementation of the President's Executive Order." He remarked, "All of us are deeply indebted to Mr. Marshall for his exposé of these conditions, which cry to high heaven for immediate correction if the prestige of our country is to be maintained and the lives of our fighting men to be saved."

After Marshall returned from Korea he was a frequent visitor to Washington, D.C., where he found a southern city still sharply segregated. The city's black population had doubled to 280,000 between 1930 and 1950 and the Washington area boasted the nation's largest percentage of black professionals: 300 physicians, 150 lawyers and judges, 2,000 teachers and faculty members. For Thurgood Marshall the hope for black America's progress rested in the nation's capital. That was where the important judicial, legislative, and executive decisions were made and where the growing political power of minorities was being brought to bear on those who made and enforced the nation's laws.

Southern congressmen fought with determination to impose their segregationist ideas on the nation's capital and the country's laws. A December 1950 article in *Harper's* magazine, "Washington: Blight on Democracy," reported: "Negroes who have lived in many parts of the country say that nowhere else in America is there such bitter mutual race hatred."

Under President Roosevelt's New Deal the federal government had expanded, but blacks were only given jobs as clerks, messengers, janitors, and chauffeurs on the lowest rung of the government's employment ladder. Segregated accommodations were still the rule, and black government workers who could not eat in government cafeterias would either have to travel uptown to U Street to eat at black restaurants, such as the Florida Avenue Grill or Harrison's, or bring lunch in a bag. Even Congressman William Dawson from Chicago, Illinois, could not eat in the Capitol's congressional dining room or drink from one of its "white" water fountains.

Segregation was so entrenched in the nation's capital that the District of Columbia's white-dominated board of recreation refused to accept ownership of the city's federally controlled golf courses and swimming pools because of a stipulation requiring they be opened to all citizens.

Marshall visited Washington frequently to see old friends at Howard University and NAACP officials, like lobbyist Clarence Mitchell II, to plan the association's civil rights strategies. He was very much at home in the city where he attended law school and he socialized with friends at the nightclubs along U Street and at the Howard Theatre.

On these trips he mixed NAACP business with pleasure, playing poker with professors Martin Jenkins, Herman Branson, attorney Wiley Branton, Ralph Bunche, and other friends he made during his student years in Washington. "Thurgood was a good poker player who had refined the art of the bluff," Branson said. "He had complete control of his face, and his heavy eyelids and the glare from his glasses made it difficult to tell if he was holding aces or if his hand was a total bust."

Gardner Bishop, "the U Street Barber," cut Marshall's hair at his popular U Street barbershop, which was a social crossroads for black men from all walks of Washington life. In addition to Marshall, his clientele had included Charles Houston and other members of the Howard University faculty.

Bishop was an activist and joined with Marshall and Houston

in developing early cases that were crucial building blocks in the school desegregation suit. A proud black man with little formal education, he had come to Washington from his Rocky Mount, North Carolina, home to work in a white barbershop in the 1930s. A short time later he opened his own shop on U Street, the black business district. He became active in civil rights when his daughter, Judine, was chased off a whites-only playground by a police officer.

Gardner Bishop now lives in northwest Washington, D.C., in a Presbyterian nursing home. He speaks often to visitors about his association with Thurgood Marshall. "Thurgood had hair like a white man," he recalled, "and he was full of jokes from the minute he got in my chair until he left the shop." Bishop remembers Marshall's self-effacing humor "that kept him in touch with the black folks on the street corners who didn't have all the college smarts he had."

Bishop said, "After he got out of the chair he would hang around the shop to read the colored papers—I used to get all of them—and talk with my other customers. He would order a slab of ribs from the Florida Avenue Grill and share them with me and my other barber, and after the shop closed we would discuss civil rights cases, Washington politics, drink bourbon, and run a few hands of poker."

But the barbershop was not the only place Marshall used his humor. On visits to the clerk's office while filing motions in Supreme Court cases, Marshall joked with the white personnel. "Well, gotta go down to South Carolina from here. Last time I was there they told me there were going to run me out of town on a rail. Better get my running shoes on," he once said.

Marshall loved to laugh. He once joked about the possibility of bringing a lawsuit against a white prostitute if she refused her services to a black man because of his race. "I wonder if a colored man could claim a violation of the Constitution's equal protection guarantees if he's turned down by a prostitute," he said.

Marshall dropped the letter g from the ends of words; he said "ax" instead of "asked" and used "dese, dat, and dose." Henry Moon, the NAACP's publicity director and Marshall's close friend, told interviewers: "It was all part of his strategy. He never wanted them to think, 'Now, this here nigger thinks he's smarter than I am.'"

Gunnar Myrdal's study of black life lends credence to Moon's theory about Marshall's use of black dialect: "Negroes do it [use dialect] to avoid appearing 'uppity' in the eyes of whites. Negroes seem to be proud of their dialect, and frequently speak it even when they know how to speak perfect English. Some upper-class Negroes do this to retain prestige and a following among lower-class Negroes."

"He could sit in the barbershop and talk like he was one of the U Street boys," Bishop said, "but everybody in the shop, even my shoeshine boy, knew Thurgood could speak perfect English, and did when he took a case to court."

Bishop recalled one of Marshall's favorite barbershop jokes. A slave had stolen a turkey from his master and eaten it. When the master came to beat the slave for eating his turkey, the slave pleaded, "You shouldn't beat me, massuh. You got less turkey, but you sure got more nigger."

ELEVEN

The Road to Clarendon County

There is no such thing as "separate but equal."
Segregation itself imports inequality.
—Charles Hamilton Houston

The onset of World War II brought the United States into violent confrontation with a racist ideology that tested America's commitment to its creed and rallied Americans around those principles valued dearly in theory, if not in practice. Adolf Hitler's declarations of Aryan supremacy, and the atrocities his regime committed against those of "lesser" genetic value, culminated in the consummate evil of the Holocaust. During its course and in its aftermath, Americans were compelled to look inside themselves. At the very least, this great soul-searching reminded Americans that this country's commitment to social justice and equality under the rule of law was worth fighting for.

For blacks, the war spawned a new resolve. Hundreds of thousands of black soldiers, sailors, and airmen volunteered or were drafted to serve in America's segregated armed forces, and they saw duty at home or abroad in North Africa, Europe, or the Pacific. Having sacrificed to defend freedom, they were no longer willing to suffer passively the patent abuse of their rights or the denial of their entitlements when they returned home to the United States. They had fought and died for this country. Their claim to the freedom that it offered was steeped in blood. African Americans were prepared to demand their rights as never before.

The nation's postwar prosperity whetted the appetite for freedom. The GI Bill bestowed upon returning veterans unprecedented opportunities to obtain federal assistance toward completing their educations, purchasing a first home, securing a job, and obtaining medical care. America's largess was its gratitude for faithful military service. Naturally, blacks wanted their fair share. As a result, the system of racial separation began to break down. There simply were not enough good houses in segregated neighborhoods for black families with the money to buy them. Similarly, there were not enough black colleges and graduate schools for those qualified and able to pay for a higher education. The African-American population increased greatly, too, which exacerbated the problem.

Equally significant were the changes that occurred in academic circles. Sociology—the study of human behavior, origins, organizations, and institutions—gained prominence in political and economic discussion. This came as a consequence of, and perhaps a reaction to, Hitler's emphasis on race and the Stalinist preoccupation with economic class, which respectively claimed that race or class predetermined history.

In the early 1940s, Swedish economist Gunnar Myrdal, who was to win the Nobel Prize in Economic Science some thirty years later, published a massive two-volume work that analyzed race relations in America. Its impact, breadth, and scope were unprecedented. Myrdal's *An American Dilemma: The Negro Problem and Modern Democracy* not only profiled the country's race problems from a historical and moral perspective; it critiqued in seemingly infinite detail the social and economic costs of maintaining a society that denied itself the full use of its human creative and scientific resources by denying blacks entry into the economic and social mainstream.

White racism, together with its economic and psychological impact on both whites and blacks, was examined by Myrdal in acute, clinical detail. Writing in a tone that was simultaneously daring and dispassionate, Myrdal challenged the very notion of race as it was applied in America. "The definition of the 'Negro race' is...a social and conventional, not a biological, concept," he declared.

He supported his assertions with those of like-minded thinkers such as Sir Henry H. Johnston, who observed, "The farcical side of the color question in the States is that at least a considerable proportion of the 'colored people' are almost white-skinned, and belong in the preponderance of their descent and in their mental associations to the white race." Had Johnston been writing specifically of Thurgood Marshall—tan-complexioned, straight-haired, and the son of a blue-eyed father—the observation would have been apt. Myrdal concluded, "The fundamental unity and similarity of mankind—above minor individual and group dif-ferentials—is becoming scientifically established."

Marshall and Houston decided to attack the separate-but-equal doctrine by establishing in a court of law, by a preponderance of scientific, biological, and sociological evidence, that there was no rational basis for race-based distinctions. After all, the law, like most fields, was interdisciplinary. The considerations that shaped judicial opinions were economic, social, and moral, as well as legal.

The Fourteenth Amendment, for example, mandates that all citizens be accorded "equal protection of the laws." Yet the U.S. Supreme Court recognized and accepted circumstances under which individuals or groups could be treated differently. As a general rule, treating some groups differently was permitted whenever there was a "rational basis" for the distinction. Whether there was a rational, or reasonable, basis for a government-imposed distinction became the focus of the Court's inquiry in any given case.

Child labor laws provided an example. These laws, which prohibited children from working as long and hard as adult men, had been challenged when they were first enacted. But the Court eventually found a rational basis for treating children and men differently, given children's relative physical and intellectual vulnerability.

At the turn of the twentieth century, an Oregon law that banned women from working as many hours as men was deemed to present a more difficult case. As the lawyer for the state of Oregon, Louis Brandeis used a plethora of sociological data to support Oregon's contention that there was a reasonable basis for distinguishing between women and men under the circumstances. Brandeis did not ask the Court to agree necessarily with the assumptions of the sociologists that he cited. Instead, he won his case, *Muller v. Oregon*, by convincing the Court that, rightly or wrongly, there was enough sociological evidence to reasonably conclude that women should not be compelled or permitted to work as hard as men.

If the Court would accept sociology at the turn of the century, perhaps it would respond to it at mid-century, especially after Hitler. There being no rational basis for racial distinctions, the separate-but-equal doctrine would have to fall. Or would it?

In 1948 Marshall argued a case before the U.S. Supreme Court, *Sipuel v. Oklahoma State Board of Regents*, that challenged the exclusion of an African-American woman, Ada Sipuel, from the University of Oklahoma's law school—not because she was a woman but because of her color. The Court found Sipuel's exclusion a violation of its ruling in *Gaines*. In *Gaines* the Court held that a state offering legal education to whites must offer it to blacks as well. Oklahoma was ordered, therefore, to make a legal education available to Sipuel immediately or close its whites-only law school until such time as it would create a law school for blacks. The Court's order was *per curiam*, meaning unsigned and without so much as a discussion of legal issues that the Court regarded settled by *Gaines*.

Marshall was confident that the Court's decision would force the desegregation of the university's law school. Oklahoma's board of regents proved stubborn, however, and refused to comply with the spirit, if not the letter, of the Court's order. Instead, they established a separate law school just for Sipuel, in a roped-off section of the state capitol in Oklahoma City, and assigned three instructors to teach her law.

Marshall was furious. Claiming that the regents' actions denigrated the Court's intent, he went back before the justices to argue that the separate treatment accorded Sipuel did not amount to an equal educational opportunity. The brief that Marshall prepared cited Myrdal and a number of other sociologists to support what was, in effect, the contention that adherence to the separate-but-equal doctrine resulted in inequality of treatment. But the underlying premises of the assertion had not been put forward and proven at the trial level.

The Court dealt Marshall a seven-to-two setback, ruling simply that Sipuel's original suit "did not present the issue of whether a state might satisfy the equal protection clause...by establishing a law school for Negroes." Ada Sipuel was left to languish alone amid her law books.

The American legal system evolved from the English common-law tradition, which placed great emphasis on the weight of precedent—that is, applying law to current situations as it has been applied in the past. The Latin term for the practice is *stare decisis*, let the decision stand. What is remarkable about the American system, however—some would say what has enabled it to survive—is a marvelous flexibility that permits judges to break with the past and rewrite the law in a way that reflects the modern world and its values.

The U.S. Supreme Court is in many ways a monastery of the intellect. To an extent, the framers of the Constitution intended it to be that way. Justices are appointed for life; they are not subject to popular recall or election; they are beholden for their jobs to no one and need not be swayed or intimidated by the passing moods, fears, fancies, or prejudices of a fickle electorate. This isolation enables the Court to protect the rights of the minority from the majority's tyranny with an impunity the system grants to neither Congress nor the president.

For the first century and a half of its existence, however, the men who sat on the Supreme Court viewed the protection of individual property rights as the Court's primary mission. Consequently, the maintenance of the status quo, meaning the system by and through which a certain minority of individuals acquired wealth, became the Court's focus. In other words, the Court was a reluctant vehicle for social change because the men who sat on the Court were, for the most part, opposed to almost any change.

Franklin Delano Roosevelt changed all that. With the nation threatened by the worst economic depression in its history, Roosevelt put forward a legislative agenda designed to change fundamentally the relationship between the federal government, on the one hand, and state governments and private individuals and corporations on the other. At first the Court resisted. For example, administrative actions that provided for shorter working hours, a minimum pay scale, and the regulation of unfair trade practices and price-cutting were declared unconstitutional. But, through his appointments to the Supreme Court, Roosevelt began to liberalize the Court's perspective.

In the process, the appointments of Hugo Black, William O. Douglas, and Felix Frankfurter, among others, shifted the Court's thinking on the race question. Black, an Alabaman who once belonged to the Ku Klux Klan, would prove, ironically, to be one of the staunchest advocates of civil rights in the Court's history. Douglas, ultraliberal, brilliant, and idiosyncratic, over the course of thirty-five years would likewise prove to be an impassioned and visionary defender of blacks.

Frankfurter, ever the Harvard law professor, judicious and often exasperatingly pedantic, had been a mentor to Houston and to others who now found themselves on Houston and Marshall's legal team. He had himself been a member of the NAACP, serving on its national Legal Committee and helping to develop the organization's litigation strategies. Obviously he was predisposed favorably to civil rights.

Roosevelt appointed others to the Supreme Court who might or might not have been as sympathetic to the cause of black equality as these men. They came and went. What was important was that the Court's evolution demonstrated that the Court's, as well as the nation's, political center was shifting.

This convinced Marshall and his colleagues in the Fund leadership following World War II that the time was propitious to move beyond the Margold strategy and challenge the separate-but-equal doctrine directly. Houston agreed. In 1947 Houston announced the policy shift in his regular *Afro-American* column, "The Highway":

The NAACP lawyers in order to get the campaign underway accepted the doctrine that the state could segregate ...provided equal accommodations were afforded.... Now the NAACP is making a direct, open, all-out fight against segregation.... There is no such thing as "separate but equal." Segregation itself imports inequality.

Later he told the Judiciary Committee of the U.S. Senate, "Segregation has to go the way chattel slavery went, and go soon."

Marshall drew a line in the dirt in Texas. Yet another Negro wanted to go to law school, a Texas mailman named Heman Sweatt. Texas law forbade his admission to the law school at the University of Texas because of his color. Instead, a state judge ordered the state to establish a law school for Sweatt at Texas Southern University, which today is named, ironically, the Thurgood Marshall School of Law. Sweatt sued. This time Marshall built the sociological argument in at the trial level. On a hot, sweaty summer afternoon in Austin, he called Robert Redfield to the stand. Redfield was the chairman of the anthropology department at the University of Chicago and held doctorates in both anthropology and law.

Over the objections of opposing counsel, Redfield dismissed the idea that blacks are somehow inferior to whites intellectually. He went on to state that segregation intensifies distrust between the races and inhibits the learning process for blacks. Marshall told the court:

"We have a right to put in evidence to show that segregation statutes in the state of Texas and in any other state, actually when examined—and they have never been examined in any lawsuit that I know of yet—have no line of reasonableness. There is no understandable factual basis for classification by race, and under a long line of decisions by the Supreme Court, not on the question of Negroes, but on the Fourteenth Amendment, all courts agree that if there is no rational basis for the classification, it is flat in the teeth of the Fourteenth Amendment."

As expected, the Texas state courts ruled against Thurgood Marshall and his client Heman Sweatt, setting the stage for a U.S. Supreme Court confrontation that would take three years to come about.

Meanwhile, Marshall pursued the same strategy in an Oklahoma case involving the University of Oklahoma's refusal to admit George W. McLaurin to its doctoral program in education.

Sixty-eight years old, McLaurin had earned a master's degree in education many years before. In 1948 Marshall took the case to a three-judge U.S. district court. A decision by such a court could be taken directly to the U.S. Supreme Court, bypassing the circuit court of appeals and thereby speeding the appellate process. The district court applied the holding in *Sipuel* and ordered Oklahoma to provide McLaurin with the opportunity to earn a doctorate in education "as soon as it does for applicants of any other group."

Oklahoma, as in *Sipuel*, complied in its own dispirited way. McLaurin was indeed admitted to the university's graduate school of education. But he was made to receive instruction on a purely segregated basis. Sipuel was consigned to a roped-off section of the state capitol. McLaurin was allowed in the same classroom as his white peers, but his seat was in an otherwise empty row separated by a railing. He was permitted to take his meals in the cafeteria but was forced to eat at different hours than the white students.

Marshall was bitterly frustrated. But he seized upon McLaurin's predicament as an opportunity for a unique challenge to the separate-but-equal doctrine. Clearly McLaurin was being offered "equal" facilities and the same academic instruction as whites. But the intangible burdens imposed on him by university officials represented a "badge of inferiority" that, it could be argued, inhibited his ability to learn, participate, and compete effectively. And there was no rational basis for treating this man differently from any other student. Even McLaurin's white classmates were affronted by the treatment he was accorded. They ripped the sign proclaiming "Reserved for Coloreds" from the railing that separated the row where McLaurin was assigned to sit.

After losing at the three-judge district court level, Marshall returned to New York, where the Fund lawyers prepared their briefs for the U.S. Supreme Court. In its *Sweatt* brief, the NAACP for the first time called upon the Court to reverse *Plessy* outright and outlaw separate-but-equal. Marshall realized, however, that *Sweatt* presented the justices with a way to sidestep the ultimate question. By ruling simply that the black facilities offered Sweatt were unequal to those provided whites, the Court could give Sweatt a victory merely by finding that Texas violated the "equal" prong of the *Plessy* doctrine. In this way, the "separate" prong could be left intact.

McLaurin left less room for waffling and maneuver. Undeniably, McLaurin's treatment was equal in the sense that he was offered the same instructors, and access to the same facilities, as whites. Therefore, the letter of the "equal" requirement was satisfied. The question was whether by its nature the "separate" treatment accorded McLaurin rendered equality unattainable. Marshall was betting that the facts of the case would require the Court to face *Plessy* squarely.

Then came what was potentially a big break. Harry S. Truman's Department of Justice filed an *amicus curiae* brief in support of the NAACP position, calling for the Court to overturn *Plessy*. For the Fund lawyers, this was a welcome, if not altogether unexpected, development. After all, Truman was the first president in American history elected on a platform that called for civil rights. As a veteran returning home to Independence, Missouri, after World War I, Truman witnessed the Ku Klux Klan in its heyday. The behavior and attitudes of the Klan convinced the future president that it was a threat to democratic institutions.

Not only did Truman become an advocate of civil rights; he practiced what he preached. Although many of his civil rights initiatives, including antilynching legislation that black leaders had sought for generations, were hamstrung by influential southerners in Congress, Truman used the powers of the presidency to advance a civil rights agenda to the extent that it was possible to do so. As commander in chief, he integrated American's armed forces. He also made the first appointment of an African American to a seat on a U.S. Circuit Court of Appeals, naming William H. Hastie, a former dean of Howard Law School and an intimate friend and associate of Thurgood Marshall's, to the Third Circuit.

Truman's appointments to the U.S. Supreme Court, however, were worrisome, at least in the beginning. Two liberal judicial activists appointed by Franklin Roosevelt—Frank Murphy and Wiley Rutledge—were replaced by Truman with Tom C. Clark, a Texan and former attorney general, and Sherman "Shay" Minton, a former Indiana senator. Clark's civil rights leanings were somewhat suspect. Minton, however, soon proved to be an activist liberal in the New Deal tradition. Also, Fred Vinson, the man Truman appointed chief justice, demonstrated some open-mindedness on the race question. In 1948 Vinson wrote the opinion of the Court in *Shelley v. Kraemer*, argued by Thurgood Marshall, holding it to be a violation of the equal-protection clause for state court or judicial officers to enforce racially restrictive housing covenants.

The Court heard oral arguments in *Sweatt* and *McLaurin* over two days, April 3 and 4, 1950. It decided both cases on the same day two months later, June 5. In the interim, Charles Hamilton Houston had died.

Over a quarter-century later, U.S. Supreme Court Justice Thurgood Marshall paid tribute to his mentor, saying, "We wouldn't have been anyplace if Charlie hadn't laid the groundwork for it." William O. Douglas, who sat on the Supreme Court longer than any other justice, called Houston a "veritable dynamo of energy guided by a mind that had as sharp a cutting edge as any I have known."

There were few, if any, men Thurgood Marshall knew better or loved more than Charles Houston. But events left him little time to grieve. Houston presaged his own death with what was one of his favorite admonitions to students who would dare enlist in his life-or-death crusade for black equality: "No tea for the feeble; no crape for the dead." He provided his own eulogy in the form of a handwritten note to his only son, left in a copy of Joshua Liebman's *Piece of Mind* by his bedside: "Tell Bo I did not run out on him but went down fighting that he might have better and broader opportunities than I had without prejudice or bias operating against him, and in any fight, some fall."

From Marshall's and the Fund's standpoint, the results of the Court's rulings in *Sweatt* and *McLaurin* were mixed. On the one hand, the holdings in both cases were groundbreaking. In *Sweatt* the Court for the first time ordered an African American admitted to a previously all-white school because the black counterpart school provided by the state was not equal to it. Based on its facilities and the caliber of its faculty and alumni, the University of Texas law school "may properly be considered one of the nation's ranking law schools," the Court stated. Therefore, the justices concluded, consigning Sweatt to a lesser law school such as Prairie View would deny him his constitutional right to "legal education equivalent to that offered by the State to students of other races."

In *McLaurin* the Court held that the different treatment accorded McLaurin—segregating him within the University of Oklahoma's graduate school of education—because of his race "handicapped [him] in his pursuit of effective graduate instruction." The Court concluded, "Such restrictions impair and inhibit his ability to study, to engage in discussions and exchange views with other students, and, in general, to learn his profession." In other words, once admission was obtained, there could be no discrimination within the school based on race.

Taken together, the rulings meant that Marshall and the Fund had made the best of what could be made of *Plessy*: That which was separate had to be truly equal.

On the other hand, the rulings were, at the same time, disheartening. The Court did not consider the ultimate issue of whether *Plessy* should be overturned. The particular cases could be decided on the basis of standing precedent; there was no need to overrule *Plessy* in order to do justice for Sweatt and McLaurin.

In conference with the other justices, Clark conceded the possibility that "at a later date our judicial discretion will lead us to hear such a case," meaning a case in which *Plessy* would have to be squarely reexamined in order to arrive at a just result. But for the time being, he argued that the "horribles" of segregation were "highly exaggerated," and he stood by the separate-but-equal doctrine. So did Reed.

Frankfurter, for his part, urged caution. He wrote to Chief Justice Vinson, "It seems to me desirable now not to go a jot beyond the *Gaines* test. The shorter the opinion, the more there is an appearance of unexcitement and inevitability about it, the better."

Black felt that unanimity was needed to "add force" to any desegregation ruling. Without unanimity the time was just not right to overrule *Plessy*. If all nine could agree only to go so far as to arrive at narrow holdings in *Sweatt* and *McLaurin*, then so be it for now.

Vinson wrote both opinions, which were unanimous. From the outset of *Sweatt*, he made plain that the Court's decisions would be limited to the particular facts of the cases at hand. "Broader issues have been urged for our consideration," he wrote, "but we adhere to the principle of deciding constitutional questions only in the context of the particular case before the Court." He went on, "We have frequently reiterated that this Court will decide constitutional questions only when necessary to the disposition of the case at hand, and that such decisions will be drawn as narrowly as possible."

By not overruling *Plessy*, the Court left Marshall in the dark as to the persuasive weight the Court would accord the kind of sociological data submitted on behalf of Sweatt and McLaurin to demonstrate that segregation was inherently unjust. As Vinson stated simply in *Sweatt*, the Court did not feel the "need" to "reach petitioner's contention that *Plessy v. Ferguson* should be reexamined in the light of contemporary knowledge respecting the purposes of the Fourteenth Amendment and the effects of racial segregation."

Ironically, then, Marshall's and the Fund's most noteworthy successes only deepened their dilemma and frustration. Marshall was gloomy. What was he supposed to do? Go around to every graduate school in the country to examine whether equal treatment was in fact being provided to each Negro enrolled there and then spend two or three years bringing to the Supreme Court every instance in which it was not?

Besides, the rulings applied only to the graduate school level. Marshall was aware of studies done by at least one noted psychologist, Dr. Kenneth Clark of Columbia University, that indicated that segregation inflicted psychological and emotional damage on blacks beginning in childhood.

He redoubled his resolve. Several weeks after the *Sweatt* and *McLaurin* decisions were handed down, he asked an NAACP conference to adopt a resolution condemning segregation in public education outright. The resolution declared that thenceforth all NAACP litigation would "be aimed at obtaining education on a nonsegregated basis and that no relief other than that will be acceptable." The NAACP board gave Marshall's position its approval. Thus strengthened and renewed, he headed for Clarendon County, South Carolina.

TWELVE

Brown v. Board of Education (Part 1)

If you show your black ass in Clarendon
County again, you'll be dead.
—An attorney for the State of South Carolina

Clarendon County sprawls across the middle of the state at the foot of the Blue Ridge Mountains. It is predominantly black, agricultural, and poor. After the Civil War, blacks were pushed inland off the magnificent coastal plantations where they had lived as slaves and onto Clarendon's unfertile lowlands. Some corn, soybeans, and tobacco can be grown there, and a few textile mills dot the landscape. Driving past pine, peach, and pecan trees, past gnarled oaks draped with Spanish moss, one realizes that this is the old South, where going to church is more important than going to school. Even today, as in Thurgood Marshall's time, there are probably four Baptist churches for every school building in Clarendon, mostly frame structures set up on bricks or stones.

On Sunday afternoon dusty black children play in the dirt in front of their ramshackle, tin-roofed houses while their grandmothers sit fanning themselves on rickety front porches in bonnets and colorful cotton print dresses, their Sunday best. Many of the children's feet bear bruises and cuts from running over the jagged edges of tin roofs that have blown off. No one could have known in 1950 that this lazy South Carolina backwater was about to serve as the focal point of the legal proceedings that would forever in the popular mind be associated with Topeka, Kansas, in the case that became known as *Brown v. Board of Education of Topeka.*

In May 1950, Harry Briggs Sr. and his wife, Liza, brought an equalization suit on behalf of one of their five children, Harry Jr., in U.S. district court. They demanded that the black schools in segregated Clarendon County be brought up to the standards of those for whites. Briggs, thirty-four, was a navy veteran who had served in the South Pacific during World War II. He pumped gas and fixed cars for a living in his hometown of Summerton. Liza was a chambermaid at a local motel.

The Briggses were joined in their legal action by the parents of other elementary-school-age African-American children in Clarendon. But the suit was named for them because their names came first in the alphabetical order of plaintiffs. As the result of their legal action, they became the targets of harassment by whites. Both were fired from their jobs when they refused to drop out of the lawsuit. Briggs was philosophical in retrospect about the risks he took. He said, "We figured anything to better the children's condition was worthwhile." When the local NAACP chapter brought the situation in Clarendon to the attention of the national headquarters in New York, Marshall decided to take on the matter. The Briggses seemed to him to be courageous people. He would do whatever he could to help.

On the face of it, they had a strong case. Over half the public school funds in Clarendon went to white schools, although the school system enrolled three times as many blacks as whites. In addition, Clarendon's annual per capita outlay for white students was almost a hundred times more than for blacks. Teachers' salaries were disparate, too, although the Briggses had won an earlier ruling that black teachers' pay be brought up to that of the white teachers in Clarendon.

Marshall seized on the favorable fact situation presented by the

case. It was uncontestable that the black and white schools in
Clarendon were unequal. He urged the Briggses to include in their
suit a claim that segregation in public education was in and of
itself unconstitutional. They agreed.

Marshall was also heartened when the judge to whom the case
was assigned turned out to be J. Waties Waring, a white native
South Carolinian who was a supporter of blacks' rights. Appointed to the bench by Franklin Roosevelt in 1942, Waring had
ruled in favor of Briggs in the suit to require equalization of black
and white teachers' pay. Before that, in 1945, Waring had struck
down the state Democratic party's attempt to bar blacks from
voting in Democratic primary elections.

Although he was not sympathetic to blacks originally, Waring's
beliefs were influenced heavily by his second wife, a native New
Yorker, who encouraged him to read Myrdal's *An American
Dilemma* and to arrive at a new understanding of the white
southerners' mentality as portrayed in such works as *The Mind of
the South* by W. J. Cash. The judge's wife even went so far as to
express publicly her view that "we don't have a Negro problem in
the South; we have a white problem."

At the November 17, 1950, pretrial conference, Waring told
Marshall that his brief should be revised so that his argument
would become a frontal attack on segregation. Years later Waring
recalled, "I pointed out to him, right there from the bench, that in
my opinion the pleadings didn't raise the issue."

Waring told Marshall, "You've partially raised the issue, but of
course the court can and may do what has been done so very, very
often heretofore: decide a case on equal facilities.... It's very easy
to decide this case on that issue." Waring suggested, however, that
the case be dismissed without prejudice and a new suit brought
attacking segregation more directly. He told Marshall, "That'll
raise the issue for all time as to whether a state can segregate by
race in its schools."

Given the demographics of Clarendon County, Marshall was
reluctant to take the approach suggested by Waring. The county
was 70 percent black. Desegregation would not only mean
allowing blacks to attend predominantly white schools; it would
also mean forcing whites to attend schools that were predomi-

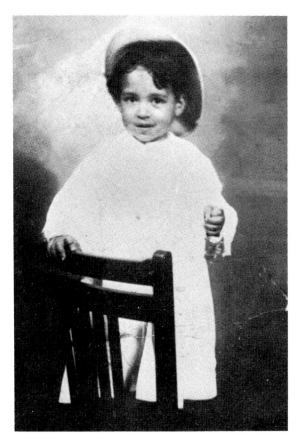

Aubrey Marshall, a physician, was two years older than his brother, Thurgood. Dr. Marshall was fifty-two when this picture was taken in 1960. He died twelve years later. (Courtesy Moorland-Spingarn Research Center, Howard University)

Thurgood Marshall, age two, in Baltimore, Maryland, in 1910. (Courtesy Moorland-Spingarn Research Center, Howard University)

Thurgood Marshall, age seventeen, in 1925, the year he entered Lincoln (Pa.) University. His mother pawned her engagement and wedding rings to help pay his college tuition and never redeemed them. (Courtesy Moorland-Spingarn Research Center, Howard University)

Thurgood Marshall's parents, Norma and William Marshall, in the living room of their Baltimore home in 1947. Marshall's father ordered him to "fight" any one who called him "nigger." (Courtesy Moorland-Spingarn Research Center, Howard University)

Vivian "Buster" Marshall was Thurgood Marshall's first wife. The Marshalls met in college and married during Thurgood's senior year. It was a childless marriage of twenty-five years that ended with Vivian's death in February 1955. Not wishing to distract Thurgood, she did not tell him she had terminal cancer until after he had argued *Brown v. Board of Education*. She died on her forty-fourth birthday. Marshall said of his wife's death, "I thought the world had come to an end." (Courtesy Moorland-Spingarn Research Center, Howard University)

Howard University Law School professor Charles Hamilton Houston, left, with Clarence Darrow, center, and Howard president Mordecai W. Johnson. Houston was Marshall's mentor and with Johnson turned Howard University's law school into a fully accredited institution in 1930. He made the law school the envy of its white counterparts by getting famous practitioners such as Darrow to lecture frequently. (Scurlock Studio)

Howard Law School professor Charles Hamilton Houston taught Marshall at Howard. As lawyers for the NAACP they travelled the dangerous South and elsewhere in the 1930s investigating lynchings and challenging segregation and discrimination. Houston's litigation strategy laid the foundation for the monumental *Brown v. Board of Education* suit that ended legal segregation in America in 1954, four years after his death. Marshall gave him credit for the victory. (Scurlock Studio)

Ruby Bates, left, with the mothers of the "Scottsboro Boys" at the Phyliss Wheatley YWCA in Washington, D.C., in 1932. The "Scottsboro Boys," nine blacks aged thirteen to twenty, were convicted of raping Bates and another white woman on a train in Alabama in 1931. Bates later recanted her accusation. The Communist Party used the case to win support among blacks to promote its political agenda. (Scurlock Studio)

Dr. W.E.B. Dubois, teacher and writer, was a founding member of the NAACP. He received the first Ph.D. degree awarded an African-American by Harvard University. (Scurlock Studio)

Mordecai W. Johnson was Howard University's first black president. He was a close associate of Supreme Court Justice Louis Brandeis, who advised him to make Howard's law school an accredited institution for civil rights lawyers. (Scurlock Studio)

Washington Attorney Leon A. Ranson, Thurgood Marshall's colleague in the 1930s and '40s, worked with Marshall and Houston on early civil rights litigation. (Scurlock Studio)

Thurgood Marshall and the NAACP worked for federal legislation to prevent lynchings like this one in Marion, Indiana. Abram Smith, nineteen (left), and Thomas Shipp, eighteen, were hanged in Public Square after they had been accused of murdering Claude Deeter and assaulting his girl friend, Mary Ball. A third juvenile, James Cameron, was spared, served four years in prison, and was recommended for a pardon a half-century later. (UPI/ Bettmann)

Thurgood Marshall, then thirty-seven, at the NAACP's annual convention in 1946 at Atlantic City, New Jersey. (Courtesy Moorland-Spingarn Research Center, Howard University)

Marshall, seated at left, represented Ada Sipuel in Norman, Oklahoma, after her application to the University of Oklahoma's law school was rejected because of her race, in 1947. Marshall won the case for Ada Sipuel on appeal to the U.S. Supreme Court, but the practical effect of the ruling was that Sipuel was left alone to study law in a roped-off section of the state capitol building instead of attending classes with other students. (Griffin Davis Photos)

Walter Lee Irvin (third from left) is defended in February 1952 by NAACP lawyers Paul C. Perkins (far left) and Jack Greenberg. Chief NAACP counsel Thurgood Marshall (far right) headed the appeals defense in Ocala, Florida, for Irwin, who was sentenced to death after his conviction for kidnapping and raping a Florida housewife. The NAACP lawyers saved him from the death penalty and considered a life prison term for him a victory. (UPI/Bettmann)

Thurgood Marshall chats with John W. Davis, his legal adversary, as the Supreme Court begins to hear *Brown v. Board of Education*, challenging segregated schools. Davis was the appellate advocate that Marshall admired most. As a Howard Law School student he cut classes to hear Davis, the 1924 Democratic presidential nominee, argue before the Supreme Court. Marshall led the team of NAACP lawyers that defeated Davis in 1954, outlawed segregated schools, and forever changed American society. (UPI/Bettmann)

The lawyers who successfully argued the case against school segregation stand in front of the U.S. Supreme Court on May 17, 1954, after the Court ruled segregation in public school unconstitutional. Left to right: George E.C. Hayes, Thurgood Marshall, and James Nabrit, Jr. (UPI/Bettmann)

Thurgood Marshall, NAACP counsel, relaxes beneath a portrait of Justice Brandeis in the Supreme Court's lawyers' lounge, after presenting his argument in the Little Rock, Arkansas, school integration case on September 11, 1958. After the Brown ruling, southern politicians launched a strategy of "massive resistance" to desegregation. Marshall represented black students from the Little Rock, Arkansas, Central High School, closed to blacks by Governor Orville Faubus. President Dwight D. Eisenhower sent armed troops to escort the students to class. (UPI/Bettmann)

nantly black. In Marshall's view this made *Briggs* a bad test case, because desegregation would be even less palatable politically and socially under these circumstances. Nevertheless, he gambled and followed Waring's recommendation.

Meanwhile, South Carolina governor James F. Byrnes prepared to defend the state's segregated school system. A former two-term U.S. senator, Byrnes had also served in the House of Representatives for a decade. He even sat on the U.S. Supreme Court briefly in 1941 before returning to the political life he loved. As a former justice, Byrnes knew the Supreme Court, and he knew that the Court's recent rulings spoke for themselves on the question of a state's obligation to provide equal educational facilities for its black residents.

The governor readily conceded that the black schools in South Carolina had endured "a hundred years of neglect." Aiming to head off a U.S. Supreme Court confrontation that he feared his state could not win, Byrnes pushed through the state legislature a $75 million bond issuance to upgrade the state's black educational facilities. "We must have a state school building program," he declared, adding, "One cannot speak frankly on this subject without mentioning the race problem. It is our duty to provide for the races substantial equality in school facilities. We should do it because it is right. For me that is sufficient reason."

At the same time, Byrnes sought authorization from the legislature to lease or sell public schools—in other words, to close or contract out public education—in the event desegregation was ordered. The Supreme Court could order public schools to desegregate, but he hoped that by privatizing education he would put the schools beyond the Court's reach in the same way that private clubs cannot have their memberships dictated by the courts. The schools would than be free to exclude blacks.

He also retained John W. Davis, the most distinguished appellate advocate of his era, to take on Thurgood Marshall and the Fund in the event the legal challenge went beyond the familiar home-field confines of the South Carolina courts.

Few men in American history have been more successful in the fields of law, politics, and diplomacy than John W. Davis. Born in Clarksburg, West Virginia, in 1873, Davis attended law school at

Virginia's Washington and Lee University and rose quickly in the legal profession, as well in the national Democratic party. From 1913 to 1918, he served as U.S. solicitor general, representing the United States in cases that came before the Supreme Court. Later he served as U.S. ambassador to Great Britain. In 1924 he became the Democratic nominee for president, selected on the 103rd ballot at a deadlocked convention.

But he waged a somewhat listless campaign against Calvin Coolidge, refusing to drop many of his wealthy "robber baron" clients, including J. P. Morgan, who were anathema to the William Jennings Bryan wing of the party. One critic predicted that, if elected, Davis would change the national anthem to "The Star-Spangled Banker." Coolidge prevailed; Davis captured only 29 percent of the popular vote. Afterward, he returned to private practice as senior partner in the law firm originally founded by him and his father, Davis, Polk, Wardwell, Sunderland & Kiendl. In addition to the House of Morgan, his clients included Standard Oil Co., AT&T, and Guaranty Trust Company of New York.

Davis, the appellate advocate Marshall admired most, had argued approximately 140 cases before the Supreme Court. Only two lawyers in history had appeared before the justices more: Walter Jones, who argued 317 cases between 1801 and 1850, and Daniel Webster of Massachusetts, who made nearly 200 appearances.

"Davis was the greatest solicitor general we ever had," Marshall, who was to hold the same post a half century later, once said. "You and I will never see a better one. He was a great advocate, the greatest." In his youth Marshall cut classes at Howard Law School to see the great John W. Davis at work before the Supreme Court. "Every time John Davis argued," Marshall recalled, "I'd ask myself, 'Will I ever, ever? No, never.'"

With Davis enlisted and in reserve, Byrnes placed the fate of South Carolina at the trial-court level in the hands of Charleston lawyer Robert McC. Figg Jr., the state's most prominent corporate attorney, and Emory Rogers, an outspoken white supremacist. In late May 1951, the two sides presented their opening arguments to a three-judge U.S. district court in Clarendon County. Figg and Rogers did not deny that the black and white schools in South

Carolina were unequal. Instead, they asked the court for "a reasonable time" to correct the inequalities. They defended segregation as a "valid exercise of legislative power" and closed on an ominous note, warning that a desegregation order would trigger "dangerous tensions and unrest" throughout the state.

Marshall, for his part, urged the court to strike down South Carolina's segregation statute as unconstitutional per se. Also, Marshall relied on recent Supreme Court rulings won by him and the Fund to support his contention that the state's promise to remedy inequalities at some future point in time was insufficient to overcome the present, existing wrongs. As *Time* magazine observed some years later, "Marshall generally has a running start on opposing lawyers....The law he made yesterday is today's precedent."

He lost. A month later, in an opinion written by Judge John J. Parker with the concurrence of Judge George Bell Timmerman, segregation in South Carolina was upheld as a valid exercise of legislative authority. The sociological data offered by the Fund lawyers was dismissed; instead, weight was given to the judicial doctrine of *stare decisis*, or precedent.

In this case, the court found, *Plessy v. Ferguson*'s separate-but-equal doctrine was the precedent that controlled the outcome; the recent Supreme Court ruling in *Sweatt* and *McLaurin* had not explicitly overruled *Plessy*. Parker concluded that it was "late in the day" to argue the validity of segregation. The court did, however, order the state to bring black schools up to par with those for whites "promptly."

Waring dissented bitterly, declaring that "segregation in education can never produce equality and...is an evil that must be eradicated." He went on, "This case presents the matter clearly for adjudication, and I am of the opinion that all of the legal guideposts, expert testimony, common sense, and reason point unerringly to the conclusion that the system of segregation in education adopted and practiced in the State of South Carolina must go and must go now." He concluded, "*Segregation is per se inequality.*"

Marshall appealed the ruling immediately to the Supreme Court. Meanwhile, South Carolina generally, and Clarendon

County in particular, embarked on a crash program to upgrade the black schools, and equalize black and white teachers' pay, across the state. For a time, appropriations for the construction of black schools totaled more than double the amount for white.

In January 1952 the Supreme Court disappointed Marshall by remanding *Briggs v. Elliott* to the South Carolina district court with instructions that it ascertain the degree of progress toward equalization of the black and white schools. Justices Black and Douglas vehemently opposed the remand, insisting that the constitutional issues raised in the case were ready for the Court's consideration. Nevertheless, by the spring of 1952 the case was back in Judge Parker's South Carolina court. Waring had retired and been replaced on the three-judge panel.

Writing for a unanimous court, Parker found that Clarendon County had "proceeded promptly and in good faith" toward equalization. By his estimation, full equalization would be achieved by the opening of the coming school year, soon enough to satisfy the Constitution and the U.S. Supreme Court.

One of the attorneys for South Carolina looked at Marshall, seated across the counsel table. In a voice loud enough for everyone in the courtroom to hear, he told him, "If you show your black ass in Clarendon County again you'll be dead."

Marshall went back to the Supreme Court and appealed Parker's ruling in the summer of that year. *Briggs* was consolidated with four other desegregation suits brought by the Fund from other states around the country. Together the cases presented just about every conceivable form and variation of segregated schooling.

From the Eastern District of Virginia came *Davis et al. v. County School Board of Prince Edward County, Virginia*, a case similar to *Briggs*. The parents of black high school students in Prince Edward County challenged Virginia's segregation law and also complained that the black schools were not equal to those for whites. As in South Carolina, a three-judge U.S. district court ruled against the blacks on the question of segregation itself, holding it to be within the state's power to order the separation of the races. The court agreed with the blacks, however, that the separate black and white schools should be made equal, and it ordered the black schools upgraded promptly.

From New Castle County, Delaware, came *Gebhart v. Belton*, brought on behalf of elementary- and high-school-age African-American children. Again, the blacks challenged the state's segregation law and in addition claimed that black schools and facilities were not equal to those for whites. This time they won. The Delaware Court of Chancery ordered blacks admitted to formerly white schools on the ground that the black schools were inferior. The Delaware Supreme Court upheld the chancellor's ruling but implied in its opinion that the schools could be resegregated once the black and white schools were equalized. The county appealed to the U.S. Supreme Court, arguing that the Delaware Supreme Court was wrong in ordering immediate desegregation.

From Kansas came the case by which the five consolidated cases became known, *Brown v. Board of Education.* In it, suit was brought on behalf of elementary-school-age children residing in Topeka, Kansas, challenging a Kansas law that permitted, but did not require, cities of more than fifteen thousand people to segregate their schools. Topeka segregated its elementary schools, although schools above the primary level were integrated. A three-judge district court took the extraordinary step of ruling that segregation had a detrimental effect on black children. Nonetheless, the court refused to order Topeka's elementary schools desegregated, since it found the black and white schools' facilities, curricula, and teachers' pay to be equal.

Last, out of Washington, D.C., came *Bolling v. Sharpe*, challenging segregated schooling in the nation's capital. Since Congress, under the U.S. Constitution, runs the District of Columbia, the question presented by this case was whether the Constitution prohibits the federal government from denying citizens equal protection. The legal issue presented by the case was quirky and somewhat technical. The Fourteenth Amendment to the Constitution contains the equal-protection clause, but the amendment applies specifically only to the states; it is the Fifth Amendment that applies to the federal government, and while the Fifth Amendment guarantees citizens due process, it does not contain an equal-protection clause.

The Court docketed oral arguments in the five cases for December 7, 1952. Marshall and the Fund lawyers spent the summer preparing and submitting their briefs. Meanwhile, John

W. Davis devoted himself and the resources of his enormous Wall Street law firm to the defense of segregation and the "Southern way of life."

Marshall took a decidedly sociological tack in his brief, as he had done in *Sweatt* and *McLaurin*. Relying heavily on the South Carolina testimony of Dr. Kenneth Clark and the published works of Clark and his wife, Mamie, Marshall tried to demonstrate the inherent evils of segregated education. Clark, who was black, was a protégé of Columbia University psychologist Otto Klineberg, one of his era's preeminent thinkers on race. He had done his undergraduate work at Howard University, where his views on social issues were influenced heavily by such instructors as Ralph Bunche and philosopher Alain Leroy Locke. He went on to earn his doctorate in psychology at Columbia.

Clark was noted for his doll tests, a technique that he and his wife, who also held a Columbia doctorate in psychology, had developed to gauge the attitudes of black children consigned to segregated schools compared with those of black children who received integrated educations. Black children of elementary school age were given dolls, some brown and others white. The children were asked, "Which doll looks most like you?"

Clark found that the children seemed to identify with the brown dolls, demonstrating an awareness of their own color or racial background. When asked which doll they liked more, or which doll was "good" and which "bad," the children demonstrated a marked preference for the white dolls, indicating unhappiness about being black, a lack of self-esteem. In other words, the children evidenced through their preferences a sense that it is better to be white than black, that white people are better than black people.

"We were really disturbed by our findings," Clark observed. "What was surprising was the degree to which children suffered from self-rejection, with its truncating effect on their personalities and the earliness of the corrosive awareness of color." He continued, "I don't think we had quite realized the *extent* of the cruelty of racism and how hard it hit."

Clark summarized many of his and his wife's conclusions in academic treatises, including a report for the White House Conference on Youth in 1950 entitled *Prejudice and Your Child*.

Davis would have none of it. In fact, he was ecstatic to read Marshall's brief and learn the extent to which it relied on what Davis referred to as sociological "fluff." He wrote in a letter to Figg, who had represented South Carolina at the lower court level, "I think I have never read a drearier lot of testimony than that furnished by the so-called educational and psychological experts." In Davis's mind, Marshall's psychological and sociological data did nothing more than demonstrate that even as early as the age of five, white children realized they were white, and black children realized they were black. "Presumably," he commented derisively, "they should have been found to ignore the evidence of their senses."

In his own brief, Davis pointed up contradictions between Kenneth Clark's South Carolina testimony and conclusions published by the Clarks in a 1947 article entitled "Racial Identification and Preference in Negro Children." Based on research that compared the attitudes of segregated southern black children with their northern counterparts from integrated backgrounds, the Clarks concluded, "The southern children,...in spite of their equal favorableness toward the white doll, are significantly less likely to reject the brown doll (evaluate it negatively) as compared to the strong tendency for the majority of northern children to do so."

Davis used the Clarks' published conclusions against them to his advantage. He asserted, "While these experiments would seem to indicate that Negro children in the South are healthier psychologically speaking than those in the North, Dr. Clark appears to disagree. In any case, the results obtained in the broader sample of experiments completely explode any inference that the 'conflicts' from which Professor Clark's Clarendon County subjects were found to suffer are the result of their education in segregated schools."

When he read Davis's brief, Governor Byrnes was moved to write to his attorney, "I liked your having Clark & Clark answer Witness Clark." Byrnes concluded, "I want you to know that this client is proud of his lawyer."

Marshall persisted on his course. In September, as the deadline for the submission of briefs grew near, he turned to Clark. What he wanted from Clark was a statement of his observations and conclusions arrived at over years of study and research regarding the harmful effects of segregation on children. Clark obliged. He wrote of the negative effects of segregation on blacks. Segregation, he concluded, produced negative, "self-destructive" tendencies, hostility, and aggression. It created feelings of inferiority that in time gave way to self-hatred. From that flowed anger, violence, and other forms of behavior that only served to reinforce existing, negative stereotypes.

Clark wrote of the harmful effects of segregation on whites as well. For white children, he determined, segregation produced "a distorted sense of social reality." It created "moral cynicism." Here, after all, was a country committed by its creed to all men being equal. Clark admitted that examining the total effect—morally, socially, and economically—of this kind of duality, hypocrisy, of double-think, double-speak, tested the bounds of scientific knowledge of the human psyche.

Marshall asked other noted psychologists, sociologists, and social scientists to endorse Clark's statement. They did. He appended to his brief in *Briggs* a concurrence in Clark's analysis signed by thirty-five of the most eminent social thinkers of their time: Jerome Bruner, Gordon Allport, and Samuel Stouffer of Harvard; Otto Klineberg, Robert Merton, and Paul Lazarsfeld of Columbia; Hadley Cantril of Princeton; M. Brewster Smith of Vassar; Arnold Rose of Minnesota; and Alfred McClung Lee of Brooklyn College, to name but a few.

The day scheduled for oral argument drew near. Marshall drove his people, an integrated staff of brilliant young men and women: Robert L. Carter Jr., his top assistant, Spottswood W. Robinson III, Louis L. Redding, Jack Greenberg, Robert Ming Jr., Constance Baker Motley, James M. Nabrit Jr., Frank D. Reeves, and others. Carter would open, arguing *Brown*. Marshall would follow with *Briggs*. Robinson would argue the Prince Edward County case, which came from his home state. Marshall would also handle the Delaware case, along with Greenberg. And so on.

He reminded everyone that Charles Houston, his mentor, had taught him there was no such thing as too much hard work, study, or preparation. He told them to assume that they were preparing for Frankfurter, known to be brilliant if pedantic and persnickety.

He was probably on the blacks' side, but he would ask the toughest questions. If they were ready for Frankfurter, they were ready for anybody.

Meanwhile, Davis was confident, if not arrogant. The law was on his side because of *stare decisis*, precedent. He set to work on his brief with zeal and relish, writing much of its himself instead of assigning it to any number of brilliant young attorneys in his law firm. "There is nothing in the Fourteenth Amendment," he insisted, "which removes from the states...control of the educational process—so long as equal facilities are accorded the children of all races...The Supreme Court has decided the question...directly in three cases and by implication in several others."

Davis genuinely believed that segregation was better for both races, especially for blacks. He refused to believe that the majority of black parents wanted to expose their children to the insults and degradation that would be heaped on them in hostile, predominantly white schools. He believed that most blacks, like most whites, would prefer to be left alone with their own kind. He could not fathom that the Court would upset such a long-standing and ingrained social convention as segregation.

His attitude surprised many people who thought they knew him. As a presidential candidate in 1924, Davis spoke out against the Klan and its vigilantism. Prior to that, as solicitor general in 1915, he won a case that overturned Oklahoma's exclusion of black voters from primary elections. In 1929 Davis was even approached by Walter White, then director of the NAACP, about the possibility of Davis's joining its board of directors or legal arm. Davis demurred. In truth, he was a white supremacist who believed in the natural inferiority of blacks. He wrote to Byrnes as he prepared for his appeal in *Brown*:

I do not believe that the only distinction between the races of mankind is to be found in the color of their skins. There are anatomical differences...I have been told, and I think it is true, that a cross-section of the hair of Mongolian races indicates that the hair is cylindrical. A similar cross-section of the hair of the Caucasian races indicates that the hair is elliptical, while a cross-section of the hair of the Negro race shows that it is flatter and more ribbon-like, hence kinky. Is it not conceivable that in addition to anatomical differences there are also differences in the intellectual processes, in tastes and in aptitudes?

Davis was beneficent enough to concede, however, that blacks should be allowed to achieve their "just level." And he thought that graduate education should be offered on a desegregated basis. He explained his views in a letter to Walter White: "I think there is a genuine distinction to be drawn in policy between the immature children in the primary schools and the more mature individuals who attend graduate schools....Meantime we should both feel satisfaction in the genuine efforts...being made to bring about equality in the schools."

Marshall's reasoning ran in the opposite direction. In his brief he not only challenged segregation based on the practice's harmful effects, he questioned the whole idea of using race as a rational basis for any type of legislative decision making.

As Tuesday, December 9, 1952, approached, both sides made final preparations for their confrontation. Davis, joined much of the time by the attorneys from South Carolina as well as from Virginia, Kansas, and Delaware, moved with his personal staff into the Sheraton Hotel, near the White House in downtown Washington.

Marshall and his staff took up residence across the street in the Statler, which was integrated. It was uncharacteristic of Marshall not to stay in the home of friends or NAACP allies instead of paying for accommodations while on the road; the NAACP's money for his expenses was severely limited. But he decided on this occasion to rely on the Statler's amenities in order to get some much-needed rest so that he could put forth his best effort in this crucial appeal.

Marshall's friend and confidant William Hastie observed, "He drove himself to and beyond the limits of the human anatomy. He was at the point of exhaustion in trying to dispel the sense of defeatism that had inflicted itself on so much of black America."

His wife recognized what was happening to him. "He's aged so in the past five years," she noted. "His disposition's changed—he's nervous now where he used to be calm. The work is taking its toll of him. You know, it's a discouraging job he's set himself." She did not add to his burden by telling him that she was dying of cancer.

Outside the U.S. Supreme Court's bronze doors, beneath the marble inscription "Equal Justice Under Law," a line began to form shortly before dawn on the day of the oral argument. Those who wanted to observe the history that was about to be made knew that the Court chamber would accommodate only about three hundred spectators. The number of would-be observers, black and white, bundled against the late-autumn chill, grew longer as the morning wore on. What began as a trickle, a few men, a few women, became a torrent of the curious and excited— one long, expectant, but well-behaved queue that by midmorning stretched down the marble front steps and spilled across the plaza onto the sidewalk.

Robert L. Carter Jr. opened the proceedings by presenting his side of the Kansas case, *Brown*. His discussion of the issues proceeded well enough until he encountered a barrage of tough questioning from Frankfurter. Basically Frankfurter tried to pry from Carter an open admission that the Court was being asked to outlaw segregation because the basis for it was nothing more than what Frankfurter referred to as "man's inhumanity to man." Yet was it not true, Frankfurter asked, that segregation had been upheld in past decisions of the Court and that Carter was therefore asking the Court to unsettle existing precedents and social customs and practices embodied in hundreds of state laws as well as in those Supreme Court precedents?

In point of fact, this was the NAACP's purpose. But after all the years of working around a direct challenge to *Plessy*, it was hard for Carter to come right out and ask directly that *Plessy* be overturned.

Marshall had no such hesitancy. After Kansas's rebuttal of Carter, he rose to argue *Briggs*. Clearly, firmly, and straightfor-wardly, he declared that segregation was humiliating and degrad-ing. He characterized distinctions based on race as "odious and invidious." The Court had outlawed segregation in transporta-tion, he contended; there was no reason not to outlaw it in education as well.

Frankfurter asked how Marshall could escape racism as a

sociological fact. What about states or school systems in which blacks constituted a majority? Should the Court order whites to attend predominantly black schools, with black teachers? Then, presaging the busing controversy that the Court would be called upon to address almost twenty years later, he asked Marshall what was to supposed to happen if whites simply resegregated themselves by moving or by gerrymandering school districts? Would the courts not have to order that the desired school desegregation be brought about? Marshall's response implied that he was prepared to accept de facto segregation if it resulted naturally from geographic circumstances.

Justice Jackson then asked Marshall to compare blacks with American Indians. Suppose the Court struck down all classifications based on race? How would such a ruling affect the treatment, rights, and privileges of Native Americans, traditionally distinguished by race?

Marshall deflected the inquiry with humor. "The biggest trouble with the Indians," he explained, "is that they just have not had the judgment or the wherewithal to bring lawsuits."

Jackson good-naturedly suggested, "Maybe you should bring some up for them."

Marshall demurred, "I have a full load now, Mr. Justice."

When Marshall finished, Davis rose to open his side of the case. A stately white-haired man of seventy-eight, his voice resounded, commanding the attention of the chamber with his formalistic, almost Victorian syntax. Paul Wilson, Kansas's young assistant attorney general, matched against Carter in *Brown*, reflected later on Davis's performance. "One need not have heard Mr. Davis's argument to know that a great lawyer was speaking. . . . The esteem of the Court was reflected in the face of each of the justices."

Davis reminded the Court that segregation had been upheld countless times and that state after state had enacted laws calling for the separation of the races. All of this had been done since the Fourteenth Amendment. He asserted that segregation was a "great national policy" and that to undermine it would subvert the deference to local self-government that was the heart of the federal system.

He asked rhetorically, "Is it not a fact that the very strength and fiber of our federal system is local self-government in those matters for which local action is competent? Is it not of all the activities of the government the one which most nearly approaches the hearts and minds of people, the question of the education of their young? Is it not the height of wisdom that the manner in which they shall be conducted should be left to those most immediately affected by it, and that the wishes of the parents, both white and colored, should be ascertained before their children are forced into what may be an unwelcome contract?"

Davis rejected Marshall's sociological assertions out of hand, dismissing them as "fragmentary expertise based on an examined presupposition." *Stare decisis* was what should count: "I respectfully submit to the Court, there is no reason assigned here why this Court or any other should reverse the findings of ninety years." He warned that equal, if separate, education was in danger of being "thrown away on some fancied question of racial prestige." It was a virtuoso performance.

Justice Harold Hitz Burton, Truman's first appointment to the Court in 1945, was a former Republican senator from Ohio whose social views were considered moderate. He challenged Davis, "What is your answer, Mr. Davis, to the suggestion...that...the Constitution is a living document that must be interpreted in relation to the facts of the time in which it is interpreted? Did we not go through with that in connection with child labor cases, and so forth?"

Davis responded that the Court should be guided by the framers of the Fourteenth Amendment and its equal-protection clause: since the framers did not end segregation, the Court should not take it upon itself to do so.

Despite this assertion, Davis, like his listeners, was well aware that constitutional interpretations changed as time went on. It was neither possible nor necessarily desirable to uncover and adhere strictly to the intention of the men who wrote the Constitution, or a particular amendment to it, every time a modern-day problem demanded. For example, the commerce clause, giving the federal government the power to regulate interstate commerce, had been expanded greatly by the Court over the years as America grew into a modern industrialized nation.

Frankfurter took up this point. "Mr. Davis," he asked, "do you think that 'equal' is a less fluid term than 'commerce between the states?'"

Davis inquired, "That what is unequal today may be equal tomorrow, or vice versa?"

"Yes, that is it," said Frankfurter.

Davis hedged. "I should not philosophize about it." He stuck to his contention, however, that the framers of the Fourteenth Amendment did not intend to outlaw segregation.

"What you are saying," Frankfurter concluded, "is that as a matter of history, history puts a gloss upon 'equal' which does not permit elimination or admixture of white and colored in this aspect."

"Yes," replied Davis. "I am saying that."

Marshall realized right away that Davis had blundered fatally. His argument failed to address Marshall's assertion that there was no *rational basis* for distinctions based on race. And without a rational basis the distinctions could not stand.

Davis was aware that Marshall's brief took this tack. But he chose to work around the argument rather than meet it head-on, relying instead on "the weight of the precedents" and Figg's earlier public-policy defense of segregation at the three-judge U.S. district court level. Davis had explained in a letter to Figg, "I have not cast [my argument] in the form of a defense of reasonableness, not wishing to adopt the battleground which the appellants evidently prefer."

In his closing remarks, Marshall rushed headlong into the breach. "It seems to me," he told the justices, "that the significant factor running through all these arguments up to this point is that for some reason, which is still unexplained, Negroes are taken out of the mainstream of American life in these states [that have segregated public education]." He continued, "There is nothing involved in this case other than race and color."

He concluded, "It seems to me that in a case like this that the only way that South Carolina, under the test set forth in this case, can sustain that statute is to show that Negroes as Negroes—all

Negroes—are different from everybody else." This, Marshall insisted, had not and could not be done.

Justice Stanley Reed, who had made clear during the Court's deliberations of *Sweatt* and *McLaurin* that he opposed overturning *Plessy*, asked Marshall what he thought of the idea that segregation was imposed by some state legislatures in the interest of maintaining law and order, in order to "avoid racial friction."

Marshall conceded that at the end of the nineteenth century racial attitudes were such that too much race mixing might have produced a violent backlash by racist elements within the South. Nevertheless, he said, "even if the concession is made that it was necessary in 1895, it is not necessary now because people have grown up and understand each other. They are fighting together and living together. I know in the South, where I spent most of my time, you will see white and colored kids going down the road together to school. They separate and go to different schools, and they come out and they play together. I do not see why there would necessarily be any trouble if they went to school together."

If went on for three days—the arguments, questions, answers, and rebuttals. When it was over, there was nothing to do but await the ultimate judgment of the Court. But at the Court's routine Saturday morning conference that followed the close of oral argument, it became clear that the justices were divided over whether to strike down the segregation statutes. Five appeared initially to be in favor of ending segregation: Black, Douglas, Burton, Frankfurter, and Sherman Minton, a liberal former Indiana senator who had been appointed by Truman in 1949. Four others leaned toward upholding *Plessy* as a matter of law: Chief Justice Vinson, Robert H. Jackson, Reed, and Clark. Frankfurter later wrote that if the Court had decided *Brown* in December 1952, the result "would have been catastrophic."

In an effort to arrive at unanimity, or at least a stronger majority, on a question with such far-reaching social implications, the Justices issued a *per curiam* order on June 8, 1953, docketing the parties to appear again for a second round of oral argument. At the reargument, and in the briefs they were to submit before then, the parties were to address themselves to five questions set forth in the order.

Essentially the questions focused on the Fourteenth Amendment: its history, the intent of the men who wrote it, and the basis of the Court's power, if any, under the amendment to end segregation, should it choose to do so. Reargument was scheduled for Monday, October 12, 1953. Each side had four months to prepare.

THIRTEEN

Brown v. Board of Education (Part 2)

I insist upon one law for all men.
—Earl Warren

John W. Davis left the Supreme Court a happy and self-confident man after the end of the first round of oral arguments in *Brown*. On his way out of the building, he commented to T. Justin Moore, counsel for the State of Virginia, "I think we've got it won, five to four—or maybe six to three."

A few days later he wrote, "Unless the Supreme Court wants to make the law over, they must rule with me." A minority on the Court might try, as Davis put it, "to rewrite the law with some high-flying remarks on the iniquity of considering the irrelevant subject of race." He was convinced, however, that no "thoroughgoing" jurist would do so.

In June 1953, his law partner Allen Wardwell was solicited for a contribution to help pay for the preparation of the NAACP brief in response to the five questions. Davis forwarded the solicitation to South Carolina's governor Byrnes with a wry note advising that Wardwell "does not feel that he can contribute....I send it on the possibility that you might be willing to." Byrnes was not amused. He reacted by asking Senator Harry Byrd of Virginia to investigate the NAACP's tax-exempt status.

Davis refused to let the State of South Carolina pay him a fee, offering his work instead as a public service. He did, however, accept a silver tea service voted him by the South Carolina legislature as an eightieth birthday present.

Davis's self-assurance was short-lived. The federal government, invited by the Court to participate in the reargument, produced a brief that took the NAACP's side in response to the five questions. Although the Eisenhower administration was reluctant to join the case, the justices' request was regarded more as an order than an invitation.

Eisenhower himself had mixed feelings about segregation. After the Court's finally ruled it unconstitutional in 1954, he told a group of southern governors, "I think personally the decision was wrong." An aide to the president claimed later, however, that while Eisenhower in fact favored the immediate desegregation of secondary schools and universities, "he did not believe this ought to be the result of any summary court order applying to immediate termination of every vestige of segregation." According to the aide, Eisenhower held the view that "in the primary schools a more gradual approach would diminish the probability that severe and very likely violent opposition would result in the event that little children were forcibly intermingled."

Nevertheless, the president allowed the Justice Department to use its own discretion in preparing the government's brief in *Brown*. Attorney General Herbert Brownell, a Nebraska native who went on to become a successful Wall Street lawyer and confidant of New York governor Thomas E. Dewey, assigned the brief to Philip Elman. Elman, a Democrat, was a Truman administration holdover who worked in the solicitor general's office.

The first thing Elman did was move to have the reargument rescheduled to give the government more time to prepare. The Court obliged, extending the date three months, to December 1953. Elman made good use of the time. Working with a staff of eight, he produced a six-hundred-page examination of the Fourteenth Amendment. The thrust of his analysis was that the amendment's history was too clouded to be used as a guide by the Court. He wrote:

"In 1868 public schools had been hardly begun in many states and were still in their infancy. School attendance was, as a general matter, not compulsory."

He went on to explain, "The Negroes had just been released from bondage and were generally illiterate, poor, and retarded socially and culturally. To educate them in the same classes and schools as white children may have been regarded as entirely impracticable."

He continued, "It is possible that state legislatures—while recognizing in the Fourteenth Amendment a clear mandate of equality—may have considered separate schools for colored children as a temporary practical expedient permitted by the Amendment. Many proponents of Negro education regarded separate schools as a more effective means of extending the benefits of the public school system to the colored people."

But, he concluded, even if nothing in its history indicated conclusively that the amendment was intended to abolish segregation in public education, it nonetheless "established the broad constitutional principle of full and complete equality of all persons under the law, and...forbade all legal distinctions based on race or color."

Meanwhile, the Supreme Court conducted its own research into the five questions, which was spearheaded by Alexander Bickel, a Harvard Law School graduate who clerked for Felix Frankfurter. Bickel spent the better part of a year working almost exclusively on this project. John W. Davis did not know it, nor did Thurgood Marshall or the government, but Bickel advised the justices that while the Fourteenth Amendment's legislative history did not specifically indicate that the framers intended to outlaw school segregation, the amendment did not prohibit Congress or the courts from outlawing the practice at some future time.

Davis read the government's brief with alarm. He and the other lawyers for the states agreed that "the Attorney General of the United States should not be consulted about this matter, as the present administration seems to be committed to do everything it can to abolish segregation in every form and we could not expect any help from that source." And Marshall's brief enraged Davis; he regarded it as a complete distortion of history.

Together with his colleagues, Davis hammered out his responses. The crux of his argument was that the framers of the Fourteenth Amendment "so clearly understood" that the amendment would not prohibit segregated schools that it was "not properly within the judicial power…to construe the Amendment so as to abolish segregation." Davis's side insisted that in a segregated school system there was no discrimination against blacks if equal facilities were provided.

But neither the government's nor Marshall's brief triggered as deep a concern on Davis's part as did the sudden and unexpected heart attack that killed Chief Justice Fred Vinson in September; Davis always counted Vinson among the votes to uphold segregation. His trepidation was compounded by Eisenhower's choice of a replacement. In the fall of 1953, a popular California politician, Earl Warren, was sworn in as the nation's fourteenth chief justice.

Warren was elected to the first of three terms as governor of California in 1942. Four years later he became the first candidate to win both the Democratic and Republican nominations for that office. A bid for the Republican presidential nomination fell short in 1948, and Warren settled for the number-two slot on the Dewey ticket. He was defeated in a second try for the Republican presidential nomination by Eisenhower in 1952.

Davis's initial reaction to Warren's nomination was "The President could go further and do better." A burly, white-haired, grandfatherly man, Warren was regarded as an honest and forthright politician, in keeping with his devoutly held Baptist beliefs. But some observers questioned his intellectual depth. John Gunther's *Inside U.S.A.* described Warren in 1947 as "a man who has probably never bothered with abstract thought twice in his life." Gunther concluded, "He will never set the world on fire, or even make it smoke."

In reality, Warren had already stirred a national debate when he demanded the internment of some 110,000 West Coast Japanese Americans during World War II. He had been a member of an anti-Asian organization, the Native Sons of the Golden West. He told a national governors' convention in 1943, "We don't want to have a second Pearl Harbor in California." President Roosevelt had acquiesced in the detentions.

Warren came to regret the decision. He said later, "Now that society in general is so much more aware of civil rights, interning them seems like a terribly cruel thing to do, and it *was* a cruel thing, especially uprooting the children from their schools, their communities and friends, and having whole families transferred out to a strange environment and a less desirable environment."

Nonetheless, blacks welcomed Warren's nomination. In a 1952 interview with the *Pittsburgh Courier,* the widest-circulating national Negro newspaper, Warren declared, "I am for a sweeping civil rights program, beginning with a fair employment practices act. I insist upon one law for all men."

During the 1948 presidential campaign, Warren called repeatedly for the enactment of voting rights and antilynching legislation. A remark made by Frankfurter suddenly took on an eerie prescience. Frankfurter called Vinson's death before the reargument of *Brown* "the first indication I have ever had that there is a God."

But Davis remained optimistic. On the eve of the reargument, he wrote to Justin Moore, "In the language of a famous general, we have got them and they will never get home."

On December 7, 1953, before a packed Supreme Court chamber, the Court began hearing three days of reargument in *Brown.*

Marshall stood by his research on the Fourteenth Amendment. He asserted that the amendment was clearly intended to "strike down all types of class and caste legislation." Segregation had to be struck down, he insisted, unless it could be shown that the framers had specifically intended to exclude segregation in public education from the class- or caste-based legislation that the amendment was enacted to prohibit.

He reiterated his contention that there is, in effect, no such thing as race and therefore no rational basis for distinguishing between individuals based on race. "Red things may be associated by reason of their redness, with disregard of all other resemblances or of distinctions. Such classification would be logically appropriate," he told the Court. But, he cautioned, "apply it further: make a rule of conduct depend upon it, and distinguish in legislation between red-haired men and black-haired men, and the classification would immediately be seen to be wrong; it would have only arbitrary relation to the purpose and province of legislation."

From this he concluded that the segregationists "would have to show—and we have shown to the contrary—they would have to show, one, that there are differences in race; and, two, that differences in race have a recognizable relationship to the subject matter being legislated, namely, public education." He asserted, "That is a rule that has been uniformly applied by this Court in all other challenges that a classification is unreasonable."

In his closing argument, he drove the point deeper. "The only way that this Court can decide this case in opposition to our position," he told the justices, "is that there must be some reason which gives the state the right to make a classification...in regard to Negroes, and we submit the only way to arrive at this decision is to find that for some reason Negroes are inferior to all other human beings."

He continued, "In order to arrive at the decision that [the segregationists] want us to arrive at, there would have to be some recognition of a reason why of all the multitudinous groups of people in this country you have to single out Negroes and give them this separate treatment."

He asserted, "It can't be because of slavery in the past, because there are very few groups in this country that haven't had slavery some place back in the history of their groups."

He went on, "It can't be color, because there are Negroes as white as the drifted snow, with blue eyes, and they are just as segregated as the colored man."

He concluded, "The only thing it can be is an inherent determination that the people who were formerly in slavery, regardless of anything else, shall be kept as near that stage as is possible, and now is the time, we submit, that this Court should make it clear that that is not what our Constitution stands for."

Davis rose for what was to be his final appearance before the Supreme Court. Now eighty, he had aged visibly in the year since the first round of oral arguments. His memory had failed some-what, and he referred to notes throughout his presentation. In addition, his voice no longer carried as once it had. He told the Court, "The horn doesn't blow as loud as it used to."

He was compelling nonetheless. Alexander Bickel later recalled, "No one hearing [Davis] emphasize how pervasive and how solidly founded the present order was could fail to be sensible to the difficulties encountered in uprooting it."

As he had in the first round of oral arguments, Davis stressed that the justices should be guided by established precedents and that segregation was a time-honored practice, sanctioned by past decisions of the Court. He insisted, "Somewhere, sometime to every principle comes a moment of repose when it has been so often announced, so confidently relied upon, so long continued, that it passes the limits of judicial discretion and disturbance." It was, in Davis's view, "late indeed in the day" to uproot segregation on any "theoretical or sociological basis."

He urged the Court to consider the practical consequences of a desegregation order. After all, it would not only mean that blacks would attend schools where whites were in the majority; it would also mean that some whites would be forced to attend schools that were predominantly black. Referring specifically to Clarendon County, where black public school children constituted the majority, he asserted, "If it is done on the mathematical basis, with 30 children as a maximum…you would have 27 Negro children and 3 whites in one school room." He asked rhetorically, "Would that make the children any happier? Would they learn any more quickly? Would their lives be more serene?"

He refuted Marshall's claim that race was not a reasonable basis for making legislative distinctions. "No man," he declared, quoting the renowned British prime minister Benjamin Disraeli, "will treat with indifference the fact of race. It is the key of history."

In his conclusion Davis assured the Court of South Carolina's intention to create equality of educational opportunity for all its residents, black and white, and implied that a desegregation order would jeopardize progress toward that end. He compared Marshall's position to that of the dog in one of Aesop's fables: "The dog, with a fine piece of meat in its mouth, crossed a bridge and saw the shadow in the stream and plunged for it and lost both substance and shadow."

He went on, echoing what he had told the Court in December 1952, "Here is equal education, not promised, not prophesied, but present. Shall it be thrown away on some fancied question of racial prestige?"

Years later, recalling Davis's performance that day, Justice Stanley Reed observed, "His argument was outstanding beyond its usual excellence." But it was Marshall, his position supported by the Justice Department, who carried the day.

At the December 12, 1953, Saturday conference that followed the reargument of *Brown*, Warren spoke first, making his feelings known unequivocally. In his view segregation was intolerable in a modern, democratic society.

"I don't see how in this day and age we can set any group apart from the rest and say that they are not entitled to exactly the same treatment as all others," he declared. The post–Civil War amendments were, as he interpreted them, "intended to make the slaves equal with all others." Addressing *Brown* specifically, he said, "Personally, I can't see how today we can justify segregation based solely on race."

He went on to assert that the separate-but-equal doctrine was based on "the concept of the inherent inferiority of the colored race." He challenged any fellow justice who believed blacks were inferior to say so openly. If no one was willing to do so, he called for a unanimous opinion to lend weight to the Court's ruling.

At first, it was not at all clear whether the new chief justice would be able to achieve the desired unanimity. Black, Douglas, Minton, and Murphy sided with him. Clark now leaned toward the NAACP position but, along with Warren and Murphy, wanted to fashion an order that would take into account conditions in different geographic areas, because a desegregation order would surely be met with strong resistance in the South.

Reed appeared still to favor segregation. Frankfurter was not allowing himself to be pinned down. He seemed to have his own ideas about how the decision should be framed, but he was keeping them to himself.

Justice Robert H. Jackson, like Frankfurter, was inscrutable. A New York aristocrat, he had served as Franklin Roosevelt's attorney general, been appointed to the Court by Roosevelt in

1941, and served as chief prosecutor at the Nuremburg trials. Initially a civil libertarian who aligned himself with Black and Douglas, he was by 1953 considered a judicial conservative.

Somehow Jackson wanted to express his view that in striking down the separate-but-equal doctrine, the Court was making a fundamentally political, rather than judicial, decision. He wrestled with the issue, drafting memorandums that indicated he might be preparing his own separate concurrence.

One of Jackson's law clerks during the early 1950s was William H. Rehnquist, an outspoken young conservative who had finished at the top of his class at Stanford University's law school. Rehnquist went on to become an associate justice, and later chief justice, of the Supreme Court. In December 1952 Jackson had asked Rehnquist to prepare a memo setting forth his views on *Brown* on the eve of the case's first oral argument.

Rehnquist's memo, entitled "A Few Expressed Prejudices on the Segregation Cases," argued that the Court should uphold *Plessy v. Ferguson* and the separate-but-equal doctrine. "To the argument made by Thurgood, not John, Marshall," Rehnquist wrote, distinguishing between the director-counsel of the Fund and America's first chief justice, "that a majority may not deprive a minority of its constitutional right, the answer must be that while this is sound in theory, in the long run it is the majority who will determine what the constitutional rights of the minority are."

Rehnquist continued, "I realize that [this] is an unpopular and unhumanitarian position, for which I have been excoriated by 'liberal' colleagues, but I think *Plessy v. Ferguson* was right and should be reaffirmed." He concluded, "If the Fourteenth Amendment did not enact Spencer's social Statistics, it just as surely did not enact Myrdal's *American Dilemma*."

When the memorandum surfaced in December 1971 during Senate consideration of Rehnquist's nomination to the Court, Rehnquist felt compelled to explain his position. In a letter to Senate Judiciary Committee chairman James Eastland, dated December 8, 1971, Rehnquist insisted, "The memorandum was prepared by me at Justice Jackson's request; it was intended as a rough draft of a statement of his views at the conference of Justices rather than as a statement of my views."

Whatever Rehnquist's role or motives, Jackson himself flirted with a concurrence that would have been, if anything, stronger than the position ultimately taken by the Court. In one internal memorandum, he wrote:

"Since the close of the Civil War the United States has been 'hesitating between two worlds—one dead, the other powerless to be born.' War brought an old order to an end but as usual force proved unequal to founding a new one. Neither North nor South has been willing really to adapt its racial practices to its professions. The race problem would be quickly solved if some way could be found to make us all live up to our hypocrisies."

Jackson went on to explain racism this way:

"The white South retains in historical memory a deep resentment of the forces which, after conquest, imposed a fierce program of reconstruction and the deep humiliation of carpet-bag government. The Negro is the visible and reachable beneficiary and symbol of this unhappy experience, on whom many visit their natural desire for retaliation."

In conclusion Jackson wrote, "That Negro segregation in the schools has outlived whatever original justification it may have had and is no longer wise or fair public policy is a conclusion congenial to my background and social and political views."

In the end, however, Warren succeeded in marshaling all nine justices behind his draft of a unanimous opinion, which he intended to be "short, readable by the lay public, non-rhetorical, unemotional and, above all, non-accusatory." This is exactly what it was. Warren read it from the bench on Monday, May 17, 1954, to an unsuspecting public and press corps.

It was the practice of the Court to deliver opinions on Mondays, with the author either reading aloud or summarizing the decision from the bench. There were few indications that this particular Monday would be the day for the delivery of *Brown*. Consequently, reporters were caught flat-footed at around one o'clock in the afternoon when Warren announced "the judgment and opinion of the Court in No. 1—*Oliver Brown et al. v. Board of Education of Topeka*." The wire services flashed the news to pressrooms around the country, and hundreds of anxious editors stopped the presses of their editions to await the details of the decision.

Warren read the decision aloud. Much of the text was devoted to a meticulous explanation of the cases' legal and historical background as well as a discussion of the value of public education in a modern society, so no one could be sure which way the Court had decided until he was two-thirds of the way through the fourteen-page opinion. As to the importance of education, he explained:

"Today education is perhaps the most important function of state and local governments. Compulsory school attendance laws and the great expenditures for education both demonstrate our recognition of the importance of education to our democratic society. It is required in the performance of our most basic public responsibilities, even service in the armed forces. It is the very foundation of good citizenship. Today it is a principal instrument in awakening the child to cultural values, in preparing him for later professional training, and in helping him to adjust normally to his environment. In these days, it is doubtful that any child may reasonably be expected to succeed in life if he is denied the opportunity of an education. Such an opportunity, where the state has undertaken to provide it, is a right which must be made available to all on equal terms."

The opinion went on to ask rhetorically, "Does segregation of children in public schools solely on the basis of race, even though the physical facilities and other 'tangible' factors may be equal, deprive the children of the minority group of equal educational opportunities?

"We believe that it does," the Court declared. "To separate [black children] from others of similar age and qualifications solely because of their race generates a feeling of inferiority as to their status in the community that may affect their hearts and minds in a way unlikely ever to be undone."

The decision quoted from the earlier decision of the Kansas court, which, despite its own findings of fact, ruled against the black plaintiffs:

"Segregation of white and colored children in public schools has a detrimental effect upon the colored children. The impact is greater when it has the sanction of the law; for the policy of separating the races is usually interpreted as denoting the inferiority of the negro group. A sense of inferiority affects the motivation of a child to learn. Segregation with the sanction of law, therefore, has a tendency to [retard] the educational and mental development of negro children and to deprive them of some of the benefits they would receive in a racial[ly] integrated school system."

Embracing the sociological perspective argued by Marshall, the Court declared, "Whatever may have been the extent of psychological knowledge at the time of *Plessy v. Ferguson*, [the Kansas court's] finding is amply supported by modern authority."

In a footnote that was to divide generations of legal scholars over the question of how much weight should be accorded authorities that are not, strictly speaking, legalistic, the Court cited as support for its proposition a number of sociological sources, including Kenneth Clark's work and Gunnar Myrdal's *An American Dilemma*.

In conclusion the justices declared, "In the field of public education the doctrine of 'separate but equal' has no place. Separate educational facilities are inherently unequal."

With this much said and done, the Court announced that it would hear reargument of the case in order to determine the appropriate remedy. On May 31, 1955, this would result in a decree that states must abolish segregation in their public education systems "with all deliberate speed."

After the decision Marshall said, "I was so happy I was numb." Not so for John W. Davis. He congratulated Marshall on the afternoon of his victory, although Davis's personal opinion was that the decision was "unworthy of the Supreme Court of the United States." Within a year of the Court's final ruling, Davis was dead. One of his law partners said that the Court's decision in *Brown* killed him.

FOURTEEN

Massive Resistance

John Marshall has made his decision; now let
him enforce it.

— President Andrew Jackson

A black reporter described Monday, May 17, 1954, the day the
Court delivered the unanimous opinion in *Brown*, as "the day we
won; the day we took the white man's law and won our case
before an all-white Supreme Court with a Negro lawyer. And we
were proud."

Felix Frankfurter, in a personal note to Chief Justice Warren,
said it was "a day that will live in glory." He added, "It is also a
great day in the history of the Court." Justice Harold Burton, also
in a note to Warren, called it "a great day for America and the
Court." The justices' law clerks remembered it as a day on which
they felt "good—and clean. It was so good."

Marshall himself saw the day as a turning point. The *Brown*
decision, he said, "probably did more than anything else to
awaken the Negro from his apathy to demanding his right to
equality." He expressed a fervent optimism that integration would
proceed in compliance with the Court's ruling.

"I think that, even in the most prejudiced communities, the
majority of the people has some respect for truth and some sense

of justice, no matter how deeply it is hidden at times," he told *Courier* magazine in August 1954. "If we keep up the educational process, as well as the legal suits, I have no doubt of our eventual victory. We now have the tools with which to destroy all governmentally imposed racial segregation. To hear some people talk, one would get the impression that the majority of Americans are lawless people who will not follow the law as interpreted by the Supreme Court. This simply is not true."

He believed the NAACP's ultimate goal was "to go out of business with a realization that race is no longer a problem." But he made clear the goal could be achieved without forcing unwanted integration on private clubs or associations. Solving the race problem, he maintained, "doesn't mean a man is not to determine who comes into his home, or his country club. There are lots of people I don't want around my house."

In his interview with *Courier*, Marshall reiterated his abiding faith in the American legal system. "Lawsuits bring home to many people the fact that Negroes have rights as Americans which must be respected." At the same time, he cautioned, "We have made tremendous inroads in the South, but this does not mean that the battle is won."

"Some states will take longer than others," he told *U.S. News & World Report*. "The length of time, I wouldn't predict. Mississippi, Alabama, South Carolina and Georgia will take quite a while. I don't think Virginia will take long."

Unfortunately, the triumph was soon dimmed by Buster's death. She died on Friday, February 11, 1955, her forty-fourth birthday, in the Marshall's apartment at 409 Edgecombe Avenue. Marshall had learned of her terminal cancer in late 1954. Theirs was a loving and devoted marriage of twenty-five years, so his reaction was not unexpected. Upon being told of her imminent death, he almost collapsed. For the next month and a half, he curtailed his NAACP activities and locked himself in their Harlem apartment, fixing meals and changing bedpans. He declined to see even his closest friends. "She would have done the same thing for me," he explained.

When she died, he said, "I thought the world had come to an end." Nevertheless, he remarried eleven months later, in December. Cecilia Suyat, "Cissy" to friends, was a diminutive woman of Filipino ancestry. Born on the Hawaiian island of Maui, she grew up in Honolulu. She moved to New York City in 1947 and, through the state employment agency, got a job as a secretary at the NAACP headquarters.

Shortly after Cecilia and Thurgood met, she wrote home to inform her family of her desire to remain in New York. Her father replied, "By all means [stay], as long as you are self-supporting." She completed a secretarial course at Columbia University, and her ambition was to become a court reporter. She recalled, "I wanted to learn how to use a stenotype. I would enjoy working." But when Thurgood asked her to forgo her career for the life of a housewife and mother, she agreed. Cissy found satisfaction in providing what she called "a restful, peaceful, comfortable home." The marriage produced two children: Thurgood Jr. and John, named after his grandfather Juan Suyat.

Cissy was called upon to share her kitchen with her husband, who still loved to cook. "I don't mind it at all," she once said. "He finds it relaxing. Heaven knows what goes in the pot, but it comes out delicious!" He soon taught her his culinary specialties. For "Turkish Delight," which he also referred to as "creoled macaroni," he simmered peppers and onions with bacon or salt pork, then added tomatoes, stuffed olives, and cheese, served with macaroni. In turn, he began to enjoy her favorite recreational activity, bowling.

Because the marriage took place so soon after his first wife's death, around the Harlem cocktail circuit there was gossip that Cissy and Thurgood had started their romance while he was married to Buster. But Ersa Poston, who was married to Ted Poston, recalled, "Cissy was a beautiful woman, and they married soon after Vivian's death because the 'death etiquette' at that time set six months as a reasonable time for remarriage. Thurgood was one of those men who needed to be married, and Cissy was very much like Vivian. She knew Thurgood was engrossed with the NAACP, and he had to make the Inc., Fund work."

Ersa Poston continued, "He was a very handsome man, and women flocked around him. Women always wanted to get to know the leader and say they slept with him, but Thurgood passed all that by. It was human nature on the part of the women, like the women who follow today's rock stars. Thurgood had a way of warming up to people. He never let anyone feel they were a stranger. He told jokes that everyone laughed at.

"Without being disparaging, some men are meant to be married. Some men need women to take care of things, to organize their personal life, take care of the laundry and dry cleaning and when you come home the food is there and all you have to do is sit down and eat. Thurgood was so involved with his work that he was that kind of guy.

"Cissy, like Buster, provided the support Thurgood needed, and her cultural background made that possible. She didn't need to be in the limelight," Poston explained. "She brought an order to his life. When a partner dies you don't just lay down and die. In our social circle we saw no indication of an affair before Buster's death. But Cissy did fill a void in his life after the death of his first wife."

His victory in *Bown* secured, his period of mourning behind him, and his new life's companion at his side, in September 1955 Marshall left for a few days of rest and relaxation in Florida and Cuba. "I'm going to Havana," he told *Time* in an interview for the magazine's September 19 cover story. "Never been there; hear they treat a man fine." It was his first vacation in eight years.

Upon his return the NAACP embarked on one of the most massive litigation programs ever undertaken, designed to force compliance with the *Brown* decree. Marshall called the strategy "gradualism," which he defined as "working out integration problem by problem until it is finally achieved," without resorting to violence or illegal acts.

On March 12, 1956, nineteen southern Senators and sixty three Southern Congressmen signed a manifesto declaring their opposition to the *Brown* decision, described as "an unwarranted exercise of power by the Court, contrary to the Constitution." The justices were accused of having "substituted their personal political and social ideas for the established law of the land." The document concluded with a pledge by its signers "to use all lawful means to bring about a reversal of this decision which is contrary to the Constitution and to prevent the use of force in its implementation."

On May 13, 1956, Marshall addressed an NAACP fund-raising rally at the Memorial Auditorium in Raleigh, North Carolina, declaring, "We are still willing to negotiate [with local officials] as to when and how desegregation will take place." But he added, "We shall not negotiate as to *whether* it will take place."

Acknowledging the resistance to the Court's desegregation order, he warned his twenty-five hundred listeners, "There can no longer be any reason to hope for compliance [with the *Brown* decision] without going to the courts." Drawing an enthusiastic response, he continued, "We shall resort to the courts and ballot when there is no other way to work out integration. And we shall do this peacefully, lawfully, and in the true American tradition."

In a September 1956 interview with *Newsweek* magazine, he described the NAACP's litigation strategy. "If the local [NAACP] offices run up against a brick wall, they take the problem to the state conference of the NAACP. If the conference agrees with the local's judgment, the case is referred to me. If I think it advisable, we go into the courts." He continued, "In some places...the local office will have a friend on the school board. This friend will say to them: 'I don't have a majority now, and if you people come in, I'll never get one. Lay off for a while and I think I can work it out.' So the local office lays off."

He explained, "In some situations legal action is called for, in others it would serve no useful purpose. The NAACP has brought no legal actions in public schools in Mississippi or Alabama, and few in Georgia or South Carolina. It has a number in Virginia, Tennessee, and others."

He tempered his conciliatory tone with a warning: "I'm the original gradualist. But let's make sure what we're talking about. If by gradualism you mean a policy of doing nothing, letting things drift and hoping for the best, I'm dead-set against it."

Meanwhile, desegregation proceeded in fits and starts. There was unexpectedly smooth progress in some areas, a disappointing lack of progress in others. In Missouri, where Marshall and Houston had won the historic *Gaines* ruling almost twenty years earlier, requiring the first admission of an African American to the University of Missouri's law school, integration of the public schools occurred virtually without incident. In West Virginia, John W. Davis's home state, integration had begun in most counties even before the Court issued its "with all deliberate speed" implementing decree in May 1955. Marshall's native Baltimore proceeded with desegregation plans, as did Washington, D.C.

The Old Confederacy, however, took up arms against the Court, its most prominent political figures vowing to fight the Court's order county by county, school district by school district. In a November 1955 interview with *U.S. News & World Report*, Senator Sam J. Ervin of North Carolina called the *Brown* decision contrary to the laws of nature. "Every day they thunder at us that racial segregation is merely the product of racial prejudice," he complained "I do not believe this. In my opinion, men segregate themselves in society according to race in obedience to a basic natural law, which decrees that like shall seek like. Wherever and whenever people are free to choose their own associates, they choose members of their own race."

In a companion interview, Senator John C. Stennis of Mississippi declared, "The overwhelming majority of the people in most areas of the South do not want to integrate our schools. They will oppose to the utmost any effort to do so."

According to Stennis, the southern opposition was rooted in the fear that school desegregation would eventually lead to interracial marriage, which some southern states legally prohibited by laws that the 1967 Supreme Court ruling in *Loving v. Virginia* would finally overturn. Stennis insisted, "One of the most compelling reasons [for the opposition to desegregation] is the deep realization that placing the children side by side over the years in primary, grammar and high-school grades is certain to destroy each race. I don't know how many generations that would take. And we all believe that the bloodstream—the racial integrity of each group—is worth saving." He defiantly predicted a "generation of lawsuits."

Marshall found the argument ludicrous. "I think there is no foundation for it at all," he said. "I don't see any connection between that [interracial marriage] and schooling."

"On the other hand," he continued, "I don't think there should be laws against intermarriage. It's a purely personal problem, and the state has nothing to do with it. After all, the white person can say no."

He went on, "This intermarriage thing has been raised in everything we've tried to do." Southerners even used it as an excuse for barring blacks from voting in primary elections, claiming that blacks and whites standing in line together at polling places would form acquaintances that would lead to interracial sex. "There aren't any figures to back it up," Marshall explained. "Even where intermarriage is permitted by law, the number is insignificant."

"But," he conceded, "in the South, it's deep in their minds."

The Deep South's official policy of opposing school integration became known as "massive resistance" or "interposition." The latter term, taken from the period following the ratification of the U.S. Constitution, referred to the view that a state government had the right to interpose itself between the federal government and the state's citizens whenever Washington pursued a policy deemed by the state government to be unconstitutional. In Arkansas, for example, a state constitutional amendment was passed in 1956 calling upon the legislature to oppose "in every constitutional manner the unconstitutional desegregation decisions of...the United States Supreme Court." Not since the Civil War had the federal system come under such attack.

Moreover, by 1956 citizens had begun to take the law into their own hands. Rural areas saw a resurgence of the Ku Klux Klan, which traditionally drew its membership and support from uneducated, lower-class whites. And white business leaders across the South drew together to form what became known as White Citizens Councils, a sort of white-collar Klan, for the specific purpose of making it "difficult, if not impossible, for any Negro who advocates desegregation to find and hold a job, get credit, or renew a mortgage."

The NAACP itself came under attack. A number of states passed laws aimed at forcing the organization to make public its membership and contributors' lists, information that could be used to target NAACP supporters for retaliation.

This threat in fact hampered the NAACP's desegregation drive. In 1957 NAACP membership stood at around 350,000. The organization's income from dues and contributions totaled approximately $1,284,189. Of this amount, $682,906 was earmarked for the parent organization, $250,000 for the local branches, and $351, 283 for the Fund. The totals represented a decline in both membership and contributions from the previous year. And the declines came at a time when the organization was matched against opponents whose litigation expenses were paid from state coffers.

There were beatings and lynchings. One of the most notorious incidents occurred in Mississippi in August 1955. Chicago teenager Emmett Till was dragged from the home of relatives he had been visiting, brutally beaten, and murdered because he had supposedly flirted with a white woman. The ghastly sight of the boy's mutilated corpse, displayed in an open casket at his Chicago funeral, shocked the nation. His accused murderers were acquitted by an all-white jury. One of the defendants, J. W. Milam, the woman's brother, explained, "I'm no bully. I never hurt a nigger in my life. I like niggers in their place. I know how to work 'em. But I just decided it was time a few people got put on notice."

The schools themselves became flash points for white rage. The riot in Sturgis, Kentucky, was typical. When nine black high schoolers attempted to enter previously all white Sturgis High on opening day in September 1956, they were met by a mob of five hundred whites shouting, "Nigger, stay home!" Governor A. B. "Happy" Chandler dispatched national guardsmen to the scene. The next day, the guardsmen, bayonets drawn, escorted the blacks through the jeering rabble. But the following day the blacks did not show up for school.

Similar incidents were reported in locales as diverse as Clay, Kentucky; Oliver Springs and Knoxville, Tennessee; and Matoaka, West Virginia. But nowhere else did the situation escalate to the level that was reached at Central High School in Little Rock, Arkansas.

Ironically, the racial climate in Little Rock was more open than in a great many southern cities. Blacks served on the police force, public facilities and transportation were integrated, and in a number of residential areas blacks and whites lived comfortably side by side. Influential businessmen, such as Winthrop Rockefeller, head of the Arkansas Industrial Development Commission, worked hard to avoid racial strife in order to foster a climate conducive to northern investment. But Governor Orval Faubus saw the race issue as a boon to his 1956 drive for a third two-year term. He exploited its vote-getting potential.

A little man with black, slicked-back hair and a wide grin, Faubus was a matchstick-chewing hick. In his youth he survived as best he could as a sharecropper and logger. To his credit, he possessed wily gumption, and though he lacked formal education, he could write. During World War II, he served in the infantry and was awarded the Bronze Star for bravery. He earned the nickname "Ernie Pyle of the Ozarks" for the war stories he sent home from the front for publication in local newspapers.

Faubus gravitated toward politics, and sometime after the war his editorial writing inspired Arkansas governor Sid McMath to hire him as his administrative assistant. Referring to Faubus's penchant for controversy, McMath once commented, "I brought Orval down out of the hills, and every night I ask forgiveness."

At the outset of his career, Faubus did not behave like a racist. In fact, he was thought to be rather fond of Negroes. He integrated the state transportation system early in his tenure as governor, and he increased the number of black employees in the state government. He appointed the first blacks to serve on the Democratic state committee and tried to have the whites-only primary abolished. By 1955, however, Faubus no longer found tolerance expedient.

Little Rock school officials responded to the 1954 *Brown* decision with, if not enthusiasm, then at least begrudging acceptance. In fact, the local school board adopted a desegregation plan in May 1955, before the Court handed down its implementation decree. Under the scheme, which became known as the "Blossom Plan," after Little Rock school superintendent Virgil T. Blossom, Central High School in Little Rock was to be desegregated immediately, meaning in the fall of 1955. Other schools would be desegregated on a delayed basis, beginning in September 1957.

The local NAACP, headed by attorney Wiley Branton, objected to any delay in implementing the Court's desegregation order. But the board insisted on proceeding with caution. "Since our school system has been segregated from its beginning until the present time," school officials explained, "the time required in the processes as outlined should not be construed as unnecessary delay but that which is justly needed with respect to the size and complexity of the job at hand." The board wanted to integrate first at the high school level, with the oldest and therefore most mature students, then use that experience as a guide for implementing desegregation at the lower levels. By so doing, it would have "the opportunity to benefit from our own experience as we move through each phase of this plan, thus avoiding as many mistakes as possible."

Branton filed suit in U.S. district court to force the total and immediate desegregation of Little Rock's schools. Branton recalled, "It became rather obvious to the NAACP that the Little Rock board really was not going to move forward unless they were forced to. I filed that suit on behalf of Negro children and their parents, running through elementary, junior, and senior high school."

The suit was dismissed by U.S. district court judge John E. Miller, who found that the Blossom Plan represented an "utmost good faith" effort to integrate, Branton then enlisted Thurgood Marshall's help in appealing Miller's ruling to the U.S. Court of Appeals for the Eighth Circuit. The appeals court held that the Blossom Plan satisfied the Supreme court's "deliberate speed" requirement. At the same time, the court made clear that it would countenance no further delays by school officials.

Marshall and Branton decided against an appeal to the U.S. Supreme Court. "We thought the [Blossom Plan[was...pretty sloppy," Branton said, "and we didn't want to run the risk of having the court adopt that one as a model for the nation."

Whatever good intentions the school board might have had were undermined by Faubus's intervention. Threatened by the growing popularity of gubernatorial candidate James Johnson, sponsor of the amendment to the state constitution that mandated opposition to court-ordered desegregation, Faubus made his move. He persuaded a private citizen's group, the newly formed Mothers' League of Little Rock Central High, to sue in state court in Pulaski County to enjoin implementation of the school board's integration plan.

Faubus himself took the stand to testify that Arkansans were now solidly opposed to integration and that violence would likely result if blacks entered Central High. He warned ominously that a number of guns and knives had already been confiscated from students, black and white, who anticipated racial clashes.

Out of deference to Faubus, state trial judge Murray O. Reed ruled in favor of the Mothers' League. "In view of the testimony and the show of the threat of violence, riots, and bloodshed, and particularly the opinion of Governor Faubus," he declared, "I feel I can only rule to grant the injunction."

Federal courts supersede state courts on constitutional questions, such as the right to an equal education, and Marshall and Branton persuaded Judge Davies of the U.S. district court to nullify the state-court injunction. It looked, therefore, as if Central High's desegregation would proceed as planned.

Not so. In a startling act of defiance, Faubus appeared on statewide television on the evening of September 2, 1957, the day before school was scheduled to open and, citing "evidence of disorder and threats of disorder," announced the dispatch of 250 national guardsmen to Central High. It became clear almost immediately that those troops were not sent to protect the nine black students who would attempt to enter Central High the following morning from the anticipated mob of angry whites. Instead, the troops were in place to turn the blacks away and thereby prevent them from exercising their constitutional right to an equal education. Faubus vowed that if the blacks attempted to enter, "blood will run in the streets."

In an interview with *Time* magazine in September 1955, Marshall spoke of his admiration for his clients. "There isn't a threat known to man that they do not receive. They're never out from under pressure. I don't think I could take it for a week. The possibility of violent death for them and their families is something they've learned to live with like a man learns to sleep with a sore arm."

In Little Rock the brunt of the threats and pressure was borne by a woman named Daisy Bates, president of the Arkansas NAACP, by nine black teenagers, and by their parents.

At the beginning of the school controversy, Bates was optimistic. She called Little Rock "a liberal southern city." Her opinion changed a year later when a brick was thrown through her living-room window with a note attached: "Stone this time. Dynamite next." But her resolve remained unshaken. On the evening of September 3, 1957, she spoke with parents of eight of the nine youngsters and arranged to escort the children to Central High, accompanied by two Little Rock police cars.

The ninth child, Elizabeth Eckford, whose parents Bates had failed to reach by phone the night before, traveled to school by bus, unescorted. Arriving before the others, she was set upon by a jeering mob. She heard someone yell, "No nigger bitch is going to get in our school. Get out of here!"

"I tried to see a friendly face somewhere in the mob," she recalled. "I looked into the face of an old woman, and it seemed a kind face, but when I looked at her again, she spat on me." She turned to the guardsmen for protection. Instead, one of them let white students pass through the ranks into the school but blocked her entrance. "I walked up to the guard who had let them [the whites] in. When I tried to squeeze past him, he raised his bayonet, and then the other guards moved in and raised their bayonets."

She heard cries of "Lynch her! Lynch her!" When she ran back to the bus stop, she heard someone shout, "Drag her over to the tree." Just then two whites intervened to avert what might have turned into a lynching. Benjamin Fine, covering events for the New York Times, and a local woman escorted Eckford away from the mob and to safety.

Meanwhile, Bates and the others heard over the radio that a black student had been attacked. They proceeded to the school, anyway, but were turned away by national guardsmen when they attempted to enter.

The unrest forced President Eisenhower's hand. Until Little Rock, Ike had skirted the school desegregation issue in a manner that was wholly characteristic of his approach to other crises, pretending that everything was normal and going about business as usual. His instinct was to distance himself from trouble and let things work themselves out.

Besides, he was ambivalent about civil rights. On the one hand, he gave free rein to the Justice Department to take the NAACP's side after the first round of oral arguments in Brown. In addition, he held the right to vote sacred and would find it "bitterly disappointing" when, in August 1957, the Senate passed an emasculated version of his civil rights bill, which was originally intended to make it easier for the Justice Department to prosecute voting-rights denials. He termed the Senate action "one of the most serious political defeats of the past four years, primarily because it was such a denial of a basic principle of the United States."

At the same time, he refused to assert the moral authority of his office to urge peaceful desegregation of the schools. For this reason, Supreme Court Justice William O. Douglas blamed Ike for much of the violent resistance to the Court's desegregation orders. "There was tragedy in [Eisenhower's] attitude," Douglas wrote in his autobiography, "for if he had gone to the nation on television and radio telling the people to obey the law and fall into line, the cause of desegregation would have been accelerated. Ike was a hero, and he was worshiped," Douglas explained. "Some of his political capital spent on the racial cause would have brought the nation closer to the constitutional standards. Ike's ominous silence on our 1954 decision gave courage to the racists who decided to resist the decision ward by ward, precinct by precinct, town by town, and county by county."

Eisenhower may indeed have emboldened Faubus and others, wittingly or not, when he told a press conference in July 1956, "I can't imagine any set of circumstances that would ever induce me to send federal troops into any area to enforce the orders of a federal court." He qualified the remark by adding, "I believe that [the] common sense of America will never require it." But then he undercut the qualification: "I would never believe that it [sending in Federal troops] would be a wise thing to do in this country."

A reporter asked Marshall whether Faubus's actions represented a direct challenge to the authority of the federal government. He replied, "I don't think there's any question about that." Despite his reservations, Eisenhower certainly saw it that way and was compelled to act.

In 1832, when President Andrew Jackson disagreed with a Supreme Court ruling that protected Cherokee Indian lands from encroachment by the state of Georgia, he commented sarcastically, "John Marshall has made his decision; now let him enforce it." John W. Davis reiterated the sentiment in one of his darker moments after his defeat in *Brown*. But Eisenhower was not so cynical about his role as chief executive, charged with enforcing the laws of the land. He wrote to a friend, "There must be respect for the Constitution—which means the Supreme Court's interpretation of the Constitution—or we shall have chaos." He vowed, "This I believe with all my heart—and shall always act accordingly."

The president began by summoning Faubus to Newport, Rhode Island, where he was vacationing with his wife, Mamie, at a U.S. naval base. After lengthy discussions in which several other southern governors also participated, Faubus went before reporters on September 14, with Eisenhower looking on. He was supposed to issue a statement that had been agreed upon, and he did: "I have never expressed any personal opinion regarding the Supreme Court decision of 1954 which ordered integration. That is not relevant. That decision is the law of the land and must be obeyed. I now declare that I will assume full responsibility for the maintenance of law and order and that the orders of the Federal court will not be obstructed..."

But then Faubus tacked on two little words that were not part of the deal: "...by me." The words left room for all kinds of unofficial maneuvering that Faubus could instigate or inspire but personally disavow. Eisenhower felt betrayed.

Marshall and Branton went back into federal court on Friday, September 20, and asked Judge Davies to order Faubus to relent. Davies ordered Faubus to withdraw the national guard. The governor complained but in a speech broadcast across the state, announced that he would comply. He demanded, however, that blacks not attempt to enter Central high until the situation calmed down.

But Daisy Bates and the nine high schoolers were not deterred. On Monday, September 23, they gathered at Bates's house to ride to school together. An angry mob waited to greet them at Central High. When a carload of black newspapermen arrived ahead of the children, they were attacked and beaten by the whites as local police looked on. While the crowd's rancor was focused on the reporters, the black students were hustled into the school through a side door. When the mob realized what had happened, it vented its rage on white journalists and photographers assigned to cover the events, assaulting them and smashing their cameras. Eventually, the blacks were removed from the school under police escort because authorities concluded they could no longer ensure the students' safety.

The next morning, when an unruly crowd of about two thousand gathered at the school, Little Rock mayor Woodrow Mann sent a desperate telegram to the president, formally requesting his help: "The immediate need for Federal troops is urgent.... Situation is out of control and police cannot disperse the mob."

Convinced that he had run out of options, Eisenhower reluctantly issued the order. By nightfall a thousand paratroopers from the U.S. Army's elite 101st Airborne Division, under the command of Major General Edwin A. Walker, had flown into Little Rock from their base in Fort Campbell, Kentucky. That night the president addressed the nation by television from the Oval Office. He conveyed his "sadness" over having to dispatch the troops. But he declared the firmness of his intentions.

> In [Little Rock], under the leadership of demagogic extremists, disorderly mobs have deliberately prevented the carrying out of proper orders from a federal court.... Whenever normal agencies prove inadequate to the task...the president's responsibility is inescapable.... Our personal opinions about the decision have no bearing on the matter of enforcement.... Mob rule cannot be allowed to override the decisions of our courts.... The foundation of the American way of life is our national respect for law.

In the morning a detachment from the 101st escorted the nine black students from Daisy Bates's house to school. When the whites moved forward against the blacks, they were dispersed by paratroopers, who advanced with drawn bayonets.

Over the coming weeks, the black students endured taunts, threats, and insults, but the desegregation of Central High School proceeded without violence. In November 1957 the last federal forces were withdrawn.

Racial tension persisted, prompting the Little Rock school board to sue in federal court in February 1958 to delay desegregation for two and a half years. This time, a U.S. district court judge granted the school board's request for an injunction, finding the situation "untolerable" (sic). As the basis for his ruling, the judge cited "tension and unrest among the school administrators, the classroom teachers, the pupils, and the latter's parents, which inevitably had an adverse effect upon the educational program."

Marshall and Branton appealed the ruling to the U.S. Court of Appeals for the Eighth Circuit, demanding that school integration proceed as planned. The appeals court held in their favor but stayed its own order so that the matter could be appealed directly to the U.S. Supreme Court by the Little Rock school board. The justices agreed to cut short their summer recess in order to hear the case, Cooper v. Aaron, in special session on September 11, 1958.

Marshall urged the justices to hold that public hostility to the Court's desegregation orders could not be used as an excuse by public officials to avoid integration. His brief stated, "This Court and other courts have consistently held that the preservation of the public peace may not be accomplished by interference with rights created by the federal constitution."

He gave no credence to Arkansas officials' contention that state authorities were incapable of maintaining law and order in the face of white resistance. Nor was he put off by threats to close the schools. "Even if it be claimed that tension will result which will disturb the educational process," he asserted, "this is preferable to the complete breakdown of education which will result from teaching that courts of law will bow to violence."

He concluded, "This case affords this Court the opportunity to restate in unmistakable terms both the urgency of proceeding with desegregation and the supremacy of all constitutional rights over bigots—big and small."

The justices met in conference immediately following the close of oral argument. To emphasize their impatience with any further delay in implementing Brown, they issued a per curiam order, meaning a simple directive that includes no discussion of legal issues, the following day. The per curiam affirmed the Eighth

Circuit appeals court; the Little Rock school board was at fault for delaying desegregation.

A complete opinion followed on September 29. In an unprecedented move designed to lend it weight and credibility, the decision was signed by all nine justices. The message was clear: Since arriving at the unanimous ruling in *Brown* four years earlier, none of the justices had wavered in their determination that the nation's schools be desegregated.

The opinion was written by Justice William Brennan and contained an impassioned defense of the federal system of government established under the U.S. Constitution. Under that system the federal courts, not the states, have preeminent power to interpret the Constitution.

Brennan used language suggested by Justice Black to state that by delaying desegregation Arkansas officials were not only depriving blacks of their right to an equal education; they were also posing a direct challenge to our constitutional form of government. He wrote, "As this case reaches us it raises questions of the highest importance to the maintenance of our federal system of government. It squarely presents a claim that there is no duty on state officials to obey federal court orders resting on this Court's deliberate and considered interpretation of the United States Constitution."

He continued, "Specifically, it involves actions by the Governor, Legislature, and other agencies of Arkansas...that they are not bound by our holding in *Brown*...that the Fourteenth Amendment forbids states to use their governmental powers to bar children from attending schools which are helped to run by public management, funds or other public property."

Brennan went on, "We are urged to permit continued suspension of the Little Rock School Board's plan to do away with segregated public schools until state laws and efforts to upset [the ruling in *Brown*] have been further challenged and tested in the courts."

He declared, "We have concluded that these contentions call for clear answers here and now."

The answers could not have been clearer. Referring to the oath of office public officials are required to take, Brennan declared,

"No state legislator or executive or judicial officer can war against the Constitution without violating his undertaking to support it."

Brennan considered the Little Rock school board's claim that hostile white resistance made it impossible to move forward with desegregation. He rejected it out of hand, stating, "The constitutional rights of [black] respondents are not to be sacrificed or yielded to the violence and disorder which have followed upon the actions of the Governor and the Legislature.... Law and order are not to be preserved by depriving the Negro children of their constitutional rights."

He blamed the hostility and resistance on the government of Arkansas: "The record before us clearly establishes that the growth of the Board's difficulties to a magnitude beyond its unaided power to control is the product of state action." This being the case, he went on, "the controlling legal principles are plain. The command of the Fourteenth Amendment is that no 'state' shall deny to any person within its jurisdiction the equal protection of the laws."

He concluded, "The *Brown* case can neither be nullified openly and directly by state legislators or state executive or judicial officers nor nullified indirectly by them through evasive schemes for segregation whether attempted 'ingeniously or ingenuously.'"

Marshall had won. But even this forceful ruling failed to put matters to rest. A little more than a year after the Court issued its decision in *Aaron v. Cooper*, Arkansas's handling of racial matters was back before the justices, framed this time as *Aaron v. Faubus*.

Within days of the Court's ruling in *Cooper*, Faubus persuaded the Arkansas legislature to cut off funding for integrated schools. In addition, integrated schools were ordered closed for the remainder of the 1958–59 school year. When these actions were struck down at the U.S. district court level, the state appealed. Yet again Marshall and Branton found themselves before the Supreme Court, in October 1958, urging the justices to hold the line against Faubus.

They did, issuing another *per curiam* order upholding the district court and requiring the schools' reopening. The desegregation of Little Rock's schools finally proceeded peacefully as planned.

From London, the *Economist* prophesied that "like the Roman general [Fabian] whose name so closely resembles his own, Mr. Faubus may one day be commemorated by a reference in a military lexicon: Faubian tactics, or the techniques of fighting a losing battle in such a way as to cause the greatest loss to all concerned."

By the end of the decade, Marshall had argued seven major cases before the Supreme Court that resulted from resistance to, or unwillingness to enforce, *Brown*. He won all of them. In addition the Court used the *Brown* ruling as the basis for requiring the desegregation of public parks and recreational facilities, local transportation, and professional athletics.

Marshall's gradualism successfully eliminated government-sanctioned segregation from most aspects of American life. But as the 1950s drew to a close, the primary focus of the civil rights struggle shifted from the courtrooms to the streets. The well-reasoned legal brief contended for center stage with the strategies of direct action and civil disobedience. Marshall would play a key role in those activities as well.

FIFTEEN

Civil Disobedience Versus the Old Guard

> I think Thurgood Marshall had this abiding concern that we didn't need to continue to put ourselves in harm's way. I think that, more than anything else, was his idea. He wasn't saying be "patient" and "wait," he was just saying that this is the way that he would do it, through the courts, and that we didn't need to have people spitting on us, pulling us off lunch-counter stools, and putting lighted cigarettes out in our hair.
>
> —Congressman John Lewis

On the U.S. Supreme Court Building's east pediment, a marble carving depicts Aesop's fable of the plodding, persistent tortoise who defeats the faster, more erratic hare in a race. Perhaps it is there to remind us that the Court moves more slowly, but more surely, than Congress. But the carving is also an appropriate analogy of events that took place in the late 1950s and early 1960s,

198

as emerging civil rights organizations, such as the Southern Christian Leadership Conference, the Student Nonviolent Coordinating Committee, and the Congress of Racial Equality, grew impatient with the NAACP's use of legal gradualism as a tool of deliverance.

The catalyst for the conflict began on December 1, 1955, in Montgomery, Alabama when Rosa Parks, a forty-two-year-old black seamstress, took a seat on the Cleveland Avenue bus. Driver J. B. Blake ordered Parks and three other black riders to relinquish their seats to standing white passengers.

"Y'all better make it light on yourself and let me have those seats," he threatened. The other black passengers moved to the rear of the bus, but Rosa Parks refused to give up her seat to a white man.

"When he saw me still sitting," Parks said, "he asked if I was going to stand up, and I said, 'No, I'm not.'"

Parks, a secretary at the local branch of the NAACP, was taken to jail. When NAACP branch secretary E. D. Nixon called to inquire about Parks, the police would not answer his questions. "They wouldn't even confirm that she had been arrested," Nixon said. Clifford Durr, a white NAACP attorney, telephoned the jail and was told Parks had been charged with violating Montgomery's bus segregation laws.

Some white local officials assumed Rosa Parks's defiance of Montgomery's laws and customs mandating that black riders sit in the back of the bus was instigated by the local branch of the NAACP. Others claimed she was the unwitting instrument of Communists seeking to parade the country's racial strife as a failed example of American democracy. Neither supposition was true. Rosa Parks simply personified black America's growing discontent and despair with segregation and discrimination.

Outraged, Jo Ann Robinson, a civic leader, and other black Montgomery women called their ministers the evening of Parks's arrest, a Thursday. They demanded some kind of public protest. A mass meeting was called for Friday night by Rev. L. Roy Bennett, an NAACP official, and a plan was made to begin a boycott of the buses Monday morning. Most of the city's bus riders were black. The ministers agreed to tell their parishioners about the proposed boycott from their pulpits Sunday morning. Montgomery did not have a black-owned radio station, so the task of spreading the word quickly to the city's fifty thousand black citizens proved a formidable one.

The twenty-seven-year-old pastor of Montgomery's Dexter Avenue Baptist Church agreed to use his church's facilities to mimeograph tracts and spread them throughout the city that weekend. His name was Martin Luther King Jr. King had preached his first sermon at the church only eighteen months earlier, on May 17, 1954. He had come to Montgomery from Atlanta after deciding—much to the displeasure of his father, Martin Luther King Sr.—not to become associate pastor at the senior King's Ebenezer Baptist Church. King's wife, Coretta, was also unhappy with her husband's decision to move to deeply segregated Montgomery. In Boston, while her husband earned a graduate degree at Boston University's School of Theology, Coretta King, a graduate of Antioch College, had been a soloist in performances at the New England Conservatory. She sang in the choir of a white Presbyterian church there and had many white friends. In Atlanta she had participated in many social and cultural events at the Atlanta University Center and taken part in musical programs at her father-in-law's church. Atlanta, though not as culturally attractive for her as Boston, was still better than Montgomery. She knew life would be much different for her in segregated Montgomery. But King convinced Coretta to move to Montgomery with him after promising her they would only be there about two years.

Three weeks before Parks's arrest, King had rejected the presidency of the Montgomery NAACP branch because he felt he had not been in the city long enough to become a community leader. In his failed effort to convince his son to remain in Atlanta, King's father had warned that Montgomery's black religious leadership would not take kindly to a young minister from Atlanta with a theological degree from a white northern college.

Thirty-five thousand fliers were distributed over the weekend. "Don't ride the buses to work, to town, to school, or anywhere," they urged. A fleet of private automobiles was organized Sunday night to carry the boycotters to work Monday morning.

The ministers formed the Montgomery Improvement Association (MIA) that week to conduct the boycott, and King agreed to direct it. The MIA's initial objective was not to end segregation on city buses, and this approach conflicted with the NAACP's standard policy of attacking segregation without qualifying reservations. The MIA's demands were simple. It wanted black riders treated with respect by white bus drivers. It wanted riders seated on a first-come basis, with black passengers seated from the back toward the front and white riders seated from the front toward the back. It asked for the employment of black drivers on routes serving predominantly black neighborhoods. On instructions from its national headquarters, the Montgomery branch of the NAACP refused to take a formal role in the boycott because the MIA was not calling for an end to segregated seating. But the city's NAACP members decided to join the boycott as individuals.

In a church basement meeting, five days after the boycott began, King told black citizens, "In spite of the mistreatment we have [met with], we must not be bitter and end up hating our white brothers." He added, "If we protest courageously, and yet with dignity and…love, when the history books are written in the future, somebody will have to say, 'There lived a race of people, of black people…who had the courage to stand up for their rights.'"

From New York, Marshall watched the boycott closely. He knew the NAACP could not continue to ignore this mass action by fifty thousand black Alabamans that was a daily story on the front pages of the nation's newspapers and the lead story each evening on network television. The NAACP's reluctance to embrace the boycott caused problems for NAACP executive director Roy Wilkins and Marshall when the association held its forty-seventh annual convention that year, in January 1956, in San Francisco.

King left Montgomery shortly after the boycott began to address the convention and received an enthusiastic welcome from the delegates, including NAACP field secretary Medgar Evers of Mississippi. While Thurgood Marshall and Roy Wilkins were taking the tortoise's cautious approach toward events unfolding in Montgomery, King's presence at the convention inspired a group of insurgent delegates, led by Evers, to call for the NAACP's immediate and unequivocal support of the bus boycott and Reverend King.

The delegates met in Evers's hotel room on the first night of the convention and drafted a three-page resolution supporting Montgomery's nonviolent bus boycott and Martin Luther King Jr. as its leader. Marshall and Wilkins were angered when they learned the delegates intended to bring their Montgomery resolution to the convention floor the following morning. They went to King's hotel room later that night to discuss the boycott and question King about his leadership.

Marshall bluntly told King the NAACP had marched, boycotted, and picketed since 1917, but none of its protests involved deliberately breaking laws or staging mass sit-ins that resulted in the arrests of hundreds of its members. He reminded King that the NAACP had just months earlier won a landmark U.S. Supreme Court decision, *Brown v. Board of Education*. Marshall asked King if he believed his tactics of civil disobedience and nonviolence could win some of the major battles the NAACP had painstakingly fought in the courts since King was a child. King quietly told Marshall he did not know.

Threatened with a runaway convention, Wilkins asked Marshall's advice. Marshall and Fund deputy legal counsel Robert L. Carter told Wilkins the Fund should agree to assume responsibility for the legal battles that would undoubtedly come from the Montgomery boycott. That, they hoped, would quiet rebellious delegates trying to force the NAACP to endorse the boycott and King.

Wilkins, the grandson of Mississippi slaves, graduated from the University of Minnesota and served as editor of the *Kansas City Call*, a black newspaper. Wilkins presented an aristocratic bearing and was prominent in Kansas City's black social world. Walter White hired him in 1932 to edit the NAACP's monthly magazine, the *Crisis*, and to direct the association's publicity campaigns and press relations. Wilkins moved to New York City and took an apartment at 409 Edgecomb Avenue, the "finest address in Harlem," where Thurgood Marshall and his wife were to live several years later. As Walter White had done earlier, Wilkins exercised an ironclad control over the NAACP. This created friction between him and NAACP branch secretaries who believed the rights organization should be governed by a more democratic process.

Marshall told Wilkins privately later that night that the NAACP would have to become involved in the Montgomery protest. Wilkins relented, but not completely. He announced on the convention floor the next morning that the NAACP would give "careful consideration" to the MIA and the Montgomery bus boycott as an example of a new civil rights tactic and that the Fund would cover the legal expenses. The delegates cheered. But he was not ready to allow the venerable civil rights organization to fully embrace Martin Luther King Jr.

After the convention the NAACP began a vigorous nationwide campaign to raise money to cover the boycott's legal fees. This campaign angered King. In a confidential letter to Wilkins, King accused the NAACP of raising money "in the name of our movement." Wilkins told King all funds raised to support the MIA should be channeled through the NAACP because Thurgood Marshall had committed the Fund to pay the boycott's legal expenses and provide bail money for protesters who were arrested. He argued that the venerable NAACP was more organized than the embryonic MIA and already had in place a national fund-raising apparatus. The NAACP was receiving thousands of dollars in small donations in the hundreds of letters pouring into its office each day from people interested in supporting the Montgomery boycott.

Wilkins warned King to keep their dispute over the money secret. "I certainly do not need to stress at this time that it would be fatal for there to develop any hint of disagreement as to the raising and allocation of funds," he wrote in a confidential letter. In a conciliatory response King said, "We are quite conscious of our dependence on the NAACP." He also mentioned that his Dexter Avenue Baptist Church had purchased a thousand-dollar institutional lifetime NAACP membership.

Though Roy Wilkins was the NAACP's executive director, in the minds of most black Americans Thurgood Marshall *was* the NAACP. It was his name that appeared foremost in newspaper stories about NAACP activities, and it was his picture that accompanied those articles. Wilkins directed the association from the security of its Fifth Avenue headquarters, while Marshall traveled as its front-line warrior through hostile southern towns, often at great personal risk.

After the *Brown* victory Marshall believed the NAACP was nearing the end of its twenty-year battle to end school segregation and integrate public accommodations. Black America now looked forward to the full implementation of the 1954 Supreme Court decision desegregating schools. Wilkins confidentially told close friends he believed the NAACP should wait until the Montgomery boycott was over before it made a public assessment of the usefulness of King's methods of nonviolence and civil disobedience.

NAACP attorney Wiley Branton said Wilkins was concerned the NAACP's involvement in the boycott would severely tax the organization's resources at a time when it needed all its strength to ensure compliance with the Supreme Court's recent *Brown* decision. "The association had just won its biggest legal battle and was now marshaling its forces and resources for the inevitable battles of implementation that were coming," Branton said. "Roy just couldn't see how the NAACP could take on a new and different kind of struggle at such a critical time."

White gangs began attacking black protesters. King and other MIA officials were arrested on charges of "disturbing the peace" and "failure to move on." Thurgood Marshall was one of the first lawyers to rush to King's defense, despite the disagreement between King and Wilkins over fund-raising. After his release King issued a statement supporting the NAACP and recognizing the work it had done.

"We must continue our struggles in the courts, and above all, we must continue to support the NAACP," King said. "Our major victories have come through the work of this organization. One thing the gradualists don't seem to understand: We are not trying to make people love us when we go to court, we are trying to keep them from killing us."

The MIA increased its demands and asked for an end to segregated seating. King felt the boycott was effective and now believed a total victory was possible, not just a still-segregated but more equitable seating policy that the MIA initially sought. Marshall agreed to take the issue of segregated buses to court.

Marshall and Carter went to Montgomery, and Carter argued the boycott case on May 11, 1956, in federal district court from a brief written by Marshall. On June 4, six months after Rosa Parks refused to relinquish her seat, the panel of three white judges ruled against segregated bus seating. The city appealed the decision to the U.S. Supreme Court. It was a strange turn of events. For the first time, southern blacks were asking the Supreme Court to uphold a decision made by white southern judges.

Four months later, in October, the Supreme Court upheld the lower court's decision. Without a hearing, the court affirmed that Alabama's laws segregating bus passengers were unconstitutional because they denied equal accommodations to all riders. Montgomery's black citizens continued to boycott until the Supreme Court order was legally executed. On December 20, federal marshals formally notified city officials that they must comply with the decision. The next day, Montgomery's citizens sat wherever they wanted to on the city's buses. A new era in civil rights was born.

"We have discovered a new and powerful weapon—nonviolent resistance," King told a victory meeting at the Holt Street Baptist Church.

The Montgomery victory spread King's reputation as a rising civil rights leader far beyond Montgomery. *Jet* magazine published his picture on its cover and called him "Alabama's Modern Moses." A *New York Times* profile described King as a speaker whose oratory "overwhelms the listener with the depth of his convictions." After a fund-raiser in New York City, a tabloid reported King received "the kind of welcome [the city] usually reserves for the Brooklyn Dodgers after more than ten thousand New Yorkers came to Concord Baptist Church to hear him speak about the Montgomery boycott.

The Montgomery victory and King's public recognition of the NAACP's historic civil rights role should have brought Martin Luther King Jr. and the National Association for the Advancement of Colored People together as allies, united against a common enemy. Instead, it drove them apart. On June 1, 1956, Alabama attorney general John Patterson won a state court order putting the NAACP out of business in Alabama. Patterson argued the NAACP was "organizing, supporting and financing an illegal boycott by Negro residents of Montgomery." The court agreed. It ordered the NAACP to stop all activities in Alabama, including fund-raising, collection of dues, and membership drives. When the NAACP resisted a corollary court order to surrender its membership lists and contribution records to Patterson, it was fined $100,000 and held in contempt.

The Alabama NAACP disbanded. Wilkins privately blamed King and the MIA. The ban had come at a critical time in the NAACP's fight to fully implement school desegregation. The association needed its state branches to develop cases to test the implementation of the *Brown* decision. It took eight years for the NAACP to win a Supreme Court order voiding the Alabama ban.

In Birmingham, Rev. Fred Shuttlesworth, an itinerant Baptist preacher who had been convicted in 1941 of producing moonshine whiskey in a backwoods still, had an idea he thought might help the NAACP continue its Alabama activities. He formed the Alabama Christian Movement for Human Rights. The NAACP now had a surrogate organization through which it could continue its activities in the state. Many former NAACP members joined. Alabama's white press charged that the creation of the new civil rights group was an obvious attempt to circumvent the court order.

The MIA's Montgomery success inspired similar assaults against segregated buses in two other southern cities. King and his volunteer workers took their nonviolent campaign to Tallahassee, Florida, and Birmingham, Alabama. Direct action and nonviolence were winning major victories quickly and thrusting King into the civil rights spotlight. But the Montgomery victory, won with the legal help of Thurgood Marshall and the Fund, did little to heal the rift between the NAACP and the SCLC.

King returned to Atlanta in 1957 to become associate pastor of his father's Ebenezer Baptist Church and to begin plans for organizing the Southern Christian Leadership Conference, which in 1968 emerged from the MIA. King's growing national recognition as a new kind of civil rights leader disturbed the city's entrenched black leaders.

"Atlanta's older black leadership did not want King to return to the city," John Lewis, who now represents Georgia in the U.S. House and who was a former chairman of the Student Non-Violent Coordinating Committee.

Atlanta had been a sleepy southern town where the white power structure catered paternally to the city's older, more moderate black leaders. The black leadership had quietly negotiated a few minor racial concessions from Atlanta's white establishment in closed-door meetings that received little public attention or fanfare.

Former *Atlanta Daily World* managing editor George Coleman said, "It [the older leadership] was proud it had been able to keep the lid on for so long, and they didn't want Martin to bring his Montgomery tactics to Atlanta and rock their safe little boat."

The few concessions the old guard had been given did little to change life for most black Atlantans. True, they convinced police chief Herbert Jenkins to hire the city's first black police officers. However, instead of working out of the Atlanta police department's headquarters on Decatur Street with the rest of the force, the sixteen recruits held roll call and maintained lockers in the basement of the black YMCA at 22 Butler Street. Black officers were assigned to the 6:00 P.M. to 2:00 A.M. shift—the "Black Watch"—and only patrolled Atlanta's black business districts, such as Hunter Street, Auburn Avenue, and Northside Drive. Black police officers could not arrest white suspects, even for murder; they could only detain a suspect until a white patrolman arrived to make the formal arrest.

At Grady Memorial Hospital there was a waiting room for white patients and one for blacks. The city's ambulances were segregated. There were segregated waiting rooms at the train and bus stations, and water fountains and restrooms were plainly marked "White" and "colored." Black students could not attend the University of Georgia at Athens or Georgia Tech in Atlanta or play on the city's whites-only tennis courts and golf courses.

Just up the street from King's church stood Wheat Street Baptist Church, an imposing concrete building that its pastor, Rev.

William Holmes Borders, called "God's mighty fortress on Auburn Avenue where the doors swing open on welcome hinges." Borders was a tall, affable preacher who wore homburg hats and chesterfield overcoats on Saturday nights when he strolled down "Sweet Auburn Avenue," taking the church's "tithe" from street-corner crap games. He had been educated at northern white colleges, but on Sunday mornings he displayed no trace of his elite educational background as he delivered electrifying call-and-response sermons in the finest tradition of the southern black Baptist preacher.

Though he was a member of the city's established black leadership, unlike most of his colleagues he was as comfortable with citizens on street corners in Vine City, Atlanta's black ghetto, as he was in the office of Mayor William B. Hartsfield. Borders was one of the first members of the old guard to support Martin Luther King Jr. and his nonviolent mass movement, and he frequently walked picket lines with college students.

Borders was a lifelong Republican, as were many of Atlanta's other most prominent black leaders, such as real estate broker Q. V. Williamson, insurance executive T. M. Alexander Sr., *Atlanta Daily World* publisher C. A. Scott, and Martin Luther King Sr.

Most of them lived on Atlanta's comfortable West Side, along Hunter Street and out on Mosely Drive, in large brick houses that sat on spacious, well-kept lawns. They bought their obligatory personal five-hundred-dollar lifetime NAACP memberships, and those who owned businesses bought thousand-dollar institutional memberships. They believed Atlanta was on a safe, if slow, path toward racial harmony and progress.

As in Montgomery, in Atlanta many conservative black leaders did not want King's massive demonstrations to promote racial progress. Atlanta called itself "the city too busy to hate," even though the Ku Klux Klan held frequent marches on Peachtree Street and burned crosses at rallies atop nearby Stone Mountain. Scott used his newspaper's editorial pages—and its news columns, too, much to the displeasure of his managing editor, George Coleman—to criticize the fast-paced civil rights movement King was bringing to the city. Scott had a standing order in his newsroom that King's picture was not to appear on the *World*'s front page.

The city's white Republican politicians, such as Alderman Rodney C. Cook, were always welcomed at Scott's office on Auburn Avenue, and *World* editorials clearly reflected Scott's embrace of the slow and cautious attitudes of the white power structure. The paper carried full-page advertisements from grocery stores that sought black patronage but would not hire black clerks and from the city's two major department stores, Rich's and Davidson's, where black women could buy two-hundred-dollar dresses but could not sit and drink a ten-cent cup of coffee in the cafeteria. "C.A.'s racial politics were tied directly to the *World*'s advertising revenues," managing editor Coleman said.

The publisher sat each Sunday morning in the Scott family pew at Ebenezer Baptist Church peering up through his horn-rimmed glasses as Rev. Martin Luther King Sr. preached fiery sermons from a high mahogany pulpit that looked like a ship's prow. In 1960, Scott approached the pastor one Sunday after church and asked him to persuade his son to confine his civil rights efforts to national issues and leave local Atlanta race relations to the older leadership. But in a few months hundreds of Atlanta's college students were launching sit-ins, and Martin Luther King Jr.'s civil rights activities continued to increase. The senior King's joining the Democratic party was the last straw. Scott left Ebenezer and joined a Methodist church on the other side of town.

Atlanta was the home of Morehouse, Clark, Spelman, and Morris Brown colleges, Atlanta University—where W. E. B. Du Bois had taught—two theological seminaries, and a school of mortuary science. Their students came from all over the United States. Martin Luther King Jr. graduated from Morehouse College in 1948. Most of the schools' northern students had not experienced overt segregation firsthand until they arrived in Atlanta. Many were from affluent families that sheltered them from even the subtle vestiges of segregation and discrimination. These students, though insulated in the sprawling, protective academic community on the Westside, which had been built with Rockefeller family money, became quickly aware of racial and political conditions in the city and the state.

"Getting off the train in Atlanta for the first time and finding myself in the 'colored waiting room' was like finding myself in another world," said divinity student Cecil L. Franklin—the brother of singer Aretha Franklin—who came to Morehouse College from Detroit as a freshman in 1957. Many of the male students worked as waiters serving the white southern aristocracy at Atlanta's Piedmont Driving Club, as Thurgood Marshall had done years earlier at Maryland's Gibson Island Club. And, like Marshall, they had been subjected to racial slurs and degradation.

On a dark night in Anniston, Alabama, the Morehouse College swimming team, traveling in the college's Ford station wagon to a meet, was refused service at a gas station. And on a trip to the Spring Hill Debate Tournament in 1960, the college's debating team was ordered to ride in the "colored" car on the Peach Queen train from Atlanta to Mobile.

At Morehouse, Harvard-educated Dr. Arthur H. Brisbane was giving his students—among them Julian Bond, who would later be refused a seat in the Georgia legislature because he opposed the Vietnam War—their first exposure to constitutional law, explaining the importance and significance of Supreme Court decisions like *Plessy v. Ferguson* and the Dred Scott decision. Brisbane explained the protections afforded black citizens under the Constitution.

On February 1, 1960, America saw its first "sit-in" demonstration. Four black students from North Carolina Agricultural and Technical College, in Greensboro, took seats at a Woolworth lunch counter. The tactic spread across southern cities.

Two months later, Atlanta's black college students were eager to participate in the "Movement," despite warnings from city officials and the entrenched black leaders that a sit-in would disrupt the city's race relations. But the students were not long inclined to march to the slow beat of Atlanta's old guard's drum. "We refused to be known as the 'students who slept' while the world changed around them," said Morehouse college student Harvey Miller.

At NAACP headquarters in New York, the rapidly developing sit-in movement concerned Thurgood Marshall and his colleagues. Marshall knew the legal expenses of what promised to be "thousands of jailed students" across the South would be much more than the NAACP could bear alone, in both money and legal talent. He called two of his old friends, Atlanta lawyers A. T. Walden and Donald Hollowell. Walden was a long-practicing attorney known as the "dean' of Atlanta's black attorneys. Hollowell was a much younger man with offices near Atlanta University and many friends among the students and faculties of the black colleges.

Walden and Hollowell told Marshall that A. D. King, Martin's brother, was holding meetings with several student-body presidents at Frazier's Restaurant on Hunter Street. They told Marshall the students had not sought advice or help officially from the local NAACP branch but were holding their own counsel with Martin Luther King Jr.—and members of his Southern Christian Leadership Conference. The lawyers said they believed it was only logical to assume that before long Atlanta would have its own sit-in demonstration.

In April 1960 a group of students met with the presidents of Atlanta's black colleges in the office of Atlanta University president Dr. Rufus Clements. The group included Marion Wright (now Marion Edleman) and Roslyn Pope, Danny Mitchell, Lonnie King, Michael D. Davis, Don Clark, James Felder, and Julian Bond. The students told the college presidents they had organized a sit-in strike and were going to launch it in two days.

Morehouse College president Dr. Benjamin Elijah Mays was not surprised by the news. He had been a fierce fighter for human rights for more than half a century and encouraged racial pride from Morehouse students in mandatory chapel sessions held each weekday morning in Sales Hall. Mays constantly reminded Morehouse students that they "must be interested in something bigger than a hamburger." Mays had been involved with the NAACP since his days as a professor of religion at Howard University in the 1930s and had known Thurgood Marshall there.

The college presidents urged caution. They were burdened with the surrogate parental responsibility for their students' welfare and safety, and they knew any sit-in demonstration could result in violence. They offered a compromise. The college presidents told the students they would raise several thousand dollars for the publication of full-page advertisements in the city's newspapers so the students could publicly express their dissatisfaction with Atlanta's segregated public accommodations. They said this would be more effective than a sit-in demonstration. The students agreed.

They went to the reading room of Treavor-Arnett Library, on the Atlanta University campus, and drafted the document "An Appeal for Human Rights," modeled on the Bill of Rights. Two days later, it appeared in the *Atlanta Constitution*, the *Atlanta Journal*, and even the *Atlanta Daily World*. The following day nearly fifteen hundred students launched the Atlanta sit-in, and three hundred were arrested. A white woman who watched the students march through downtown Atlanta told the Associated Press, "I didn't know there were that many niggers in college."

Again, Benjamin Mays was not surprised. Nor did he feel betrayed by the students. In fact, Mays had anticipated the students' actions; shortly after the meeting with the students adjourned, he had called his friend Thurgood Marshall to seek his legal help. Mays knew the students were impatient with what they saw as the futility of waiting for the courts to move and the slow and only partial implementation that often followed court decisions. Mays later said the college presidents knew "in our collective wisdom that, advertisement or no advertisement, the students were going to sit-in."

Mays also called members of Atlanta's old guard the day of the student meeting. He told them he believed a sit-in was imminent and asked them to support the student demonstrations. The old guard called its white friends in city government—Mayor William B. Hartsfield and police chief Herbert Jenkins—to make sure the students would be peacefully arrested and not attacked with police dogs, billy clubs, and water hoses, as had been done in other southern cities. Marshall called Walden and Hollowell—the NAACP's "Atlanta attorneys"—and they arranged to bail the students out of jail and plead their defense.

Walden, Hollowell, and a third attorney, Horace Ward, now a federal district court judge in Atlanta, arrived at the Atlanta City Jail with Morehouse College dean Brailsford R. Brazeal as the first bus load of arrested students drove up. Surprisingly, three members of Atlanta's old guard came, too. T. M. Alexander Sr., Q. V.

Williamson, and Rev. William Holmes Borders brought money and the deeds to their property to pledge as collateral for the students' release. Atlanta had weathered its first mass demonstration.

On April 15, 1960, the Student Nonviolent Coordinating Committee (SNCC) was organized at Shaw University in Raleigh, North Carolina. As civil rights demonstrations and white resistance to them increased that year, the Congress of Racial Equality (CORE) and SNCC began "Freedom Rides" to test the enforcement of federal laws banning segregation in interstate bus terminals, restaurants, and waiting rooms. For years black riders had traveled on buses throughout the South carrying jugs of water and bags of fried chicken because they could not eat in terminal restaurants. Southern interstate bus routes were called "the chicken bone express" by black travelers.

The first Freedom Ride left Washington, D.C., on April 28, 1961, when seven black and six white passengers began a trip through Virginia, the Carolinas, Alabama, Georgia, and Mississippi on the way to a CORE conference in New Orleans. When the Greyhound bus arrived at the terminal in Anniston, Alabama, an angry mob pounded on the doors with pipes and chains and slashed the tires. The mob was angry because the riders had attempted to use the facilities in the Anniston terminal. Most terminals remained segregated despite the law. City police officers escorted the bus out of town, where it was chased along Highway 78 by fifty cars carrying about two hundred white men. The driver pulled the bus off the highway when the tires began to go flat. He leaped from the bus and fled into a nearby field.

The mob descended on the crippled bus, breaking the windows with axes and trying to force open the doors. A firebomb was tossed through the broken back window. Flames raced through the bus. The passengers tried to force open a door, but it was barricaded by the mob.

Alabama state investigator E. L. Cowling, who had followed the bus, quickly realized what was about to happen. He drew his pistol and held the mob at gunpoint while the riders escaped the burning bus. But as they ran, coughing from the acrid smoke, they were struck with clubs and chains. A few minutes later, the

Alabama State Police arrived, and the mob dispersed after the troopers fired a volley of warning shots into the air. Injured riders were taken to the Anniston hospital and treated for their injuries and smoke inhalation.

Undaunted by violence in Alabama, more than a thousand Freedom Riders continued the protests across the South. In Montgomery six hundred federal marshals were called to protect Freedom Riders. In Mississippi three hundred Freedom Riders, including fifteen Catholic priests, were jailed. The rides resulted in the desegregation of 120 interstate bus terminals when, five months after the rides began, the Interstate Commerce Commission enforced its order to end segregated buses and the use of segregated terminal facilities.

Wilkins remained concerned about the tactics of the newer civil rights organizations despite the fact that Marshall and the Fund were now handling most of the Movement's legal matters. Wilkins was offended by some student leaders who were calling the NAACP "ineffective" and "conservative." He often said that CORE and the SCLC "get people in jail, and we have to get them out."

Thurgood Marshall was critical of King, though King's growing national prominence was not as threatening to Marshall as it was to Wilkins, who held the nation's premier civil rights position. Marshall said school desegregation was "men's work" and that King and his followers were using "the bodies of children" to achieve their civil rights objectives. Marshall characterized King as "a boy on a man's errand." When one of King's aides, Ella Baker, took two student leaders to visit Marshall, he told the students that he disapproved of the tactic "jail without bail" and that the Fund's job was to "get people out of jail, not get them in." In remarks to his legal colleagues, Marshall referred to King as an "opportunist," a "first-rate rabble-rouser," and a "coward." Those were strong words of disapproval from a man who nearly thirty years earlier had sat with other black students in the whites-only section of a Pennsylvania movie theater, who had been chased from rural southern towns by angry whites, and who had masqueraded as an Alabama sharecropper while investigating a lynching.

Marshall speaking before a group of black veterans in New York City on September 23, 1956. During the Korean War Marshall travelled to Japan and Korea to investigate complaints that black servicemen had been unjustifiably court-martialed. He was critical of General Douglas MacArthur's treatment of black troops. (AP/Wide World Photos)

NAACP lawyers Thurgood Marshall, left, James A. Nabrit, Jr., and Jack Greenberg announce plans in March 1960 to defend more than one thousand lunch counter demonstrators who were arrested in the South. Marshall initially opposed the direct confrontation strategy of civil rights leaders like Martin Luther King, Jr., because he believed it was safer to win these victories in the courts. (UPI/Bettmann)

A Birmingham, Alabama, police officer uses a dog to chase civil rights demonstrators on April 7, 1963. Civil rights demonstrators were subjected to attacks by police armed with dogs, clubs, and water hoses. (UPI/Bettmann)

Six students who attended the Little Rock, Arkansas, Central High School in 1958 sit on the steps of the Supreme Court with Thurgood Marshall in August 1958. The NAACP won a Supreme Court ruling assuring black students would be admitted when the school opened on September 9, 1958. From left are: Melba Patillo, 16; Jefferson Thomas, 15; Gloria Ray, 15; Mrs. Daisy Bates, president of the Little Rock NAACP; Thurgood Marshall, NAACP chief counsel; Carlotta Walls, 15; Minnie Jean Brown, 16, and Elizabeth Edkford, 16. (UPI/Bettmann)

Thurgood Marshall confers with members of the Senate Judiciary Subcommittee on July 12, 1962, during confirmation hearings on his nomination to the U.S. Court of Appeals for the Second Circuit. President John F. Kennedy and his brother, Attorney General Robert F. Kennedy, struck a deal with Mississippi Senator James O. Eastland, agreeing to appoint a racist Mississippi judge to federal district court in order to secure Marshall's appointment. Marshall is shown here with New York Senators Jacob Javits (left) and Kenneth Keating (right), standing. Seated are Judge Samuel Rosenman (left) and Thurgood Marshall. (UPI/Bettmann)

Federal Appeals Court Judge Thurgood Marshall (second from left) is welcomed by Kenya Minister of Justice Tom Mboya (center) on his arrival at Nairobi Airport on July 10, 1963. At left is Berl Bernhard, staff director of the U.S. Commission on Civil rights; second from right is Kenya Minister for Commerce and Industry, Dr. Kiano; and far right is U.S. counselor general in Nairobi, L. V. Juge. Marshall was beginning a tour of Kenya, Tanganyika, and Uganda at the request of President John F. Kennedy. Marshall had served as a consultant in 1960 to Kenya's constitutional convention. (AP/Wide World Photo)

Thurgood Marshall at home with his young sons, Thurgood Jr., left, and John. (Courtesy Moorland-Spingarn Research Center)

President Lyndon Baines Johnson congratulates Thurgood Marshall after announcing he was nominating him to be U.S. solicitor general on July 7, 1965. With them is Mrs. Penelope Thunberg, whom the President had appointed to the U.S. Tariff Commission. (UPI/Bettmann)

Thurgood Marshall takes the oath of office for Solicitor General on August 24, 1965, from Associate Supreme Court Justice Hugo Black. President Lyndon B. Johnson (center), Mrs. Cecilia Marshall, his second wife, and the Marshall boys, Thurgood Jr. and John, watch the ceremony. (UPI/Bettmann)

Thurgood Marshall on August 24, 1965, in the White House Cabinet Room, shortly after he was sworn in as the nation's first black solicitor general, representing the United States in cases before the Supreme Court. Marshall used the office to continue his fight to win equality for all Americans. His wife, Cecilia, and son Thurgood Jr., 9, are on the left. John, 7, is on the right. (AP/Wide World Photo)

President Lyndon Baines Johnson announces his nomination of Thurgood Marshall as the first African-American Supreme Court justice on June 13, 1967. (UPI/Bettmann)

Marshall appears before a Senate Judiciary hearing on July 7, 1967, on his appointment as an associate justice of the Supreme Court. Seated next to Marshall is his wife, Cecilia Marshall. (UPI/Bettmann)

New Supreme Court Justice Thurgood Marshall with his family on September 1, 1967, in front of the Supreme Court building. With Marshall are his wife, Cecilia, and their sons, John, 9, foreground, and Thurgood Jr., 11. (AP/Wide World Photo)

Justice William O. Douglas with his fourth wife, Cathy, in his chambers during the early 1970s. Marshall refused to give Douglas the fourth vote needed to bring the question of the Vietnam War's constitutionality before the Court. When Marshall overturned Douglas's order to halt the bombing of Cambodia in 1973, Douglas called the action taken by Marshall "lawless." (Supreme Court Historical Society)

An anti-death-penalty demonstrator stands with a sign in front of the Supreme Court building on January 17, 1977. Throughout his career Marshall remained adamantly opposed to the death penalty, which he felt was "cruel and unusual punishment" under the Constitution's Eighth Amendment. (UPI/Bettmann)

Demonstrators protesting legal abortion march in front of the Supreme Court building on January 22, 1990. Marshall voted with the majority in *Roe v. Wade* in 1973, establishing women's constitutional right to abortion. Later, he called for government funding of abortions for indigent women. (UPI/Bettmann)

Justices Brennan and Marshall, the conservative Rehnquist Court's liberal holdovers, at the dedication of the Clarence Mitchell courthouse in Baltimore, Maryland, on March 8, 1985. As a conciliator and consensus builder on the Warren and Burger Courts, claimed the *National Review* in 1984, Brennan had had a more sustained impact on American public policy than anyone. When Brennan resigned from the Court in July 1990, Marshall declared that his friend and colleague "cannot be replaced." Marshall's grandson was named after Brennan. (Ray Lustig)

The members of the Supreme Court sit on November 9, 1990, for their annual photo. Bottom row (left to right) Associate Justices Harry Blackmun and Bryon White, Chief Justice William Rehnquist, Associate Justices Thurgood Marshall and John Paul Stevens. Top row (left to right) Anthony Kennedy, Sandra Day O'Connor, Antonin Scalia, and David Souter. (Reuters/Bettmann)

King received a letter from NAACP board member Jackie Robinson asking him not to criticize the NAACP in public. Robinson urged him to control statements by "individuals who are knocking the NAACP and promoting the SCLC." King felt it was the NAACP that was "knocking" the SCLC, and in his response he made it clear he was aware of Thurgood Marshall's verbal attacks on him:

> I have no Messiah complex, and I know that we need many leaders to do the job. I have refused to fight back or even answer some of the unkind statements that I have been informed that NAACP officials said about me and the Southern Christian Leadership Conference. Frankly, I hear these statements every day, and I have seen efforts on the part of NAACP officials to sabotage our humble efforts.... I am sure that if criticisms were weighed it would turn out that persons associated with the NAACP have made much more damaging statements about SCLC than persons associated with SCLC have made concerning the NAACP.... The job ahead is too great to be bickering in the darkness of jealousy, deadening competitions and internal ego struggles.

Morehouse College president Benjamin Mays also attempted to resolve the differences between the NAACP and the SCLC. He privately asked King and Wilkins to "discourage anyone in your organization from taking a crack at either the NAACP or the SCLC."

Robinson's letter asking King to help end the conflict between the SCLC and the NAACP did not reveal the former baseball player's deeper concern for the future of the NAACP and his realization that it needed to change with the times. That came later, in an interview with writer Louis Lomax:

> The NAACP must adopt mass action as a matter of policy or accept the consequences. There are no two ways about it. The students and many of the adults want mass action. Either we employ it or suffer. We are not meeting the needs of the masses. We don't know the people; the people don't know us. I have been asked by many people to form a new

civil rights organization that would be closer to the masses. I am all for a new organization if we can do it without interfering with what the NAACP is doing. We must do something. We can't go on as we are today.

Dr. John Morsell, executive assistant to Roy Wilkins, disagreed with Robinson: "We [the NAACP] can hardly advocate or condone a policy of mass civil disobedience except under extreme conditions because that would require the complete abandonment of the philosophy of operations which has sustained us for fifty years."

But Marshall's criticisms of King and mass demonstrations were tempered by his willingness to defend members of the Movement and Martin Luther King Jr. himself. It was clear Marshall and the NAACP would soon have to fully support the Movement, and Marshall was the force from within that changed the NAACP's position.

"The NAACP was not just the 'old guard,'" said attorney Juanita Jackson Mitchell, whose mother, Lillie Mae Jackson, had been president of the NAACP's Baltimore branch in the 1930s and 1940s and whose husband, Clarence Mitchell II, was the NAACP's Capitol Hill lobbyist in the 1950s and 1960s. "It was the 'old folks guard,' and if it was to survive it had to attract younger members, the students walking the picket lines, sitting-in and going to jail, people who were joining and working in the more progressive rights groups, and Thurgood Marshall and Jackie Robinson knew this long before Roy did."

Thirty-two years later, Congressman John Lewis, offered his perspective on the evolution of Marshall's position:

I think it was difficult for some of the old guard leaders to understand the nature of a mass movement. They didn't understand the power, the philosophy of nonviolence. They had reservations about Montgomery and the leadership of Dr. King, but even there I think they tried to be supportive. I think some of them felt threatened on the local level as well as on the national level. This was something new, this was something different, they didn't know how to deal with it. White southerners didn't know how to deal with it and the black leadership, the old guard, didn't know how to deal with it because we had been programmed or taught that we should use the court to seek to redress our concerns, our grievances.

Lewis said that in the summer of 1961 Marshall told students on the campus of Fisk University in Nashville, Tennessee, that the Freedom Rides should be discontinued and a test case challenging segregated buses taken to court. "I don't think some of the NAACP leaders and Thurgood Marshall understood at that time the importance of creating a mass movement," Lewis said. "In a mass movement you can involve more than just the plaintiffs, more than the lawyers, the sort of just professional civil rights workers, but you can involve the masses to help increase the tempo of change." However, Lewis continued, "I think later Thurgood Marshall came to appreciate the power of mass movement."

Lewis said he attended meetings where Marshall, Wilkins, and Whitney Young of the Urban League debated civil rights tactics.

"The NAACP was not there in the beginning, but later, when we needed help, needed someone to go into federal court, we had the NAACP Legal Defense Fund," Lewis said. "So on many occasions when we got arrested, when we went to jail, the NAACP responded with lawyers like Donald Hollowell, A. T. Walden, and James Nabritt. The NAACP had lawyers all across the South, so when we would go to jail, even though Thurgood Marshall disagreed with our techniques, he would make available the legal expertise and the legal resources of the Inc. Fund, Jim Nabrit, Constance Baker Motley, Robert Carter, and a battery of just very bright and very smart people."

Lewis attributed Thurgood Marshall's verbal attacks on Martin Luther King Jr. to Marshall's fear that King's tactics "invited violence. I think Thurgood was concerned more than anything else about the young people's well-being. He did not want to see us get hurt, he didn't want to see us get killed, and he knew that jail was not a pleasant place. He didn't want to see young people, young college students and these pretty young women from Fisk University and Spelman College, stay in jail. Thurgood was a very warm, humane, and humorous person.

"There was a young lady named Diane Nash, a student from Howard University who transferred to Fisk. She was from Chicago, a very beautiful, a very charming woman, who was a coordinator of the Freedom Rides, and even today when I see Thurgood he asks me, 'John, what happened to Diane Nash, what happened to that beautiful woman?' He saw these young people and was concerned about them. He thought the South was so crazy, so backward, that something could happen to a group of young people in the jails of Mississippi, Alabama, and Georgia. And he was right. People did get shot. People did get killed."

Lewis concluded, "I think Thurgood Marshall had this abiding concern that we didn't need to continue to put ourselves in harm's way. I think that, more than anything else, was his idea. He wasn't saying be 'patient' and 'wait,' he was just saying that this is the way that he would do it, through the courts, and that we didn't need to have people spitting on us, pulling us off lunch-counter stools, and putting lighted cigarettes out in our hair. I think that was his overriding concern, because Thurgood Marshall was one of those and still is one of these imposing figures. To hear him and see him during my days in Nashville come to a little church or to the Fisk University gym was an inspiration. I grew up hearing about Thurgood Marshall, and the first time I met him was like meeting a legal savior."

At NAACP conventions the question continued to be asked: Should the NAACP use direct action as official policy to make further progress against discrimination and segregation? The delegates had seen it work in Montgomery and other cities, but the NAACP's legal gradualism was still getting results in the courtroom without the violence often generated by mass demonstrations.

The NAACP was slow to change because its bureaucracy made change difficult. Convention delegates could offer resolutions but could not make policy. Rank-and-file members had no role in setting the association's civil rights agenda because the executive board was reluctant to relinquish its absolute control over policy. It refused to directly address the issue of mass actions.

In March 1960, Marshall called sixty-two lawyers, representing more than one thousand mass-demonstration defendants in the

South, to a conference in New York City. Marshall told the *New York Times* on March 20, "The state use of disturbing the peace laws to convict demonstrators...would be challenged as a violation of the 14th Amendment." On April 7 Marshall said "the whole force of NAACP" would be committed to the students.

Marshall's promise signaled a dramatic change in the NAACP's position on mass demonstrations. Marshall's prior support of the Movement had come through his work as the director of the Fund—legally a separate organization—but now he was speaking for the NAACP.

The change signaled by Marshall's words of commitment were soon followed by the NAACP's actions. The NAACP sent Herbert Wright, its national youth secretary, south to conduct legal training classes for young people participating in sit-ins.

In March 1961 Roy Wilkins publicly supported the newer rights organizations and their activities for the first time. He said that school desegregation was still the most important tool in the long struggle for equality but that there was room in the struggle for other tactics. In an address to Atlanta's black students at Sisters chapel on the Spelman College campus he praised the nonviolent protests but held fast to the NAACP's contention that school desegregation was the "cornerstone" of civil rights progress. "Everything, of course, is tied to the school desegregation suit, not only here, but throughout those southern areas still resisting the inevitable."

On December 4, 1961, Gloster Current, national director of branches, sent a memorandum to NAACP offices in major cities telling them to press for jobs for blacks in national retail stores such as Sears and Montgomery Ward. Current's directive told NAACP members the association would support picket lines. It was further evidence the NAACP was recognizing the power of direct action.

Earlier that year Marshall and the Fund took the legality of sit-ins to the Supreme Court in *Garner v. Louisiana*. Garner and fifteen other students were arrested in Baton Rouge after they refused to leave a Kress department store, a drugstore, and a bus terminal. The charge alleged their actions "would foreseeably disturb or alarm the public." The students were found guilty and given thirty-day jail terms and hundred-dollar fines. The convictions were upheld by Louisiana's supreme court. NAACP lawyers Marshall, Jack Greenberg, A. P. Tureaud, and Johnnie A. Jones appeared before the Supreme Court on December 31, 1962. Marshall headed the team and wrote the brief, and Greenberg argued the case.

Marshall's brief contended the state court's decision affirming the convictions was not based on evidence of guilt and therefore conflicted with recent Supreme Court decisions. He said the students were neatly dressed and quiet, that no one was "disturbed or alarmed," and that there was no disorder. Furthermore, he contended, the students were convicted under a state law that was "vague and indefinite." In conclusion Marshall argued that "disturbing the peace" statutes could not be used to enforce racial segregation in public facilities: "The lower court's decision, if allowed to stand, would be completely subversive of the numerous decisions throughout the federal judiciary outlawing state-enforced racial distinctions. Indeed, the segregation here is perhaps more insidious than that accomplished by other means, for it is not only based upon a vague statute which is enforced by the police according to their personal notions of what constitutes a violation and then sanctioned by state courts, but it suppresses freedom of expression as well."

The Supreme Court reversed the convictions of all defendants. Chief Justice Earl Warren, writing for the majority, said, "The undisputed evidence shows that the police...were left with nothing to support their actions except their own opinions that it was a breach of the peace for the petitioners to sit peacefully in a place where custom decreed they should not sit. Such activity...is not evidence of any crime and cannot so be considered either by the police or the courts."

The NAACP quickly took credit for winning the sit-in case, but those inside the civil rights movement knew it was Thurgood Marshall who had welded legal gradualism to the mass movement. Juanita Jackson Mitchell said, "It was Thurgood Marshall, more than anyone else, who changed the NAACP's position on Martin Luther King Jr., the sit-in movement, and direct protest action.

Even during his time in Baltimore, when we boycotted stores and walked picket lines on Pennsylvania Avenue, Thurgood was always two or three steps ahead of the established leaders."

Marshall's performances before the Supreme Court had won him respect, even from enemies of the civil rights movement; Senator Richard B. Russell, a Georgia Democrat, said Marshall exercised "an almost occult power" over the Supreme Court justices.

The NAACP had concentrated most of its civil rights efforts in the South because discrimination in the North was less extreme and less insidious. In the South the association focused on schools, voting, and public accommodations. In the North voting and public accommodations were not such pervasive problems, so the emphasis was on employment opportunities, housing, and the elimination of de facto segregation in schools caused by racial housing patterns.

The nation's first census, in 1790, reported that blacks constituted 20 percent of the population and that 90 percent of them lived in the South. At the beginning of World War I, 80 percent of the nation's blacks lived in the eleven states of the Old Confederacy, but the nation's racial geography was rapidly changing. Lured by employment opportunities in labor-short defense plants and shipyards, blacks broke the shackles that had bound them to southern sharecropping fields for generations. By 1960 nine million, or 48 percent, of the nation's black population lived in the North or the West. There were half a million blacks in Philadelphia; blacks comprised 23 percent of Chicago's population, 14 percent of New York's, and 51 percent of Washington, D.C.'s; and five hundred thousand blacks lived in the Los Angeles metropolitan area.

Racial segregation and discrimination in the middle of a free society was still a paradox in the 1960s, and the Montgomery bus boycott provided an opportunity to display the power of direct protest and ultimately brought divergent civil rights organizations together. A proliferation of protest organizations had emerged where in the past one or two had carried the burden. New leaders and different strategies gained prominence. Protest was now a symbol of social conflict and a medium through which blacks could let white America know how deeply they resented segregation and discrimination.

On August 28, 1963, 250,000 black and white Americans converged on Washington, D.C., to participate in a day of protest before the Lincoln Memorial. They came from all parts of the country to protest unemployment, police brutality, and discrimination in housing and employment and to support President John F. Kennedy's civil rights bill, then in Congress. It was the largest protest demonstration in the history of the United States. The march was the idea of A. Phillip Randolph, militant head of the Brotherhood of Sleeping Car Porters and Maids, and was organized by Bayard Rustin, former field secretary of CORE. Every black civil rights organization was represented, along with integrated organizations representing labor, churches, and civic associations.

SCLC's Martin Luther King Jr., CORE's James Farmer, the NAACP's Roy Wilkins, Randolph, and SNCC's John Lewis were the principal speakers. The march offered evidence there was support in America for an open, desegregated society. It culminated with King's historic "I Have a Dream" speech, which ended, "And when this happens...we will be able to speed up that day when all God's children, black men and white men, Jews and gentiles, Protestants and Catholics, will be able to join hands and sing the words of the old Negro spiritual, 'Free at last! Free at last! thank God Almighty, we are free at last!'"

The March on Washington brought most of the nation's civil rights organizations together. It forged a united front that was ready to abandon the jealous rivalries and disputes over techniques and tactics that had threatened to dissipate their collective energies. A breed of new leaders took their place on the civil rights battlefield with the older warriors.

SIXTEEN

A Strange Trio: Thurgood Marshall, James Eastland, and Robert Kennedy

Tell your brother...I will give him the nigger.
—Senator James O. Eastland

In 1961, Thurgood Marshall wanted Attorney General Robert F. Kennedy to recommend that the president appoint him to the U.S. Court of Appeals for the Second Circuit. Years later, he related the story of his confrontation with the attorney general to a Columbia University interviewer, speaking matter-of-factly, without any trace of the bitterness he had felt at the time:

Kennedy told him, "Well, you can't go on the Court of Appeals."

Marshall responded, "There is an opening."

Kennedy said, "But that's already filled."

Marshall replied, "So."

Instead, Kennedy offered to recommend Marshall for a U.S. district court judgeship. "You don't seem to understand," Kennedy said. "It's this or nothing."

Marshall answered, "I do understand. The trouble is that you are different from me. You don't know what it means, but all I've had in my life is nothing. It's not new to me. So good-bye." With that, Marshall walked out.

Marshall wanted nothing less than a seat on the appeals court, which he regarded as an important position.

At the time, the federal court system was comprised of eleven judicial circuits. The Second Circuit encompassed New York, Connecticut, and Vermont.

The appeals court for each circuit took appeals from the circuit's district, or trial, courts. There were nine appeals court judges for the Second Circuit. They usually sat in panels of three to hear the cases brought before them. Appeals from circuit court decisions could be taken directly to the U.S. Supreme Court, the apex of the pyramid that is the federal judiciary.

The job Kennedy offered Marshall was a step below the appeals court level. At the time of Marshall's conversation with Kennedy, there were forty-three district court judgeships in the Second Circuit alone. Appeals court judgeships were, of course, much rarer, and by 1961 only a single black, William H. Hastie, had ever been appointed to one.

Hastie had become the first black to serve in the federal judiciary when President Roosevelt named him to a district judgeship in the Virgin Islands in 1937. President Truman's appointment of Hastie to the Third Circuit, in Philadelphia, in 1949 made him the first black circuit court judge.

U.S. Supreme Court justices are commonly, but by no means exclusively, appointed from among the ranks of federal appeals court judges. When Associate Justice Charles E. Whittaker resigned in the spring of 1962, the president met in the Oval Office with his top advisers to discuss a possible replacement, and Hastie was mentioned. Kennedy had won the black vote in the 1960 election; in return for this black voter support, civil rights groups expected him to appoint African Americans to influential positions.

Presidential confidant Clark Clifford opposed naming Hastie to the High Court. He argued that while Hastie's performance on the bench was distinguished, it fell short of greatness, and he did not feel that the president should name a black just for the sake of naming a black.

After some discussion of other possible candidates, including Harvard law professor Paul Freund, Secretary of Labor Arthur Goldberg, and Texas lawyer Leon Jaworski, Kennedy decided to nominate from within his own White House circle a young assistant attorney general, Byron R. White. A former Rhodes scholar from the University of Colorado and Yale Law School, White had been a star running back for the National Football League's Pittsburgh Steelers and Detroit Lions. He seemed to personify the president's New Frontier ideal of the well-rounded, liberal scholar-athlete.

Meanwhile, despite whatever he might have said to Marshall in person, Robert Kennedy lobbied furiously to win Marshall's Second Circuit appointment. As Burke Marshall (no relation), assistant attorney general for civil rights during the Kennedy administration, noted, "Marshall was a very distinguished lawyer...and his appointment [to the federal bench] was, accordingly, meaningful in terms of the desirability of appointing the best qualified judges." Moreover, Kennedy wanted to reward Marshall for his gradualist approach to civil rights.

For Marshall, the implication of an appeals court appointment was obvious: He would be but a step away from a seat on the U.S. Supreme Court.

Ordinarily, a man of Marshall's reputation and stature would have been a welcome addition to any court. Yet it took an unsavory but necessary compromise on the part of President Kennedy and his attorney general to win the U.S. Senate's confirmation of Thurgood Marshall's first appointment to the federal bench, which in fact turned out to be the seat on the U.S. Second Circuit Court of Appeals that he wanted.

In the summer of 1962, blacks remained frustrated by the slow pace of progress toward equality. Martin Luther King Jr.'s SCLC, SNCC, and other groups, with their strategy of direct action involving boycotts, civil disobedience, nonviolent sit-ins, and mass demonstrations, had succeeded in dramatizing American racial injustice in the South and in focusing the attention of the nation and the world on it. This caused considerable embarrassment for the Kennedy administration at a time when America sought to compete effectively worldwide with Soviet communism and other repressive ideologies. At the United Nations and in other international forums, Soviet leader Nikita Khrushchev, Cuban ruler Fidel Castro, and other Communist spokesmen pointed to the racial turmoil in America as evidence of American hypocrisy in human rights.

In the mind of the president, direct action, with its cycle of escalating black demands followed by increasingly violent white backlash, threatened to rend America's tenuous social fabric. Black and white Freedom Riders were attacked and brutally beaten, their buses sometimes burned, by angry white mobs wielding ax handles, bicycle chains, and baseball bats. Local law enforcement authorities, sympathetic to the rabble, frequently stood by idly as the violence transpired or even conspired to bring it about.

Meanwhile, resistance to court-ordered desegregation gathered momentum. In Mississippi, Governor Ross Barnett resisted the efforts of a black man named James Meredith to enroll in the all-white University of Mississippi. Rioting by segregationist whites ensued. Again federal marshals were called to the scene of what was but one of dozens if not thousands of efforts to evade or defy civil rights decrees. After fewer than two years on the job, the president found himself confronted with the prospect of fighting the Civil War all over again.

Throughout the 1960 presidential campaign, John Kennedy had dramatized the plight of blacks. In Wisconsin, for example, Kennedy admonished his supporters, "The Negro baby has one-half, regardless of his talents, statistically has one-half as much chance of finishing high school as the white baby, one-third as much chance of finishing college, one-fourth as much chance of being a professional man or woman, four times as much chance of being out of work." He promised that if elected he would use the power and the prestige of the presidency to help.

At the Democrats' national convention in Los Angeles, he issued an appeal to black delegates. "My friends," he told them, "if you are sober-minded enough to believe, then—to the extent that these tasks require the support, guidance, and leadership of the president of the United States—I am bold enough to try." The black delegates responded with their support, backing Kennedy over liberal Minnesota senator Hubert Humphrey, an outspoken, long-time civil rights advocate.

On the eve of the election, Kennedy again demonstrated his commitment to black Americans. In doing so, he may have saved Martin Luther King Jr.'s life.

In October, King and thirty-six other demonstrators were arrested and charged with trespassing during a sit-in at Rich's department store in Atlanta, where when they had demanded to be served at the whites-only lunch counter. The incident occurred at a time when the city was beset with racial unrest. In fact, Mayor William B. Hartsfield had proposed a two-month period of calm, during which time he promised to review the demands of the protesters for the desegregation of Atlanta's public accommodations.

After his arrest at Rich's, King was charged by DeKalb County officials with violating the conditions of a probationary sentence he had received for a minor traffic violation the previous May. He was detained at the Fulton County Jail.

King's attorney, Donald L. Hollowell, worked feverishly to secure King's release. Hollowell was shocked when King was unexpectedly brought before DeKalb County judge Oscar Mitchell on October 25 in handcuffs and leg irons. Judge Mitchell declared that King's "trespassing" at Rich's was a violation of his probation on the traffic charge. He sentenced King to four months at hard labor and remanded him immediately to Georgia's Reidsville State Prison.

Hollowell returned to his Hunter Street office and worked through the night preparing a brief designed to prevent King from being transported to Reidsville the next morning. But when he took it to the DeKalb County courthouse shortly before 8:00 A.M., he was told that King had already been taken to Reidsville during the night. For King, it was a harrowing journey along obscure and isolated Georgia back roads where cross burnings and lynchings were not uncommon.

Hollowell, King's aides, and the King family feared that King would be murdered on the way to the prison. Hollowell was confident that he could get Judge Mitchell's ruling overturned, but he feared for King's immediate safety. Prisons in the Deep South were notoriously dangerous, and Reidsville, in rural Tatnall County, had earned a reputation for being one of the worst. King's supporters feared a lynching or some scenario in which King would be shot while allegedly trying to escape. Even without the authorities' complicity, the Baptist minister might find himself at the mercy of violent, racist inmates.

News of King's predicament spread. The White House was flooded with requests for federal intervention. Northern senators, congressmen, and governors called on President Eisenhower to order a federal investigation. In a show of unity, all the major civil rights organizations called for King's immediate release. The national elections were just a few days away.

Eisenhower drafted a statement affirming King's right to protest segregated facilities and remarking that the sentence for the traffic violation appeared unusually severe. But for some reason, the statement was never released. Meanwhile, the Republican presidential nominee, Vice President Richard M. Nixon, remained silent, fearing the loss of the southern white vote. The Democratic nominee, John Kennedy, decided to act.

One of Kennedy's Atlanta advisers, attorney Morris Abrams, suggested that Kennedy issue a statement supporting King, an idea endorsed by Kennedy's adviser on minority affairs, Harris Wofford. Then Kennedy called Coretta Scott King in Atlanta to try to allay her fears; he told her that he understood that she was worried about her husband's safety and that he shared that concern and wanted to help. Next, Robert F. Kennedy, who was his brother's campaign manager, called Judge Mitchell. The following day, October 27, Mitchell agreed to King's release.

News of Kennedy's phone call to Coretta Scott King spread quickly across the nation. CBS and NBC chartered small planes and flew correspondents and camera personnel to Reidsville to cover King's release. At a press conference held in front of the prison, the voice of a black inmate rang out from inside the walls: "Long live the King!"

Later that day Hollowell received a telephone call from Thurgood Marshall. Marshall kidded him, "Say, Hollowell, they tell me that everybody got King out of jail but the lawyers." He told Hollowell that the NAACP would pay the legal expenses arising from the Rich's sit-in and King's alleged probation violation.

King expressed his gratitude for Kennedy's efforts: "I am deeply indebted to Senator Kennedy, who served as a great force in making my release possible. It took a lot of courage for Senator Kennedy to do this, especially in Georgia....He did it because of his great concern and humanitarian bent." King's father was grateful as well. A lifelong Republican because a Republican president freed the slaves, he promised to deliver Kennedy a "basketful of votes."

On election night black voters demonstrated their appreciation and affection at the polls, thereby guaranteeing Kennedy's election. Black support helped put Illinois, Michigan, Texas, South Carolina, and arguably Louisiana into Kennedy's electoral vote column. Without some combination of these states, Kennedy would not have won what turned out to be the closest presidential race in U.S. history, with the two candidates separated by a slim 112,881 popular-vote margin. John F. Kennedy owed African Americans a political debt.

The day he was inaugurated was one of the happiest days in the history of black America. It was also one of the most bitterly cold January days in memory. But the sky was clear, and sunlight bathed the east front of the capitol. The nation's leaders—senators, congressmen, the nine justices of the Supreme court, the ranking members of the military and civilian departments of government—were assembled in top hats and tails to observe an occasion fraught with symbolism. The oldest man ever to serve as president was departing; the youngest man ever elected to the office was about to assume it. In his inaugural address, Kennedy stated: "The torch has been passed to a new generation of Americans—born in this century, tempered by war, disciplined by a hard and bitter peace, proud of our ancient heritage, and unwilling to witness or permit the slow undoing of those human rights to which this nation has always been committed, and to which we are committed today at home and around the world."

The energy, the vitality, the devotion, with which this new generation would set about the task of defending freedom would "light our country and all who serve it," he vowed. And, he promised, "The light from that fire can truly light the world."

For blacks Kennedy's message offered hope that America would break with the discriminatory practices of the past and adhere to the nation's ideals: justice, freedom, equality for all, life, liberty, property, and the pursuit of happiness. Almost a century had elapsed since the post-Civil War amendments to the Constitution bestowed full citizenship upon the eighteen million Americans of African descent whose forebears were emancipated by Lincoln. But on the frigid January day on which John Kennedy became the thirty-fifth president, there were few blacks among the assembled dignitaries: no black senators, no black cabinet officers, no black Supreme Court Justices. African Americans were not even conspicuous by their absence from the ranks of the powerful.

It was a fact of life: Racial inequality permeated American society at every level, from the rural South to the teeming ghettos of the great northern cities. Thurgood Marshall had indeed won *Brown v. Board of Education*. Segregation violated the law of the land. In custom and in practice, however, segregation was the rule—in housing, in the workplace, and in education. In the South blacks were routinely denied the right to vote, as well as access to public facilities and accommodations. Violence and coercion against blacks were common, and commonly unpunished.

A lot was expected and demanded. In an article for the *Nation* that appeared soon after the president's inaugural, Martin Luther King, Jr., called for "really far-reaching" progress in civil rights, including the passage of a major civil rights bill. As a practical matter, however, Kennedy regarded this as an impossibility. Like every American president since Reconstruction, Kennedy was forced to confront the power and influence of southerners in the Congress, where the actual work was done in powerful committees whose chairmen, chosen on the basis of seniority, in effect set Congress's legislative priorities. Because they controlled key committees, southern senators and congressmen hostile to civil rights had the power not only to block specific civil rights legislation but also to undermine the president's entire legislative agenda.

Kennedy was frank with King about political realities. He warned that efforts to get a civil rights bill through Congress might prove counterproductive: "If we go into a long fight in Congress, it will bottleneck everything else, and still get no [civil rights] bill." By "everything else" Kennedy meant legislative items, such as the increased minimum wage and federal aid to education, that were not directly related to civil rights but considered of great importance to blacks.

For much the same reason, Kennedy balked at King's demand that the president fulfill his campaign pledge to "give segregation its death blow through the stroke of a pen" by issuing executive orders banning discrimination in the award of federal contracts, in federally financed housing, in hiring on federally supported hospital and highway construction, and more.

Nevertheless, Kennedy was aware of the political debt he owed the nation's blacks. He also knew that the civil rights movement represented an awakening of the minds and spirits of African Americans that could not be ignored or reversed. Besides, both he and his attorney general were men who operated on the basis of moral imperatives, not just political expedients. They believed deeply that, at a minimum, every American is entitled to expect that his or her rights will be protected and enforced. As attorney general, the nation's top law enforcement officer in charge of the federal government's law enforcement apparatus, including the FBI, Robert Kennedy was the administration's point man on civil rights. Even in the enforcement and execution of those laws already in effect, he would find his power wanting.

On the surface there was little indication that Robert Kennedy had much familiarity with, or concern for, civil rights or the black American predicament. He confided as much to his biographer Arthur M. Schlesinger Jr., admitting, "I won't say I stayed awake nights worrying about civil rights before I became attorney general." During the early 1950s, Kennedy focused his energy on rooting Communist influences out of the government, serving as special counsel to Senator Joseph McCarthy's Senate Investigative

Committee on Un-American Activities. Later in the decade, he turned his attention to organized crime, earning a reputation for ruthlessness as the crime-busting chief counsel to the Senate rackets committee. He played a major role in exposing Mafia influence in the organized labor movement, especially within the United Brotherhood of Teamsters; its president, Jimmy Hoffa, became one of his most celebrated antagonists.

Besides, Robert Kennedy was skeptical about the feasibility of creating brotherhood by government fiat, demanding racial tolerance at the point of a gun. He told Schlesinger, "People have grown up with totally different backgrounds and mores, which we can't change overnight." In time, he believed, blacks would simply be absorbed into the melting pot like other ethnic groups, including his own Irish. Whatever might have been his initial instincts or predilections, however, he expressed to Schlesinger soon after his appointment his "fundamental belief that all people are created equal." From that he said, "it follows that integration should take place today everywhere." The challenge was how to bring integration about.

First, Kennedy realized that he would have to overcome obstacles that existed within the very Department of Justice that he headed. The department was, quite simply, not geared up to go to war for civil rights. Zealous litigation on behalf of blacks denied the right to vote, or against school systems that continued to discriminate, would be essential. So would leading by example. Yet out of almost one thousand Justice Department lawyers based in Washington, only ten were African Americans.

Moreover, FBI director J. Edgar Hoover was outright hostile to civil rights. This partially explained why there were no black FBI agents by 1961. Recruiting black agents was crucial to investigating civil rights violations in the South. Southern blacks feared local white law enforcement officials because many of them were sympathetic to the Klan. For the same reason, blacks were reluctant to share information with white FBI agents, especially since they knew that those agents cooperated frequently with local officials.

Getting Hoover to agree to make changes presented its own peculiar set of problems. Hoover disliked the Kennedy brothers as much as he disliked their civil rights policies. He undercut the attorney general's credibility by questioning his qualifications. He once remarked sarcastically that Kennedy was well equipped to be the nation's top lawyer: He had never practiced law or tried a case in court. When Bobby Kennedy sought Hoover's advice about whether to accept the appointment, Hoover remarked dryly that being attorney general was a good job and, since it was offered, he should take it. Later it became standard practice for tour guides at the FBI Building in Washington to inform visitors that J. Edgar Hoover's tenure as FBI director began in 1924, a year before the attorney general, Hoover's ostensible superior, was even born.

At the same time, however, firing Hoover was out of the question. Members of the Kennedy family, including the new president, had been subjects of FBI surveillance. As a result, Hoover possessed incriminating information that, if made public, would cause considerable embarrassment for the nation and the Kennedy family. It was insinuated that John Kennedy, before he became president, had had affairs with actress Marilyn Monroe and Judith Campbell, whose other lovers included entertainer Frank Sinatra and Sam "Mo Mo' Giancana, a Chicago mobster.

Besides, civil rights was not the only item on Robert Kennedy's personal agenda. He realized that he would need Hoover's experience, credibility, and connections in order to achieve his declared, immediate, and overriding national law enforcement objective: the infiltration and subversion of the Mafia in America.

Second, the extent to which federal marshals could be used to protect civil rights activists from vigilante violence in the South was limited. Marshals were often little more than deputized citizens, ill equipped and untrained for the sheer numbers and violence of the southern mobs. The president could federalize the national guard, but beyond a point the loyalty of local guardsmen could not be guaranteed. At the extreme was the option of calling out the U.S. Army and imposing martial law. But that would be tantamount to fighting the Civil War all over again, and one could argue that by the end of Reconstruction the outcome of the first Civil War had at best yielded mixed results.

It was clear that the entire federal law enforcement apparatus needed to be reformed. What was called for in the face of massive southern resistance was in effect a national police force, which did not exist and would, even if it did, be suspect from a constitutional standpoint. Even legal scholars as committed to civil rights as Thurgood Marshall conceded this point. "The law is quite clear that the federal government is not the policing authority," Marshall admitted. "That...some of us can understand, but the average layman cannot understand it."

Eventually the attorney general and his advisers concluded that the best solution to the civil rights problem in the South was to guarantee the voting rights of African-American citizens. Through the vote blacks could exercise a considerable degree of power over their own destinies by electing officials who would use the power of the state to expand and enforce, rather than limit or altogether deny, their freedom. The Justice Department during the Kennedy years in fact undertook an unprecedented amount of litigation to ensure voting rights enforcement.

Until change could be secured through the ballot box, the president would have to take whatever measures he could to improve the lives of blacks. Foremost among these, the attorney general recommended, should be the appointment of judges sympathetic to the need to protect the rights and physical safety of all American citizens. Certainly the courts had made a positive difference for blacks. While the Congress had failed to enact sweeping civil rights legislation and while presidents had been personally hostile to civil rights or restricted in their options, the courts had responded. As the efforts and successes of Thurgood Marshall and other advocates demonstrated over the years, the courts could serve as an effective force for social change in America.

For these reasons, Robert Kennedy recommended Thurgood Marshall's appointment to the Second Circuit Court of Appeals. What could send a better message to the president's black supporters than the appointment of such a fine civil rights lawyer to the federal bench? In addition, there were few, if any, stronger messages that the president could send to those who opposed his commitment to civil rights. As Burke Marshall later put it, the nomination was indeed "symbolic in a very important and useful way."

Nevertheless, the appointment of a single black judge, even if he were to become only the second black ever named to a U.S. court of appeals, seemed like a token gesture. Privately some of Marshall's supporters wondered whether he would be able to advance the cause of black equality from the bench as effectively as he had as a lawyer.

Marshall himself had mixed feelings about the move. "I had to fight it out with myself," he admitted. "But then I knew I had built up a staff—a damned good staff—an excellent board, and the backing that would let them go ahead. And when one has the opportunity to serve his government, he should think twice before passing it up." He went on, "I've always felt the assault troops never occupy the town. I figured after the school decisions, the assault was over for me. it was time to let newer minds take over."

What stood between the president and Marshall's appointment was a Mississippi senator, James O. Eastland.

Eastland was a senior Democrat who since 1956 had chaired the Senate's Judiciary Committee, to which all judicial appointments, as well as all civil rights legislation, were referred. Through his use of that position, Eastland came to personify the southern political establishment's irrevocable hostility to black advancement. "What are the two southernmost points in the United States?" pundits asked rhetorically. "Key West, Florida, and James O. Eastland."

A wealthy landowner, Eastland was from the Mississippi Delta's Sunflower County, which boasted the registration of less than 3 percent of its eligible black voters. The county had become the focus of the nation's attention a few years earlier as the result of Emmett Till's being lynched there.

Eastland himself indulged in the most rudimentary race baiting. He charged that the NAACP was Communist oriented and backed by organizations "of all shades of red, the blood red of the Communist party." During a reelection campaign, he bragged that as chairman of the Senate Judiciary Committee's Subcommittee on Civil Rights he had bottled up 127 pieces of civil rights legislation. "Not one [of those bills] ever emerged" to go before the full committee and Senate, he told his supporters. *Time* magazine called Eastland the "nation's most dangerous demagogue." Clarence Mitchell, an NAACP leader, branded him a "mad dog loose in the streets of justice."

The young attorney general was surprised to find the Mississippian in a conciliatory mood on the subject of Marshall's appointment when he discussed it with him early in the Kennedy administration. Eastland signaled that he might be amenable to a deal. If the president appointed Eastland's college roommate Harold Cox to a recently vacated district judgeship in the South, in the Fifth Circuit, where most of the civil rights "agitation" was occurring, Eastland would allow the Marshall nomination to go to a full committee vote. Later, when Eastland met with Robert Kennedy, he told him, "Tell your brother that if he will give me Harold Cox, I will give him the nigger."

Kennedy agreed. Harold Cox of Mississippi became the president's first nominee to the federal bench. Shortly thereafter, on September 23, 1961, the president forwarded Marshall's nomination to the U.S. Senate. Despite his promise, Eastland maneuvered to keep the Marshall nomination form coming to a committee vote for almost a year. In the interim the president gave him a recess appointment.

The hearings conducted by the Judiciary Committee's Subcommittee on Nominations dragged on over the course of six days, scattered throughout May, July, and August in the spring and sweltering summer of 1962. Marshall found himself subjected to a grilling by southern senators and committee counsel L. P. B. Lipscomb. The legitimacy of the Fund's tax-exempt status was called into question. Marshall himself was charged with violating the American Bar Association's Code of Professional Responsibility by soliciting clients for desegregation cases. He also came under attack for his alleged involvement with the Lawyer's Guild, which was backed by the Communist party, and for alleged Communist influence within the NAACP.

The dramatic high point of the hearings came when Lipscomb challenged Marshall's handling of the five questions posed by the Supreme Court at the end of the first round of oral arguments in

Brown in 1953. Lipscomb based his accusations on a paper delivered by Professor Alfred H. Kelly of Wayne State University at the annual meeting of the American Historical Association in Washington, D.C., in December 1961.

In his paper, "An Inside View of *Brown versus Board*," Kelly set out his account of the summer he and scores of other noted historians and academicians worked with Marshall and other Fund lawyers helping to frame the NAACP's answer to the five questions, which related to the intention of the framers of the Fourteenth Amendment. Kelly wrote:

"I was trying to be both historian and advocate...and the combination, as I found out, was not a very good one. I tried to draw conclusions which were at odds with the thing which most impressed me at the time—the damning modifications of the civil rights bill in the House and its apparent identity in purpose with the Fourteenth Amendment. I was facing for the first time in my own career the deadly opposition between my professional integrity as a historian and my wishes and hopes with respect to a contemporary question of values, of ideals, of policy, of partisanship, and of political objectives. I suppose if a man is without scruple this matter will not bother him, but I am frank to say that it bothered me terribly."

Lipscomb's goal was clearly to cast doubt on the integrity of the work that was the basis for the NAACP's brief. He also tried to use Kelly's paper to raise doubts about Marshall's character and his personally held views of whites. He implied that Marshall was a racist. He directed the subcommittee's attention to a section of Kelly's paper that described Marshall's personality:

"The sudden shifts of mood he displayed on occasion were nothing short of astonishing. One morning in his office, he related to John Hope Franklin of Yale and myself, with tears in his eyes and a voice dulled with the cumulative grief of three hundred years, the experiment of a leading sociologist with a group of little colored girls, who were given their choice of playing with two sets of dolls, one white or Caucasian, one black or Negro. Even at three years of age, he said, the little colored girls preferred the white dolls, describing the black dolls as 'bad' and 'not nice' and the white dolls as 'pretty' and 'good.'"

"As Marshall told the story, he seemed bowed down under an unbearable burden of tragedy.

"Sometimes Marshall could reveal a mood of sudden savagery and bitterness. Customarily he referred to the Mason and Dixon line as 'the Smith and Wesson line.'

"On one occasion he read with savage delight from an Iowa frontier paper which portrayed a local Negro community as a mass of illiterate apes. For him, he made clear, this epitomized the white man's attitude toward his people.

"On still another occasion at an evening session at which I found myself playing devil's advocate with a bit too much enthusiasm and lack of tact, Marshall stopped suddenly and speaking into the growing silence around the table said:

"'Alfred, you are one of us here and I like you. But'—and this in a voice of terrible intensity—'I want you to understand that when us colored folks take over, every time a white man draws a breath, he'll have to pay a fine.'"

When Lipscomb finished reading the passage he paused a beat, then looked across at Marshall and asked, "Is it still your conviction that when the colored folks take over that every time a white man draws a breath he will have to pay a fine?"

Marshall responded, "That has never been my conviction, is not now and never will be."

When asked whether Kelly had misquoted him, Marshall replied, "I am certain he has on that point."

Subcommittee chairman Olin D. Johnston of South Carolina, who was opposed to the nomination, requested that Kelly be called to testify in person. The hearings were then adjourned until Kelly could be located and brought to Washington.

It had been almost a decade since Kelly and Marshall had met. During that time, the historian had lost none of his admiration for the man he helped win *Brown*. Kelly opened his testimony before the subcommittee with a ten-minute statement that immediately dashed any hopes the segregationists might have had of finding in him a willing and supportive ally.

"First," he began, "let me emphasize very strongly my firm belief in the integrity, honor, and decency of Judge Thurgood Marshall." He went on, "It is my opinion that he is a man of the highest professional standards and ideals and that he is a credit to the American bar and to the federal judiciary."

Next, Kelly defended the NAACP's interpretation of the Fourteenth Amendment's legislative history. He stated, "The argument in the brief was not history; it was advocacy. It was, in short, a lawyer's brief...This does not mean that the brief falsified facts, that it lied, or even that it necessarily reached false conclusions. Within a large sense, most Reconstruction historians believe it did not... The important thing here is that within the ethics of the legal profession, Thurgood Marshall's professional obligations required him to handle his available evidence in this fashion...Again, he was functioning as an advocate, not as a historian."

Kelly added, "It may be worthwhile to observe, by the way, that the brief prepared by the late John W. Davis for the respondents in *Brown v. Board* is, from a technical historical point of view, every bit as far from a balanced constitutional history of Reconstruction as is the NAACP brief. Again, Mr. Davis's brief was not history; it was advocacy. Yet no one has indicted him for having argued his case adequately for his clients. No doubt he would have been open to a charge of professional dereliction and malpractice had he done otherwise."

Kelly dispelled the notion that Marshall harbored racist sentiments. He testified that he did indeed recall Marshall saying that "when we colored folks take over, every time a white man draws a breath he'll have to pay a fine." But he insisted the remark was "mordant humor, given exclamation by a man possessed of a powerful sense of humor, and who expresses something of the excitement of verbal exchange in humorous hyperbole of this kind." He assured the subcommittee, "To lift the remark out of context and treat it as a threat or even a philosophical observation is absurd, even grotesque, in its bizarre distortion of reality."

Asked about Marshall's feelings about communism, Kelly said, "I have...heard Marshall express personally his powerful conviction that communism and Marxism are fatal pitfalls for the American Negro which must be avoided like the plague....On more than one occasion Marshall in my presence bespoke his intense conviction that the destiny of the American Negro is to be fulfilled in terms of the American constitutional system. What he wanted for the Negro, he made clear, was first-class citizenship. I have heard him say, 'We want no more; we will not take less.'"

In conclusion Kelly stated, "It is my conviction that Thurgood Marshall's victory in *Brown v. Board*, consistent as it was with the highest ethics of the legal profession, has already earned him a permanent position of honor in American history. And as a constitutional historian, I believe strongly that in his new capacity as a federal judge, he will prove to be an outstanding and preeminent judicial figure."

The Judiciary Committee passed Marshall's nomination on to the full Senate without recommendation. On September 11, 1962, he was confirmed for the Second Circuit seat by a vote of fifty-four to sixteen. The deal was complete. Eastland got Cox; Kennedy got Marshall.

Cox proved to be one of President Kennedy's most embarrassing judicial appointments. The man was a racist, and an injudicious one at that. He complained bitterly when the Justice Department brought suit to defend blacks' voting rights. From the bench on one occasion, he called black litigants in a voting rights matter "a bunch of niggers...acting like a bunch of chimpanzees." Cox turned out to be what Roy Wilkins predicted at the time of his nomination: "Another strand in the barbed-wire fence of Negro Mississippians, another cross over their weary shoulders, and another rock in the road up which their young people must struggle." No judge was ever overruled more on appeal of civil rights cases than Harold Cox of Mississippi.

By contrast, Thurgood Marshall found himself in the judicial mainstream on the U.S. Second Circuit Court of Appeals in New York City. During his four-year tenure, he wrote ninety-eight majority opinions, none of which was reversed by the U.S. Supreme Court, and contributed eight concurrences. He wrote only twelve dissents.

In one case, *United States v. Wilkins*, he broke new ground regarding double jeopardy, protecting criminal defendants from being tried more than once for essentially the same crime. Marshall's opinion held that the Fifth Amendment protection against repeated prosecutions at the federal level also applied to the states by virtue of the Fourteenth Amendment's guarantee of due process. In *United States v. Denno*, Marshall concurred in the trial court's ruling that an accused's lawyer should have been present in the hospital room where the defendant was taken to be identified by a crime victim. Subsequently, in *Stovall v. Denno*, the Supreme Court adopted the position taken by Marshall.

Several other cases indicate Marshall's emerging liberal perspective. In *Keyishian v. Board of Regents of the University of the State of New York*, he wrote for the majority that New York Laws requiring members of the state university's faculty to sign loyalty oaths raised significant questions under the U.S. Constitution. The Supreme Court agreed and struck the laws down, ruling that they violated the First Amendment by unnecessarily restricting free speech and vital thought.

In *People of the State of New York v. Galamison*, Second Circuit judges found themselves confronted with the kind of case that cut close to Marshall's heart. Galamison and about fifty others were arrested and prosecuted under a number of laws for disrupting road and subway access to the New York World's Fair. Their objective, according to their attorney William Kuntsler, was to protest "the denial of equal protection of the laws to Negroes in the City, State and Nation with reference to housing, education, employment, police action and other areas of local and national life too numerous to mention." A majority of the court upheld the protesters' convictions.

Marshall wrote a lengthy dissent arguing that since the protesters were challenging the denial of rights provided by law, they were in effect acting under the color of the law's authority. He was careful to draw a distinction between peaceful protest and criminal conduct:

"For example, if the petitioners arrested and prosecuted for violating the truancy law had merely sought to induce parents not to send their children to a segregated school which denies the 'equality of law' guaranteed by the Constitution, this in my opinion could be [protected activity] while, on the other hand, a charge of third degree assault might very well not be covered."

He also insisted that each demonstrator should have been given a separate hearing to determine the demonstrator's motivations.

This would have imposed a substantial burden on the court system and thereby discouraged prosecution.

But it cannot be said that he unwaveringly followed a liberal line. A common generalization about liberal jurists is that they are sensitive to the rights of the minority when those rights conflict with the majority's will. Naturally, Marshall was sensitive to civil rights issues, yet he did not always side with minorities against the government.

For example, in *Seneca Nation of Indians v. United States*, he upheld the government's power to condemn land on an Indian reservation for the Allegheny Reservoir Project. At issue was the secretary of the army's decision to widen a road through Seneca territory. Writing for the court's majority, Marshall stated simply, "It is hard to see how a four-lane road will interfere with communication among the Senecas so much more than a two-lane road." In dissent, Judge Moore pointed out that the land was given to the Senecas by treaty and declared, quoting Justice Hugo Black, "Great nations, like great men, should keep their word."

Another common characterization of liberals is that they are quick to uphold criminal defendants' rights. This was true of Marshall, who knew firsthand that in the South "uppity" blacks were routinely harassed or scapegoated by law enforcement authorities. In *United States v. Fay*, he argued in dissent that the Supreme Court ruling prohibiting the use of illegally seized evidence in criminal prosecutions should be applied retroactively. This would have made anyone convicted with illegally seized evidence eligible for a new trial. The Supreme Court ultimately rejected Marshall's view, concluding that opening up past convictions to challenge would "tax the administration of justice to the utmost."

His concern about the government using its power to violate the rights or privacy of individuals did not necessarily extend beyond the criminal justice arena, however. In *United states v. Rickenbacker*, he upheld the conviction of a man who refused to provide census data, dismissing the appellant's claim that a 1960 census questionnaire constituted "an unnecessary invasion of my privacy." Instead, he concluded, "The authority to gather reliable statistical data reasonably related to governmental purposes and functions is a necessity if modern government is to legislate intelligently and effectively."

Overall, his Second Circuit performance managed to silence, for the most part, critics who claimed that, because his expertise as a lawyer was in civil rights litigation, he lacked sufficient familiarity with other fields of law to function effectively as a judge. Writing for the *New York Times Magazine*, columnist Sidney Zion noted, "In some of the early tax cases Thurgood's lack of knowledge was embarrassing. I recall one case where a question he asked indicated that he didn't even understand the *concept* of a corporation. It was not a nice moment for anyone in the courtroom."

Newsweek praised him, however, for broadening his academic scope "to fill in the blanks from tax law to admiralty law." In *Mertens v. Flying Tiger Line, Inc.*, for example, his majority opinion maneuvered deftly through the intricacies of international law, allowing survivors of an international airplane crash to collect more damages than they would otherwise have been allowed under the Warsaw Convention. Summing up his Second Circuit tenure, *Newsweek* concluded that Marshall "acquitted himself well enough."

Well enough for what? The answer came on a humid afternoon in July 1965 when a lunch with friends was interrupted by a phone call from President Lyndon Baines Johnson.

SEVENTEEN

Solicitor General, a Position of Power

If Martin Luther King wants to catch up with
me, he has to get up early and march fast.
—President Lyndon Johnson

On the evening of Friday, July 2, 1965, President Lyndon Baines Johnson's wife, Lady Bird, made an entry in her personal diary. "Lyndon admires Thurgood Marshall and spoke [today] of the possibility of asking him to be solicitor general, and if he proved himself outstanding, perhaps when a vacancy on the Supreme Court opened up he might nominate him as a justice—the first of his race."

Ten days later, on Monday, July 12, Marshall's law clerk anxiously interrupted him during lunch with friends in a New York City restaurant to tell him the president had called.

"The president of what?" Marshall barked, annoyed.

The clerk said President Johnson had phoned a few minutes earlier and wanted Marshall to return his call. Marshall leisurely finished his lunch, returned to his chambers in the U.S. appeals court, and called the White House. The president told Marshall he

244

wanted him to become the thirty-third solicitor general of the United States. He would replace Archibald Cox, who had resigned to join the Harvard Law School faculty.

The decision Thurgood Marshall faced created a profound personal dilemma. If Marshall gave up his U.S. appeals court judgeship to become the nation's top-ranking courtroom advocate, it would mean a reduction of his annual salary from $33,000 to $28,500. Perhaps more important, as the fifty-seven-year-old father of two sons not yet teenagers, he would have to relinquish the comfortable security of a lifetime federal judgeship to serve at the pleasure of a president who might not seek a second term.

"I told Cissy that it would call for some belt tightening, that it might mean she couldn't get a new dress for a year, and all she said was 'So?'" Marshall confided to his friend, Ted Poston. "I told the boys they would have to cut back, too, but all they asked was if they would get to see me in court with my cutaway."

Marshall's decision would also affect every other black American. Marshall's acceptance of President Johnson's offer would again put their own advocate on the front lines of the civil rights battle, this time in a powerful position to ensure compliance with emerging civil rights legislation. There would be an important collateral benefit, too: direct access on their behalf to the president of the United States.

The solicitor general is the nation's only public official, including Supreme Court justices and the attorney general, required by statute to be "learned in the law." Congress created the Justice Department on June 22, 1870, and provided that "there shall be...an officer learned in the law, to assist the attorney general in the performance of his duties, to be called the solicitor general." The legislation was introduced by Republican congressman Thomas Jenckes of Rhode Island, who wrote, "We propose to have a man sufficient of learning, ability and experience that he can be sent to New Orleans, or to New York, or into any court wherever the government has any interest in litigation, and there present the case of the United States as it should be presented."

The solicitor general has offices in the Department of Justice but also maintains a chamber in the Supreme Court. He or she argues the government's cases before the Court and also executes an influential behind-the scenes role in helping the Court decide what cases it will hear and how those issues will be framed for discussion. The Court relies heavily on the solicitor general for the accurate presentation of facts and legal issues. This dual responsibility prompted Justice Lewis Powell to tell author Lewis Kaplan in 1987 that he considered the solicitor general to be the Court's "tenth justice."

The Twenty-fourth Amendment, ratified in 1964, prohibited poll taxes in national elections, but some southern states and their municipalities still found guileful ways to circumvent the anti–poll tax laws. This was particularly evident in Alabama, Mississippi, and Virginia. Since 1957, Congress had taken a more active role in guaranteeing the political and civil rights of black people and other minorities. Thurgood Marshall's civil rights career had been a testimony to those changing legislative attitudes and the restructuring of crucial local political power bases that put those guarantees in place. The Civil Rights Acts of 1957, 1960, and especially 1964 were important legal instruments in the continuing struggle for equality, but they were only as strong as the government's will to enforce them. The responsibility for enforcement rested with the Justice Department and its five thousand lawyers under Attorney General Nicholas B. Katzenbach, including the department's Civil Rights Division, headed by Assistant Attorney General Burke Marshall.

The previous July, President Johnson had signed the nation's most comprehensive civil rights bill, the Civil Rights Act of 1964. It prohibited job discrimination by employers and labor unions with more than twenty-five workers or members on the basis of race, sex, or religion. It gave the Justice Department authority to bring school desegregation suits and to eliminate racial segregation and discrimination in all programs receiving federal funds. The act's most controversial section, Title II, banned racial discrimination in public accommodations engaged in interstate commerce: hotels, motels, restaurants, service stations, bus and train terminals, and places of entertainment.

Civil rights activists put Title II to the test and in most instances found a moderate amount of compliance. But on Forsyth Street in the heart of Atlanta, Georgia's soon-to-be-governor Lester Maddox stood with a pistol in his hand in the doorway of his Pickwick restaurant chasing away students from the city's black colleges. Maddox sold autographed ax handles attached to small Confederate flags to white patrons and encouraged their use if blacks attempted to enter his restaurant. Ironically, on Saturday nights white patrons flocked to the black-owned Pascals' restaurant and its adjoining Carousel jazz nightclub on West Hunter Street. They came to eat a more succulent version of southern fried chicken than the "skillet chicken" Maddox served at his Pickwick. They would sit at the Carousel's round bar and listen to jazz saxophonist Lou Donaldson play "Funky Momma." Or they might hear Roland Kirk, Billy Taylor, Lloyd McNeil, or a new young singer from Atlanta's Westside, Gladys Knight.

Title II met some resistance, and in two major cases Katzenbach responded successfully on behalf of the Johnson administration. In *Heart of Atlanta Motel, Inc. v. United States* and *Katzenbach v. McClung*, the Supreme Court said businesses that offer public accommodations and are engaged in interstate commerce must end their discriminatory practices.

It was clear the Johnson administration intended to enforce civil rights legislation rigorously, which Thurgood Marshall understood and appreciated.

Cissy Marshall packed Thurgood's overnight bag, and on Tuesday morning, July 13, 1965, he left his wife and two sons in their seventeenth-floor cooperative apartment in Morningside Gardens on Harlem's West 123rd Street. He was on his way to the White House, where he told President Johnson that he had discussed the nomination with his "chief adviser," Cissy, and that they had agreed he was ready to become the nation's first African-American solicitor general.

When a reporter asked why he was leaving the security of a federal judgeship, Marshall answered, "Because the president asked me to." Then he added, "I believe that in this time especially, we do what our government requests of us. Negroes have made great advancements in government, and I think it is time they started making some sacrifices." Marshall gave old friends Sterling Brown, Wiley Branton, and John P. Davis a different version of his decision to accept the nomination: "I was reluctant at first, but when the president was through with me I was ashamed I hadn't volunteered."

When reporters asked President Johnson his reason for nominating Marshall, he said, "I want the world to know that when the United States government speaks it does so through the voice of a Negro." Johnson, like Marshall, had his private version of Thurgood's nomination. He told close associates, "I want folks at the Justice Department to walk down the hall and see a nigger sitting there."

There was public conjecture that President Johnson had already decided to appoint Marshall to the next Supreme Court vacancy and had named him solicitor general to increase his national visibility, smoothing the path for that step. Johnson never admitted, and Marshall has always denied, such an agreement. "We made no promises, we didn't even discuss that," Marshall insisted. "And I can tell you, it just isn't in the cards." Lady Bird Johnson's July 2 diary entry, however, shows that the idea had at least already crossed her husband's mind.

When Marshall was asked if he had an interest in eventually sitting on the Supreme Court, he brusquely told the Associated Press, "Please, one job at a time." In a subdued aside he added, "There's not a lawyer in the country who wouldn't snap at the chance."

To most black Americans, Lyndon Johnson had become a president whose positive actions spoke louder than his sometimes unfortunate words. He said "nigger," and he could be patronizing, as when he commented during a 1964 campaign trip to his native Texas: "When I get out of that car you can just see them light up and feel the warmth coming up at you.... Those Negroes go off the ground. They cling to my hands like I was Jesus Christ walking in their midst."

The hope African Americans held for a place on the New Frontier died in Dallas in 1963 with the assassination of John F. Kennedy. Now black Americans looked to President Johnson, if not for Christian salvation, at least for a pew of dignity, respect, and equality in his promised Great Society. In a May 1964 speech, Johnson described his vision for the country: "The Great Society rests on abundance and liberty for all. It demands an end to poverty and racial injustice, to which we are totally committed in our time."

African-American novelist Ralph Ellison said of Johnson's civil rights record: "When all the returns are in, perhaps President Johnson will have to settle for being recognized as the greatest American president for the poor and for the Negro, but that, as I see it, is a very great honor indeed."

Lyndon Johnson was proud of his efforts to create equality for black Americans. On the July day Lady Bird Johnson recorded his remarks about Marshall in her diary, she also noted this reflection of her husband's view of his contribution to the nation's racial progress: "Lyndon said, 'If Martin Luther King wants to catch up with me, he has to get up early and march fast.'"

Marshall's appointment as solicitor general came at a time when black America's moderate old guard, including the National Urban League and the NAACP, had been challenged by an emerging younger and more aggressive group of black leaders and organizations. Dr. Martin Luther King Jr. and his SCLC had moved the fight for civil rights from the subdued world of the courtroom to the mean streets of white America. Their tactics of nonviolence and civil disobedience were met with beatings, bombings, and murders. Voter registration drives, lunch-counter sit-ins, and other protest demonstrations unleashed a virulent white backlash not only in southern cities but in western and northern ones as well.

The "black power" voices of even more militant leaders, such as H. Rap Brown and Stokely Carmichael of SNCC and CORE's Floyd McKissick, were rising, urging even swifter redress for racial injustices.

And black nationalists, with their perspective of separateness, were urging African Americans to halt their efforts to integrate the country. Thurgood Marshall had learned several years earlier to take their desire for separateness in stride. During an ugly confrontation in the early 1960s, Black Muslims called him a "half white son of a bitch" because he was a staunch advocate of integration. Marshall said that he met Black Muslim leader

Malcolm X one rainy night on the corner of New York's 125th Street and Amsterdam Avenue. Some months later "we spent the whole time calling each other a bunch of sons of bitches."

After Marshall was threatened by several Black Muslims on a Harlem street corner in 1960, New York City police commissioner Stephen P. Kennedy came to Marshall's apartment and offered him a snub-nosed .38 caliber Smith & Wesson revolver. "I turned it down," Marshall said. In 1991 Marshall still held no brief for the late Muslim leader. "I still see no reason to say he [Malcolm X] is a 'great person, a great Negro,' and I ask a simple question. What did he ever do? Name me one concrete thing he ever did."

The legal ramifications of the racial violence that spread across the nation the year Thurgood Marshall became solicitor general consumed much of his time. On March 7, 1965, more than two hundred Alabama state troopers with nightsticks, whips, tear gas, and dogs assaulted demonstrators, led by Dr. Martin Luther King Jr., marching from Selma to the state capital in Montgomery. For a month the black citizens of Selma had tried to exercise their basic constitutional right to vote. They were turned away by registrars, and more than two thousand prospective voters were arrested in demonstrations and registration lines.

President Johnson met with Alabama governor George Wallace, but Wallace would not agree to Johnson's request to let the marchers continue their protest peacefully under police protection. They went ahead along the red-dust roads to Montgomery, anyway, now joined by several movie stars, singer Harry Belafonte, and UN undersecretary Ralph Bunche. Wallace accused the federal judge who approved the march of "prostituting our law in favor of mob rule while hypocritically wearing robes." The marchers were not concerned with the black robes of judges but with the white robes of the Ku Klux Klan along the road to Montgomery.

Wallace told the president that he would not provide state police protection for the marchers and that Alabama did not have the money to employ its national guard. Johnson sent three thousand army troops armed with bayoneted M-1 rifles to protect the twenty thousand marchers on their five-day trip to the "cradle of the Confederacy." On the final day of the march, Mrs. Viola Liuzzo, a white woman driving a black civil rights worker in her car, was shot to death by four members of the Ku Klux Klan on the outskirts of Montgomery.

A year after the march, Thurgood Marshall addressed a group of college students in Atlanta. A black youth accused him of not being "militant enough" and asked him why he did not march with other civil rights leaders in Selma. He told the student, "I was there before you were born, and your father didn't have guts enough to walk across the street," Marshall said angrily. "Why, you see, you people forget things like that. That's why I like to mention them, to find out how far we came.... We've come a long ways."

Selma was not the only confrontation between black and white on the eve of Thurgood Marshall's elevation to solicitor general. Between June 11 and 15, police in Chicago arrested 526 anti-segregation demonstrators protesting the rehiring of the city's school superintendent, who had been accused of failing to integrate Chicago's schools. More than twenty thousand protesters, led at times by Dr. King, marched for forty-two days. In the ensuing months racial violence would break out in other major cities.

President Johnson wanted Marshall confirmed without delay, and Senate Judiciary Committee hearings were scheduled for July 29, 1965, just two weeks after the nomination. Marshall again left Cissy and his sons, nine-year-old Thurgood Jr. and seven-year-old John William, in New York City. He moved into a small, temporary apartment in southwest Washington. He was prepared to encounter what he thought would be the hostile examination of the sixteen-member committee packed with southern senators, as he had three years earlier, when his U.S. appeals court nomination stalled in the committee for several months.

President Johnson was not going to have his nominee subjected to that kind of senatorial abuse. Johnson was a consummate politician who knew how to get what he wanted from an often hostile and cantankerous Congress. He had won approval of his controversial bills on voting rights, federal aid to education,

Medicare for senior citizens, and wilderness parklands protection. Thurgood Marshall was the man he wanted for his solicitor general, and he made this clear to his fellow southerners.

According to Virginia senator Charles S. Robb, who was to become the president's son-in-law, Johnson used his powers of political persuasion to ensure Marshall would not "again be denigrated" by the committee. He privately threatened to close military bases and reduce federal projects that employed thousands of local workers in the districts of Senators up for reelection. They quickly got the point.

Democratic congressional leader Mike Mansfield and Republican senator Everett M. Dirksen told Johnson they saw no reason why Thurgood Marshall should not be confirmed. But aging senator Spessard L. Holland called the nomination "unwise." The Florida Democrat, who had served as his state's governor from 1941 until 1945, said, "To make him [Marshall] the special pleader for the whole government opens the matter up to controversy."

Questions on Marshall's personal life did come from another quarter, the inquiring and amused media. Reporters were eager to know about his reputation as a drinker who "polished off three cocktails at lunch," something Marshall freely admitted and joked about often. "Well, not when I am working, just one, but maybe two more before dinner."

Others inquired about the legendary all-night poker and pinochle games and about his fondness for baseball, western movies, and chain-smoking. "Now isn't that something else?" he asked a reporter. "My newspaper friends keep saying all those things, and I wish to hell it was up to date. Once in a while I'll catch a western on television, and I am still waiting to see one where the Indians win, and poker, ha, I haven't pushed a chip in ten years. You know what cards I'm down to now? I play War with my two boys. Now that's hot action for you, isn't it?"

There were also more serious questions for the man who had truculently prodded the white establishment and was now about to become one of its most powerful members. *Washington Star* editor Sidney Epstein told reporter Mary McGrory to ask Marshall about his judicial philosophy. "I'm certainly not a conservative," he told her.

On the afternoon of July 29, 1965, it took the Senate Judiciary Committee just twenty-nine minutes to approve Marshall's nomination by a vote of eleven to five. The next day, he was confirmed by the Senate by a vote of sixty-nine to eleven.

Marshall's swearing-in ceremony was scheduled for August 11, but Johnson put him right to work. Shortly after his confirmation, he boarded an Air Force 707 jet at Andrews Air Force Base in suburban Maryland and flew to Stockholm as head of the U.S. delegation to the UN Congress on the Prevention of Crime and Treatment of Offenders. White House press secretary Bill Moyers said Marshall's assignment to lead the delegation "underscores the president's deep interest in the problems of crime and of the need for a massive attack on its roots in this country."

Johnson named several other black men to the UN delegation. They included Marshall's former NAACP colleague Robert L. Carter, now NAACP general counsel; UN ambassador Franklin H. Williams; New York City youth commissioner Lawrence R. Pierce; and federal judge Wade McCree. High over the Atlantic Ocean, en route to Stockholm, they told Marshall he should have had their plane designated "Turkey One" in honor of his nickname.

On August 11, Marshall arrived at the White House to take the oath of office administered by Associate Justice Hugo Black. "He has good policy judgment and the power of self-control," Black said later. "I know he will do a fine job."

President Johnson stood at his nominee's right. Next came Cissy, Thurgood Jr., and John. Cissy wore a demure pink dress with a short jacket, white gloves, a single strand of pearls, and double pearl earrings. The four-foot-one-inch Cissy Marshall was dwarfed by the two six-footers, Johnson and Thurgood. The Marshall boys wore fresh summer cord suits, which they probably appreciated because of the swamplike mugginess of Washington summers. Thurgood wore a dark blue three-button suit that pinched his spreading paunch. The Marshall boys would have to wait to see their father in his cutaway.

That day came on the first Monday in October when Marshall, accompanied by his family and Attorney General Nicholas Katzenbach, received an official welcome from the Supreme Court.

Notorious for keeping things plain and simple, Thurgood Marshall nevertheless admitted owning the traditional formal dress of the solicitor before his appointment. "Now isn't this the silliest getup in the world?" he asked.

When asked if he considered wearing a business suit to the court, he said, "No, no. I'm too old to worry about changing all that now. If I had to go out and buy a new one, maybe I'd think about changing the tradition. I am already ahead of them. I've already got the outfit. I bought it when I attended the inauguration of President Tubman in Liberia around 1960. I told the tailor that I was going to Africa, but he lined the vest, anyway—and in that climate."

As solicitor general, Marshall had a comfortable office in the Justice Department and a staff of twenty-three lawyers. One October afternoon he sat at his desk fiddling in vain with the dials of a large brown speaker. He was trying to get the 1965 World Series game between Los Angeles and Minnesota, but the only thing he heard was a congressional budget hearing.

"How the hell do you work that noise box in my office? I can't get the World Series anywhere," he yelled. A secretary patiently explained that the speaker was not a radio but a monitor connected to hearing rooms at the Capitol. The next morning he found a radio on his desk.

Marshall brought a ceremonial leopard-skin cape, which he had received when he was made an honorary Kibiyu tribal chief, to his office and draped it over a chair. Five years earlier, in January and February 1960, he had been a consultant to the Constitutional Conference on Kenya in London and Nairobi as Kenya prepared to gain its independence from Britain. It had been a crown colony and protectorate since 1920.

Newsman Eric Sevareid recalled Marshall's performance at the conference. "What stayed with me, what was to me impressive and humbling, was that in everything the man said…in his every expression and gesture, one was made conscious of the presence of an American, period."

Marshall had been careful to write protections for the white minority into Kenya's constitution, and he made sure it contained a due process clause. But he had difficulty explaining that legal concept to Masai tribesmen, who feared whites would take over the rich plateau known as the White Highlands and regarded by Kenya's Kibiyu people as their land. After hours of futile explanation, a tribesman said to him, "If they come, we kill them."

"Now you've got it!" Marshall roared.

When the former British colony became independent, on December 12, 1963, Marshall represented the United States at the celebrations. In August 1978, when his friend Jomo Kenyatta, Kenya's first president, died, Marshall headed the U.S. funeral delegation.

The ceremonial cape was a reminder of his African heritage. His great-grandfather had been an African tribal chief. But there was also a bust on his desk of Maryland native Frederick Douglass, the former Maryland slave, orator, author, ambassador, and journalist who had urged Abraham Lincoln to proclaim emancipation for slaves.

On November 9, 1965, Thurgood Marshall put on the cutaway and argued his first major case before the Supreme Court, *United States v. Price.* He was trying to convince the nine justices that acts of racial terrorism should be made federal crimes. Marshall felt at home in the high-ceilinged chamber with its red velvet draperies, wrought-iron grilles, and marble pillars; he had been there many times before.

At the end of the day a friend asked if he had been nervous during his first appearance as solicitor general. Marshall replied, "Hell, I ain't had the jitters in the Supreme Court since de day I was admitted to practice nearly thirty years ago. But dat day, oh boy! You coulda heard mah knees knockin' way out in de hall."

But when Thurgood stepped on the Court's polished wooden podium to begin his argument, it was his baritone voice, not his "knees knockin'," that was heard throughout the courtroom and "way out in de hall." He was barrel-chested and weighed about 210 pounds. His mustache was neatly trimmed, and his hair was graying at the temples. His voice carried through the chamber as he opened his argument on racial terrorism.

"People don't conspire to do good," he quipped. To make his point, Marshall imitated a white-supremacist accent and attitude. "Look," he said, conjuring up a Ku Klux Klan or White Citizens'

Council meeting, "we are going to plan all this for the purpose we are just sick and tired of what's going on."

Marshall was telling the justices about the murders of three civil rights workers who were killed in June 1964 while attempting to register black voters in Philadelphia, Mississippi. James E. Chaney, a twenty-one-year-old black Mississippian, and two white New York residents, Andrew Goodman, twenty, and Michael H. Schwerner, twenty-four, had been shot to death and dumped in an earthen dam.

Three officers of the Neshoba County sheriff's office and fifteen members of the Ku Klux Klan were charged with having conspired on June 21, 1964, to commit the murders. The U.S. Grand Jury for the Southern District of Mississippi returned indictments against the men, but the state's district court dismissed charges against all the defendants except the three law enforcement officers. Marshall took the case directly to the Supreme Court and argued that the lower court's decision to dismiss the indictments should be reversed and charges reintroduced against all defendants.

Washington Star reporter Mary McGrory was impressed with his performance. "Thurgood Marshall was, predictably, in excellent form as he argued his first major case before the Supreme Court. "He was at ease, quick with the law, and able to command the acceptable joke."

The opposing counsel representing the state of Mississippi, H. C. Watkins, was a young lawyer from Meridian, with a crewcut. He argued in a barely audible voice that the Court should not interfere with Mississippi law. He said murder was a state, not a federal, crime.

"Marshall dominated the long and often dry proceedings, principally because he could, unlike the other participants, always be heard," McGrory said. "Thurgood told the Court federal laws were being circumvented 'by shooting Negroes, by killing, by pressuring them by burning crosses in public at night.'"

Across Capitol Plaza in the Congressional Caucus Room, the House Committee on Un-American Activities was scheduled to begin its own investigation of the Ku Klux Klan at the same hour Marshall stood up before the Supreme Court.

The Justice Department was conducting a separate investigation of the Klan's involvement in the death of Lt. Col. Lemuel E. Penn, a black National Guardsman who was director of adult and vocational education for the District of Columbia's public school system. Penn was killed by shotgun blasts as he drove along an interstate highway on the outskirts of Athens, Georgia, on July 11, 1964. Six people were indicted for his murder by the U.S. Grand Jury in the Middle District of Georgia for criminal conspiracy in violation of Penn's rights, but the Georgia court dismissed the charges.

Solicitor General Thurgood Marshall was anxious to find a way to ensure justice would be served and the killers of Penn and the three civil rights workers not go unpunished. He cited the Enforcement Act of 1870 to force the courts to bring the murder suspects to trial. The pertinent provisions of the 1870 act, which had been refined since its inception and were now known as Sections 241 and 242 of Title XVIII of the U.S. Code, prohibited interference with the rights of citizens under the privileges-and-immunities clause of the Fourteenth Amendment.

Mississippi's attorney, Watkins, argued that the state court was correct in dismissing charges against the fifteen civilians because the defendants, unlike the officers, were not government employees acting under the authority of the state.

The Supreme Court disagreed with Watkins. It unanimously reversed the Mississippi court's decision and remanded the case to the state's district court. The defendants were tried, and the three officers, along with four of the civilians, were convicted and sentenced to ten-year jail terms. The other defendants were found not guilty. The case became the subject of a 1990 motion picture, *Mississippi Burning.*

In a companion case the same day, *United States v. Guest*, Marshall persuaded the court to reinstate charges against the six Georgia men accused of killing Lieutenant Colonel Penn. Several months later they were tried. Two of the defendants were convicted and sentenced to ten-year prison terms. The four other defendants were found not guilty.

Between 1965 and 1967, Thurgood Marshall won fourteen of the nineteen cases he argued for the government as solicitor general. Most of those cases dealt with civil rights and privacy. His legal approach was in sharp contrast to that of his predecessor, Archibald Cox, an urbane and scholarly Harvard Law School graduate who spoke in a low voice and used subtle wit. Cox addressed the Court as if it were a law school seminar. By contrast, Marshall was a forceful speaker whose humor often brought the staid justices to the verge of laughter. By comparison, former solicitor general Cox was concerned with small academic points of law. Marshall's approach took a broader view of the law and addressed problems of human dignity.

In 1965, Marshall tackled Fair Housing by pleading the government's position in a California case, *Reitman v. Mulkey*, asking the Court to declare California's Proposition 14, a 1964 anti–fair housing amendment to the state's constitution, invalid. A black couple, the Mulkeys, had sued a white couple, the Reitmans, under California's Civil Code for refusing to rent them an apartment because they were black. Marshall said popular initiatives were unconstitutional if they in effect promoted racial discrimination. "Everybody knows minority groups do not have the strength to win a popular statewide vote," he said. Marshall argued Proposition 14 made California a partner in a discriminatory act because it excused the state from compliance with statutes enacted to end housing discrimination. The U.S. Supreme Court unanimously agreed with him.

In 1966 Marshall argued *Evans v. Newton*, asking the Court to integrate a public park in Macon, Georgia. The 1911 will of Senator Francis A. O. Bacon deeded a tract of land to the city of Macon to be used as a public park. Bacon's will stipulated the park would be governed by a white board of managers and black citizens would be barred. After passage of the Civil Rights Act of 1964, Macon officials did not enforce the terms of Senator Bacon's will, and for two years white and black citizens used the park in harmony.

Then Bacon's heirs and the park's board of managers forced the city to resign as trustee and enforced the will's racial restriction. When black citizens sued to once again integrate the park, the Supreme Court of Georgia upheld the ban. Macon's police officers chased little black children from the playground's swings and slides. The appeal reached the U.S. Supreme Court, and Marshall argued that though the park was "technically private," it performed a "public function" and therefore could not remain segregated under the equal-protection clause of the Fourteenth Amendment.

In its seven-to-two decision, the Court agreed. Associate Justice William O. Douglas said in the majority opinion: "Under the circumstances of this case we cannot but conclude that the public character of this park requires that it be treated as a public institution...regardless of who now has title under state law."

President Johnson's Voting Rights Act of 1965 authorized the Justice Department to register voters and to ensure their ballots were properly counted. It banned literacy tests in states where voting discrimination was evident. The Justice Department presented evidence in 1966 that the states of Alabama, Florida, Georgia, Louisiana, Mississippi, North Carolina, South Carolina, and Tennessee were not in compliance with the act.

South Carolina v. Katzenbach challenged the voting rights law and took it to the Supreme Court. Attorney General Nicholas B. Katzenbach decided to personally argue the government's case, and Thurgood Marshall wrote the government's brief. He asked for the dismissal of South Carolina's complaint, contending the Voting Rights Act was a proper implementation of the Fifteenth Amendment. He said neither the Seventeenth Amendment nor the Constitution empowered a state to grant or withhold voting rights on any conditions it wished to put in place and that the Constitution expressly prohibited imposing such conditions on the basis of color or race.

Again, the Court agreed with the government in a unanimous decision. Chief Justice Earl Warren rejected South Carolina's claim that its powers over the electoral procedure had been "usurped":

"Congress may use any rational means to effectuate the constitutional prohibition of racial discrimination in voting. After enduring nearly a century of widespread resistance to the Fifteenth Amendment, Congress has marshalled an array of potent weapons against the evil, with the authority in the Attorney General to employ them effectively...Hopefully, millions of non-white Americans will now be able to participate for the first time on an equal basis in the government under which they live."

Later that year, another section of the Voting Rights Act was contested by voters in New York State. The act prohibited states from denying voting rights to qualified Puerto Rican New York residents who had successfully completed the sixth grade of an accredited school and were literate in Spanish but could not read and write English. An "accredited school" included accredited schools in the fifty states and U.S. territory and American schools in the Commonwealth of Puerto Rico "in which the predominant classroom language was other than English." This section voided a provision of New York State's constitution extending voting rights only to persons able to, "except for physical disability," read and write English.

A suit to stop Puerto Ricans from voting was brought by Kings County, New York, residents John P. and Christine Morgan. Their complaint, filed in the U.S. District Court for the District of Columbia, sought to enjoin the Justice Department and the New York City board of elections from enforcing the Voting Rights Act. The Morgans contended that nearly 50 percent of the seven hundred thousand Puerto Ricans in New York could read and write only Spanish and that their unfamiliarity with English made them ignorant of political issues.

In November the New York's local courts declared a portion of the act unconstitutional and issued an order restraining the Justice Department and New York City's board of elections from enforcing it. Katzenbach appealed the decision to the Supreme Court.

Thurgood Marshall argued the government's case in *Katzenbach and the United States v. Morgan*. His brief illustrated the historical relationship between the United States and Puerto Rico, explaining that from the time of Puerto Rico's acquisition by the Treaty of Paris in 1898 until 1952, Congress had the power to determine the political and civil rights of Puerto Rico's citizens and was responsible for the island's governance. Marshall wrote that Congress conferred citizenship on Puerto Ricans when it passed the Jones Act of 1917, thereby easing the migration of Puerto Ricans to the U.S. mainland.

He noted there were nearly one million Puerto Ricans in the country and about 70 percent of them lived in New York City. He said the literacy rate in Spanish was high in Puerto Rico, nearly 85 percent, but two-thirds of the people could neither speak, read, nor write English. Marshall said the act was valid because it represented Congress's lawful discharge of its duty to Puerto Ricans who came to the U.S. mainland because Congress had made them citizens despite their "language handicap." He cited other states with multilingual minorities—Hawaii, Louisiana, and New Mexico—that were complying with the act.

In its seven-to-two decision, the Supreme Court struck down the lower court's judgment and upheld the validity and enforcement of the act, saying it was a proper use of congressional power under the Fourteenth Amendment. Associate Justice William Brennan wrote: "It is enough that we perceive a basis upon which Congress might predict a judgment that the application of New York's English literacy requirement...constituted an invidious discrimination in violation of the Equal Protection Clause."

A group of black Virginians argued in 1966, in *Harper v. Virginia Board of Elections*, that the state's poll tax violated their "equal protection" under the Fourteenth Amendment and that the Twenty-fourth Amendment, approved in January 1964, had specifically made poll taxes illegal. A local court had dismissed their complaint on the ground that the right to vote in local elections was given by the state, not the federal government, and that Virginia had sole authority to set reasonable requirements for Virginia voters.

Thurgood Marshall took the case before the Supreme Court. He said Virginia could not impose poll taxes on citizens who wanted to vote. The Court's six-to-three decision invalidated the poll tax.

The right of privacy was another issue Marshall strongly defended during his career. *Olmstead v. United States*, in 1928, and subsequent Supreme Court decisions had strengthened the Fourth Amendment's protection against unreasonable search and seizure and extended those protections to speech as well as material goods. Several decisions suggested that utilization of listening devices constituted a "physical intrusion or trespass" and that recorded evidence obtained by "bugging" was inadmissible in federal courts. Wiretaps were also prohibited under the Federal Communications Act of 1934.

Marshall had often wondered if his own telephones had been subject to government eavesdropping. "All they would have heard was me cussing and my wife gossiping," he said.

Marshall believed all electronic eavesdropping was illegal because it constituted "an illegal trespass." While preparing for *Black v. United States* in 1966, Marshall learned that the government had acquired evidence in the tax case by listening surreptitiously to telephone conversations between the defendant and his attorney. At Marshall's request the Court set the judgment aside and returned the case to the district court for review.

In the same year, Marshall spoke to the Association of Federal Investigators and told them all electronic eavesdropping must stop if they expected to win convictions in federal courts. He noted that the Supreme Court's trend appeared to be to reverse convictions obtained by wiretaps. He said, "The evil is in the eavesdropping and not the device being used. It is unfair to U.S. prosecutors and the government for investigators to make illegal moves which may crop up years later in court and prevent what otherwise would be a solid conviction."

In February 1967 Ramsey Clark was appointed attorney general. His father, Associate Justice Tom C. Clark, announced his resignation from the Supreme Court to prevent any appearance of conflict of interest now that his son was the nation's chief legal officer. President Johnson had a vacancy to fill.

EIGHTEEN

The Supreme Court Nomination

As I see it, I've moved the Negro from D+ to
C— He's still nowhere. He knows it. And
that's why he's out in the streets. Hell, I'd be
there too.
                              —President Lyndon Johnson

It was not at all unusual for President Lyndon Baines Johnson to
meet with advisers or reporters during his morning toilet. So it
came as no surprise to Joseph Califano and several other top
domestic-policy advisers when they were instructed to join the
First Couple in the president's White House bedroom suite one
morning in March 1967. As Johnson emerged dripping from his
high-pressure shower, he reached for a towel and asked Califano
whom he should appoint to the Supreme Court to replace retiring
Associate Justice Clark.

Califano was mindful of Johnson's commitment to appointing
blacks to high office. Johnson had already made Robert C. Weaver
the first black cabinet officer by naming him secretary of the
Department of Housing and Urban Development. He also appointed U.S. army major Hugh Robinson the first black military
aide to a president. Therefore, Califano was not surprised when

LBJ rattled off the names of several blacks as potential Supreme Court nominees.

What did catch Califano off guard, however, was Johnson's sudden musings about appointing the first woman instead. Lady Bird pricked up her ears; she was intrigued by the idea. After all, she interjected, "Lyndon has done so much" already for black people. A California judge, Shirley Hufstedler, was mentioned as a possible choice. But sometime during the course of brushing his teeth and combing his hair, LBJ decided to nominate Thurgood Marshall.

During the following weeks, Johnson tested the reaction to his choice. Among those whose opinions he valued, Marshall was well thought of and the idea of nominating him well received. Acting attorney general Ramsey Clark gave Marshall a strong recommendation, stating, "I have no doubt that his future contributions will add even more prominence to his already well established place in American history."

Earl Warren, whose tenure as chief justice had begun in 1953, the year the Court heard Marshall reargue *Brown,* told the president that he was "very happy" with Marshall's nomination. Warren said, "He has had a tremendous amount of experience of the kind that will be very helpful to the Court."

Associate Justice Tom C. Clark, the man Marshall would replace, thought highly of him. When President Truman elevated Clark, a Texas Democrat, to the Court from the attorney general's post in the early 1950s, Clark was perceived as a conservative on racial issues. He had been impressed with the quality and thrust of Marshall's advocacy in *Brown* and other desegregation suits.

In June 1966 Solicitor General Marshall was awarded the Distinguished Service Award of the Conference of Prince Hall Grand Masters of America, a black Masonic organization. The organization commended him for acumen "far beyond the average American lawyer in his presentations to the courts of the nation."

Clark spoke at the testimonial dinner in Marshall's honor. He told the audience, which included Justices Hugo Black and William J. Brennan Jr., "No man has given himself to the brotherhood of man more than Thurgood Marshall. We salute him as Mr. Civil Rights."

Marshall used the award ceremony to explain his own thinking on civil rights, emphasizing the development of positive attitudes within the black community. He declared that while civil rights gains had been made, "we still have a terrific job to do, and that job is making sure that our community is ready, by raising the sights of our young people.... We have got to show them—even where they are segregated and pushed around—that there is a future." Rather than use the occasion merely to honor him, he urged his audience, "Let this night be a beginning of what has to be done; as President Johnson has said, 'We're too close to the end to give up now!'"

Cissy Marshall was at home on June 13, 1967, a weekday like any other. She got up and made eggs and bacon for her husband and their two sons, now eleven and eight. Then she drove her husband to the Justice Department and headed uptown with the boys to the Georgetown Day School, an exclusive private school on MacArthur Boulevard in upper northwest Washington. She returned home to the rented town house in the city's southwest quadrant and was engaged in housekeeping chores when, at around 11:00 A.M., the phone rang. It was her husband, calling from the Oval Office of the White House.

"Take a deep breath and sit down slowly," Thurgood told her. "Now, wait just a minute." The next voice on the line was that of President Johnson, telling her that he had asked her husband to join the Supreme Court.

"Mr. President, I am simply speechless," said the wife of the justice designate. She was glad she had sat down and taken a deep breath. "Thank you for having so much faith in my husband."

Later, when the joy and excitement subsided, she was able to contemplate developments from a more mundane perspective. She commented wryly, "I drive Thurgood to work and then take the boys on to school. I enjoy it. I doubt that our lives will change very much because of this appointment."

Her younger son, inspired by his father's success, told his mother, "Mom, I want to be a judge, too, when I grow up." He added, "But can't I let my hair grow long right now like the Monkees?"

Georgetown Day School enjoyed a liberal reputation. The

children of Washington's socially liberal white power elite studied there. The school was noted for the wide latitude it gave students in terms of their personal appearance. Many showed up for school wearing jeans or T-shirts and with long hair. If Cissy Marshall had let her mixed-race children's hair grow long, it would have grown straight, like mops sported by the popular rock band John William referred to, not into the kinky Afro hairstyle, the "bush," that black militants of the era regarded as a statement of pride in their African heritage.

But she was not lax when it came to her boys' grooming. Her husband was African American, and she knew that despite his station in life, blacks, if they wished to succeed ultimately in the white man's world, were not accorded the same social latitude as whites. She was outnumbered by her sons, but in family matters her lone dissent overrode any majority vote. She told John William he would have to wait until he was twenty-one to go without a haircut.

Both boys were clean-cut and wore scratchy, uncomfortable suits and freshly shined shoes for the ceremony in the White House Rose Garden the following week. The president, beaming, introduced his nominee to the press. Gesturing toward Marshall, who stood behind him in the brilliant sunlight, LBJ declared, "I believe he earned that appointment, he deserves the appointment. He is best qualified by training and by very valuable service to the country. I believe it is the right thing to do, the right time to do it, the right man and the right place."

Warned by Johnson to keep his remarks short in order to avoid controversy pending Senate hearings on his nomination, Marshall appeared laid back, almost laconic, when he stepped forward to address reporters. Asked to grade his performance as solicitor general, he replied, "I guess it's been about as good as anybody else's, maybe better than some." When he was bombarded with a barrage of other inquiries on a wide range of subjects, the nominee demurred, saying simply, "The president speaks for me."

Dozens of men have served on the U.S. Supreme Court. The historical significance of Marshall's nomination was that he was the first African American to do so. Yet there, in the Rose Garden, no reference was made to Marshall's race. Later, Senate minority leader Everett Dirksen predicted Marshall's speedy confirmation by the Senate, telling reporters, "He's a good lawyer. The fact of his color should make no difference."

Yet whether they cared to admit it or not, his color made all the difference, both to his supporters and detractors. For his part, Johnson saw Marshall's nomination as a way to revive his flagging social agenda for the Great Society, a booming, vibrant America unfettered by poverty and racial discrimination. Lady Bird was right: Her husband had done a lot for blacks.

Shortly after his landslide victory over Barry Goldwater, Johnson signed the Civil Rights Act of 1964, the most sweeping civil rights legislation of the modern era. He then pushed through Congress the Voting Rights Act of 1965. At the bill's nationally televised signing ceremony in the Capitol Rotunda, Johnson addressed the nation's black citizens directly.

"To every Negro in this country" he said, "You must vote. Your future, and your children's future, depend upon it. If you do this, then you will find, as others have found before you, that the vote is the most powerful instrument ever devised by man for breaking down injustice and destroying the terrible walls which imprison men because they are different from other men."

There was more. The president sent to Congress a fair housing bill that would outlaw racial discrimination in the sale and rental of residential property. He threw the full weight of the Justice Department behind efforts to break down the massive resistance to school desegregation that had persisted since Marshall's victory in *Brown* the decade before; during Johnson's elected term of office, the number of blacks attending desegregated schools across the South tripled. Beyond all this, he formulated ambitious plans to rebuild America's blighted urban areas. Johnson called it his "model cities" program.

By 1967, however, the president's social policies no longer enjoyed an enthusiastic mandate. Rioting in the nation's urban centers had fueled a white backlash that threatened racial progress.

The predominantly black Watts area of Los Angeles exploded first. Rioting there began on the evening of August 11, 1965, when a California highway patrolman arrested an unemployed twenty-one-year-old black man for drunk driving. The man's mother rushed from her house into the street, screaming at the policeman. A crowd gathered. More police arrived. The crowd grew into the hundreds. Bottles and rocks flew toward the police. By the time it was over four days later, approximately twenty people were dead, six hundred injured, and fourteen hundred arrested. It took fifteen thousand police and National Guardsmen to reclaim the streets from five thousand black rioters, snipers, and looters.

In Newark, New Jersey, on the evening of July 12, 1967, police arrested a black cab driver for a traffic violation. Rumors spread that the driver had been beaten and died in police custody. Looters, snipers, and arsonists took to the streets. The National Guard was ordered into the city. Before order was restored on July 19, fifteen people were dead, and over a thousand had been arrested.

The most serious rioting took place in Detroit less than two weeks later. On July 23, 1967, police raided an after-hours club on the city's West Side. It was rumored that an unarmed man and woman were brutally beaten by police during the raid. Rioters, looters, and arsonists again went into action. Police and firemen came under sniper attack. President Johnson ordered federal troopers into the city, but five days passed before calm was restored. In all, forty people died, two thousand were injured, five thousand were arrested, and another five thousand were left homeless.

Newsweek magazine interviewed Dr. Kenneth Clark for an August 21, 1967, special report "The Hard Core Ghetto Mood." Clark, whose doll tests had been used by Thurgood Marshall in the *Brown* case to show that segregated schools made black children feel inferior, was asked to explain the psychology of the urban rioters. "The chronic riot of their day-to-day lives is, as far as they're concerned, no better than the acute riots," Clark explained. "They don't have anything to lose, including their lives. It's not just desperation—it's what-the-hell."

The fatalism of a jobless nineteen-year-old Chicagoan seemed to confirm Clark's observations. He told his *Newsweek* interviewer,

"I don't mind gettin' killed. When I'm dead, they'll tell my kid, 'He died for a good cause.'"

A high school dropout living in Harlem expressed similar sentiments. Ed Bowen, twenty-six, told *Newsweek,* "People have been begging for years for a decent place to live, a job, some food, but they ain't got nothing, so they burn things down and maybe they'll get it."

Another Harlem resident, a young woman of eighteen, added, "I hope you don't expect me to rap Rap [black power advocate H. Rap Brown]. He's kinda crazy—but it's a feel-good crazy."

Dr. Alvin Poussaint, a black Harvard-trained psychiatrist, summarized his perceptions. The rioters, he concluded, ranged "from the plain damn angry to those with fantasies of taking over, to those who want a TV set, to those angry at their father and mother, to those caught up in hysteria, to those who will act only when they see the cops shoot someone."

President Johnson blamed the white backlash on urban rioting, black militancy, and black power advocates such as H. Rap Brown and Stokely Carmichael. He compared the behavior of rioting blacks to that of the black senators and congressmen elected just after the Civil War who "ran into the chamber with bare feet and white women," in Johnson's words, squandering the chance to make real and lasting progress during Reconstruction. "Negroes will end up pissing in the aisles of the Senate," he complained. "The Negroes will once again take unwise actions out of frustration, impatience, and anger."

In the wake of the riots in Watts, Detroit, Newark, and other cities, Johnson was shocked to find among the moderate black leadership—including Martin Luther King Jr., the Urban League's Whitney Young, and Roy Wilkins, head of the NAACP—an utter sense of powerlessness to control or even influence young blacks in the ghettos. Johnson saw a critical need to bolster the stature of moderate black leaders and to show that, frustrating though the pace of progress might be, gradualism was in fact producing concrete results. Johnson counted on translating these results into black votes in his 1968 reelection effort.

At the same time, however, the president understood why hope was losing out to despair among poor blacks. "I moved the Negro from D + to C −," he told his biographer Doris Kearns Goodwin. "He's still nowhere. He knows it. And that's why he's out in the streets. Hell, I'd be there too."

Johnson believed that racial prejudice was not based on skin color but on fear. He told Goodwin, "Anyone who's afraid of losing his job to another man will soon turn to hate that other man." He concluded that economic growth, the creation of enough jobs and wealth to go around, was the antidote for racial turmoil.

Conditions in the nation's ghettos were beyond the short-term reach of LBJ's policies. His own Department of Labor conducted a survey of ghettos in ten cities and reported, "No conceivable increase in the gross national product would stir these backwaters. Unemployment in these areas is primarily a story of inferior education, no skills, police and garnishment records, discrimination, fatherless children, dope addiction, hopelessness."

In addition, Congress was reluctant to "reward" rioters. Lawmakers began to refuse funding for Johnson's antipoverty initiatives. A month after Marshall's nomination, in July 1967, the President's Rat Extermination Act was defeated in the House of Representatives. The bill, which passed committee easily enough, would have provided federal assistance to cities for rodent extermination in ghetto areas. But after the riots in Newark and Detroit left dozens of people dead and caused millions of dollars in property damage, the mood on Capitol Hill changed. The legislation was derided as a "civil rats bill," a cynical derision of LBJ's Texas twang.

What the House did consider, however, was legislation that would have made it a federal crime to cross state lines to instigate civil disturbance. This antiriot law was clearly aimed at agitators who, like Brown and Carmichael, traveled the country urging violent resistance to racial discrimination. Ironically, Brown used vermin infestation to arouse the people he sought to incite. On one occasion, he told a crowd in Cambridge, Maryland, a small blue-collar community on the eastern shore of the Chesapeake Bay, "Burn this place down! You won't be killin' nothin' but a bunch of rats! Every night they truck more rats down here from Washington. They back trucks up to the FBI building and load them up with rats, then they bring them down here and turn them loose in the black community. Burn this fuckin' place down! Burn it down!"

Johnson realized that rats in fact posed a serious threat to ghetto dwellers, especially children. He urged Congress to reconsider his rat bill. "Thousands of children—many of them babies—are bitten by rats in their homes and tenements," he stated. "Some are killed. Many are disfigured for life.... We are spending federal funds to protect our livestock from rodents and predatory animals. The least we can do is give our children the same protection we give our livestock." But by the middle of 1967, lawmakers were more concerned with black power than black powerlessness.

"When I appointed Thurgood Marshall to the Supreme Court," Johnson told Goodwin, "I figured he'd be a great example to younger kids. There was probably not a Negro in America who didn't know about Thurgood's appointment. All over America that day Negro parents looked at their children a little differently, thousands of mothers looked across the breakfast table and said: 'Now maybe this will happen to my child someday.' I bet from one coast to the other there was a rash of new mothers naming their newborn sons Thurgood."

Goodwin's research showed otherwise. In her book *Lyndon Johnson and the American Dream*, she noted that birth certificates on file in New York City and Boston "revealed seven Martins, ten Luthers, eleven George Washingtons, and fifteen Franklin Delanos, but not a single Thurgood."

Blacks were, in fact, divided over the nomination, to the extent that they even knew or cared about it. Some militants were elated. Floyd McKissick, director of CORE, declared, "This has stirred pride in the breast of every black American."

But others dismissed Marshall's appointment as a cynical act. One man's role model is another man's token. The week the nomination was announced, deadly racial disturbances rocked Tampa, Florida, and Cincinnati and Dayton, Ohio. In Dayton, H. Rap Brown continued his call for young ghetto blacks to arm. "The honky [white man] is your enemy," he told them. "How can you be nonviolent in America, the most violent country in the world? You better shoot the white man to death."

Meanwhile, the Supreme Court that Marshall was about to join dealt the proponents of nonviolent protest a setback. By a five-to-four vote, the Court ruled that Martin Luther King Jr. would have to spend time in an Alabama jail for defying a state court's order not to conduct a civil rights march in Birmingham back in 1963. Justice Potter Stewart, an Ohio Republican appointed by Eisenhower, stopped just short of referring to King by name when he wrote for the majority, "No man can be judge in his own case, however exalted his station, however righteous his motives, and irrespective of his race, color, politics or religion."

Justice Brennan, joined by the chief justice and Justices William O. Douglas and Abe Fortas, wrote a bitter dissent, stating, "We cannot permit fears of 'riots' and 'civil disobedience' generated by slogans like black power to divert our attention from what is here at stake—arming the state courts with the power to punish as a 'contempt' what they otherwise could not punish at all."

Privately, President Johnson began to wonder whether he could get his nominee confirmed by the Senate.

The southerners on the Senate Judiciary Committee plotted their anti-Marshall strategy. They would not use Marshall's color—at least not explicitly—as the basis for their opposition to him. Instead, they would try to paint him as a liberal who was soft on crime. In August 1965, while awaiting Senate confirmation to become solicitor general, Marshall served as head of the U.S. delegation to the Third UN Congress on Crime Prevention.

Marshall made his views on crime clear in a speech to the delegates. He defined the "great dilemma" confronting law enforcement as how to provide a "fair balance between the freedom of the individual and the fair interest of society." He went on to attribute criminal activity to social factors such as poverty and discrimination. He opposed harsh prison sentences, warning, "There is substantial danger that imprisonment, deprivation of self-respect, and alienation from the community will produce new recruits to criminal culture."

Marshall's emphasis on the sociological aspects of crime had become unpopular. At a time when the nation, its cities aflame, cried out for law and order, Marshall sounded like a man as predisposed to the perpetrator as to the victim. A recent report by a conference of state supreme court chief justices had criticized the Warren Court for not exercising "judicial self-restraint." Specifically, the report attacked Warren Court rulings that freed a convicted murderer because his lawyer was not present at his voluntary confession, required states to provide free trial transcripts to convicted felons in order that they could appeal their convictions, and struck down municipal ordinances designed to supervise ex-convicts.

The confirmation hearings wore on for five days, July 13, 14, 18, 19, and 24, 1967. The questioning ranged from the penetrating to the absurd, from the philosophical to the kind of esoterica found in a law school exam. At one point Marshall was asked, "Do you know who drafted the Thirteenth Amendment to the U.S. Constitution?" He could not remember. At another point he was asked to explain, "Of what significance do you believe it is that in deciding the constitutional basis of the Civil Rights Act of 1866, Congress copied the enforcement provisions of this legislation from the Fugitive Slave Law of 1850?"

Marshall maintained his composure, punctuating his testimony with acerbic wit. He insisted that recent Supreme Court decisions were not responsible for any rise in the nation's crime rate. "I don't believe that any court decisions, by the decisions themselves, have increased crime," he declared.

Beyond that, he refused to discuss any matter that he might have to rule on as a member of the Court. He asked rhetorically, "Any statement I make...would oblige me to disqualify myself in those cases, would it not?"

The southerners were incensed. Senator Sam J. Ervin of North Carolina demanded to know, "How can this committee, or how can the Senate, perform its duty and ascertain what your constitutional or judicial philosophy is without ascertaining what you think about the Constitution?"

Marshall told him, "Well, one way, you can look at my opinions."

Ervin pressed on, anyway, with questions about the Court's ruling in *Miranda v. Arizona*. He wanted Marshall to say that the

Court had overstepped its authority, in effect amending the Fifth Amendment, which only the Congress and the state legislatures can properly do. In *Miranda* the Court ruled that police must inform criminal suspects that they have the right to remain silent, that anything said can be used against them, and that they have the right to have an attorney present before questioning, appointed by the state if they cannot afford one themselves.

Ervin, who referred to himself as "a plain old country lawyer," was in fact a graduate of Harvard Law School. He demanded of the nominee, "Can you point out a single syllable in the provision of the Fifth Amendment, which says that no person shall be compelled in any criminal case to be a witness against himself, that embraces the requirements announced and the system of warnings laid down by the majority opinion in the *Miranda* case for the first time on June 13, 1966?"

Marshall replied, "I have to repeat, sir, I do not want to comment upon that decision."

Senator John L. McClellan of Arkansas attacked Marshall's stand on wiretapping. "Wiretapping or electronic surveillance has become a matter of national concern; but I think it is something that is vital," McClellan stated. "I think under proper regulations and court direction that it is absolutely indispensable to an effective war on organized crime and on some of the more heinous crimes that are committed."

Marshall conceded that it might be possible to write a law to permit electronic eavesdropping that would pass constitutional muster. But he said he would have to see it to believe it.

On the final day of the hearings, McClellan exploded. "Look at the riots everywhere. A sentiment has been built up over the country to the point where some people feel that if you don't like the law, violate it. And the Supreme Court takes the position that . . . they can change the law. They don't feel very strongly bound to enforce it, to observe it and to follow it. . . . No wonder the fellow out in the street thinks that if the Supreme Court has no regard for precedent in law and can change it when it wants to, why can't I do as I please?" The complaint about the Court's lack of regard for precedent was an allusion to the Court's ruling in *Brown*.

McClellan concluded, "You may lecture me if you want to. I have told you what I think."

Marshall responded, "Far be it from me to lecture you, sir."

When the hearings were finally over, the committee majority commented in its report, "There probably has never been any nominee for any judicial position who has received more minute and searching examination." By an eleven-to-five vote, the committee recommended full Senate confirmation. The majority report concluded, "The Senate will do itself honor, the Court will be graced, and the nation benefited by our confirmation of this nominee to the Supreme Court."

Ervin wrote a report for the minority that was concurred in by McClellan, Eastland, and Strom Thurmond of South Carolina. (Senator George A. Smathers of Florida voted against confirmation but did not sign the minority report.) Labeling Marshall a "constitutional iconoclast," the report warned that his confirmation would add to the Court's "judicial activist" majority of Warren, Black, Douglas, Brennan, and Abe Fortas.

On August 30, 1967, the Senate confirmed Marshall's appointment by the overwhelming margin of sixty-nine to eleven. Senate majority leader Mike Mansfield of Montana called the action "a confirmation of the vitality of the democratic system." He added, "Thurgood Marshall's rise to the Supreme Court reaffirms the American ideal that what counts is what you are and not who you are, or whom your antecedents may have been."

Republican senator Thomas H. Kuchel of California made a rare direct reference to Marshall's race. He called Marshall's confirmation "part of a larger process in which not only Negro Americans but Americans from all minority racial and religious backgrounds have begun to participate in the affairs of the nation."

From his office at the Justice Department, Marshall issued a statement saying he was "greatly honored by the appointment and its confirmation." He went on, "Let me take this opportunity to reaffirm my deep faith in this nation and its people and to pledge that I shall be ever mindful of my obligation to the Constitution and to the goal of equal justice under law."

Ironically, while Marshall was expressing his faith and gratitude, another black American, Stokely Carmichael, was on the other side of the world communicating contradictory sentiments. On the same day that the Senate approved Marshall's appointment to the Supreme Court, Carmichael met in Hanoi with leaders of the North Vietnamese National Assembly. He told them that U.S. blacks and the Vietnamese people were engaged in a struggle against a common enemy: U.S. imperialism. He pledged to the leaders American blacks' support.

After issuing his formal statement to the press, Marshall telephoned the president to thank him personally for the appointment. He was disappointed and somewhat perplexed to discover that Johnson did not share his unbridled enthusiasm. Johnson told him, "Well, congratulations, but the hell you caused me. Goddammit, I never went through so much hell."

Years later, in January 1973, Johnson spoke with Marshall by phone from his Texas ranch. The men had developed a friendship, combining their similar political views with their passions for bourbon and cigarettes. The former president told Marshall that he believed appointing the first black to the Supreme Court caused his political demise. "He thought that moving me here [to the Court] was what killed him off," Marshall recalls. "He felt they used the Vietnam War as the excuse. He told me that as late as about a week before he died."

"I loved that man," Marshall said of LBJ.

Meanwhile, Cissy Marshall began to peruse interior design magazines and started window-shopping for ideas. It would fall to her to decorate her husband's new chambers at the Supreme Court. What did Thurgood know about chairs, rugs, and draperies? The royal blue decor chosen by Marshall's predecessor Tom Clark would have to go. She decided instead on deep red with black leather. But for the time being, all of that would have to wait. She and the boys would have to prepare for the swearing-in ceremony.

NINETEEN

A Liberal on a Liberal Court

> Move, but move within the Constitution, and
> find new ways of moving nonviolently within
> the Constitution, bearing in mind that there
> are many of us in this country who are not
> going to let it go down the drain. We are not
> going to continue to stand for anarchy, which
> is anarchy which is anarchy.
>
> —Thurgood Marshall

T hurgood Marshall Jr. was asked to describe his father's mood on the morning of Monday, October 1, 1967. The eleven-year-old replied, "He acted generally normal, kinda jumpy."

"Is he normally jumpy?" a reporter asked.

"No," said the boy, "he isn't normally jumpy."

Cissy Marshall was asked to describe how she felt. "I'm still up in the air," she admitted. "This is something you hope for but think will never happen."

But it did happen. In the same ornate chamber where as lawyer for the NAACP he had won cases that shaped the future of America's multiracial democracy, Thurgood Marshall was about to be sworn in as the first Afro-American Supreme Court justice.

The mood was ethereal. The setting lends itself to that. The courtroom is magnificent, the most majestic chamber in the land. It is surrounded by marble columns that support a ceiling so high there seems to be no ceiling at all, only the pensive gaze of the gods above. At the same time, the room is heavy, solemn. It pulses with the history and the high drama played out there. At the front of the room is the long, elevated bench behind which the nine justices sit. Their judgments are delivered from on high, a reminder that no one is above the law.

The Supreme Court begins its term on the first Monday in October. Attorneys docketed for oral argument, their families, friends, interested parties, the press, and the general public gather inside the courtroom by 10:00 A.M. On this particular day, the spectators seated in the family section, the second row of the red-cushioned mahogany pews, included Marshall's wife and children; his brother, Aubrey; a sister-in-law, Mrs. Phillip Acoba of Honolulu; and his aunt Mrs. Cyrus W. Marshall. Seated with the family were Arthur Spingarn, a founder of the NAACP and former president of its board of directors, and Tom C. Clark, the man Marshall replaced.

At precisely 10:01 A.M., another spectator arrived and sat in the middle of the front row: President Lyndon Baines Johnson.

The Court's enigmatic rituals and traditions inspire an awed bewilderment in some onlookers, a bemused curiosity in others. After the president was seated, the marshal of the Court, T. Perry Lippett, rose from his chair at the far end of the bench and gaveled the chamber to its feet. "Oyez, oyez, oyez!" he announced. "Persons having business before the Honorable, the Supreme Court of the United States are admonished to draw near and give their attention, for the Court is now sitting." He closed his eyes and bowed his head. "God save the United States and this Honorable Court."

From behind three sets of massive red velvet draperies, one at each end of the bench and the other in the middle, the black-robed justices emerged in groups of three and took their seats, except for Marshall, who sat at the end of the dais in a chair next to Lippett. Chief Justice Warren opened the session with the announcement of Marshall's appointment, followed by words of praise for his predecessor, Clark. Alluding to Clark's sons's ascension to the attorney generalship, Warren said, "While we still feel the loss of his [Justice Clark's] wisdom and companionship, the felicitous reason for his retirement compels us to forgo the regret which we would otherwise have."

John F. Davis, clerk of the Court, stood and read Marshall's commission. Marshall rose, dressed in the robe he wore on the Second Circuit court of appeals. Lippett stood with him and administered the ceremonial oath of office. He swore to "administer justice without respect to persons and do equal right to the poor and to the rich."

It was Marshall's second swearing in. The first, and official one, occurred on September 1 in a private ceremony in senior justice Hugo Black's chambers. At that time, Marshall was sworn in by Black and took an oath to "support and defend the Constitution," his brown hand resting resolutely on a weathered Bible that belonged to the former Ku Klux Klansman.

Lippett escorted the new justice to his seat at the end of the bench. The seating of the justices is based on seniority. The chief justice sits in the middle. The longest-serving member sits to his immediate right; the second-longest-serving member to the chief's left; then right again to the third most senior justice; left for the fourth; and so on. Marshall, the most junior member, found himself at the far left end of the bench, next to Justice White.

The brief ceremony over, the president left without comment. It was 10:06 A.M.

The Warren Court was lambasted by its critics for its judicial activism. It greatly expanded the power of the federal courts over matters traditionally left to the states, and it stressed the rights of individuals, including those suspected of criminal activity, against the power of state and federal government. The breadth of the changes in American society brought about by Warren Court rulings was indeed monumental. Among the most notable decisions were *Brown v. Board of Education* (1954) and its progeny, outlawing segregation; *Mapp v. Ohio* (1961), excluding illegally seized evidence from criminal prosecutions; *Baker v. Carr* (1962) and *Reynolds v. Simms* (1964), mandating "one person, one vote" in local and congressional elections, respectively; *Gideon v.*

Wainwright (1963), entitling indigent criminal defendants to legal representation paid for by the State; *New York Times v. Sullivan* (1964), restricting the right of public officials to sue the press for libel; *Griswold v. Connecticut* (1965), expanding the right of privacy to protect married couples' use of contraceptive devices; *Miranda v. Arizona* (1966), establishing guidelines for the arrest and interrogation of criminal suspects; and *Loving v. Virginia* (1967), striking down state laws against interracial marriage.

Because Supreme Court justices are appointed for life unless impeached, they are beholden to no one politically. Therefore, it is difficult if not impossible to predict how a justice will vote once elevated to the Court. Even past records can be deceptive. Eisenhower, for example, appointed Warren because of Warren's Republican "middle of the road philosophy." Warren's middle proved to be Eisenhower's left lane, and Ike later lamented the appointment as "the biggest damned-fool mistake I ever made."

But Marshall surprised no one. His critics complained that he would add to the Court's liberal majority, and in fact he did. From 1967 until the end of the Warren era in 1969, he contributed a number of views and opinions that meshed with those of the liberal bloc consisting of Warren, Black, Douglas, Brennan, and Fortas. White was considered a swing vote, somewhat unpredictable. Justices Stewart and John Marshall Harlan, an Eisenhower appointee whose grandfather and namesake wrote the famed lone dissent in *Plessy v. Ferguson,* were the Court's most conservative members.

For example, in his first major majority opinion, *Interstate Circuit, Inc. v. City of Dallas* (1968), Marshall demonstrated a solicitous attitude toward First Amendment freedoms. In *Interstate* the Court considered the constitutionality of a Dallas city ordinance that set up a board of censors to review motion pictures to determine whether they were "suitable" for viewing by persons under sixteen years of age. At issue was an erotic film, *Viva Maria,* banned by local officials.

For some years the Court had grappled with the regulation of pornography and struggled to arrive at a workable definition of obscenity. Pornography restrictions posed a threat to the First Amendment guarantee of free speech, which had to be balanced with the desire to uphold community values.

Marshall enjoyed the debate in his own inimical way. Always a gregarious man, he indulged his ribald humor even within the stodgy confines of the Court. Each week the justices gathered with their law clerks in a basement room next to the pages' room to watch the adult movies they were called upon to review. This irreverently became known as "Dirty Movie Day." Marshall always took a front-row seat and wisecracked loudly throughout the viewings, especially if he had had a few drinks at lunch, which was not unusual. If the action on-screen got especially heated, he would commend the performance and even ask for a copy of the film so he could have it to show his kids when they reached college age.

Black and Douglas never attended the showings. They believed that the First Amendment, which provides that "Congress shall make no law...abridging the freedom of speech," was *absolute*. To them "no law" meant *no* law. Black ridiculed the attempt at formulating pornography restrictions. He derided his brethren, as the justices refer to themselves, as the "Supreme Board of Censors." He wondered what men the brethren's age could presume to know about sexuality, anyway, and he said that if they wanted to watch dirty movies they should go to the theater and pay the cost of admission just like everybody else.

Marshall's opinion in *Interstate* focused on free expression, striking down the Dallas ordinance as unconstitutionally vague. He contended that such terms as "sexual promiscuity" lacked specificity and could be interpreted entirely too broadly. "It may be unlikely that what Dallas does in respect to the licensing of motion pictures would have a significant effect upon filmmakers in Hollywood or Europe," he wrote. "But what Dallas may constitutionally do, so may other cities and states."

In another First Amendment case, the Court expanded free speech protections to privately owned shopping malls. Suburban malls were fast replacing the old-fashioned downtown business districts like the one Marshall grew up knowing in his native Baltimore. In privately owned shopping malls, there are no public streets or sidewalks on which to stand or demonstrate in order to effectively protest a particular store's hiring or employment practices. Writing for a six-to-three majority in *Amalgamated Food Employees Union v. Logan Valley Plaza* (1968), Marshall upheld a labor union's right to picket peacefully in front of a store in a privately owned mall, stating that such protests may not be banned on private property that is devoted to public use.

In criminal justice matters, he followed the majority's emphasis on protecting the rights of the accused. In *Barber v. Page* he wrote for a unanimous Court in support of the right of a suspect to be confronted by his accuser at a preliminary hearing. The case originated in Oklahoma, where a man was convicted of armed robbery based on the transcript of a statement made against him by his accomplice. Marshall concluded that, even for the preliminary hearing, the accomplice should have been taken to Oklahoma from his federal prison cell in Texas to testify in person. He wrote, "The right to confrontation is basically a trial right. It includes both the opportunity to cross-examine and the occasion for the jury to weigh the demeanor of the witness."

He broke with the majority on the question of forced confessions, however. His first dissent came in April 1968. Robert L. Johnson was a bank robber condemned to death for the murder of a Boston policeman. He was never informed of his right to counsel, and his confession was obtained after continuous interrogation by thirty-two police officers left him with a bleeding head wound and in need of brain surgery. The Court dismissed Johnson's claim, citing a 1964 ruling that the "totality of the circumstances" could be taken into consideration when deciding whether a confession obtained under duress should be admitted into evidence. In a dissent joined by Warren and Fortas, Marshall wrote, "I had thought that more recent decisions of this Court would have made it abundantly clear that a confession obtained under the circumstances present here would be involuntary and constitutionally inadmissible."

By 1968 former vice president Richard M. Nixon was again running for president. His "law and order" campaign theme struck a sensitive and responsive nerve among voters nationwide. He appealed directly to white southerners, who traditionally voted Democratic, with his promise that he would appoint to the Supreme Court "strict constructionist" southern jurists who would interpret the Constitution more narrowly, limiting the rights of criminal suspects and reversing the Court's judicial activist trend.

To the right of Nixon was former Alabama governor George C. Wallace. Wallace launched a formidable third-party presidential effort that attracted disillusioned whites in both the North and the South by directly attacking integration and the emphasis on equal opportunity and affirmative action policies that he claimed threatened whites' jobs.

LBJ responded to the rising concern over crime by proposing the Safe Streets and Crime Control Act in 1967. As submitted by Johnson, the bill would have provided federal grants to local law enforcement authorities to upgrade equipment and facilities, including police academies and correctional centers. The president also asked Congress to pass comprehensive gun control legislation.

He was forced to compromise in order to finally get the safe streets bill passed in 1968, agreeing to an antiriot provision insisted upon by Congress. The bill was also stripped of a provision that would have prohibited wiretapping and electronic surveillance except where the national security was deemed to be at risk. Meanwhile, he watched his gun control initiatives die in the House of Representatives.

But while Johnson moved to quiet those calling for stricter law enforcement, he pressed ahead with efforts to further liberalize the Supreme Court. In the spring of 1968, Warren, approaching eighty and suffering from a heart condition, informed the president of his intention to resign in mid-June, giving the president the opportunity to appoint a liberal replacement before the presidential election.

Johnson nominated Abe Fortas to take Warren's place. He picked a fellow Texan, Homer Thornberry of the U.S. Court of Appeals for the Fifth Circuit, to fill the seat made vacant by Fortas's elevation.

Fortas was appointed to the Court by Johnson in 1965. A former Yale Law School professor and a founder of the prestigious law firm of Arnold and Porter in Washington, D.C., he was regarded by LBJ as "the best lawyer I know." He had represented Johnson in the challenge to LBJ's victory in the 1948 Texas Democratic primary election for the U.S. Senate. Fortas won the case when it went to the Supreme Court. From then on, he was one of LBJ's closest advisers and confidants.

Thornberry had succeeded Johnson in the U.S. House of Representatives when Johnson won the Senate seat. During his fifteen years in the House, he earned a reputation as a liberal legislator. On the bench, first as a federal district court judge and later on the court of appeals, he became known as an ardent enforcer of civil rights.

Both nominations were doomed virtually from the start. Throughout his tenure on the Court, Fortas had continued to advise Johnson on matters ranging from economic policy to the conduct of the Vietnam War as well as on matters pending or likely to come before the Court. When this came to light, he was accused of ethical indiscretions that called his fitness into question.

One such indiscretion involved Marshall, albeit indirectly. In 1966 Marshall, as solicitor general, drafted a brief for a Supreme Court case challenging the merger of the Pennsylvania and New York Central railroads (Penn-Central), opposed by the Justice Department on antitrust grounds. The consolidation was popular in New York among wealthy Democratic party campaign contributors, however, and Johnson wanted the deal to go through. He called Fortas at the Court and asked him what to do.

Fortas advised the president that the agencies in charge of regulating interstate transportation should set the government's policy regarding the merger. In other words, Secretary of Transportation designate Alan Boyd, known to favor the deal, should have final say as to the government's position, not Solicitor General Marshall. LBJ instructed Boyd to tell Marshall to rewrite his brief.

At first Marshall balked. He complained, "It is inconceivable that the solicitor general could fail to take a position before the Supreme Court." But in the end he did what he was told, dropping his opposition to the merger. He rewrote the brief to say, "We emphasize that...we do not quarrel with the merits of the Penn-Central merger proposal itself. Indeed, the agencies of the Executive Branch that have substantive responsibilities for the formulation of economic and transportation policy believe that the merger is in the public interest and that its consummation should be promptly effected."

The Court remanded the case for further consideration by the Interstate Commerce Commission over the vigorous dissent of Fortas, who was joined by Harlan, Stewart, and White. The case eventually came back to the Court and was decided in January 1968. Marshall recused himself because of his earlier involvement as solicitor general. Fortas had the temerity to write the majority opinion approving the merger.

When Johnson failed to muster the two-thirds vote needed to cut off the Senate filibuster that blocked Fortas's appointment, Fortas asked that his nomination as chief justice be withdrawn. For the time being, he remained on the Court as an associate justice. Warren stayed on as chief pending the qualification of a successor.

Meanwhile, Johnson had decided not to seek a second term. His support within his own party had been eroded by challenges from Minnesota's Senator Eugene McCarthy and New York's Senator Robert F. Kennedy, and the country was divided over both his civil rights policies and the Vietnam War. He told the nation on March 31, 1968, "I shall not seek—and will not accept—the nomination of my party for another term as your president." Richard M. Nixon went on to defeat Vice President Hubert H. Humphrey in one of the closest presidential elections in history.

The spring of 1969 found Marshall despondent. As he saw it, his life's work, everything he stood for, was threatened by Nixon's ascendancy. He could easily imagine nightmare scenarios that would deliver Nixon three, maybe even four, conservative appointments to the Court during his first year or two in office.

Warren's resignation was already on Nixon's desk. In addition, Black and Douglas were in failing health. Black was in his early eighties and had suffered a stroke that left his short-term memory impaired. His gait was now a mere shuffle, and he broke wind uncontrollably on the bench and in conference. Douglas, seventy, had recently married his fourth wife, Cathy, a twenty-five-year-old law student at American University. The couple met one evening when she waited on his table in a Washington restaurant. But while Douglas was still alert and of a youthful mind, he was known to suffer from a heart condition that would eventually require the implantation of an electronic pacemaker.

Moreover, the Nixon Justice Department was targeting the members of the Court's liberal bloc, probing for evidence of misconduct to use for impeachment or to force resignations. Questions had been raised about Douglas's relationship with Albert Parvin, a Las Vegas casino owner. Douglas served as director of the Albert Parvin Foundation. Fortas was under scrutiny as well, and ugly rumors were surfacing about his financial dealings both on and off the bench. It looked as if Nixon would succeed in forcing him off the Court. Even Brennan was threatened. Investigators were looking into a fifteen-thousand-dollar real estate investment he had made with Fortas and several lower court judges.

Beyond all this, the country was experiencing an inexorable shift to the right. Marshall was convinced that black militancy and the riots that followed Martin Luther King Jr.'s assassination in April 1968 had altered the political climate for the worse. Then, of course, there was the Vietnam War and the disillusioned young people who so stridently opposed it. The hippies, the Yippies, the drug culture, those who preached "Never trust anyone over thirty"—all posed challenges to the established social order, which, in his mind, resulted in retrenchment by the white middle class, the great "silent majority" that had brought Nixon to power.

Far from being a radical, Marshall could relate to middle-class fear and frustration. At the very least, he understood the need to be sensitive to middle-class concerns. He had, after all, come from the middle class, from people who worked hard all their lives for what they had and did not want to lose it. What was wrong with that? As Paul Gewitz, a former law clerk for Marshall and now a professor of law at Yale, said, "He had a strong distaste for flag burners and others who attacked our country."

Shortly after he was elevated to the Court, Marshall defended the young people who criticized "the Establishment," defiantly growing their hair long and launching the 1960s countercultural revolution. At a Women's National Press Club reception given in honor of him and his wife at the International Club in Washington on December 6, 1967, he reminded his audience that the young have always been restless for change.

"These young people with their hair down to here—we worry about these youngsters," he said, "but it is nothing new." He offered a humorous reminiscence: "I was in college four years and participated in four strikes. I led three of the strikes and was into a fifth strike, only to find we were trying it too early in the season. The dean called us in and told us our timing was wrong. He said he had enough additional applicants to fill our places. He suggested we wait until at least Thanksgiving."

He went on to speak of his life as an advocate devoted to changing many of the fundamental assumptions and social practices in America, such as segregation. He called his Supreme Court appointment "a real challenge that gives me the opportunity to put up or shut up."

By the spring of 1969, his attitude was less sanguine. He decided to speak out against the destructive trend of the protest movement. In his mind, it was one thing to criticize or dissent, quite another just to tear things down. He had credibility, and his credentials in the struggle for change were unimpeachable. It was time for someone like him to take a stand against the stridency and militancy that were fueling the white middle-class backlash. Otherwise, there was no telling to what extent the drive to turn the clock back on social progress would succeed.

He contemplated an appropriate forum. Because of its relative obscurity, he chose what seemed an unlikely venue: Dillard University, a small, traditionally black, predominantly female Methodist school located in a residential section of New Orleans. The occasion for which he was invited to speak was the institution's centennial celebration on May 4, 1969.

Speaking extemporaneously, referring occasionally to a few handwritten notes, he attacked black separatism and those who would seek to bring about revolution or social reform through violence.

"Every country in the world is seething with young people on the move. What I want to talk to you about this afternoon," he told his undergraduate audience, "is not to stop it, not to stop this energy, but to channel it toward a decent end." He went on, "I remember a congressman, a Negro congressman, who said, 'The trouble is that you don't follow the right theory. Don't get mad—get smart!'"

Saying that there had been "a whole lot of progress" in race relations over the previous decade, he defended America despite her faults. "I've never had to defend my country by lying about it," he declared. "I can tell the truth about it and still be proud. I'm not going to be completely satisfied. I'll be dead before I'll be satisfied."

He assailed the movements for a separate homeland in the United States just for blacks and for curricula based exclusively on black studies. "I don't believe that everything that's black is right and everything else is wrong. I think that we Negro Americans have just as many beautiful in mind and body, as well as skin, as any other group. And I am sure we have just as many stinkers as there are in every other group."

He reaffirmed his belief in the American dream. "Our country is based on equality—that all men are created equal—or the Fourteenth Amendment, which is actually a conjugation of the Judeo-Christian ethnic of the equality of man—his individual equality. And I say you can't destroy that by setting up one group as superior to everybody else."

He then turned his assault on those who perpetrated riots and civil disorder, attributing their motives to social irresponsibility and cowardice. "I don't believe you can use color for an excuse for not doing what you know should be done," he declared. "I don't think race should be an excuse not to take care of your children and bring them up properly, even if they are still in segregated schools. I think that race is not an excuse for not keeping your house up properly."

He went on, "As you look around the world today, you'll find that anarchy is what's wrecking country after country, pulling down, tearing down, building not. And in this country we don't approach it yet. But the seeds of it remain. Nothing will be settled with a gun. Nothing will be settled with a fire bomb. And nothing will be settled with a rock, because the country cannot survive if it permits it to go unpunished. It's that simple. It takes no courage to throw a rock. Rather, it takes courage to stand up on your own two feet and look anyone straight in the eye and say, 'I will not be beaten.'"

Alluding to the riots precipitated by King's death, he pondered aloud, "I wonder how many people who burned whole areas of towns like Washington and Chicago ever even thought of voting or going to church or doing any of the things that our country was founded upon."

He concluded by offering encouragement, tempered with a warning: "Move, but move within the Constitution, and find new ways of moving nonviolently within the Constitution, bearing in mind that there are many of us in this country who are not going to let it go down the drain. We are not going to continue to stand for anarchy, which is anarchy which is anarchy."

Voltaire once said, "I may not agree with what you say, but I will defend to the death your right to say it." Marshall was that kind of man, committed to free speech under the First Amendment, notwithstanding his personal beliefs and sentiments. During the Court's 1968–69 term, he joined in a *per curiam* order overturning an Ohio law making it a crime to advocate violent acts. He also voted to uphold the right of a white supremacist organization to espouse its views at a public rally despite the likelihood that violence would result.

The investigations of Douglas and Brennan yielded nothing of substance. But by mid-May government investigators had un-covered incontrovertible evidence of a financial arrangement between Fortas and Leonard Wolfson, a wealthy industrialist. Fortas was to receive twenty thousand dollars a year for life from a foundation that Wolfson funded. Fortas's widow was to continue receiving payments after his death. Fortas had apparently prom-ised to use his influence to derail a Securities and Exchange Commission investigation of Wolfson that eventually resulted in Wolfson's indictment and conviction. Forced by Attorney General John N. Mitchell to choose between resigning from the Court or facing impeachment and possible criminal prosecution, Fortas resigned on May 14, 1969.

Meanwhile, Nixon had settled on a replacement for Warren. In late June the Senate confirmed his nomination of Warren E. Burger, a judge on the U.S. Court of Appeals for the District of

Columbia Circuit, to be the nation's next chief justice. Next, Nixon turned his attention to candidates for the seat vacated by Fortas. In office less than a year, Nixon was already in a position to reshape the Court with his two appointments.

Four years later, on July 9, 1973, Earl Warren died of cardiac arrest at Georgetown University Hospital. Marshall was deeply saddened by the passing of the man he referred to as the "Super Chief," who, in his opinion, had done more to bring about racial equality than anyone else in the twentieth century. He said, "When history is written, he'll go down as one of the great chief justices the country has ever been blessed with. I think he is irreplaceable."

In the meantime, he found himself in the unenviable position of trying to carry on the Warren Court's legacy with the ranks of his liberal compatriots on the Court ailing and dwindling.

TWENTY

A House Becomes a Home

It's a private matter where I make my home.
—Thurgood Marshall

In November 1968 Thurgood and Cissy Marshall were looking for a new house. They had decided to move from their predominantly black neighborhood on Fourth Street in southwest Washington, D.C., to the Virginia suburbs. When President Johnson had appointed Marshall to the post of solicitor general, in 1965, Cissy had been reluctant to move her family to Washington. Thurgood Jr., almost nine, and John, seven, were attending the Dalton School, a private school on Eighty-ninth Street in New York City.

"I don't feel that now is the time to pull up roots here in New York as far as the boys are concerned," she said. "I feel we ought to take our time and find a good school in Washington for the boys before making any move." But she finally agreed, and the family came to Washington that year.

Now, three years later, Cecilia Marshall asked Attorney General Ramsey Clark and his wife to help them find a house in the Clarks' neighborhood, an all-white subdivision in Falls Church, Virginia. The Marshalls had been guests at the Clarks' home and believed the area would be a pleasant place to live and raise their two sons, now twelve and ten.

Mrs. Vincent Augliere, a saleswoman for Regent Realty, had helped the Clark's find their own house several years earlier. She soon discovered a contemporary ranch-style home with five bedrooms and three baths on curving Lakeside Drive, overlooking the 114-acre Lake Barcroft, priced at $52,000. She thought the Marshalls might like it. Mrs. Augliere had no reservations about showing the house to the Marshalls. She had been one of only a few northern Virginia real estate agents to speak out openly in favor of Fairfax County's open housing ordinance. The owner of the house told his neighbors the Marshalls' had decided to purchase his property; he said only one objected.

That neighbor told the *Washington Star:* "I'm not happy about it at all, because this might be encouragement for more of the same."

Thurgood and Cissy liked the house, and soon they moved in with their sons and became the first black family on the block. Marshall refused to discuss the purchase and his integration of the neighborhood with reporters from the *Washington Post* and the *Washington Star.* "It's a private matter where I make my home," he said.

But most of the Marshalls' new neighbors were not distressed by their arrival. Ramsey Clark's wife said, "I think most people around here were just delighted. The only thing I was afraid of was that the Marshalls would be overwhelmed with hospitality."

In the summer of 1969 it was the Marshalls' own hospitality and the pungent, rising smoke from Thurgood's backyard barbecue pit that "overwhelmed" Lakeside Drive homeowners as Thurgood and Cissy welcomed their new neighbors, including the Clarks and Barefoot Sanders, legislative assistant to President Lyndon B. Johnson, to hearty feasts of chicken, spare ribs, and steaks.

Cissy turned the house into a comfortable home, using one of its five bedrooms for Thurgood's den. She filled bookcases with copies of the U.S. Code and plastered the walls with Thurgood's large collection of photographs, pictures, plaques, and awards, among them the NAACP's Spingarn Medal.

The Marshalls' new house was a short drive from Washington's Maine Avenue waterfront, where on summer Saturdays Thurgood purchased bushels of Maryland blue crabs, one of his favorite delicacies. He had learned the secret of cooking them—a little steaming water, half a cup of apple cider vinegar, and the famous Old Bay Seasoning, manufactured in his native city, with a dash of black pepper—in his maternal grandmother's kitchen. He knew how to eat them, too—separating the back fin's lump of meat from the delicate cellophane membrane—because he acquired that indigenous Maryland skill as a teenager.

Marshall planned and presided over elegant dinner parties for old friends, among them singers Harry Belafonte and Lena Horne. "Thurgood cooks the best pigs' feet in the world," Lena Horne said. Belafonte's former wife, Marguerite Mazique, remembers that at the Marshall home "you ate better than if you had gone to one of Washington's best restaurants."

His closest friend on the Supreme Court, Associate Justice William Brennan, was also a frequent guest at the Marshall dinner table. But, following tradition, Marshall limited his social contacts with friends in the legal profession. He said his formerly large circle of friends became smaller when he joined the Supreme Court because most of them were civil rights lawyers "and would probably have business before the Court."

The sixty-year-old Marshall was seen frequently in his backyard tossing a softball or playing touch football with his two young sons. He often joked that was all the exercise he did. The neighborhood children were friendly to the Marshall boys, who had inherited their father's light skin and straight hair and their mother's soft Asian features.

Thurgood also pursued another lifelong interest, the racetrack. At nearby Maryland tracks, such as Laurel, Bowie, and Pimlico, he would often meet another rail bird, former Lincoln University classmate Cab Calloway. Calloway, who still goes to Laurel, said Marshall had a special interest in following Maryland-bred horses. "He was never a heavy bettor," Calloway remembered. "And he was a pretty good handicapper."

Thurgood and Cissy made frequent trips to Atlantic City after

casino gambling was legalized there. Thurgood played blackjack
and roulette at Bally's and Resorts for small stakes and reluctantly
admitted he lost six hundred dollars one weekend; he never
discussed his winnings.

Marshall spent many evenings in his paneled family room
watching reruns of his favorite western movies. And he enjoyed
watching baseball games, especially when the Baltimore Orioles
were playing. Like most people in the Washington metropolitan
area, the Marshalls were avid Washington Redskin fans, often
joining the crowd on Sunday afternoons at Robert F. Kennedy
Stadium to wave burgundy-and-gold pennants and root for the
capital's football team.

Thurgood's interest in music ranged from jazz to symphonies. "I
don't know all the titles and composers," he confessed. "I just like
it." His fondness for jazz began in the 1930s, when he lived in
Harlem and counted among his friends bandleader Duke
Ellington, a native of Washington, D.C., and singer Lena Horne.

Supreme Court security guard Lloyd D. Roberts, who is now
retired, frequently drove Marshall to and from the Court.
Roberts, who is black and now pastor of Ebenezer Baptist Church
in Alexandria, Virginia, recalled the twenty-five minute trips
across the Fourteenth Street Bridge, spanning the Potomac River.

"Unlike some of the other justices, he treated me as an equal. He
would sit in the back of the car, and if he wasn't reading a case, we
would talk about the importance of his position as the only
minority on the Court, and he often told me his presence on the
Court made a difference, even as he became a member of the
Court's minority. Sometimes, when we arrived at his home late at
night from a social function or a late court session, he would
invite me in, and Mrs. Marshall would serve us coffee and cake.
She, like the judge, is a very congenial person."

According to Roberts, Marshall knew how to drive and owned a
gray Cadillac, but stopped driving at the age of seventy-one,
"about 1979, when he had increasing medical problems and
cataracts." Justices Powell and Blackmun were the only other
justices who spoke to Roberts as equals when he drove for them,
he said. "Blackmun and Powell didn't treat me like just a

chauffeur, and when Justice Powell, a real Virginia gentleman, heard I was graduating from Howard University's divinity school, he sent me a hundred-dollar graduation present."

Roberts said the conversations he had while driving Justices White, Rehnquist, and Burger were much different. "They would only talk to me about the weather or sports, like baseball, football, or boxing, because they thought that was all I was interested in or was able to understand, but Thurgood Marshall was never demeaning or condescending."

The Marshall family's 1968 transition to the "Better Homes and Gardens" life actually started twenty-four years earlier, when Marshall won a Supreme Court decision striking down restrictive covenants that legally sanctioned all-white neighborhoods.

At an NAACP meeting in 1944, Marshall sharply criticized the Federal Housing Administration for the racial restrictions it placed on rentals in a new government housing project in Detroit. Its eight hundred units designated for white occupants stood vacant while thousands of black citizens lived in substandard housing. In Detroit's suburbs black families could not buy or rent homes from white owners. The situation was not much different in the rest of the nation.

Even in Marshall's native Baltimore, where shortly after the turn of the century black and white families had lived side by side, black families could not purchase or rent property in some of the city's better neighborhoods, such as Park Heights, and on Liberty Road across the Baltimore County line.

The racial exclusivity of white neighborhoods was protected by restricted covenants: written agreements, enforceable by state laws, between white buyers and sellers that they would never sell or rent their property to someone of a different race or, sometimes, a different religion. In some states entire towns signed restrictive covenants. The bans had been challenged many times in the courts, and their legality was always upheld. As early as 1926, in *Chicago v. Buckley* the Supreme Court said that restrictive covenants were actions between private parties neither governed nor sanctioned by the state and that, though they were discriminatory, they were not illegal. The Court said the Constitution did not "prohibit private individuals from entering into contracts respecting...their own property."

In 1947 Thurgood Marshall combined three restrictive-covenant suits that had been lost in the lower courts. Marshall asked the Supreme Court to consider the complaint of Orsel McGee and his wife, who bought a house in a racially restricted Detroit neighborhood from a white owner who ignored the covenant. When a white homeowner named Sipes learned of the sale, he rushed to obtain a court order prohibiting the McGees from moving into their new home. The order was upheld in Michigan's highest court.

The Supreme Court heard the combined restrictive-covenants cases as *Shelley v. Kraemer* in 1948. Attorney General Tom Clark, on instructions from President Truman, filed an *amicus curiae* brief on behalf of the United States, asking the Court to strike down restrictive covenants.

Marshall argued, "This case is not a matter of enforcing an isolated private agreement. It is a test as to whether we will have a united nation or a nation divided into areas and ghettos solely on racial and religious lines." Ruling restrictive covenants illegal, he argued, would "allow a flexible way of life to develop in which each individual will be able to live, work, and raise his family as a free American."

In May 1948 all six sitting judges agreed that restrictive convenants were unconstitutional. Reed, Jackson, and Rutledge recused themselves from the case without giving a reason. It was believed, however, that they declined to hear the case because each of them owned property covered by restrictive covenants.

"These are not cases, as has been suggested, in which the states have merely abstained from action, leaving private individuals free to impose discriminations as they see fit," wrote Chief Justice Fred M. Vinson. "Rather, there are cases in which the states have made available to such individuals the full coercive power of government to deny petitioners, on the grounds of race or color, the enjoyment of property rights in premises which the petitioners are willing and able to acquire and which the grantors are willing to sell." Vinson continued, "Equal protection of the laws is not achieved through indiscriminate imposition of inequalities."

Though black Americans still faced formidable obstacles in

purchasing decent housing, there was noticeable progress. Two years after Marshall won the case that struck down restrictive covenants, the 1950 census disclosed that nonwhites were living in 459 more of the 3,887 residential blocks in Washington, D.C., than in 1940. Chicago's Commission on Human Relations reported four years after the covenant case that twenty-one thousand black families had purchased or rented property in neighborhoods from which they were formerly excluded. It was this decision and its implementation that eventually made it possible for the Marshalls to buy their Lake Barcroft home.

Thurgood's marriage to Cissy was considered an interracial marriage by the U.S. Census Bureau and the Commonwealth of Virginia. If the Marshalls had bought their home in 1967 instead of 1968, they would have been in violation of Virginia's 210-year-old antimiscegenation law that made it a crime for mixed-race couples to live in the state.

Cissy, who was Hawaiian-born and of Filipino ancestry, turned down Thurgood's initial proposal of marriage. "They called me a foreigner, and with his position I didn't want to bring any controversy into it." Their marriage was noted by a Mississippi newspaper that wrote that Thurgood Marshall had "admitted his racial prejudice by marrying a white woman."

"And I wrote back to them," Marshall recalled, "and I said, 'Not that I object to it, but I just think you ought to be accurate. And I don't know which wife you are talking about, but I have had two wives and both of 'em were colored.'"

The editor scrawled a two-word reply on the back of the letter. "So what?"

In 1958, ten years before the Marshalls moved to Virginia, Richard Loving, a white man, and his seventeen-year-old black bride, Mildred, moved to Virginia's rural Caroline County. They had been married in the District of Columbia. In the middle of a July night, the Caroline County sheriff rousted the Lovings from their bed and took them to the courthouse in Bowling Green. They were charged with violating Virginia's antimiscegenation laws. Judge Leon A. Bazile found the Lovings guilty and sentenced them to a year in jail. Bazile said he had to uphold Virginia's "racial integrity."

He agreed to suspend the sentence if the Lovings left Virginia and did not return for twenty-five years. The Lovings moved to Washington and retained Bernard S. Cohen, an attorney for the American Civil Liberties Union, to challenge the law. They began a lengthy court battle that did not end until 1967, when the U.S. Supreme Court, in *Loving v. Virginia,* ruled the miscegenation laws of Virginia and fifteen other states unconstitutional.

Black men had been lynched for making complimentary remarks to white women. Love across the color line was one of racism's strongest taboos. A 1991 Gallup Poll disclosed that 44 percent of white Americans approved of interracial marriages and 45 percent disapproved.

The *Loving* case was to have another implication for the Marshall family. The two Marshall boys married white women. When questioned about the marriages, Thurgood Marshall Sr. responds with a defiant "So what!" and refuses to discuss it further.

The Marshall's sons chose law enforcement careers initially. They both say their father did not influence their decisions. John W. Marshall, Thurgood and Cissy's younger son, is a state trooper. Marshall was disappointed when his boy quit college to become a Virginia State Police officer. "He didn't downgrade me or talk down to me," declared Sgt. John W. Marshall, who teaches the use of firearms and survival tactics at the Virginia State Police Academy. "I know him well enough, I could tell when he is disappointed. I felt pretty bad about it. I told myself I was going to go back to school."

John returned to Georgetown University in Washington, D.C., part-time and in 1989 received his degree in government and sociology. He kept his school attendance a secret from his parents. They did not know about it until they received an invitation to his graduation. "My dad yelled for joy," John said.

John Marshall is considering attending law school. "Of course, I'd want to be a prosecutor, I'd want to be on the prosecuting side," he said. "My dad, he'd shake his head again, I guess."

Thurgood Marshall Jr. received his undergraduate and law degrees from the University of Virginia and worked for a while as a federal prosecutor in the U.S. Attorney's office in Washington, D.C., before becoming judiciary counsel on the staff of Massachusetts senator Edward M. Kennedy. His wife, Colleen, is an attorney with the Securities and Exchange Commission.

Marshall, who spent most of his professional life fighting for equal treatment of blacks by the white law enforcement establishment, does not think it ironic that he has a son who served as a prosecutor and another son who is a police officer.

"I didn't give advice to either one of my boys," he said. "I had a deal with them: I would answer any question, but I wouldn't volunteer advice. And it ends up that one of them gave up a job paying $100,000 with the biggest law firm here to go to work for Ted Kennedy.

"I said, 'With all the money I spent on your education, why did you take that?'"

"You know what he said? 'I know somebody else who didn't give a damn about money, too.'"

His son's remark was probably accurate. In 1989 financial disclosures statements that made public the assets of Supreme Court justices, Marshall listed his holdings as between $50,000 and $100,000. He reported owning a $2,500 Steuben glass piece he received as a gift from the Judicial Friends of New York City. By contrast, Justice Sandra Day O'Conner listed her assets as between $1.3 and $2.6 million. Justices Harry Blackmun, Anthony Kennedy, William Rehnquist, William Brennan, John Paul Stevens, Antonin Scalia, and Byron White said their assets were close to $500,000. Financial reporting procedures do not require justices to list the value of real estate they use as a personal residence.

"And my other son is a state trooper, a state policeman, and he had the same kind of education, he graduated from Georgetown," Marshall continued. "And you know what he said? 'I want to work for the people.'"

Marshall does not seem concerned that his sons are not worried about earning large salaries. "So that's their way, not based on money," Marshall explained. "I mentioned it to Lewis Powell on our Court, and Lewis said, 'Yeah, I understand you, but I just remembered that a friend of mine who was the president of the biggest bank in Richmond was a former state trooper.'"

"So I said, 'I have something to look forward to.'"

TWENTY-ONE

Marshall and the Burger Court

> Somewhere in our history—though not inten-
> tionally—we slowly moved from a government
> of the people to a government of a chosen few
> ...who, either by birth, family tradition or
> social standing—a minority possessing all the
> wealth and power—now...control the destiny
> of mankind.
>
> —An American GI in Vietnam

Warren E. Burger had a regal bearing. He was six feet one, broad-shouldered, and husky, a handsome Minnesotan with an erect, measured gait, a deep voice, and thick white hair. He was an adept debater and a politically astute, skillful behind-the-scenes maneuverer who never shied away from a confrontation with those who posed a threat to his conservative, midwestern mores and vision for America.

He began his career as a trial lawyer in St. Paul, Minnesota, where he became active in politics. In 1952 he managed St. Paul attorney Roger Kennedy's unsuccessful campaign to unseat Democratic congressman Eugene J. "Gene" McCarthy. In 1968 McCar-

300

thy, by then a U.S. senator, forced the split within the Democratic party that contributed to Lyndon Johnson's downfall by running for president as a peace candidate opposed to the Vietnam War.

During the 1952 campaign, Burger was accused of bolstering Kennedy's bid by employing the scare tactics of a fellow Minnesotan, Senator Joseph McCarthy. Appearing as a last-minute substitute for Kennedy at a debate at St. Paul's Hamline University, Burger questioned Gene McCarthy's patriotism because the congressman opposed the expulsion of Communists from university faculties, action he saw as a threat to academic freedom. In her memoir *Public Faces/Private Places,* McCarthy's ex-wife Abigail recalled, "Burger, whose legal approach used every trick of courtroom debate, so confused the audience that Gene was never able to make his position clear." The tone of the campaign turned nasty. Fliers attacking McCarthy's loyalty appeared all over the city. They asked rhetorically: "Is YOUR CONGRESSMAN A TRAITOR?"

Burger supported Dwight D. Eisenhower's effort to win the Republican presidential nomination in 1952, although he had originally gone to the national convention in Los Angeles as a delegate for perennial presidential hopeful Harold Stassen, then Minnesota's governor. Eisenhower brought him to Washington as an assistant U.S. attorney general, then in 1956 appointed him to the U.S. Court of Appeals for the District of Columbia Circuit, which for the most part hears appeals of suits brought against the federal government.

Nixon met Burger at the 1948 Republican national convention. When he began his search for Earl Warren's replacement, Burger's name came to mind. During his tenure on the appeals court, Burger was an outspoken critic of what he saw as the court's liberal activism. He called instead for "judicial avoidance," meaning deference to the legislative and executive branches of government in matters of social and economic policy. Also, in speeches and interviews, Burger advocated administrative reform of the judicial system, which he felt was burdened with unnecessary safeguards and delays that made prosecutions and sentencings of criminal defendants unduly cumbersome.

Nixon liked him. So did the Senate. By a vote of seventy-four to three, he was confirmed in June 1969 as the nation's fifteenth chief justice.

At the Court it did not take him long to earn the nickname "Imperial Burger." He insisted on being introduced as the "chief justice of the United States" rather than "chief justice of the Supreme Court." He also began the practice of delivering a "State of the Judiciary" address to the American Bar Association each year, a counterpart to the president's annual State of the Union message to Congress.

At the Court he consulted with architects and interior designers about upgrading the Court's environs to project a loftier aesthetic, a more pronounced and dignified sense of history, prestige, and purpose. The building did, in fact, resemble a mausoleum suffering the neglect of an absentee caretaker. Its stark white-marble corridors were cavernous and bare. For the edification of tourists and visitors, he ordered portraits hung, busts of former justices displayed, and Court memorabilia exhibited under glass.

The courtroom itself needed at least a minor renovation. It was poorly lit and had a shadowy eeriness about it. Burger installed better lights and upgraded the sound system.

In addition, the bench behind which the justices sat was straight. Burger wanted it to curve so that the justices could see each other during oral argument. The justices went along with the redesign, although Marshall quipped privately that in his opinion they saw each other enough and, frankly, there were some brethren he would prefer to see less of.

Other reforms were supercilious. Burger thought the chief justice's chambers were too small, so he appropriated the adjacent conference room, where the nine met each week to discuss and vote on cases, for his own use when entertaining dignitaries or luncheon guests. There was grumbling that the move was "undignified" and "inappropriate."

Also, he ordered two of the Court's four pages—formerly on call in the basement page room when Court was not in session to perform messenger, clerical, and housekeeping duties for any of the nine justices' offices—stationed in the chief's chambers throughout the day for his exclusive use. Among other duties, the pages were to serve him and his three secretaries Earl Grey tea punctually at 4:00 P.M. from silver trays, in china that bore the seal of the chief justice. There were gripes that this, too, was "selfish" and "inappropriate."

But it was not until he tried to change the justices' chairs that he provoked open dissension. By tradition, each justice sat in his own chair behind the bench. Some preferred high-backed swivel rockers. Other chairs had lower backs or were big, upright, and square. Burger thought the chairs should all be the same, projecting an aesthetic uniformity. But the justices flatly refused to give up their chairs.

For the most part, Burger's imperiousness was tolerated with a certain pained amusement, or it was ignored. Douglas, for example, was a rugged outdoorsman whose passions included hiking and mountain climbing even into his later years His own chambers were cramped with books and souvenirs, including Indian headdresses and big overstuffed pillows on which were embroidered such phrases as "Here come de judge," all set against a bright green and yellow decor. He paid the chief no mind at all.

Neither did Brennan, whose long-haired law clerks plastered the walls of his chambers with the kind of posters usually associated with college dormitories, some emblazoned with antiwar or black power slogans.

Always a gregarious man, Marshall did not allow the Imperial Burger's decorousness to inhibit his raucous demeanor and ribald wit. The pages, for example, were high schoolers required to maintain straight-A averages at the Capitol Page School, located across the street from the Court in the Library of Congress. When he encountered them passing through his chambers or in the hall, he would corner them and complain loudly about his own sons' grades if one of them had recently brought home a report card that displeased him.

"A C minus! Damn! A C minus, not even a C, a C *minus*. You can't get much lower than that, can you?" he would ask. "They haven't changed what grades stand for since I was in school, have they?"

Or he could be found in the hallways, sharing his favorite jokes with guards and messengers at the Court. One that he particularly liked was about the golfers who go back to the clubhouse to change after playing eighteen holes. When one puts on a woman's girdle, his pal asks, "When did you start wearing that?' The other golfer responds, "Ever since my wife found it in my glove compartment."

Nixon had difficulty filling the seat vacated by Fortas. His nomination of Clement F. Haynesworth Jr., chief judge on the U.S. Court of Appeals for the Fourth Circuit, in the South, failed to win Senate confirmation in April 1970. Nixon was indebted to the southern white voters who, abandoning their traditional allegiance to the Democratic party, delivered him the South in the 1968 election. But Haynesworth was undermined by the Senate's Democratic majority, which challenged his civil rights record and also questioned his ethics for participating in a case that involved a company in which he owned stock.

Nixon's second choice, G. Harold Carswell, a judge on the Fifth Circuit court of appeals, covering northern Florida, was rejected by the Senate the following month. He was accused of harboring segregationist views. In a speech to an American Legion group in 1948, Carswell had stated, "Segregation of the races is proper and the only practical and correct way of life in our states. I have always so believed and shall always so act."

In addition, when Carswell drafted the charter for Florida State University's boosters' club in 1953, he included in the document a "for whites only" clause. In 1956 he assisted in converting a municipal golf course to private ownership in order to avoid desegregation of the facility. Civil rights lawyers complained that Carswell was openly antagonistic toward them from the bench during civil rights cases throughout his tenure as a judge.

Charging that the Senate's regional prejudice against southern jurists was insurmountable, Nixon again looked north and nominated another Minnesotan in May 1970. His name was Harry Andrew Blackmun, and he had been serving on the U.S. Court of Appeals for the Eighth Circuit since 1959.

Blackmun was born in a small town in southern Illinois but grew up in St. Paul, Minnesota, where he and Burger were boyhood friends. A graduate of Harvard College and Harvard

Law School, he mused fondly that if he had his life to live over again, he would become a doctor instead of a lawyer. He was gratified when, in 1950, he was named general counsel to the prestigious Mayo Clinic in St. Paul, a position for which he abandoned a lucrative private practice specializing in tax, wills, and trusts and estates. Blackmun's time at Mayo would prove significant. Because of his expertise in forensic law, in 1973 he was assigned to write the Court's landmark ruling in *Roe v. Wade*, establishing a woman's constitutional right to an abortion.

During the confirmation hearings that followed his nomination to the Supreme Court, Blackmun came across as an honest, amicable man, a nonideologue. He promised to do his best for the "little people." He once said, "What comes through most clearly is the utter respect which the little person has for the Supreme Court of the United States. The little person feels this is a real bastion for the protection of his rights." He was confirmed by the Senate unanimously in May 1970.

Suddenly the Court looked very different. What was to have been the Fortas Court, consisting of a solid six-member liberal majority comprised of Fortas, Black, Douglas, Brennan, Marshall, and Thornberry, was now the Burger Court, on which conservatives appeared to hold sway. The liberals, Black, Douglas, Brennan, and Marshall, were now aligned against a conservative majority composed of Burger, Stewart, Harlan, White, and Blackmun.

But while the personnel had changed, many of the issues remained the same. For example, during its 1968–69 term, the Court was again confronted with a pornography case, *Stanley v. Georgia*, which pitted First Amendment protections against community values.

In Georgia, the home of a man named Stanley was searched for evidence of illegal bookmaking activities. During the search, police came across and confiscated several rolls of pornographic film in Stanley's bedroom. Stanley was subsequently arrested and charged with violating Georgia's antiobscenity law.

Black and Douglas held to their absolutist view that the First Amendment protected Stanley from prosecution. But theirs seemed an extremist stance that a majority of the Court would not accept. Marshall stepped in and won unanimous support for overturning the conviction. He conceded that obscenity was not protected by the First Amendment, but he emphasized that broader liberties were jeopardized by the violation of Stanley's right of privacy. This enabled him to use the case as a forum for an impassioned defense of First Amendment freedoms.

Writing for the Court, he declared that the "right to receive information and ideas, regardless of their social worth, is fundamental to our free society." Stanley, he went on, "is asserting the right to read or observe what he pleases—the right to satisfy his intellectual and emotional needs in the privacy of his own home. He is asserting the right to be free from state inquiry into the contents of his library."

He concluded, "If the First Amendment means anything, it means that a State has no business telling a man, sitting alone in his own house, what books he may read or what films he may watch. Our whole constitutional heritage rebels at the thought of giving government the power to control men's minds."

During the 1969–70 term, the Court was yet again confronted with persistent resistance to the implementation of its ruling in *Brown*, even though fifteen years had passed since the justices had ordered separate, or dual, school systems for blacks and whites abolished "with all deliberate speed." In *Alexander v. Holmes County Board of Education*, suit was brought on behalf of fourteen black Mississippi schoolchildren whose NAACP lawyers argued that Mississippi was taking too long to effect desegregation in thirty-three school districts.

Shortly after his elevation to the court, Marshall learned that the "all deliberate speed" language had been included in the 1955 *Brown* implementing decree at Frankfurter's insistence. Justice Black had long since come to regret the use of the phrase, which, he lamented, "has turned out to be only a soft euphemism for delay."

"In my opinion," Black once stated, "there can be no more disastrous educational consequence than the continuance for one more day of an unconstitutional dual school system such as those in this case."

The other eight justices agreed. On October 29, 1969, the Court issued a unanimous *per curiam* order mandating integration of the

Mississippi school districts "at once." Writing for the Court, Justice Brennan stated that the "continued operation of segregated schools under a standard of allowing 'all deliberate speed' for desegregation is no longer constitutionally permissible....The obligation of every school district is to terminate dual school systems at once and to operate now and hereafter only unitary schools."

But while the Court maintained its unanimous commitment to school desegregation as a matter of law, the justices began to break ranks over the methods that could properly be employed to achieve integration. On October 12, 1970, the Court heard oral arguments in *Swann v. Charlotte-Mecklenburg Board of Education,* an appeal from a ruling by U.S. District Court judge James B. McMillan, who had approved busing as a means to achieve racial balance in North Carolina's Charlotte-Mecklenburg school district, which encompassed the city of Charlotte and surrounding Mecklenburg County.

During the 1968 presidential election, Richard Nixon ran on a platform opposed to busing. He called instead for "freedom of choice"; allowing parents to send their children to neighborhood schools, regardless of the racial imbalance that resulted from residential housing patterns, otherwise known as de facto segregation. After he became president, Nixon issued a defiant statement regarding federal court-ordered busing. "Unless affirmed by the Supreme Court," Nixon declared, "I will not consider [busing orders] as precedents to guide administrative policy."

At first, Nixon's new chief justice appeared to share the president's view. He told his law clerks that *desegregation* and *integration* had different meanings, though the terms were frequently used synonymously. Desegregation prohibited the denial of rights or opportunities because of race; integration implied race mixing and achieving numerical racial balances or quotas, which busing promoted. Burger doubted whether it was within the power of the federal courts to order busing as a remedy for dual school systems.

Douglas disagreed. In his opinion, integration was the only way to eliminate "the stigma—the stamp of inferiority." During the 1968–69 school year, Charlotte had roughly eighty-four thousand students attending 107 schools. Of this total, approximately twenty-four thousand pupils, or 29 percent, were black. Fourteen thousand of these blacks were enrolled in twenty-one all-black schools.

Douglas's longtime ally Black shared his skepticism. On March 25, 1971, Black circulated a memorandum to the other justices in which he stated that he "gravely doubt[ed] this Court's Constitutional power...to compel a state and its taxpayers to buy millions of dollars worth of buses to haul students miles away from their neighborhood schools and their homes." For the Court to issue a busing order would be, as Black put it, "bizarre." Brennan joked privately that Black, an absolutist who adhered strictly to the literal language of the Constitution whenever possible, opposed busing because the word *bus* does not appear in the Constitution.

Marshall had made his feelings unequivocally clear in a memorandum to the justices dated January 12, 1971: "The time has come for the era of dual school systems to be ended. And when school boards fail to meet their obligations it is up to the courts to find remedies that effectively secure the rights of Negro children. He went on, "Innovation and unrefined techniques are necessary when the work of sixteen years has to be done in one." He concluded, "The techniques used in the District Court's order were certainly within the Court's power to provide equitable relief."

Brennan sided with Marshall and Douglas. White, Harlan, Stewart, and Blackmun, the newest justice, remained undecided. Over the course of the ensuing months, after much negotiation and discussion, Marshall managed to prevail, winning the Court's unanimous support for upholding McMillan's busing order.

Burger himself wrote the opinion, which was issued on April 20, 1970. In it he declared that the "assignment of children to the school nearest their home serving their grade would not produce an effective dismantling of the dual school system." He continued, "In these circumstances, we find no basis for holding that the local school authorities may not be required to employ bus transportation as one tool of school desegregation." He concluded, "Desegregation plans cannot be limited to the walk-in school." Coming sixteen years after *Brown*, *Swann* was to be the Court's last major, unanimous school desegregation ruling.

The Vietnam War divided the Court much as it did the nation as a whole. While the Court refused to rule directly on the war's constitutionality, it nonetheless found itself embroiled in the swirl of conflicting passions that the war generated.

In April 1971 an antiwar group, Vietnam Veterans Against the War, encamped on the Mall in downtown Washington and vowed to shut down the city unless the government redressed their grievances. One of the group's demands was that the justices consider whether the president could commit American military forces in Vietnam without a formal declaration of war by Congress.

Douglas had urged the Court since 1967 to rule squarely on the question. He felt that the American public had been lied to and misled about the nature and scope of the military's Vietnam involvement, and consequently he saw the war as a direct contravention of the nation's democratic principles. In his 1969 book *Points of Rebellion,* in which he offered a passionate defense of the younger generation's protest movement against "the Establishment," Douglas quoted a letter he received from a young American soldier serving in Vietnam.

"Somewhere in our history—though not intentionally—we slowly moved from a government of the people to a government of a chosen few...who, either by birth, family tradition or social standing—a minority possessing all the wealth and power—now ...control the destiny of mankind," the GI wrote. He explained, "You see, Mr. Douglas, the greatest cause of alienation is that my generation has no one to turn to." He ended with a plea: "With all the hatred and violence that exist throughout the world it is time someone, regardless of personal risk, must stand up and represent the feelings, the hopes, the dreams, the visions and desires of the hundreds of thousands of Americans who died, are dying, and will die in the search of truth."

In Douglas's opinion the war was illegal, but in conference he consistently failed to muster the four votes needed for the Court to hear any of the cases challenging the American military involvement.

Burger, White, Blackmun, and Marshall, an appointee and admirer of the president's whose name became synonymous with the war, were considered hawks, supportive of America's military effort. Black and Brennan opposed the war but were reluctant to involve the Court in what they regarded as fundamentally a political question. In Brennan's view, Congress's continued funding of the war amounted to tacit approval of the war's conduct. The Court should not step in, he thought, unless the president defied or resisted congressional actions intended to bring the war to an end. Black shared Brennan's view, though he considered the American involvement in Vietnam a mistake the country would ultimately regret. Surprisingly Stewart and Harlan, considered two of the Court's most conservative members, sided with Douglas.

Marshall refused to provide Douglas with the fourth vote needed to bring the question of the war's constitutionality before the Court. At the same time, he took umbrage at what he saw as an attempt to use the Court to silence and intimidate antiwar protesters.

On the morning of April 20, 1971, the Vietnam Veterans Against the War conducted one of the most emotional protests ever staged in the nation's capital. Some four-to-five-hundred veterans broke camp on the Mall and proceeded to the Capitol. Out of concern that the protest would turn violent, the Capitol police had sealed off the Capitol grounds during the night, padlocking the iron gates at each entryway. In defiant rejection of the nation's Vietnam policy, veterans who had been decorated for valor in combat, many of them amputees or in wheelchairs, tears streaming down their faces, hurled their medals over the padlocked gates.

The men then moved across the street to the Supreme Court, which was in session. The day before, at the Justice Department's request, the chief justice had signed an order evicting the veterans from their camp on the Mall, and the full Court was scheduled to hear an appeal of that order. Several veterans managed to gain admission to the Court chamber before the start of the oral argument. A scuffle with Court police ensued when one of the men rose to his feet, his clenched fist thrust in the air, and shouted, "Remember the Vets!" He was forcibly ejected from the courtroom.

That evening the Court issued a short ruling that unanimously upheld the chief justice's order. Douglas was forced to recuse himself in the matter because the lawyer for the veterans, former attorney general Ramsey Clark, also represented Douglas in impeachment proceedings, later dropped, that had been initiated by conservative Republican congressman Gerald Ford of Michigan.

Next morning, April 21, some 150 to 200 veterans returned to the Court, this time demanding that the justices take up the question of the war's constitutionality. Fearing violence or disruption, Burger for the first time in the Court's history ordered the building closed to the public. He told the Court police to remove the veterans from the premises, which they did with the help of the District of Columbia riot police, who moved in and arrested the demonstrators.

Marshall was deeply troubled. He had voted along with the others to uphold the chief's eviction of the veterans from the Mall. But now things had gone too far, and his conscience bothered him. The veterans were being hauled off to jail for what amounted to no more than a peaceful protest against the war. They were being incarcerated not for what they had actually done but for suspicions about what they might do.

It seemed to Marshall that Burger had brought with him a Nixonian paranoia about protest and dissent. The chief traveled incognito, and it was common knowledge that his chauffeur carried a gun. Burger himself had recently answered a reporter's knock on his door at home with pistol drawn. He was, like Nixon, disdainful of the press generally and had promised to fire immediately any law clerk seen with a reporter.

What Marshall did not know was that the chief's paranoia had spread throughout the building, supplanting the amiable if sterile gentility that characterized relationships among the staff at the Court. Earlier in April, for example, Burger's newly appointed head of building security, Paul Taggert, had called one of the pages, Mark Albertson, into his office for questioning about a brown substance that had stained a tabletop in the page room. The pages had, over the years, acquired a reputation as pranksters and smart alecks around the Court. But now Taggert was accusing

Albertson of something more serious: defecating on government property as some weird form of protest. When Albertson asked why he was a suspect, Taggart responded that secret dossiers were kept on all the pages and that the security people knew that Albertson's father, a professor of history at the University of Massachusetts, had leftist, antiwar leanings. The substance on the table proved to be varnish remover, spilled by a maintenance crew.

Fearing that the Court was being manipulated by Nixon and the Justice Department to suppress antiwar activism, Marshall sat down on the evening of April 21 and composed a blistering memorandum to the other justices, castigating the chief without mentioning him by name. There was, he asserted, no legitimate basis for the veterans' arrests. He claimed that the tactics employed against the demonstrators were unconstitutional and brought disgrace to the Court as an institution. He insinuated that the veterans had ample grounds for challenging the arrests in court and wondered how the Court would feel if called upon to rule on its own improper conduct.

Subsequently, charges against the veterans were dismissed in the U.S. District Court for the District of Columbia. "Inconvenience alone," the district court judge held, "does not warrant a criminal prosecution." The government did not appeal the ruling, so the Court was never called upon to sit in judgment of its own behavior.

Douglas's contention that the government had lied to the American people about Vietnam was proved correct just two months later. In June 1971 the *New York Times* and the *Washington Post* began publishing excerpts from the Pentagon Papers, a forty-three-volume history of America's Vietnam involvement commissioned by former secretary of defense Robert S. McNamara. The documents, which were classified top secret, were provided to the newspapers by Daniel Ellsberg, a former employee of the Rand Corporation, who had participated in the study.

Citing national security concerns, the Justice Department obtained court orders halting publication. On June 24, 1971, the Supreme Court heard the newspapers' challenges to those injunctions. The case was framed as *New York Times Co. v. United*

States. Just six days later, on June 30, the Court issued a *per curiam* order overturning the injunctions and affirming the newspapers' right to print. The decision was six to three, with Burger, Harlan, and Blackmun dissenting.

Most memorable for its soaring eloquence was Black's concurrence in the final result: "Paramount among the responsibilities of a free press is the duty to prevent any part of the government from deceiving the people and sending them off to distant lands to die of foreign fevers and foreign shot and shell. In revealing the workings of the government that led to the Vietnam War," he continued, "the newspapers did precisely that which the Founders hoped and trusted they would do."

Marshall also wrote a separate opinion, concurring in the result but taking a narrower tack. He argued that Congress had given the president power to criminally prosecute acts of espionage but not to stop newspapers from publishing the kind of information contained in the Pentagon Papers. He concluded, "When Congress specifically declines to make conduct unlawful it is not for this Court to redecide those issues—to overrule Congress."

Two years later, the Court would find that it was not yet finished with the Vietnam controversy.

Meanwhile, Marshall had set to work formulating what would be his most significant contribution to constitutional jurisprudence, the idea that courts should strike down governmental actions that have a disproportionately detrimental impact on the poor.

During the 1960s the Court began to recognize certain rights as "fundamental" even though they were not specifically mentioned in the Constitution. For example, the Court ruled that there is a fundamental right to counsel, obliging the government to provide legal representation for indigents in criminal, as well as in some civil, proceedings. The government was also required to provide free trial transcripts to indigents for use in appeals and to waive filing fees for the poor in divorces.

Throughout the 1970s Marshall tried to broaden the number and nature of fundamental rights. He elaborated his views on the fundamental rights of poor people in a decision handed down on April 6, 1970, *Dandridge v. Williams.*

In *Dandridge* the Court was asked to decide whether the State of Maryland could put a ceiling on monthly benefits paid to welfare families under the Aid to Families with Dependent Children program, financed jointly by the states and the federal government. Maryland limited the total allowable benefit to $250, regardless of the size of the family or its actual need. Under the scheme, welfare families with fewer children would have proportionately more money for each child; larger families would have less money to go around.

Justice Stewart, writing for the majority, upheld the Maryland plan. The federal courts, he concluded, have "no power to impose upon the States their views of what constitutes wise economic or social policy."

Marshall vehemently disagreed. He wrote in a dissent joined by Brennan: "This...process effected by the maximum grant regulation produces a basic denial of equal treatment. Persons who are concededly similarly situated (dependent children and their families) are not afforded equal, or even approximately equal, treatment under the maximum grant regulation."

He went beyond theoretical policy considerations to the actual effect of the Maryland plan. "In theory, no payments are made with respect to needy dependent children in excess of four or five as the case may be," he wrote in a footnote. "In practice, of course, the excess children share in the benefits that are paid with respect to the other members of the family." But, he went on, "the result is that support for the entire family is reduced below minimum subsistence levels."

In other words, some needy children were provided enough money to subsist; others were not. He asserted, "The only distinction between those children with respect to whom assistance is granted and those children who are denied such assistance is the size of the family into which the child permits himself to be born." There being no rational basis for such a distinction, the Maryland plan violated the equal-protection clause, in Marshall's view. He insisted, "The State may not, in the provision of important services or the distribution of governmental payments, supply benefits to some individuals while denying them to others who are similarly situated."

In another footnote Marshall went so far as to imply that there is a constitutional right to subsistence under both the due-process and equal-protection clauses of the Fourteenth Amendment. That being the case, a rational basis, even if one existed, would not constitute sufficient grounds for upholding the Maryland plan.

Marshall maintained that the traditional rational-basis test was adequate for judging the legitimacy of distinctions made among businesses or business interests. But he argued that to determine whether a law unfairly discriminates against a class of individuals, the Court should apply a heightened scrutiny, something tougher to satisfy than the mere rational-basis test. He asserted, "If the classification [of a group of persons] affects a 'fundamental right,' then the state interest in perpetuating the classification must be 'compelling' in order to be sustained." To apply this heightened scrutiny, he explained, "concentration must be placed upon the character of the classification in question, the relative importance to individuals in the class discriminated against of the governmental benefits that they do not receive, and the asserted state interests in support of the classification."

Applying this rationale in *Dandridge,* he concluded, "The basis of that discrimination—the classification of individuals into large and small families—is too arbitrary and...the impact on those discriminated against—the denial of even a subsistence existence—too great and the supposed interests served too contrived and attenuated to meet the requirements of the Constitution."

In a later case, *Wyman v. James,* decided on January 12, 1971, he dissented from the Court's six-to-three ruling that a state may cut off a welfare recipient's benefits for refusing to allow home visitations by a welfare case worker without a search warrant. Joined by Brennan, he wrote, "This Court has occasionally pushed beyond established constitutional contours to protect the vulnerable and to further basic human values. I find no little irony in the fact that the burden of today's departure from principled adjudication is placed upon the lowly poor." He concluded, "Perhaps the majority has explained why a commercial warehouse deserves more protection than does this poor woman's home. I am not convinced; and, therefore, I must respectfully dissent."

In *James v. Valtierra,* decided on April 26, 1971, the Court by a five-to-three majority upheld California's requirement that community consent be obtained by referendum prior to the construction of low-income public housing. Marshall, joined by Brennan and Blackmun, filed a dissent. He complained, "Publicly assisted housing developments designed to accommodate the aged, veterans, state employees, persons of moderate income, or any class of citizens other than the poor, need not be approved by prior referenda." He declared, "An explicit classification on the basis of proverty [is] a suspect classification...[and] demands exacting judicial scrutiny."

Justice William Brennan wrote for the November 1991 edition of the *Harvard Law Review* that what made Thurgood Marshall unique as a justice was the "special voice he added to the Court's deliberations and decisions." Brennan explained, "His was a voice of authority: he spoke from firsthand knowledge of the law's failure to fulfill its promised protections for so many Americans." This unique quality was exhibited by Marshall's graphic dissent in *United States v. Kras*, decided by the Court on January 10, 1973.

Kras, an indigent, sought to file for bankruptcy but could not afford the fifty dollars in filing fees. Citing an earlier ruling by the Court that relieved indigents of the obligation to pay filing fees in divorce proceedings, Kras sought to have the bankruptcy fees waived. But the Court, by a five-to-four vote, distinguished divorce, which related to marriage and therefore involved a fundamental right, from bankruptcy, reasoning that there is no constitutional right to a discharge of one's debts. Justice Blackmun, joined by Burger, White, Powell, and Rehnquist, wrote for the majority that paying the fees in installments would cost Kras only $1.28 per week, which "should be within his able-bodied reach."

Marshall was livid. "It may be easy for some people to think that weekly savings of less than $2 are no burden," he wrote. "But no one who has had close contact with poor people can fail to understand how close to the margin of survival many of them are."

He went on, "A sudden illness, for example, may destroy whatever savings they may have accumulated, and by eliminating a sense of security may destroy the incentive to save in the future."

He continued, "A pack of cigarettes may be, for them, a luxury indulged in only rarely. The desperately poor almost never go to see a movie, which the majority seems to believe is an almost weekly activity. They have more important things to do with what little money they have—like attempting to provide some comforts for a gravely ill child, as Kras must do."

His conclusion was biting. "It is perfectly proper for judges to disagree about what the Constitution requires. But it is disgraceful for an interpretation of the Constitution to be premised upon unfounded assumptions about how people live."

If anything exceeded his sensitivity to the way poor people live, it was his concern over the way so many of them died. No legal issue was more important to Thurgood Marshall than capital punishment, which the Burger Court addressed directly during the 1971–72 term.

TWENTY-TWO

Compassion in Time of Crisis

> My wife Cissy is after me and thinks we should
> string 'em all up.
>
> —Thurgood Marshall

Throughout his twenty-four-year tenure on the Supreme Court, Thurgood Marshall remained adamantly opposed to capital punishment. The Eighth Amendment to the U.S. Constitution provides, "Excessive bail shall not be required, nor excessive fines imposed, nor cruel and unusual punishments inflicted." In Marshall's view, capital punishment was unconstitutional because it violated the Eighth Amendment's strictures. He considered the death penalty excessive, cruel, and unusual.

He regarded the death sentence as "excessive" because it did not deter the crimes it was intended to punish. He cited the hanging of pickpockets in seventeenth-century England to support his point. He once observed, "While spectators were looking up at the hangings, they had their pockets picked."

Besides, most murders resulted from family squabbles or were committed in the blind heat of passion without regard for, or consideration of, legal consequences. He told his law clerks, "Hell,

318

if the death penalty was a deterrent, there never would have been a second execution after the first one."

He thought capital punishment was "cruel" because if the death sentence did not deter criminal conduct, the motivation for its imposition had to be something else. And what other motive existed than the desire to wreak vengeance and retribution? He considered these impulses abhorrent, wanton, morally repugnant—in a word, cruel, and therefore disallowed under the Eighth Amendment.

The Constitution itself contemplates death as a criminal sanction. The Fifth Amendment extends to those accused of capital crimes a special modicum of procedural protection by providing, "No person shall be held to answer for a capital, or otherwise infamous crime, unless on a presentment or indictment of a grand jury." But in 1792, at the Eight Amendment's inception, branding, butchering of ears, and flogging were also sanctioned. Marshall argued society's values and mores had changed.

"A penalty that was permissible at one period in our nation's history is not necessarily permissible today," he maintained. He frequently cited former chief justice Earl Warren's 1958 opinion in *Trop v. Dulles* that the Eighth Amendment was not "static" but changed with "evolving standards of decency that mark the progress of a maturing society." He noted that since the end of World War II, Canada and the Western European democracies had carried out fewer and fewer executions.

Marshall found the death sentence "unusual" because, in the dictionary sense of the word, it was imposed haphazardly, arbitrarily, freakishly. A man convicted of rape in Nebraska might be sentenced to prison. A man convicted of the same crime, under similar circumstances, might be sentenced to death in Alabama.

He called capital punishment the "ultimate form of discrimination," contending it was invoked disproportionately against minorities, the poor, and the uneducated. He had stood over the burned and mutilated bodies of black men lynched by angry mobs. He had seen black men convicted of capital offenses by all-white juries in trials that violated constitutional guarantees. And he also knew that in many instances black defendants had been given harsher sentences than white defendants for similar crimes.

In 1951, in Korea and Japan, he successfully defended black soldiers unjustly sentenced to death on false charges of dereliction of duty. He had those sentences reduced or reversed after bringing the facts of each case to the attention of military officials and President Harry S. Truman. Marshall's firsthand knowledge that America's criminal and military justice systems were prone to grievous errors and prejudice was alone evidence enough for him to personally oppose capital punishment.

His opposition to the death penalty was also based on an early personal experience. As a young attorney in private practice, he defended an acquaintance charged with robbery and murder. "The reason why I took the case was that it was a classmate of mine in high school," Marshall explained. He lost, and his client went to the gallows. Marshall had every intention of going to the Maryland penitentiary on Baltimore's cobblestoned East Eager Street to witness the hanging on Monday, August 8, 1936. He recalls, "When the time of execution came up, I felt so bad about it—that maybe I was responsible—that I decided I was going to go and see the execution." But he changed his mind.

"A white reporter from the daily *Morning Sun* newspaper [the *Baltimore Sun*] was a good friend of mine. "And when I told him he said, 'Now wait a minute. You do whatever you want to do, but I am required to go,' and he gave the number [of hangings] he had been to, something like a dozen or more." At that time, state law required the presence of at least one newspaper reporter at executions. Marshall went on, "He told me, 'I have been to blank number of executions, and I have puked at every one of them. Now, if you feel you want to go, go ahead,' and I chickened out." Asked years later if the execution of his classmate precipitated his lifelong opposition to capital punishment, Marshall said, "Well, I don't know whether that...well, it did. It did because I lost the death penalty case in private practice."

Furman v. Georgia, argued before the Court on January 17, 1972, presented Marshall the opportunity to convince the other justices that the death penalty was unconstitutional. William Furman had been sentenced to death for killing the father of five children when the victim discovered Furman in his home one morning. Two other cases consolidated into *Furman* involved the imposition of the death penalty for forcible rape. The common practice among states that had capital punishment was to delegate to juries unfettered discretion to impose the death sentence. The issue before the Court was not capital punishment per se, but whether what was done in the three cases presented in *Furman* violated the Eighth Amendment.

The composition of the Court changed during the months leading up to the *Furman* oral argument. On September 17, 1971, Hugo Lafayette Black resigned at the age of eighty-five because of ill health. He died a few days later, on September 25. John Marshall Harlan also stepped down, resigning on September 23, 1971, at the age of seventy-one. He had served sixteen terms on the Court. The oral argument in *Furman*, originally scheduled for that fall, was postponed until January 1972, pending the appointment of Black's and Harlan's replacements.

Nixon contemplated what would be his third and fourth appointments to the Court. As a replacement for Black, Burger recommended to Attorney General John N. Mitchell a sixty-four-year-old southerner, Lewis Powell of Richmond, Virginia, a former president of the American Bar Association. A Phi Beta Kappa graduate of Washington and Lee College, Powell had attended law school at Washington and Lee and done postgraduate work at Harvard. He was considered a political moderate.

To replace Harlan, Nixon chose William H. Rehnquist, then an assistant attorney general and a Goldwater Republican. At the relatively youthful age of forty-seven, Rehnquist could be counted on to influence the Court for years to come with his conservative views.

Powell was confirmed by the Senate on December 6, 1971, by a margin of eighty-nine to one. Rehnquist faced rougher going. His civil rights views were called into question after it was revealed that he had written a memorandum to Justice Robert Jackson recommending that *Plessy* be upheld while serving as Jackson's law clerk during the 1951–52 term, when *Brown* was being considered by the Court. In that memorandum Rehnquist had stated, "I realize that [this] is an unpopular and unhumanitarian position, for which I have been excoriated by 'liberal' colleagues, but I think *Plessy v. Ferguson* was right and should be reaffirmed." As mentioned earlier, Rehnquist claimed later that the memorandum was written to reflect Jackson's views, not his own.

He survived the ensuing controversy, however, and was confirmed by the Senate on December 10, 1971, by a vote of sixty-eight to twenty-six.

Powell suffered from a mild heart condition and had been advised by his physician to exercise regularly by taking walks. Marshall, overweight and disdainful of physical exertion, had been given the same advice by his doctor. Following Powell's elevation to the bench, the two would frequently pass each other in the Court's corridors during their daily constitutionals. As they approached each other from opposite directions, Marshall would sometimes quip, "I'm gainin' on you."

During one such meeting, Marshall inquired of the junior justice, "Lewis, do you have your *Furman* opinion written yet?" Referring to his own opinion, which he had written but not yet circulated to his colleagues, Marshall said, "My wife Cissy is after me and thinks we should string 'em all up."

Over the following weeks, Marshall lobbied hard to win Powell's vote for overturning the death penalty. There was little chance of swaying Rehnquist, who solidly supported capital punishment. In the end, Marshall's efforts to woo Powell on the issue proved fruitless.

Nevertheless, Marshall managed to muster the majority that he needed. By a five-to-four vote, the Court on June 29, 1972, issued a *per curiam* order declaring the sentencing procedures used in the *Furman* cases unconstitutional. Each justice wrote a separate opinion. Douglas, Brennan, Stewart, White, and Marshall concurred in the final judgment. The four Nixon appointees, Burger, Blackmun, Powell, and Rehnquist filed dissents.

The result of the widely varied opinions was a mishmash of conflicting rationales. Only Marshall and Brennan asserted that the death penalty was per se unconstitutional as "cruel and unusual punishment" under the Eighth Amendment. Burger, in dissent, empathized with Marshall's and Brennan's view as a matter of personal opinion, but not as a matter of law.

Burger wrote, "If I were possessed of legislative power, I would either join with Mr. Justice Brennan and Mr. Justice Marshall or, at the very least, restrict the use of capital punishment to a small category of the most heinous crimes. Our constitutional inquiry, however, must be divorced from personal feelings as to the morality and efficacy of the death penalty, and be confined to the meaning and applicability of the uncertain language of the Eighth Amendment."

Overall, what emerged under the Court's ruling was that the sentencing procedures under the existing laws resulted in arbitrary imposition of death sentences. Juries should have been informed clearly of available sentencing alternatives and instructed to take mitigating and aggravating circumstances into consideration in each case.

In dissent, the Nixon appointees argued that jurors in each case had in fact been provided sufficient information to make informed sentencing decisions. The opinions of the four, as expected, reflected Nixon's staunch law-and-order advocacy at a time when many Americans felt threatened by rising violent crime.

The late constitutional scholar Alexander Bickel said the Court employed "passive virtues" in the *Furman* decision because it struck down the sentencing procedures while at the same time acknowledging the principle of capital punishment. Bickel referred to the ruling as the "ultimate of legitimization and invalidation." *Furman*'s effect was to impose an immediate moratorium on the pending executions of nearly six hundred condemned prisoners.

Marshall's sixty-page concurrence in the *Furman* result was a masterly product of exhaustive, painstaking research. He wrote most of it himself, trusting little of it to his clerks. Many court observers regard it as the finest opinion he produced during his years on the Court.

He emphasized the irrevocable nature of the death penalty, expressing his fear for the innocent person wrongly convicted. He wrote, "Just as Americans know little about who is executed and why, they are unaware of the potential dangers of executing an innocent man. Our 'beyond a reasonable doubt' burden of proof in criminal cases is intended to protect the innocent, but we know it is not foolproof. Various studies have shown that people whose innocence is later convincingly established are convicted and sentenced to death.

"Death is irrevocable," he reminded. "Death, of course, makes rehabilitation impossible; life imprisonment does not. In short, death had always been viewed as the ultimate sanction and it seems perfectly reasonable to continue to view it as such. It must be kept in mind, then, that the question to be considered is not simply whether capital punishment is a deterrent, but whether it is a better deterrent than life imprisonment."

He wrote, "Statistics show that the deterrent effect of capital punishment is no greater in those communities where executions take place than in other communities."

He went on, "In fact, there is some evidence that imposition of capital punishment may actually encourage crime, rather than deter it. And, while police and law enforcement officers are the strongest advocates of capital punishment, the evidence is over- whelming that police are no safer in communities that retain the sanction than in those that have abolished it."

Some criminals, he maintained, would prefer death to spending the rest of their lives in prison.

As for using the death penalty to exact retribution, he wrote, "At times a cry is heard that morality requires vengeance to evidence society's abhorrence of [a criminal] act. But the Eighth Amendment is our insulation from our baser selves."

He went on, "The 'cruel and unusual' language limits the avenues through which vengeance can be channeled. Were this not so, the language would be empty and a return to the rack and other tortures would be possible in a given case."

He presented an array of historical and sociological evidence to argue that punishments are deemed "cruel" if excessive and that when judged by modern-day standards, the death penalty is excessive.

Summing it up, he wrote, "There is no rational basis for concluding that capital punishment is not excessive."

Marshall offered authoritative documentation to support his assertion that the death penalty was enforced more often against certain classes of people, especially minorities and the poor. He had kept a special notebook in his chambers with the number of death-row prisoners described by race, sex, and national origin, regularly updated by his law clerks.

"Regarding discrimination," he wrote, "it has been said that '[i]t is usually the poor, the illiterate, the underprivileged, the member of the minority group—the man who, because he is without means, and is defended by a court-appointed attorney—who becomes society's sacrificial lamb....' Indeed, a look at the bare statistics regarding executions is enough to betray much of the discrimination. A total of 3,859 persons have been executed since 1930, of whom 1,751 were white and 2,066 were Negro. Of the executions 3,334 were for murder; 1,664 of the executed were white and 1,630 were Negro; 455 persons, including 48 whites and 405 Negroes, were executed for rape. It is immediately apparent that Negroes were executed far more often than whites in proportion to their percentage of the population.

Moreover, he did not believe that race and economic or social standing were the only criteria for the inequitable imposition of the death penalty. Sex was also a factor. "There is also overwhelming evidence that the death penalty is employed against men and not women," he wrote. "Only 32 women have been executed since 1930, while 3,827 men have met a similar fate. It is difficult to understand why women have received such favored treatment since the purposes allegedly served by capital punishment seemingly are equally applicable to both sexes."

He pointed out in a footnote, "Men kill between four and five times more frequently than women.... Hence, it would not be irregular to see four or five times as many men executed as women. The statistics show a startlingly greater disparity, however."

He agreed that "the criminal acts with which we are confronted are ugly, vicious, reprehensible acts. Their sheer brutality cannot and should not be minimized."

Nevertheless, he went on, "at a time in our history when the streets of the nation's cities inspire fear and despair, rather than pride and hope, it is difficult to maintain objectivity and concern for our fellow citizens. The measure of a country's greatness is its ability to retain compassion in time of crisis. No nation in the recorded history of man has a greater tradition or revering justice and fair treatment for all its citizens in time of turmoil, confusion and tension than ours. This is a country which stands tallest in troubled times, a country that clings to fundamental principles, cherishes its constitutional heritage, and rejects simple solutions that compromise the values that lie at the roots of our democratic system."

Associate Justice William Brennan Jr. summarized Marshall's view of the death penalty for the November 1991 edition of the *Harvard Law Review*. "Thurgood and I, of course, were alone on the Court in believing that capital punishment was in all cases barred as "cruel and unusual punishment' under the Eighth Amendment. Justice Marshall canvassed a vast array of historical and social science materials to demonstrate that punishments are deemed 'cruel' if excessive and that when judged by any acceptable theory of punishment, the death penalty is excessive."

Brennan continued, "Justice Marshall held to that view.... He never became complacent in his opposition, rather...he challenged the majority view on its own terms by arguing that there were insufficient safeguards to ensure the 'reliability' of capital sentencing, safeguards that several other justices found constitutionally necessary."

Death-penalty opponents had hoped the *Furman* decision would mean the end of capital punishment. Fourteen states and the District of Columbia abolished their death penalty laws. But thirty-five others revised their capital punishment statutes in an effort to satisfy the procedural guidelines laid down in *Furman*.

Marshall was disheartened by the new legislation. He conceded that the swift passage of revised laws put in doubt his long-held assumption that capital punishment was "morally unacceptable to the people of the United States at this time in their history," though he maintained that "if they knew its history and application, they would oppose it."

Far from laying the capital punishment question to rest, *Furman* rekindled the debate. The Court would be forced to reconsider the issue four years later.

Meanwhile, the Court was forced to revisit another matter: the Vietnam War.

On July 1, 1973, Congress cut off funding for the war in Southeast Asia by declaring that "on or after August 15, 1973, no funds...may be obligated or expended to finance directly or indirectly combat activities by United States military forces in or over or from off the shores of North Vietnam, South Vietnam, Laos or Cambodia." New York congresswoman Elizabeth Holtzman, joined by several air force officers serving in Asia, immediately filed suit in U.S. district court in New York, seeking an injunction to halt further U.S. air operations over Cambodia at once, ahead of the August 15 deadline.

President Nixon had announced on April 30, 1970, that the Cambodia raids were being conducted "to clean out major enemy sanctuaries on the Cambodia-Vietnam border." Subsequently evidence surfaced indicating that the raids had actually begun some time before the president's announcement. In any event, American ground forces had been withdrawn from Cambodia in June 1970, as required by the so-called Fulbright Proviso, enacted by Congress.

The district court judge ordered the bombing halted but stayed, or delayed, implementation of the order until July 27, 1973, to give the U.S. Court of Appeals for the Second Circuit time to hear an appeal. The Second Circuit appeals court extended the delay of the bombing halt and scheduled a hearing on the matter for August 13, 1973—two days before the congressional action would take effect, stopping the bombing, anyway.

Under federal law, each justice of the Supreme Court is designated to sit as a circuit justice, hearing appeals of circuit court rulings when the Supreme Court is not in session. Marshall was assigned to hear appeals of Second Circuit rulings during the Court's 1973 summer recess.

Holtzman and the air force officers appealed directly to Marshall to vacate, or void, the stay and allow the bombing halt to take effect immediately. They claimed that America's Vietnam involvement was unconstitutional because it had been entered into without a formal declaration of war by Congress, required under Article I, section 8, of the Constitution.

On August 1, 1973, Marshall issued his opinion in the case, framed as *Holtzman v. Schlesinger*. He had never given Douglas the fourth vote needed in conference to bring the question of the war's constitutionality before the Court, but over the years his views on the war had somewhat softened. He wrote in *Holtzman*, "When the final history of the Cambodian war is written, it is unlikely to make pleasant reading."

Quoting Hugo Black's eloquent concurrence in the Pentagon Papers case, he went on, "The decision to send American troops 'to distant lands to die of foreign fevers and foreign shot and shell'...may ultimately be adjudged to have been not only unwise but also unlawful."

Nevertheless, he refused to order an immediate bombing halt. "[I]f the decision were mine alone," he explained, "I might well conclude on the merits that continued American military operations in Cambodia are unconstitutional, and its decisions reflect the views of a majority of the sitting Justices."

He went on, "It follows that when I sit in my capacity as a Circuit Justice, I act not for myself alone but as a surrogate for the entire Court, from whence my ultimate authority in these matters derives. A Circuit Justice therefore bears a heavy responsibility to conscientiously reflect the views of his Brethren as best he perceives them...and this responsibility is particularly pressing when, as now, the Court is not in session."

Ordinarily, when a motion is denied by a circuit justice, it can be appealed to the full conference when the justices are in town, or a special conference can be called. When a full conference cannot be called, an appeal can be taken to another circuit justice. On August 2, Holtzman and the air force officers appealed Marshall's ruling to Douglas in his capacity as circuit justice for the Ninth Circuit.

Douglas, vacationing at his Goose Prairie, Washington, retreat, held a hearing on the matter in the federal courthouse at Yakima on August 3. Later that day, he reversed Marshall and ordered the bombing halted immediately.

Douglas applied a rationale designed to exploit Marshall's sensitivity over the death penalty. "The classic capital case," he wrote, "is whether Mr. Lew, Mr. Low, or Mr. Lucas should die. The present case involves whether Mr. X (an unknown person or persons) should die."

He continued, "No one knows who they are. They may be Cambodian farmers whose only 'sin' is a desire for socialized medicine to alleviate the suffering of their families and neighbors. Or Mr. X may be the American pilot or navigator who drops a ton of bombs on a Cambodian village. The upshot is that we know that someone is about to die."

He went on, "When a stay in a capital case is before us, we do not rule on guilt or innocence.... If there is doubt whether due process had been followed in the procedures, the stay is granted because death is irrevocable."

Under the Fifth Amendment to the U.S. Constitution, "life, liberty, or property" cannot be taken "without due process" of law. Douglas concluded that due process had not been followed because war had not been declared by Congress.

Douglas assumed his order would stop the bombing until the full conference of justices convened in October. But back in Washington, D.C., Marshall acted. He contacted the other justices by telephone. Then, on August 4, claiming that the other seven justices agreed with him, he issued an order delaying the bombing halt as if he had never seen or heard of Douglas's Yakima order. The effect was that the bombing proceeded. Not a single scheduled mission was abandoned or delayed.

Douglas dictated a scathing dissent from Goose Prairie. "If we who impose law and order are ourselves to be bound by law and order, we can act as a Court only when at least six of us are present. Seriatim telephone calls," he contended, "cannot, with all respect, be a lawful substitute."

He complained, "Those of the Brethren out of Washington, D.C., on August 4, 1973, could not possibly have studied my opinion in this case. For, although I wrote it late on August 3, it was not released until 9:30 A.M. on August 4; and before 3:00 P.M., August 4, I was advised by telephone that eight Members of the Court disagreed with me."

Declaring that Marshall's was "not a lawful order," he invoked divine providence, asserting, "Under the law as it is written, the order of Mr. Justice Marshall of August 4, 1973, will in time be reversed by that Higher Court which invariably sits in judgment on the decisions of this Court."

Summarizing the episode in his autobiography, *The Court Years (1939–1975),* Douglas wrote that the action taken by Marshall was "lawless. I hesitate to say this," he wrote, "but I believe that some Nixon men put the pressure on Marshall to cut corners. Sad to say, he did so and thus emulated the 'law and order' men during the Watergate period."

Privately he began referring to Marshall, his liberal ally in so many other matters that came before the Court, as "spaghetti spine." Marshall, for his part, found Douglas's self-righteousness annoying. In Marshall's eyes, Douglas was guilty of a cardinal sin: He took himself too seriously.

Marshall had his disagreements with fellow brethren, but generally speaking, he regarded the Court as exactly what he had called it in *Holtzman*, a "collegial institution." In actuality, he was close to no one personally except Brennan, the jovial, diminutive, twinkle-eyed Irishman from New Jersey. Brennan, like Earl Warren, had disappointed Ike, the Republican president who appointed him, with his liberal social views. Marshall was friendly with Potter Stewart, too, and the two men chatted incessantly in chambers and in the halls on the way to or from conferences and oral arguments. He even liked Rehnquist, commenting once, "I don't agree with him on much, but he's a great guy."

But Douglas insisted on being different, on holding himself away from and above the others socially, politically, and intellectually. Without question, he was a legend, a giant, and since Black's death, the lone giant on the Court. He strode the halls like a brooding colossus, his gait stiff and erect from the polio he suffered as a child, absorbed in thought, projecting an impenetrable aura. One could stand next to Douglas at an elevator and feel as though Douglas were the only person standing there in the hall.

On the bench, he was a grab bag of ticks and quirks. Sometimes he flapped the back of his right ear with his hand like a cocker spaniel scratching fleas. Or, suddenly, he would rub the side of his face vigorously with his palm, as if his face were an appendage that had fallen asleep. He wrote almost thirty books during his career, on subjects ranging from political dissent to foreign policy, as well as memoirs, plays, and journals of travels across America, Russia, Asia, and the Himalayas. This total did not include the dime-store cowboy novels he penned under an assumed name to pay his way through law school at Columbia University.

He scribbled feverishly during oral arguments, tearing sheet after sheet off his long yellow legal pad and handing them behind him to the pages to take back to his office for typing by his secretaries. He kept the pages scurrying back and forth between the bench, his office, and the library, fetching him books, journals, atlases, everything. Yet somehow he managed never to lose track of the arguments being presented, interrupting with questions here and there, all the while popping cherry-red Luden's cough drops.

Marshall watched him in fascination. One day he asked a page what flavor cough drops Douglas liked, and he requested that a box of the same kind be placed in his own drawer on days of oral argument.

He began to mimic another of Douglas's habits. On Fridays, when the justices met in conference, Douglas had his messenger Harry Datcher bring him a glass of buttermilk for his ulcer at precisely 10:30 A.M. Datcher would arrive outside the conference-room door with the milk and a napkin on a silver tray. A page would knock on the door, and Douglas would emerge, stand just outside the door, and down the buttermilk in one go.

One day, Marshall's messenger showed up at 10:30 along with Datcher, also with a glass of white liquid on a silver tray. Marshall emerged from the conference room behind Douglas, and the two men stood next to each other, downing their drinks, not saying a word, each imbibing as if the other were not there. The ritual was repeated for several weeks.

The pages knew that buttermilk was in Douglas's glass—Datcher had told them. But their curiosity had grown about what was in Marshall's. Noticing their perplexed looks, Marshall one day turned to them and, after Douglas had gone back into the conference room, pointed to his empty glass, then to his rear end, playing a charade. No one got it. Frustrated, he said, "It puts a firecracker up my ass."

"Aha!" said one of the pages. "A laxative!"

Marshall and Douglas clashed again during the ensuing 1973–74 term, this time over the question of affirmative action. The case, *DeFunis v. Odegaard*, was brought by a white law school applicant—Marco DeFunis Jr.—his wife, and his parents after DeFunis was denied admission to the University of Washington Law School. His suit was based on the fact that, while he had been rejected, blacks with lower entrance examination scores had been admitted under the school's affirmative action plan.

The two had feuded over the issue before *DeFunis*. The Court had considered a similar challenge to affirmative action during the 1971–72 term. In *Johnson v. Committee on Examinations*, a white law school graduate appealed the denial of his admission to the Arizona state bar. The white applicant had failed to reach the bar examination passing grade of 70 percent on three separate occasions, but blacks who had also received failing grades had been admitted to practice.

President Lyndon Johnson had laid the groundwork for affirmative action policies in a speech to Howard University's graduating class in 1965. At the time, half of all black teenagers came from broken homes. Johnson asserted that this "breakdown of the Negro family structure," for which, "most of all, white America must accept responsibility," had left blacks socially and economically disadvantaged. He compared the situation to a race in which both runners are required to start at the same place, although one has been allowed to train while the other's legs have been kept in chains.

Affirmative action triggered white resentment from its inception. Beneficence toward blacks was regarded as reverse discrimination by whites who watched jobs and university admissions denied them in favor of less qualified minority applicants.

In conference, Douglas had tried to persuade the justices to hear the *Johnson* appeal, but none was prepared to address the explosive issue. When Douglas asserted that discrimination against whites was as unconstitutional as discrimination against blacks, Marshall responded, "You guys have been practicing discrimination for years. Now it is our turn."

The Court agreed to hear oral arguments in *DeFunis* and did so on February 26, 1974. On April 23, 1974, it handed down a decision that again skirted the issue. Because DeFunis had since been admitted to law school at the University of Washington and was about to complete his three-year course of study, the Court concluded the case was moot and declined to address the central questions raised by it. In dissent, Douglas argued strongly against race-based admissions policies.

Blacks have never had a stronger proponent on the Supreme Court than William Orville Douglas. Hugo Black once wrote of him, "I suspect that [Douglas] must have come into the world with a rush and that his first cry must have been a protest against something he saw at a glance was wrong or unjust." Growing up in Yakima, Washington, Douglas encountered few blacks but was outraged by prejudice against the Yakima Indians. Throughout his extensive travels as an adult, he was drawn to the problems and concerns of the nonwhite peoples he came across.

In June 1953, before the reargument of *Brown*, John W. Davis tried to predict which justices could be counted on to uphold segregation. He was unsettled by the publication of a book by Douglas that called for Malaya to integrate its Chinese, Japanese, Australian, English, and Indian schools. In fact, Douglas had voted to overturn segregation when the Court first considered *Brown* in 1952.

During the 1960s, he became a vocal advocate of black rights both on and off the bench. He believed the riots that followed Martin Luther King Jr.'s death resulted from "a century of neglect, aided and abetted by the Court."

He continued in *The Court Years*, "The fault was not that of the 'uppity Negro' but the 'unreconstructed white'—and the latter did not live in the South alone."

He made his case against the white Establishment on behalf of blacks plain in *Points of Rebellion*. "Negroes want parity as respects human dignity—parity as respects equal justice and parity in economic opportunities," he wrote. Then he declared, "Police practices are anti-Negro. Employment practices are anti-Negro. Housing allocation is anti-Negro. Education is anti-Negro."

But he simply did not believe in affirmative action. In his *The Court Years*, Douglas expressed understanding of the reasoning behind affirmative action, which was that "black people were at such a disadvantage in the educational system in America that they needed some concessions in order to have black lawyers and judges, black dentists and doctors." Yet he considered it "a wholly un-American practice, quite inconsistent with equal protection" because, in his view, it promoted aristocracy. He referred to it "not as an aristocracy of race, but an aristocracy of talent, the best talents being recognized in all minority groups and each entitled to take his or her place at the top."

His point was that affirmative action should not be used to reserve places in the professional classes for certain people just because of their race—for example, the sons and daughters of minority members who through their own struggles had already gained access to the middle or upper class. Rather, it should be used to accommodate entry into the social and economic mainstream for individuals whose talents would otherwise go neglected or unnoticed because of their underprivileged backgrounds, irrespective of their color.

He explained his thinking in his DeFunis dissent. He wrote, "A black applicant who pulled himself out of the ghetto into a junior college may thereby demonstrate a level of motivation, perseverance, and ability that would lead a fair-minded admissions committee to conclude that he shows more promise for law study than the son of a rich alumnus who achieved better grades at Harvard. That applicant would be offered admission not because he is black, but because as an individual he has shown he has the potential, while the Harvard man may have taken less advantage of the vastly superior opportunities offered him."

He continued, "Because of the weight of the prior handicaps, that black applicant may not realize his full potential in the first year of law school, or even in the full three years, but in the long pull of a legal career his achievements may far outstrip those of his classmates whose earlier records appeared superior by conventional criteria."

He went on, "There is currently no test available to the Admissions Committee that can predict such possibilities with assurance, but the Committee may nevertheless seek to gauge it as best it can, and weigh this factor in its decisions. Such a policy would not be limited to blacks, or Chicanos or Filipinos, or American Indians, although undoubtedly groups such as these may in practice be the principal beneficiaries of it. But a poor Appalachian white, or a second generation Chinese in San Francisco, or some other American whose lineage is so diverse as to defy ethnic labels, may demonstrate similar potential and thus be accorded favorable consideration by the Committee."

He concluded, "The difference between such a policy and the one presented by this case is that the Committee would be making decisions on the basis of individual attributes, rather than according a preference solely on the basis of race."

In *The Court Years*, he expressed the view that racial preferences can work to the ultimate detriment of the minorities they are intended to benefit. He stated, "I feel that if blacks or any other minority are poorly prepared for the legal profession but are nevertheless admitted, the situation of the minorities will worsen."

He used the following hypothetical to make his point: "Many law schools admit blacks even though their credentials are not up to par, and this leads to the following tragedy: the black student graduates, enters the job market and is hired, perhaps as a law clerk. It is soon apparent, in these instances, that he cannot research a problem, or prepare a relevant memo, or draft a contract or a will. Years pass and he goes from one law firm to another and finally ends up in the street—a wholly discredited professional person. This has a more deadly, killing impact than if he had been turned down at the entrance of the law school because he possessed inadequate credentials. Having reached the top and entered the market, he is told in no uncertain terms that the society that needs lawyers has no place for him."

He asserted that Marshall was appointed to the Court "simply because he was black," although he conceded that "in the 1960's that was reason enough," owing to the paucity of black lawyers and jurists.

He explained, "At that time, few black people studied law, and those who did seldom reached the top. Marshall attained the pinnacle for conspicuous service in civil rights—not civil rights generally, but civil rights in the field of race. The public needed a competent black on the Court for symbolic reasons; none was needed to put the Court right on racial problems. Where would a black judge stand on mergers, on Sherman Act cases, on 'Communists' in defense plants or schools, on public aid to parochial schools, on civilian control over the military, on the right of the police to search without a warrant, on whether being an 'active Communist' can be made a crime? No one knows the answer."

His point was that the appointment of a black because of his color did not, of itself, guarantee that the interests of the poor, the suppressed, or the politically unpopular would be adequately expressed or represented. "Being a black was no clue," he explained, "for blacks, like Jews, Germans, English and others, can be reactionary."

Alluding to Marshall's Vietnam stance, he added, "Moreover, a black reaching the top was likely to be anxious to prove to society that he was safe and conservative and reliable. That at least had been the history of most black appointees to judicial posts."

And yet nothing exemplified the barriers to the entry of minorities and women into America's upper echelons more than the Court itself. At the time the Court first began its consideration of affirmative action in the early 1970s, there were no black law clerks, and only one law clerk was female, a white woman from Georgetown Law School, hired by Marshall. The law clerks were selected from among the top students at the nation's most prestigious law schools and usually worked as editors of their schools' law reviews.

In fact, throughout the entire history of the Court up to that time, there had been only one black law clerk, William Coleman, who had clerked for Frankfurter after finishing Harvard Law School. As an associate of Marshall's during the 1950s, he had participated in the *Brown* litigation. He went on to become secretary of transportation in the Nixon administration.

In addition, none of the justices had a black secretary, considered the prestige administrative/clerical position. Among the Court police, there were no blacks above the rank of sergeant. At the same time, all the justices' messengers were black. The messengers were more or less personal valets who performed menial tasks, such as serving lunch or tea, driving justices to and from home, and running personal errands. Also, most of the Court's maintenance personnel, the janitors, were black, but their supervisors were white.

While he was chief justice, Earl Warren had imposed at least one affirmative action policy at the Court. Of the four pages, he decreed, two were to be black. There was no lowering of the academic standards for eligibility, just a guideline, a quota, for selecting among those equally qualified.

The pages were chosen from schools located in Washington, D.C., which was about 90 percent black during the early 1970s. It was a prestigious appointment, carrying with it the imprimatur of the Court. Tenure as a Court page usually opened doors to the top technical or Ivy League universities, especially when a page's application was backed up by a recommendation from a justice.

The justices themselves, to a man, held individual academic achievement in the highest esteem. In the fall of 1971, when Douglas learned that one of the black pages, Hunter R. Clark, was applying to Harvard College, he enthusiastically offered to write a recommendation. Chief Justice Burger authorized his secretary to write one as well. When news circulated in the spring of 1972 that Clark had been accepted to Harvard and awarded an academic scholarship, each justice at one time or another called him into his chambers and personally congratulated him.

Burger went further. He took all four pages to lunch at the Federal Bar Association on Pennsylvania Avenue. Afterward, he chatted with Clark privately, offering his advice as to how Clark might one day return to the Court as a law clerk, explaining how the system worked, and emphasizing the importance of getting published or making law review. He encouraged Clark to keep everyone at the Court informed of his progress.

Four years later, on Justice Marshall's recommendation, Clark was accepted at Harvard Law School.

Douglas's aversion to affirmative action policies did not alter his steadfast commitment to equal educational opportunity or his opposition to the way the death penalty was applied in this country. Marshall soon found himself allied once again with his old ally on these and other issues, including sex discrimination and abortion, when they came before the Court.

TWENTY-THREE

The Rehnquist Court: A Sharp Right Turn

> My father came to this country when he was a
> teenager. Not only had he never profited from
> the sweat of any black man's brow, I don't think
> he had ever seen a black man.
>
> —Antonin Scalia

Sex did not inhibit Thurgood Marshall. He enjoyed it. He laughed about it. And he joked about it. But he was angered by it when it was used as an excuse to deny women their constitutional rights.

Marshall's African-American background gave him a unique perspective on feminine equality, much as it did about race. He grew up in the black middle class, which has a long tradition of working women. His mother was a schoolteacher, and his grandmother Annie, owner of a small Baltimore grocery store with his grandfather, was an independent entrepreneur.

Also, Marshall's attitudes were shaped by the forceful black women whose contributions to the civil rights movement he had witnessed. Lillie Jackson, president of the Baltimore NAACP in the 1930s, helped organize an effective boycott of white-owned businesses that refused to hire black clerks. Daisy Bates, president of the Little Rock, Arkansas, chapter of the NAACP during the 1950s, risked her home and personal safety to achieve the successful desegregation of Central High School. Constance Baker Motley, who served on Marshall's Fund staff, assisted in the preparation of *Brown*. These were but a few of the women who were prominent in Marshall's professional life.

Motley, who went on to become senior U.S. district judge for the Southern District of New York, finished law school at Columbia University at a time when few law firms hired women attorneys. She found it difficult to crack the discriminatory job market until Marshall persuaded the NAACP board to hire a woman lawyer for the Fund staff in 1945. She wrote of the personal debt she owed Thurgood in the November 1991 edition of the *Harvard Law Review*, recalling that, at the time she was hired, "nobody had to tell [Marshall] that African-American males were on the bottom rung of the ladder in every conceivable professional endeavor and that African-American women were not even on the ladder."

She worked for the Fund until 1965. When the Senate confirmed her nomination to the U.S. district court in 1966, she became the first black woman ever appointed to the federal bench. "If it had not been for Thurgood Marshall," she wrote, "no one would ever have heard of Constance Baker Motley."

Marshall had insisted that any classification of individuals by the government should be subjected to heightened, or strict, judicial scrutiny. The government, he felt, should be required to put forward a compelling reason for any classification that resulted in the denial of a right or benefit.

He was unable to persuade the majority that strict scrutiny should be applied to laws or government actions having a disproportionately detrimental impact on the poor—in other words, that poverty should be a suspect classification. Instead, the Court clung to the old rational-basis test for judging actions that affected the poor. But during the 1972–73 term, in *Frontiero v. Richardson*, he was joined by Douglas, Brennan, Stewart, and

White in the view that classifications based on sex were inherently suspect.

Sharron Frontiero was a lieutenant in the U.S. Air Force. Her husband, Joseph Frontiero, was a full-time student at Huntington College in Montgomery, Alabama. Lieutenant Frontiero brought suit against the government when she was denied an increased housing allowance and medical and dental benefits for her husband as a dependent. Male air force officers were granted the benefits under similar circumstances.

In a strongly worded opinion written by Justice Brennan, the majority concluded that the air force was according "dissimilar treatment for men and women who are...similarly situated." Brennan went on, "There can be no doubt that our nation has had a long and unfortunate history of sex discrimination."

Traditionally, such discrimination was rationalized by an attitude of "romantic paternalism" which, in practical effect, put women "not on a pedestal, but in a cage."

The minority, composed of Powell, Burger, and Blackmun, based its dissent on the fact that the Equal Rights Amendment (ERA) had been submitted to the states for ratification. The three dissenters asserted that the Court should not establish sex as a suspect classification unless or until the ERA's acceptance.

Frontiero was a turning point, a landmark victory in the struggle for women's rights. But by far the most controversial women's rights issue to come before the Court was abortion.

"Jane Roe" claimed she was gang-raped on the way home from work one summer evening in 1969. She said she was pregnant as a result and sought an abortion, but abortions were illegal under the laws of her home state of Texas, except when the life of the mother was at risk.

Roe decided to challenge the Texas abortion law. When the U.S. Supreme Court heard oral arguments in the matter for the first time, on December 13, 1971, the case had become known as *Roe v. Wade*. The justices requested that the case be reargued during the 1972–73 term. The reargument was held on October 11, 1972.

At the time, no one knew, nor was it really relevant, that Jane Roe's real name was Norma McCorvey and that no gang rape had taken place. McCorvey simply wanted to terminate an unwanted pregnancy. She had used an alias to protect her privacy. At issue was whether a woman has a constitutional right to abort an unwanted fetus.

At the heart of the abortion debate were two fundamental questions: Is a fetus a person and, if so, what are its rights? Under what circumstances, if any, should abortions be allowed?

Because Blackmun had acquired an expertise in forensic law, the relationship between law and medicine, during his years as general counsel to the Mayo Clinic, Burger assigned him to write the Court majority's opinion.

Blackmun was a quiet, congenial man with a professorial manner. He wore sweaters instead of suit coats and did most of his work not in his chambers but in the Court's second-floor library, which reminded him fondly of Langdell Law Library at Harvard, his alma mater. He liked to write with no. 2 pencils that had been shortened. The pages would break new pencils in half, then sharpen them, for his use.

He devoted the better part of a year to researching the subject. He had a keen sensitivity to the issue, since his own daughter had had an abortion, over which she had agonized as the most difficult decision of her life.

Blackmun's research proved inconclusive as to the first question, "When does life begin?" It seemed that since the beginning of recorded history, from the Hittites in 1300 B.C., to Aristotle's Greece, to St. Augustine in the fifth century A.D., civilizations had answered the question differently based on their own ethical, theological, medical, and legal considerations.

The Hittite Code, for example, imposed a sliding scale of fines for abortions that increased from the fifth to ninth month of pregnancy. Aristotle believed that abortion should be permitted until a fetus acquires "sense and life," which he said occurred at the fortieth or ninetieth day of pregnancy for unborn males and females, respectively. St. Augustine regarded any abortion as damnable sin but only considered the abortion of "formed," as opposed to "unformed," fetuses murder. In his view, a fetus was formed after six and a half weeks.

At one end of the spectrum of the debate in *Roe* were those who maintained that life begins at conception. At the other end were those who argued that a fetus does not become a person and acquire legal rights until viable, capable of surviving outside the mother's womb. Between the two poles were those who spoke of "quickening"—the point at which the fetus begins to move inside the womb—or those who, for whatever reason, designated some number of months after conception. Others defined the moment when life begins in more metaphysical terms, such as "ensoulment," the acquisition, emergence, or manifestation of a soul.

The second question was equally difficult. Under what circumstances was abortion justified? From antiquity to the present, abortion was generally abjured. As late as the eighteenth century, abortion was punishable under the Napoleonic Code and English common law as murder. The more modern trend, however, was to permit abortions under certain circumstances. In this country at the time of *Roe*, all but one state, Louisiana, permitted abortions to save the life of the mother. Some states also allowed it in cases of rape or incest.

Interestingly, a poll taken in 1990 showed that 77 percent of all Americans favored abortion, and another poll taken in the same year indicated that an equal percentage of Americans regarded abortion as murder.

Unable to arrive at definitive answers, Blackmun aimed for an acceptable balancing of interests. As he saw it, what was at stake were the interests of the mother, the unborn child, and the state.

For purposes of establishing the legal rights of the interested parties, Blackmun divided pregnancy into three trimesters. In his scheme, during the first trimester, a woman's right to an abortion, based on a constitutional right of privacy, was absolute. During the second trimester, the state could regulate abortion, but only to protect the woman's health. By the end of the second trimester, the sixth month of pregnancy, the fetus was considered viable, and the state, in order to promote its interest in protecting unborn life, could proscribe abortion except when necessary to protect the life or health of the mother.

Marshall agreed with Blackmun's approach and analysis. Along with Burger, Douglas, Brennan, Stewart, and Powell, he joined in the seven-to-two majority decision. White and Rehnquist filed dissenting opinions that would have upheld the Texas statute. The result was considered a watershed victory by women's rights groups, but it served to fuel, rather than resolve, the abortion debate, which has divided the country.

Three years later, Marshall broke with the Court majority over the question of abortion funding. *Roe* established a woman's constitutional right to choose to have an abortion; it said nothing about the government having to pay for it. The pro-life, antiabortion movement therefore focused its energy on limiting the exercise of the abortion right, of a woman's right to choose, by blocking state and federal funding of abortions.

On January 11, 1977, the Court heard oral arguments in *Beal v. Doe*, challenging Pennsylvania's decision to provide Medicaid funds only for therapeutic abortions, meaning abortions certified by a physician to be necessary to protect the life or health of the mother. Health benefits provided under the Medicaid program are paid for jointly by the states and federal government.

On June 20, 1977, the Court upheld the Pennsylvania restriction, six to three. Writing for the majority, Justice Powell concluded that the state's interest in encouraging normal childbirth permitted the restriction. Marshall dissented. He was joined by Blackmun, *Roe*'s author. Brennan filed a separate dissenting opinion.

The tone of Marshall's dissent reflected his deeply held view that the Court should strike down government regulations that had a disproportionate impact on the poor. Clearly, poor women, singled out as a group, were disadvantaged by the Court's ruling. Women of means could afford to pay for their own abortions.

Also, Marshall looked beyond the impact on women to the effect the *Beal* decision would have on the children of the poor, born into the world unwanted by both their mothers and society at large. "The enactments challenged here brutally coerce poor women to bear children whom society will scorn for every day of their lives," he wrote. "I am appalled at the ethical bankruptcy of those who preach a 'right to life' that means, under present social policies, a bare existence in utter misery for so many poor women and their children."

He accused the majority of pulling "from thin air a distinction between laws that absolutely prevent exercise of the fundamental right to abortion and those that 'merely' make its exercise difficult for some people." He pointed out that while an abortion performed during the first trimester was, at the time, a relatively inexpensive procedure, costing around $200, "even this modest sum is beyond the means of most Medicaid recipients. He added in a footnote, "If one does not have it and is unable to get it the fee might as well be one hundred times as great."

In the wake of *Beal*, Congress adopted the "Hyde Amendment," prohibiting the use of federal funds to pay for Medicaid abortions, in August 1977. In addition, thirty-seven states adopted laws similar to Pennsylvania's, permitting state Medicaid funds to be used only for abortions needed to save the life of the mother or in the cases of incest, rape, or fetal deformity.

Meanwhile, as the Court moved to limit the exercise of the abortion right, it also set limits on the methods employed by federal judges to eradicate dual school systems. On February 27, 1974, the Court heard oral arguments in *Milliken v. Bradley*, in which the State of Michigan asked the justices to overturn a U.S. district court order requiring the busing of schoolchildren between Detroit and its surrounding suburbs to achieve racial balance.

The district court judge determined that, over the years, Detroit school officials had adopted policies designed to effectuate *de jure* racial segregation, meaning segregation brought about by law or official government action. There was no evidence that suburban school officials had done the same, but residential housing patterns had produced suburban schools that were virtually all white, while Detroit's schools remained overwhelmingly black— in other words, *de facto* segregation. Seeing no alternative means of eliminating the dual school systems, the judge ordered cross-district busing between Detroit and fifty-three of eighty-five surrounding suburban school districts.

For the majority of the Court, the order went too far. It would have involved busing as many as 779,000 schoolchildren, 503,000 from the suburbs and 276,000 from Detroit.

In addition, the five-to-four majority opinion, written by Chief Justice Burger and delivered on July 25, 1974, held that the district court judge had read the Court's ruling in the North Carolina case, *Swann v. Charlotte-Mecklenburg*, incorrectly. *Swann*, according to Burger, required desegregation, not a particular racial balance.

Furthermore, the majority rejected the idea of holding suburban school districts responsible for the actions of Detroit officials who had fashioned the city's segregated school system. There was no evidence of wrongdoing by the suburbs, so they should not have been involved in a Detroit remedy.

Marshall, Douglas, Brennan, and White dissented. To Douglas, the distinction between *de jure* an *de facto* was a chimera. He saw it was a threat to desegregation in the North, where there was rarely a history of state-imposed segregation but where segregation nonetheless flourished as the result of economic circumstances and more insidious government actions, such as discriminatory zoning, restrictive racial covenants, and racial steering in residential housing sales. He preferred doing away with the distinction altogether.

"It is inconceivable that ghettos develop on their own without any hint of state action," he wrote. "The issue is not whether there should be racial balance, but whether the state's use of various devices that end up with black schools and white schools brought the Equal Protection Clause into effect."

Marshall accused the Court of wavering in its overall commitment to integration in the face of unavoidable complexities and public opposition. "Desegregation is not and was never expected to be an easy task," he chided. "Racial attitudes ingrained in our Nation's childhood and adolescence are not quickly thrown aside in its middle years."

He continued, "But just as the inconvenience of some cannot be allowed to stand in the way of the right of others, so public opposition, no matter how strident, cannot be permitted to divert this Court from the enforcement of the constitutional principles at issue in this case."

He went on, "Today's holding, I fear, is more a reflection of perceived public mood that we have gone far enough in enforcing the Constitution's guarantee of equal justice than it is the product of neutral principles of law."

He concluded, "In the short run, it may seem to be the easier course to allow our great metropolitan areas to be divided up each into two cities—one white, the other black—but it is a course, I predict, our people will ultimately regret."

To critics of the decision, *Milliken* represented the high-water mark of the Court's school desegregation efforts. It sent an ominous signal that the Court, now controlled by a solid conservative majority, might even go so far as to retreat from *Brown*.

Both this concern and the trepidation that the Court's decision in *Beal* raised within the women's rights movement were deepened the following year by the resignation of William O. Douglas.

At around 7:30 P.M. on New Year's Eve, 1974, Douglas suffered a massive stroke in his hotel room in Nassau, the Bahamas, where he was vacationing with his wife, Cathy. He was seventy-six years old. A few hours later, he was flown back to Washington, D.C., on a military aircraft graciously dispatched by Gerald Ford, his old nemesis, who, as a Michigan congressman, had tried unsuccessfully to have him impeached in the early 1970s. Ford had ascended to the presidency, replacing Richard Nixon, who resigned in disgrace on August 9, 1974, in the aftermath of the Watergate scandal.

At first, Douglas's recuperation at Walter Reed Army Hospital proceeded fairly well, though he had lost the use of his left arm and leg and was confined to a wheelchair. He was present for oral arguments at the beginning of the Court's 1975–76 term in the fall of 1975. But his condition deteriorated, and it became clear that he would be unable to continue on the Court. He resigned on November 18, 1975, having served thirty-six and a half years, longer than any other justice.

In farewell, he penned a free-verse poem entitled "Keep the Faith" to the Court's staff:

Keep the faith in the rule of law not only for our own people but for the people of the world.

Keep the faith in a unity of mankind irrespective of race, intellect, color, religion, or ideology.

Keep the faith in the informed citizenry who can govern wisely and justly.

Keep the faith in the system that allows a place for every man no matter how lowly or how great.

Keep the faith in a system which does not leave every issue of human rights to the ups and downs of the political campaigns.

His departure provided a Republican president with the opportunity to appoint yet another conservative justice. Ford nominated John Paul Stevens, a judge on the U.S. Court of Appeals for the Seventh Circuit (covering Illinois, Indiana, and Wisconsin), as Douglas's replacement. Considered somewhat moderate, Stevens, a native of Chicago, had finished first in his class at Northwestern University Law School and afterward had clerked for Supreme Court justice Wiley Rutledge from 1947 to 1949. During his time as Rutledge's clerk, he met Douglas, whom he greatly admired. At the time of Stevens's appointment by Rutledge, Douglas had already been on the Court for eight years.

Stevens subsequently went into private practice, specializing in antitrust law. He made his mark in 1969, serving as general counsel to a commission investigating judicial corruption in Illinois. The investigation forced the resignations of two Illinois State Court judges.

Nixon appointed him to the Seventh Circuit court of appeals in 1970, as a favor to Illinois senator Charles Percy. On the bench, Stevens earned a reputation for thoroughness. Ford was attracted to his conservative midwestern outlook and his reputation as a hard worker. He also hoped that Stevens's relative anonymity would make the nomination noncontroversial. He was right. Although women's groups complained that the time was right for the first appointment of a female to the High Court, Stevens won unanimous Senate approval in December 1975.

The two had feuded, but Marshall rued Douglas's departure. Now he found himself aligned with Brennan against an overwhelming conservative majority composed of Burger, Stewart, White, Blackmun, Powell, Rehnquist, and Stevens. He could rely on Blackmun to vote to uphold abortion, and both Stewart and White sometimes joined the liberals. But he could foresee no set of circumstances in which he would be guaranteed a five-to-four majority.

Moreover, Douglas's retirement could not have come at a worse time, for the Court was about to reconsider the issue Marshall held closest to his heart: capital punishment. On March 31, 1976, the Court heard oral arguments in *Gregg v. Georgia*, a consolidation of cases from states that had revised their sentencing procedures to satisfy the guidelines established in *Furman*.

The Court was asked to decide if the revisions the states had made in their sentencing codes after the 1972 *Furman* decision were constitutional. Since *Furman*, fifteen states had rewritten their sentencing guidelines to require juries to consider mitigating and aggravating circumstances, and twenty had revised their codes to provide for mandatory death sentences for certain crimes, such as murder for hire or killing a correctional officer.

In January 1976, the justices agreed in conference to review fifty petitions. Burger wanted to review only cases involving the most heinous crimes, one of them a razor mutilation, but he did not have the three other votes needed to limit review. Agreement was reached, however, to hear only homicide convictions.

The conference decided to review one case from each of five states. The Georgia case, *Gregg v. Georgia*, was the appeal of Troy Leon Gregg, sentenced to die for the robbery and murder of two men. None of the cases to be reviewed involved the question of racial prejudice or other collateral concerns.

Marshall and Brennan were disturbed by this approach. Marshall had successfully raised the racial question in the *Furman* case and believed it was still a crucial factor for consideration in the cases now before the Court. But this time he failed to get enough votes in conference to have the race of the defendants taken into consideration.

The cases came from Georgia, Florida, North Carolina, Texas, and Louisiana. Georgia required a jury to review aggravating circumstances before imposing capital punishment, and the sentence had to be approved by the state supreme court.

Florida initiated separate sentencing trials after conviction of first-degree murder so a jury could consider aggravating and mitigating circumstances. This allowed a jury's sentence to be overturned by the trial judge or by Florida's supreme court.

North Carolina invoked a mandatory death penalty for all premeditated murders, or murders committed in the commission of a felony, to meet the objection that death sentences were often arbitrarily imposed.

Texas imposed the death penalty only in certain kinds of murders—contract killings, the murder of a prison employee, or deliberate and unprovoked murders—or where there was a belief that a defendant would kill again. This, too, was done to meet the concern raised in *Furman* that death sentences were often meted out arbitrarily.

Louisiana sanctioned a mandatory death penalty for all first-degree murder convictions but allowed juries to consider lesser sentences for second-degree murder or manslaughter. Lawyers for Louisiana believed this revision satisfied *Furman*'s requirement that juries be informed of available alternative sentences.

The Court's deliberations took a bizarre turn when Douglas, from his retirement chambers, insisted on being present at the oral arguments and participating as a "tenth justice." Eventually he was persuaded that there was no legal provision for him to take part in the Court's proceedings.

On July 2, 1976, the court delivered a lengthy, splintered ruling, with Justice Potter Stewart speaking for the majority. The upshot of the decision was that, by a seven-to-two vote, the Court held the death penalty did *not* constitute "cruel and unusual" punishment under the Eighth Amendment. In ruling on the constitutionality of the revised criminal codes passed by the five states, the majority pointed to Georgia's as a model statutory scheme, although Burger, White, and Rehnquist voted to uphold all five new laws. Marshall and Brennan were alone in dissent, maintaining that capital punishment was per se cruel and unusual.

What especially angered Marshall was the assertion by several members of the *Gregg* majority that retribution was an acceptable reason for imposing the death sentence because it discouraged lynchings and other acts of vengeance. He wrote in his dissent, "It simply defies belief to suggest that the death penalty is necessary to prevent the American people from taking the law into their own hands."

As the result of the Court's ruling in *Gregg*, states were free to resume executions of the nation's seven hundred death-row prisoners. Executions in fact resumed on January 17, 1977, when Gary Gillmore, thirty-six, convicted of murder during a robbery, was shot to death by a Utah firing squad.

Courtroom observers said Marshall was visibly shaken as the decision in *Gregg* was read. He left the Court early that day. Later that night, six days away from his sixty-eighth birthday, he suffered a mild heart attack.

Heart attacks change people's lives. Cancers can be surgically removed, or treated with chemotherapy or radiation, and often life can be resumed almost as if nothing had ever happened. But heart attacks can profoundly affect life-styles, regardless of how mild they are said to be.

A weakened heart increases the work of the other organs. Inevitably, if unnoticeably at first, the lungs and kidneys especially are called upon to work harder. Fluid builds in the lungs; unsupported by a vigorous heart, they are unable to expel it. So lasix or other diuretics are administered on a regular basis, thereby increasing the strain on the kidneys.

Meanwhile, limbs and joints begin to ache from the reduced rate at which blood is pumped through the body, carrying strength-giving oxygen. The constant discomfort can make a person irritable. Together with the psychological impact of confronting one's own mortality and advancing years, this condition can sour even the sweetest disposition.

Moreover, smoking, with the damage it causes the heart, becomes suicidal, and Thurgood Marshall loved to smoke. A lot of favorite foods are proscribed because of their salt or cholesterol content, and Thurgood Marshall loved eating all the wrong things. Liquor becomes criminally suspect, and Marshall still enjoyed bourbon. To quit smoking and drinking and to diet strictly, all in combination, was difficult. It is hard for anyone to change the habits of a lifetime.

He felt sorry for himself in his own humorous, self-deprecating way. As the nation's hard-working solicitor general, he once described himself to Sidney Zion of the *New York Times* as "a hedonist with no time for pleasure." After his heart attack, he was a hedonist lacking even the constitution for self-indulgence.

He was forced to reevaluate his career, its strains and, lately, frustrations. There was still the need to carry on the fight for his beliefs and principles on behalf of the poor. But, paradoxically, there was, at the very same time, the need to find greater distance from all the stress, in order to better preserve his strength and to survive, so that he could prolong the years he had left to devote to the struggle. Survival was the key.

He harbored no hope of shifting the conservative direction of the Court. This situation angered him greatly. Lyndon Johnson was right when he told biographer Doris Kearns Goodwin, "No matter how well you may think you know a Negro, if you really know one, there'll come the time when you look at him and see how deep his bitterness is."

Yet Marshall refused to let his bitterness consume him. He held it at bay, kept it in check, as he had his fear of death. He was alone now except for his good friend Brennan. That realization imbued him with serenity. He took solace in it.

He softened his days. He went to work a little later, left a little earlier.

Meanwhile, he girded for what he saw as his last remaining battles. He could not win, but surrender was unthinkable. He focused on his legacy.

The threat to American democracy, as he saw it, was the danger that history was about to repeat itself. In the decades that followed the Civil War, America craved absolution for its sins against the Africans dragged to these shores in chains and held in dehumanizing slavery. The Thirteenth, Fourteenth, and Fifteenth Amendments to the Constitution, the Reconstruction and Civil Rights Acts, and the multitude of federal agencies, such as the Freedmen's Bureau, set up to assist the newly freed slaves and their descendants, were well-intentioned efforts to supplant dehumanization with equality. In short, to make amends.

But like a vaccination that did not take, repentance gave way to baser sentiments, fear, prejudice, and cruelty. It did not take long for the country to reverse course.

Marshall saw the Court's conservative trend presaging civil rights reversals that would obliterate the gains made during the

1950s and 1960s. In his view, the same thing had happened when the retrenchment of the 1870s, 1880s, and 1890s undid much of what Reconstruction had achieved.

Marshall made his feelings known during the 1977–78 term when the Court decided for the first time to address squarely the question of affirmative action. On October 12, 1977, the justices heard oral arguments in *University of California Regents v. Bakke.*

Alan Bakke was denied admission to the medical school of the University of California at Davis in 1973 and 1974. Both years, he had failed to achieve the cumulative score—based on grade-point average, admissions test performance, interviews, and recommendations—that was required under the school's general admissions program.

The school also ran a special admissions program for disadvantaged minorities, who could gain admission despite lower cumulative scores. Each year, sixteen out of one hundred places were set aside for special admissions. Bakke claimed the special admissions program operated as reverse discrimination in violation of the equal-protection clause.

On June 28, 1978, the Court issued a mixed ruling. The justices refused to order Bakke's admission because he failed to show that he would have been admitted but for the special admissions program. But the court struck down Davis's separate admissions program as a violation of equal protection. A plurality of the justices maintained, however, that race was one of many factors that could be taken into consideration for purposes of determining admission.

Justice Powell, writing for the Court, pointed to Harvard College's admissions program as a model. Harvard did not have a separate admissions process for minorities, but in order to promote diversity within its student body, Harvard took into consideration an applicant's race.

Under the Harvard program, race was accorded some weight along with grade-point average, entrance examination scores, extracurricular interests, recommendations, and geographic background. Harvard's reasoning was that a ghetto black might not have done as well on the Scholastic Aptitude Test (SAT), or attended as prestigious a secondary school, as a white from a more affluent background. Yet the black applicant, in rising above his circumstances, might have demonstrated resourcefulness and academic commitment in the face of unfavorable odds that reflected an admirable strength of character and resolve. In addition, because of his underprivileged background, the black applicant might lend to Harvard's academic community unique perspectives on American society that would enrich intellectual thought and discussion.

Harvard's program was different from a selection process that chose people just because they were black, although Harvard did choose some people just because they were excellent hockey players or just because they played the violin well. The joke around Harvard after the *Bakke* ruling was that a black applicant from Salt Lake City who could play hockey and was also a virtuoso violinist was a shoo-in for admission, irrespective of his SAT scores.

Marshall regarded the ruling as a setback for affirmative action. He dissented from the part of Powell's opinion that invalidated separate admissions. But he concurred that race was one of many factors that could legitimately be taken into consideration in making admissions decisions.

His carefully crafted concurrence set forth the entire history of discrimination against blacks as he saw it, from slavery to the present day. "I do not agree that petitioner's admissions program violates the Constitution," he wrote. "For it must be remembered that, during most of the past 200 years, the Constitution as interpreted by this Court did not prohibit the most ingenious and pervasive forms of discrimination against the Negro. Now, when a State acts to remedy the effects of that legacy of discrimination, I cannot believe that this same Constitution stands as a barrier."

If affirmative action programs, set-asides, or quotas accorded blacks some degree of privileged treatment, then so be it. In Marshall's view, blacks needed special protection. He pointed out, "Although Negroes represent 11.5% of the population, they are only 1.2% of the lawyers and judges, 2% of he physicians, 2.3% of the dentists, 1.1% of the engineers and 2.6% of the college and university professors. The relationship between those figures and the history of unequal treatment afforded to the Negro cannot be denied. At every point from birth to death the impact of the past is reflected in the still disfavored position of the Negro."

Marshall charged, "The racism of our society has been so pervasive that none, regardless of wealth or position, has managed to escape its impact."

He distinguished blacks from others. "The experience of Negroes in America has been different in kind, not just in degree, form that of any other ethnic groups. It is not merely the history of slavery alone but also that a whole people were marked as inferior by the law. And that mark has endured. The dream of America as the great melting pot has not been realized for the Negro; because of his skin color he never even made it to the pot."

He concluded, "These differences in the experience of the Negro make it difficult for me to accept that Negroes cannot be afforded greater protection under the Fourteenth Amendment where it is necessary to remedy the effect of past discrimination."

A few months later, he took the extraordinary step of speaking out publicly, breaking a self-imposed, ten-year moratorium on public statements about race. On November 18, 1978, Marshall returned to his alma mater, Howard University, and warned his listeners not to be complacent about civil rights.

Speaking forcefully to a gathering of five hundred in Howard's Cramton Auditorium, he alluded to reports of a resurgence of the Ku Klux Klan, declaring that bigots "in every phase of American life are still laying traps for us." He cautioned, "The Klan never dies. They just stop wearing sheets because sheets cost too much."

He told his listeners, "Be careful of the people who say, 'You've got it made. Take it easy. You don't need any more help.' Today we have reached the point where people say, 'You've come a long way.' But so have other people."

He asked, "Has the gap [between blacks and whites] been getting smaller? No. It's getting bigger."

He refused to let his own success belie the pervasiveness of racial prejudice. "These Negro kids are not fools," he stated. "They know that if someone says they have a chance to be the only Negro in the Supreme Court, the odds are against them."

He expressed his frustration over the slow pace of change, saying that he used to assure people that "things are going to get better." But in recent years, he said, the response he most often heard was "You not only told me that but you told my father too and he's no better off. Are you going to tell my children that, too?"

Advising his audience that blacks have to be better than whites in order to succeed in a prejudiced society, he quoted his mentor Charles Houston: "You've got to be better, boy. You've got to move better." He chided, "Don't listen to that myth that inequality has been solved. Take it from me, it has not been solved."

Nevertheless, the Court continued its inexorable retrenchment. On April 22, 1980, the justices upheld, six to three, an at-large system for electing city commissioners in *City of Mobile, Alabama v. Bolton*. Blacks had charged that Mobile's at-large electoral framework unfairly diluted black voting strength, the result being that whites, not blacks, got elected.

Writing for the majority, Justice Stewart concluded that blacks have no constitutional right to elect blacks. Instead, the Constitution prevented merely the purposeful, or intentional, denial of the right to vote. The Court failed to find in the Mobile voting scheme evidence of an intent to discriminate.

Marshall dissented. He argued that discriminatory impact alone violated the Constitution. Requiring the victims of discrimination to demonstrate governmental intent to discriminate against them imposed an insurmountable burden, in Marshall's view.

He wrote, "An approach based on motivation creates the risk that officials will be able to adopt policies that are the products of discriminatory intent so long as they sufficiently mask their motives through the use of subtlety and illusion."

He warned of social unrest: "If this Court refuses to honor our long-recognized principle that the Constitution 'nullifies sophisticated as well as simple-minded modes of discrimination,' it cannot expect the victims of discrimination to respect political channels of seeking redress."

Meanwhile, Republican Ronald Reagan was waging a successful campaign in the 1980 presidential election. A number of key factors contributed to his landslide victory over incumbent Democrat Jimmy Carter. Among them were a faltering economy, with double-digit inflation and unemployment, and foreign policy setbacks, including the taking of American hostages in Iran.

But the crux of Reagan's appeal was a pledge to unleash a conservative "revolution" that would restore American greatness by bringing about a return to "traditional" social and moral values, which he claimed had been eroded by government policies dating back to Franklin Roosevelt's New Deal of the 1930s.

Reagan attacked racial preferences in university admissions and job hiring and promotions. He exploited the popular view that affirmative action programs, for which "quotas" became the catchword, amounted to reverse discrimination, in effect punishing individual whites unjustly for the sins of their forebears.

In addition, he aligned himself with the pro-life movement, pledging to commit his best efforts to reversing the Court's decision in *Roe v. Wade.*

Nevertheless, Marshall won a key victory on July 2, 1980, when the Court decided *Fullilove v. Klutznick.* By a six-to-three vote, with Stewart, Rehnquist, and Stevens dissenting, the Court upheld federal regulations establishing a set-aside program for minority contractors. Minorities were defined to include "Negroes, Spanish-speaking, Orientals, Indians, Eskimos, and Aleuts."

Under the regulations, state and local governments were required to set aside for minority business enterprises (MBEs) 10 percent of the federal funds allotted them for local public works projects. The contract awards were to be made even if the MBEs were not the lowest bidders on contracts, based on the assumption that MBEs were forced to cover costs inflated by the present effects of past discrimination. For example, minority businesses were typically forced to pay higher rates for loans and insurance.

In his concurring opinion, Marshall, joined by Brennan and Blackmun, hailed the ruling. "It is clear to me," he wrote, "that the racial classifications employed in the set-aside provision are substantially related to the achievement of the important and congressionally articulated goal of remedying the present effects of past racial discrimination."

Not long after Reagan was elected, however, the Court dealt pro-choice advocates another setback with its ruling in *H.G. v. Matheson,* decided on March 23, 1981. By a six-to-three vote, with Marshall, Brennan, and Blackmun dissenting, the justices upheld a Utah law requiring physicians to "notify, if possible," the parents or guardian of minors seeking abortions. Minors who did not wish to have their parents notified could instead seek the consent of a judge.

Writing for the majority, Chief Justice Burger concluded, "The possibility that some parents will not react with compassion and understanding upon being informed of their daughter's predicament...does not undercut the legitimacy of the State's attempt to...enhance the probability that a pregnant young woman exercise as wisely as possible her right to make the abortion decision."

Again looking beyond legal principles to the practical effect of the Court's ruling, Marshall dissented. He insisted, "This [parental notification] scheme forces a young woman in an already dire situation to choose between two fundamentally unacceptable alternatives: notifying a possibly dictatorial or even abusive parent and justifying her profoundly personal decision in an intimidating judicial proceeding to a black-robed stranger. For such a woman, this dilemma is more likely to result in trauma and pain than in an informed and voluntary decision."

Reagan was provided with the opportunity to make his first appointment to the Court just three months after he was sworn in as president. In April 1981, Potter Stewart announced plans to retire, after twenty-two years. Reagan used Stewart's departure to fulfill his campaign promise to appoint the first woman justice. Her name: Sandra Day O'Connor.

The president announced the nomination on July 7, 1981. Said one Reagan Justice Department official, O'Connor "was the most conservative woman we could find."

A native of Arizona, O'Connor had graduated from high school at the age of sixteen and completed both undergraduate and law studies at Stanford University in just five years. She graduated near the top of her law school class, several places behind William Rehnquist, who finished first. After graduation, O'Connor found her job options limited by sex discrimination. Despite her impressive academic credentials, none of the major law firms in San Francisco or Los Angeles would offer her more than secretarial positions. She recalls, "None had ever hired a woman as a lawyer, and they were not prepared to do so."

She went to work for a small law firm in Phoenix, then left to be a housewife and raise her three sons. Subsequently, she got involved in state politics, eventually becoming majority leader of the state senate in the early 1970s. In 1979, she was named to the state court of appeals by Democratic governor Bruce Babbitt. When Reagan announced her nomination, she was fifty years old.

During her confirmation hearings, O'Connor refused to answer whether she would vote to overturn *Roe v. Wade*. But she told the Senate Judiciary Committee that she found abortion "personally repugnant." In July 1981, the Senate approved her nomination by a vote of ninety-nine to zero.

Over the next two terms, O'Connor typically joined with the conservative majority, often providing the decisive fifth vote in cases that limited the rights of criminal defendants. In addition, she voted with Burger, White, Rehnquist, and Powell in a controversial 1984 decision that upheld the constitutionality of government-sponsored nativity scenes, regarded by critics as a significant weakening of the wall traditionally separating church and state.

Again, Marshall felt compelled to speak out, criticizing publicly the Court's reactionary trend. In September 1984, he delivered an address to a conference of Second Circuit appeals court judges in Hartford, Connecticut. He used the occasion to accuse the Court of denying adequate remedies to victims of constitutional rights violations, charging that the Court's conservative majority was turning the Bill of Rights into "an unenforced honor code."

He made specific reference to a ruling that upheld a New York law permitting preventive detention of any juvenile suspected of being a "serious risk" to commit another crime. The Court conceded that prison conditions exposed juveniles to the threat of violence and sexual assault. But the majority concluded that juvenile victims of such abuses could seek damages after the fact in lower courts. Marshall stated, "Given [the possibility of violence], I find it shocking that rather than make an assessment of how likely those evils were under the New York system, it instead validated the scheme as a whole and offered a hollow remedy for individual abuses."

He went on to criticize the Court for a ruling he regarded as insensitive to the needs of the handicapped. In a Vermont case, the justices conceded that lengthy delays in processing Social Security benefits caused the handicapped great hardship, but the decision left it to Congress to remedy the situation. He warned, "Decisions that [fail to offer effective remedies] will erode the faith in the law of those who rely on the law's protection."

His open dissent was echoed by Stevens and Blackmun, both regarded as conservative justices. In an August 1984 speech dedicating a new building at the University of Chicago Law School, Stevens accused the Court of overstepping its authority.

A month later, Blackmun told an audience at the Cosmos Club in Washington, D.C., that the Court's conservative majority was arriving at its rulings "by hook or by crook." He also complained that the Court had lost its collegiality, saying there was "very little humor" left among the justices.

Despite O'Connor's conservative reputation, civil rights groups had hoped that, as a past victim of discrimination, she would harbor liberal sentiments regarding issues related to affirmative action. She disappointed them. For example, she joined with a plurality of the justices to hand Marshall a defeat in a crucial case, *Wygant v. Jackson Board of Education*, decided on May 19, 1986.

In *Wygant* the Court struck down a collective-bargaining agreement between the Jackson, Michigan, school board and the teachers' union. The agreement was part of a concerted effort by Jackson officials to compensate for the underrepresentation of minorities by increasing the number of minority teachers and administrators.

The agreement provided that, in the event of layoffs, those hired last would be fired first, except that the percentage of minority personnel laid off would not be allowed to exceed the total percentage of minorities employed by the school system. In other words, if minorities constituted 10 percent of the total work force, no more than 10 percent of those minorities could be laid off. The result was that, when layoffs occurred, some minority school-teachers were retained ahead of white teachers with more seniority.

Marshall dissented. He conceded his belief that the layoffs were "unfair." Nevertheless, he stated, "unfairness ought not to be confused with constitutional injury."

He reasoned that any scheme basing job retention on seniority would have a disproportionately negative impact on minorities, since minorities had only recently gained access to previously discriminatory job markets. He declared, "I believe that a public employer, with the full agreement of its employees, should be permitted to preserve the benefits of a legitimate and constitutional affirmative-action hiring plan even while reducing its work force."

Reagan won an overwhelming reelection victory over the Democratic candidate, former Vice President Walter Mondale, in November 1984, carrying forty-nine of fifty states. He was handed two more Supreme Court appointments halfway through his second term. During a private conversation in the White House in May 1986, Warren Burger, seventy-nine, expressed to Reagan his desire to step down after having served seventeen years as chief justice. Burger told the president he wished to direct his full-time energies to chairing the commission that was organizing the upcoming bicentennial celebration of the Constitution's ratification.

Reagan chose Rehnquist to replace Burger as chief justice. Throughout his tenure as an associate justice, Rehnquist had demonstrated his unwavering fidelity to conservative principles. To fill the seat made vacant by Rehnquist's elevation, Reagan selected an outspoken, if unheralded, ideologue with impeccable academic credentials: Antonin Scalia, who became the first Italian American nominated to the High Court.

Antonin Scalia, "Nino" to family and friends, was born on March 11, 1936, in Trenton, New Jersey. His father was an Italian immigrant who taught romance languages at Brooklyn College and was an authority on Dante. His mother, a first-generation Italian American, was an elementary school teacher.

Scalia graduated from a Jesuit high school, the St. Francis Xavier Military Academy in Lower Manhattan, as valedictorian. He finished college at Georgetown University at the top of his class. He went on to become an editor of the *Harvard Law Review*, again finishing first in his class at Harvard Law School in 1960. After law school, he went to work for one of the nation's largest and most prestigious law firms, Jones, Day, Reavis, and

Pogue. He left private practice after six years to teach law at the University of Virginia in Charlottesville.

During the Nixon administration, he served as general counsel for the Office of Telecommunications. Under President Ford, he became head of the Justice Department's Office of Legal Counsel, a post at one time held by Rehnquist.

After Ford was defeated by Jimmy Carter in 1976, Scalia became a scholar in residence at the American Enterprise Institute (AEI), a right-wing think tank that, like the Hoover Institute in Palo Alto, California, generated many of the ideas and policies that fueled the Reagan revolution. He left the AEI to teach law at the University of Chicago.

A devout Roman Catholic and father of nine children, he opposed abortion. He was also an impassioned opponent of affirmative action. In fact, he loathed the concept. From Scalia's Italian-American perspective, affirmative action programs were nothing more than self-serving attempts by "Aryan" judges and justices to assuage their liberal guilt over wrongs done to blacks at the expense of less privileged, hard-working white ethnics.

Scalia felt no such guilt. In a 1979 lecture at the University of Chicago, he explained, "My father came to this country when he was a teenager. Not only had he never profited from the sweat of any black man's brow, I don't think he had ever seen a black man."

He said he was "entirely in favor of according the poor inner-city child, who happens to be black, advantages and preferences not given to my own children because they don't need them. But," he went on, "I am not willing to prefer the son of a prosperous and well-educated black doctor or lawyer—solely because of his race—to the son of a recent refugee from Eastern Europe who is working as a manual laborer to get his family ahead."

In summary, he condemned affirmative action "because it is based upon concepts of racial indebtedness and racial entitlement, rather than individual worth and individual need, and that is to say, because it is racist."

Reagan appointed him to the U.S. Court of Appeals for the District of Columbia Circuit in 1981, shortly after he became president.

The Republican-controlled Senate approved both Supreme

Court nominations on September 17, 1986. Nine days later, Rehnquist and Scalia were sworn in. With Rehnquist in charge, bolstered by Scalia, Reagan was confident the Court's rightward movement would accelerate.

Two weeks later, the beginning of the 1986–87 term ushered in the era of the Rehnquist Court. Marshall found himself aligned with Brennan against six conservatives—Rehnquist, White, Blackmun, Powell, Stevens, and O'Connor—and one ultraconservative, Scalia.

Anxious to rid the Court of the remaining liberals, critics began to insinuate that Marshall's age and ill health had rendered him uninterested in his work. Some went so far as to assert that Marshall rarely wrote his own opinions and had, in effect, relinquished power to his law clerks, operating as a justice in name only.

According to Gay Gellhorn, a professor at the District of Columbia School of Law who clerked for Marshall during the mid-1980s, nothing could have been further from the truth. Gellhorn recalled, "He never lost interest in his work." In Gellhorn's words, Marshall maintained a "litigator's attentiveness," a nuts-and-bolts interest not just in legal issues but in how advocates structured their cases and presented them to the Court.

Moreover, Gellhorn was impressed by Marshall's "voluminous retention" of cases. She said he "never forgot anything he read. While discussing a point of law with us, he might say, 'Now wait a minute, isn't there a Second Circuit appeals court ruling that addresses this point?' We might not recall having seen it. But whenever he told us something was there, and we went to look for it, we found it."

Glen M. Darbyshire, a Savannah, Georgia, attorney who clerked for Marshall during the Court's 1986–87 term, expressed similar views in a September 1991 article for the *ABA Journal*, "Clerking for Justice Marshall." According to Darbyshire, Marshall accorded his clerks "creative freedom" to draft opinions after defining the central focus and rationale that he wanted them to use. "Nonetheless," wrote Darbyshire, "his review of draft opinions could be exacting."

Darbyshire explained, "He edited with a thick blue pencil that could, with a single stroke, obliterate pretentious or ineffective wording.... His law clerks, before submitting drafts to him, followed a detailed procedure for reviewing and editing them for substantive or grammatical errors—all in a determined effort to avoid the blue pencil."

Despite his obvious frustrations, both Gellhorn and Darbyshire remember Marshall as a lively wit and consummate raconteur— "a great schmoozer," as Gellhorn put it—who enjoyed relating his life's adventures, from his early days as a struggling, young Baltimore attorney, to hitting after-hours parties with heavy-weight champion Joe Louis and his Harlem entourage.

Darbyshire recalled a get-acquainted cocktail party at the Court at the beginning of the 1986–87 term. "Twenty minutes into the affair, nearly half of the clerks were gathered around him listening to raucous tales while the rest of us discussed our law schools and geographic origins with other justices."

A year later, Marshall exhibited his feistiness in a September 1987 television interview with journalist Carl Rowan. Rowan asked him to grade the civil rights records of recent presidents. Marshall's candor ignited a controversy when he dismissed Ronald Reagan as "the bottom," calling his administration a throwback to the era "when we [blacks] really didn't have a chance."

He said of Franklin Delano Roosevelt, "I don't think [he] did much for the Negro." He criticized Dwight D. Eisenhower as well, saying, "I don't think [he] did anything except try to undermine the *Brown* decision."

Of his beloved Lyndon B. Johnson, he declared, "His [civil rights] plans were just unbelievable," which, according to Marshall, explained why "they...[got] rid of him." He reserved faint praise for Jimmy Carter, commenting, "His heart was in the right place, but that's the best I can do with him."

At first, Reagan, who was close to Marshall's age, tried to dismiss the unprecedented criticisms of a sitting president by a Supreme Court justice with characteristic humor. He remarked offhandedly, "A young fellow like me is not going to get angry at an old fellow like him."

Later, the president assumed a more defensive posture. At a state dinner for Swedish prime minister Ingvar Carlsson on September 9, he responded, "I hope he [Marshall] will be informed that that isn't my record, and I will point to the record we had not only in this administration but as governor of California, and I was raised in a household where the greatest sin was prejudice. From boyhood on, I have been on the side of civil rights and no discrimination and I am just sorry that he is not aware of that."

Time magazine commented wryly in its September 21, 1987, edition, "It's best that the president, 76, keeps his sense of humor. Marshall, 79, vowed not to retire from the court as long as Reagan remains in the White House."

A year later, in an August 10, 1988, address to the National Bar Association (NBA) convention in Washington, D.C., Marshall reiterated his view that Reagan administration policies and the conservative Court posed a threat to hard-won advances made by blacks.

"We're not gaining ground, my friends. We might be losing," Marshall told the assembled delegates.

The National Bar Association was formed in 1925 as an alternative to the American Bar Association, which, until 1952, did not admit African-American lawyers. At the time of Marshall's speech, the NBA claimed ten thousand members.

Asked to justify a separate bar association for blacks "at this late date," Marshall replied, "The answer is simple: It's not that late."

On January 23, 1989, the Rehnquist Court dealt advocates of affirmative action the major blow Marshall had long expected. In *City of Richmond v. J. A. Croson*, Justice O'Connor delivered on behalf of the Court a splintered decision striking down the Virginia city's set-aside program for minority contractors.

Anthony Kennedy, the newest justice, voted with the plurality to overturn the Richmond plan. A graduate of Stanford University Law School, Kennedy was appointed to the U.S. Court of Appeals for the Ninth Circuit, covering a number of western states, including California, by President Gerald Ford in 1975. He had replaced Justice Lewis Powell on February 18, 1988, following Powell's retirement.

Under the Richmond plan, prime contractors awarded city construction contracts were required to subcontract at least 30 percent of the total dollar amount of each contract award to MBEs. The city council had adopted the plan based on evidence that despite the fact that Richmond was 50 percent black, only 0.67 percent of the city's prime construction contracts had been awarded to MBEs in recent years.

A plurality of justices objected to the Richmond scheme because there was no showing of past discrimination by the city itself. In addition, the plan was held to be too broad in its reach. It made MBEs nationwide eligible for the set-aside, not just those based in Richmond. Moreover, no MBE was required to show that it had itself been the victim of discrimination. In other words, the plan, designed to remedy broad-based societal discrimination, lacked the required specificity.

The Court distinguished between the federal government, on the one hand, and states and localities, on the other. In the Court's view, the federal government had the power under the Fourteenth Amendment to use racial classifications to enact broad-based remedies for past discrimination; state and local governments did not.

In an eloquent concurrence, Justice Scalia bitterly attacked all remedial measures that employ racial quotas or preferences.

He wrote, "It is plainly true that in our society blacks have suffered discrimination immeasurably greater than any directed at other racial groups. But those who believe that racial preferences can help to 'even the score' display, and reinforce, a manner of thinking by race that was the source of the injustice and that will, if it endures within our society, be the source of more injustice still."

He continued, "The relevant proposition is not that it was blacks, or Jews, or Irish who were discriminated against, but that it was individual men and women, 'created equal,' who were discriminated against. And the relevant resolve is that it should never happen again."

He went on, "Racial preferences appear to 'even the score' (in some small degree) only if one embraces the proposition that our society is appropriately viewed as divided into races, making it right that an injustice rendered in the past to a black man should be compensated for by discriminating against white. Nothing is worth that embrace."

Scalia left the door open for race-neutral programs that grant preferences based on a showing of economic disparity rather on race. He reasoned, "Since blacks have been disproportionately disadvantaged by racial discrimination, any race-neutral remedial program aimed at the disadvantaged *as such* will have a disproportionately beneficial impact on blacks." In other words, since a disproportionate number of black people are poor, any program aimed at helping the poor will benefit blacks most. He concluded, "Only such a program, and not one that operates on the basis of race, is in accord with the letter and the spirit of our Constitution."

Marshall, joined by Brennan and Blackmun, filed a bitter dissent. He complained, "Today's decision marks a deliberate and giant step backward in this Court's affirmative-action jurisprudence. Cynical of one municipality's attempt to redress the effects of past racial discrimination in a particular industry, the majority launches a grapeshot attack on race-conscious remedies in general. The majority's unnecessary pronouncements will inevitably discourage or prevent governmental entities, particularly States and localities, from acting to rectify the scourge of past discrimination." He declared, "The battle against pernicious racial discrimination or its effects is nowhere near won."

Nine months later, Marshall traveled to Bolton Landing, New York. On September 9, 1989, he told the conference of Second Circuit appeals court judges that recent decisions of the Court "put at risk not only the civil rights of minorities but the civil rights of all citizens."

He stated, "It is difficult to characterize last term's decisions as the product of anything other than a deliberate retrenchment of the civil rights agenda. We could sweep it under the rug and hide it, but I'm not going to do it. We have come full circle [since *Brown*]. We are back where we started."

His despair was deepened by the resignation of William J. Brennan on July 20, 1990. In 1978, Brennan had undergone radiation treatments for a malignant tumor in his throat. The following year, he had suffered a stroke. At the age of eighty-four, he cited "advancing age and medical condition" as his reasons for stepping down.

Overshadowed throughout his long and illustrious tenure by the likes of Earl Warren, Hugo Black, and William O. Douglas, Brennan had served as one of the Court's key consensus builders during the Court's liberal heyday. In a begrudging accolade to a formidable adversary, the conservative *National Review* in 1984 offered the following assessment of Brennan's work: "There is no individual in this country, on or off the Court, who has had a more profound and sustained impact upon public policy in the United States."

Marshall told ABC News in July 1990, "There's nobody here that can persuade the way Brennan can persuade. Brennan will sit down with you and talk to you and show you where you're wrong. Well, there's nobody with that power on the court today." Brennan, he insisted, "cannot be replaced." He had become Marshall's closest ally, and also his dearest friend. Thurgood's grandson was named after him.

All human beings have their limits. There is only so much that anyone can take. Pride and purpose crumble under the crush of age and illness, punctuated by resignations and deaths. Enduring marriage provides comfort and solace. Children and the births of grandchildren provide momentary joy. But each graveside shovelful of dirt, each good-bye, is a loss. And the cumulative effect of the losses is overpowering. Brennan's departure left Thurgood Marshall disconsolate.

He contemplated his own retirement. But first, he decided to indulge in one last affront to a conservative Republican president.

In a July 1990 interview with ABC News, he ridiculed President George Bush's nomination of David H. Souter, an obscure New Hampshire Supreme Court judge, to be Brennan's replacement. His remarks were broadcast nationwide on the July 26 edition of ABC's "Primetime Live."

"When his [Souter's] name came down, I listened to television," Marshall said. "And the first thing, I called my wife and asked, 'Have I ever heard of this man?' She said, 'No, I haven't either.' So I promptly called Brennan because it's his circuit. And his wife answered the phone, and...she said, 'He's never heard of him either.'"

Marshall was asked whether he would vote for Bush if he ran for reelection. He replied, "It's said that if you can't say something good about a dead person, don't say it. Well, I consider him dead." He went on to express his opinion that Bush's peripatetic chief of staff, John H. Sununu—a former New Hampshire governor who had in fact recommended Souter's nomination—was "calling his [Bush's] shots." (Sununu would resign within the space of a few months amid charges of unethical conduct relating to personal travel at government expense.)

Bush refused to comment directly on the remarks, attributing his reticence to his "very high regard for the separation of powers and for the Supreme Court."

But Bush's attorney general, Richard Thornburgh, said Marshall's comments "saddened" him. He added that to his knowledge it was "the first time any Supreme Court justice has ever criticized in our history an appointment and, indeed, the president who made the appointment."

In Congress, Senate minority leader Robert J. Dole accused Marshall of taking "cheap shots" and making "partisan and demeaning political statements" about Souter and the president.

Souter's nomination was confirmed by the Senate on October 2, 1990, by a vote of ninety to nine. He joined Marshall on the bench for the start of the Court's 1990–91 term.

That term was to be Marshall's last. On June 27, 1991, he announced his retirement.

TWENTY-FOUR

Marshall's Legacy

Thurgood Marshall was the legal conscience
for all Americans, not just black Americans.
—Attorney Juanita Jackson Mitchell

Thurgood Marshall was rolled in a wheelchair to the jaws of a construction fork lift and hoisted with all deliberate speed to the stage of Philadelphia's Independence Mall. He was guest of honor at the city's 1992 Fourth of July celebration of the nation's 216th birthday. Marshall, who had celebrated his eighty-fourth birthday two days earlier, appeared more infirm than he had thirteen months earlier, when he retired from the Supreme Court. But on this day his voice still flashed with the fiery indignation that had wilted two generations of segregation foes.

"The battle has not yet been won; we have barely begun," he said. "Americans can do better.... America has no choice but to do better to assure justice for all Americans, Afro and white, rich and poor, educated and illiterate....Our futures are bound together." The racially mixed crowd cheered loudly and stopped only after Thurgood waved his cane and shouted, "Enough, enough."

Thurgood Marshall was the fourth recipient of the Liberty Medal, established in 1988 to honor "an individual or an organization from anywhere in the world that has demonstrated leadership and vision in the pursuit of liberty of conscience or freedom from oppression, ignorance and deprivation."

In 1989, the medal's first recipient was Lech Walesa, Poland's president and founder of the Solidarity movement. Former U.S. president Jimmy Carter received the award in 1990, and it was shared by past Costa Rican president Oscar Arias Sanchez and the French medical organization Médecins Sans Frontières (Doctors Without Borders) in 1991.

Martin Meyerson, chairman of the Liberty Medal Award Selection Committee, opened the ceremony by saying, "Activists from Benjamin Franklin to Martin Luther King Jr. would have appreciated today as we recognize the distinguished American patriot Thurgood Marshall." There probably was no better place for Thurgood Marshall to be on this Independence Day than the birthplace of the U.S. Constitution. He had spent most of his life vigorously defending constitutional principles while angrily reminding America that its founding document was flawed.

Five years earlier, in 1987, during the bicentennial celebration of the Constitution, Marshall made clear his displeasure with the original document. The nine Supreme Court justices had been asked to reenact the drafting of the Constitution. Marshall refused to participate, noting that the Constitution had failed to abolish slavery. He told the brethren, "If you are going to do what you did two hundred years ago, somebody is going to have to give me short pants and a tray so I can serve coffee."

He explained, "I cannot accept this invitation, for I do not believe that the meaning of the Constitution was forever 'fixed' at the Philadelphia Convention. Nor do I find the wisdom, foresight, and sense of justice exhibited by the Framers particularly profound. To the contrary, the government they devised was defective from the start, requiring several amendments, a civil war, and momentous social transformations to attain the system of constitutional government, and its respect for the individual freedoms and human rights we hold as fundamental today. When contemporary Americans cite 'the Constitution,' they invoke a concept that is vastly different from what the Framers barely began to construct two centuries ago."

In fact, the Constitution had required more than a "civil war and momentous social transformations" to perfect it. It was a document that at its inception excluded black slaves who could not vote and were counted for representation purposes as three-fifths of a person. And it would be more than 130 years after the original document's ratification before women, black or white, could vote.

Thurgood Marshall had a panoramic view of American life, from the powerful Oval Office of the White House and the majestic marble corridors of the Supreme Court to the tar-paper and tin-roofed shacks of Virginia, Alabama, Tennessee, Georgia, Mississippi, Florida, Texas, the Carolinas, and Arkansas, where black Americans lived in fear of night riders and in frustration with a system that denied them the basic decencies of life and at times life itself. His twenty-four-year tenure as an associate justice of the U.S. Supreme Court epitomized the battle of black Americans for equality, but his reputation as the most powerful civil rights advocate of the century had been authenticated long before he joined the Court in 1967.

As a young attorney on the streets of his native Baltimore Maryland, in the 1930s, Marshall used the NAACP, the powerful civil rights organization conceived the year he was born, as an instrument for social and legal change. Its anachronistic name— "N Double A C P"—and the whispered phrase "Thurgood is coming" struck fear in the hearts of white southerners who had tried to keep the racist shackles of segregation clamped firmly around the ankles of millions of black Americans. He came to personify the NAACP as an organization that stirred pride in the souls of black folk who looked to it for succor.

During his career as director-counsel of the NAACP's Legal Defense and Educational Fund, he became the most successful lawyer in Supreme Court history. Together with his team of Fund lawyers, he was responsible for striking down the barriers to voting rights for African Americans. In addition, he successfully challenged laws preventing black students from receiving quality educations and black families from purchasing homes in previously all white neighborhoods, like Lake Barcroft in Fairfax County, Virginia, where he and Cissy raised their sons. His victory in *Brown v. Board of Education* in 1954—overturning *Plessy v. Ferguson*'s separate-but-equal doctrine, which had given legal sanction to racial segregation, American apartheid—stands as a singular, monumental achievement unmatched in its scope and social impact.

Juanita Jackson Mitchell, Marshall's friend from Baltimore who was an active NAACP attorney, spoke of his career two weeks before she died, in July 1992. "He brought a vitality and a sense of mission to the NAACP that it would not otherwise have had. Thurgood was the legal conscience for all Americans, not just black Americans."

Marshall went on the become one of the most effective advocates on behalf of the U.S. government during his tenure as solicitor general. His opposition to the government's use of evidence obtained illegally through electronic eavesdropping and surveillance devices struck a principled blow upholding the privacy and civil liberties of all citizens.

As the first African American to sit on the Supreme Court, he never lost touch with or respect for the common man or woman. He was always praised for his humanity. "I like people," he said. "I like to have them around me."

He was especially sensitive to the plight of the poor. His association with poor Americans—black and white—during the years he traveled across the nation as an NAACP attorney gave him a unique insight into the problems of the less fortunate that was not shared by his Supreme Court colleagues. As the last liberal holdover from the Warren court, he construed the Bill of Rights and the Constitution's civil rights amendments as instruments to protect the powerless and the disadvantaged.

In 1970, for example, an attorney asked the Supreme Court to overturn a lower-court ruling that would have forced local governments to increase welfare payments to indigent families. Marshall took the lawyer to task. "Is the argument that there is not enough money available a proper one for the most affluent nation in the world today?" he asked.

When the lawyer replied, "The pit is not bottomless," Marshall inquired, "Do you want us to note that this government is unable to pay people enough to eat?" Marshall said the question was not economics "but the vital interest of a powerless minority, poor families without breadwinners and the stuff which sustains children's lives, food, clothing and shelter."

By the end of his Supreme Court career, he had written over eighteen hundred dissents, more than any of his colleagues. At times he was joined by only one or two other justices. After Marshall's appointment new justices named by Presidents Nixon, Ford, Reagan, and Bush held different views on the rights of individuals and justice. The result was that the philosophical distance between Marshall and his Supreme Court colleagues became greater as the Court moved to the conservative right. Yet he never despaired at finding himself in the minority because of his strong conviction that his opinions were morally correct.

He failed in his efforts to persuade the Court's majority that poverty should be regarded as a "suspect classification" and that government actions having a disproportionately negative impact on the poor should be struck down. He also failed to muster the needed votes for his view that, having established a constitutional right to abortion, governments should be required to finance abortions for indigent women in order that they might effectively exercise that right.

His greatest defeat was on the issue of capital punishment. Only his close friend and liberal ally William Brennan came to share his view that the death penalty is cruel and unusual punishment. As a Supreme Court justice, Marshall always voted for stays of execution when eleventh-hour death-penalty appeals came before the Court. He left standing instructions with his law clerks to call him at any hour of the night so he could record his vote to grant a stay of execution, even when he knew the Court's majority would deny the doomed petitioner's request. Court records indicate Marshall filed more than 250 dissents from capital punishment denials of certiorari, the discretionary procedure the Court uses to decide which cases it will hear on appeal from lower courts.

On the day Marshall retired, there were more than two thousand death-row prisoners in the United States, and the pace of executions had begun to increase as the Court began swiftly reducing the number of death-penalty cases it would hear on appeal. In June 1992, there were 2,588 condemned prisoners in the United States, according to the National Coalition Against the Death Penalty. Of this number, 1,316 were white and 1,008 were black, along with 47 Native Americans, 14 Asians, and 13 condemned prisoners whose race was unknown. Forty-one women were included in this total.

Nevertheless, while Marshall was unsuccessful in abolishing the death penalty, he succeeded in making some major reforms in death-sentencing procedures. His 1985 majority opinion in *Ake v. Oklahoma* allowed indigent defendants to have a psychiatrist present for their insanity defenses to murder charges. And in *Ford v. Wainwright*, in 1986, Marshall persuaded a majority of the Court that the execution of mentally ill prisoners violated the Eighth Amendment. In that opinion he noted "the natural abhorrence civilized societies feel at killing one who has no capacity to defend himself."

Shortly after his 1991 retirement, Marshall reiterated his opposition to capital punishment in simple terms: "I am not for the death penalty. I don't see what's gained by it."

At the same time, Marshall failed to escape criticism from the left. Opponents of the Vietnam War have justifiably assailed him for his refusal to support William O. Douglas's repeated efforts to have the Court take up the issue of the war's constitutionality. For many antiwar activists, the battle cry of the 1960s and early 1970s was "If you're not part of the solution, you're part of the problem." For them, Marshall was part of the problem on Vietnam. In hindsight, it is difficult to justify his refusal to bring before the Court for full airing and discussion one of the most divisive legal, social, and political issues of the day.

Meanwhile, militant blacks accused him of failing to appreciate their contribution in the struggle for equal rights. One thing the militants did was lend credibility to Marshall's moderate call for working for change within the system. Before Malcom X's call for liberation "by any means necessary" and Martin luther King's strategy of mass protest and civil disobedience, Marshall had himself been labeled a radical for calling on blacks to seek redress through the courts. For whites, King's activism increased Marshall's appeal; Malcolm X's emergence made Marshall an even more politically palatable alternative.

In addition, Marshall's unequivocal commitment to racial preferences as an effective tool for remedying the effects of past discrimination may well prove misguided. The privilege of preference is limited to but a select few who are qualified to take advantage of the opportunities that preferences open up for them. In this regard, the direct reach of affirmative action, noble as its aims may be, is too restricted to lift up or eliminate the black underclass, the masses of disfranchised African Americans who are most in need of basic skills and equal educational opportunity.

However, affirmative action can be used to guarantee the representation in the ranks of the privileged classes of poor people whose talents, because of their underprivileged status, might otherwise have gone unnoticed. Exposure to their perspectives, which are shaped by poverty and struggle, may bear the fruits of increased understanding and compassion for the poor.

Yet skin color alone is no guarantee that a person will think in a certain way. In fact, the color and background of a man like Clarence Thomas, nominated by President Bush to replace Marshall, betrays most liberal assumptions about affirmative action's benefits.

A black graduate of Yale Law School, Thomas, forty-three years old at the time of his appointment, was born in rural poverty in segregated Pin Point, Georgia. At the age of seven, he went to live with his grandfather in Savannah, Georgia, where for the first time he had indoor plumbing. He acquired a Catholic education and, for a time, considered entering the priesthood, enrolling in the Immaculate Conception Seminary in northeastern Missouri after high school. Later, he attended Holy Cross College in Worcester, Massachusetts, before entering law school at Yale.

In 1974, he went to work for Missouri attorney general John Danforth, who was later elected to the U.S. Senate. Then, after three years as an attorney for the Monsanto Corporation, he rejoined Danforth in Washington, D.C., as a legislative assistant from 1979 to 1981. He served briefly in the civil rights division of the Department of Education in 1981 before Ronald Reagan appointed him head of the Equal Employment Opportunity Commission (EEOC).

Thomas complained of racial slights and insults throughout his growing up, and he was a beneficiary of Yale's commitment to affirmative action. But he infuriated liberals early in his EEOC tenure by attacking racial preferences in hiring.

"I am unalterably opposed to programs that force or even cajole people to hire a certain percentage of minorities," he told a *New York Times* interviewer in July 1982. "I watched the operation of such affirmative action policies when I was in college, and I watched the destruction of many kids as a result. It was wrong for those kids, and it was wrong to give that kind of false hope."

Instead, he called for increased black self-reliance. He told a *Washington Post* interviewer in July 1983, "I'll put the bottom line on you: I don't think we caused our problem, but we're damn sure going to have to solve it."

He was also critical of the civil rights movement. In an October 1987 review of Harvard Law School professor Derrick Bell's book *And We Were Not Saved*, Thomas wrote, "The tragedy...is that as blacks achieved the full exercise of their rights as citizens, government expanded and blacks became an interest group in a coalition supporting expanded government. Instead of reflecting the diversity of the black community, blacks' political views have become homogeneous. Yet black ambitions need not be so closely wedded to ever-expanding government."

As EEOC chairman, Thomas shifted the commission's focus away from class-action litigation to investigating more limited, specific acts of discrimination. He also rejected the use of statistics on minority hiring as evidence of employer bias. Once, in an appearance before a congressional committee, he asked rhetorically whether Georgetown University's all-black basketball team was proof of discrimination against whites.

In 1990, Bush appointed him to the U.S. Court of Appeals for the District of Columbia Circuit, where he served just sixteen months before being nominated to the Supreme Court.

At first, Thomas's nomination appeared to be a shrewd political move on the part of the president. By making effective, if cynical, use of the skin color of a nominee opposed to racial preferences, Bush threatened the Democratic coalition of liberals, women's groups, and blacks. Liberals and feminists were aligned against Thomas because of his conservatism and outspoken opposition to abortion. At the same time these groups risked antagonizing blacks whose paramount goal was to have an African American succeed Marshall. The white liberal leadership of the Democratic party knew that by opposing Thomas, they also risked further alienating white middle-class voters—the so-called Reagan Democrats—who regarded racial preferences as reverse discrimination.

But developments took a stunning and unexpected turn during Thomas's confirmation hearings. Anita Hill, a black thirty-five-year-old University of Oklahoma Law School professor, appeared before the Senate Judiciary Committee and a shocked national television audience to charge Thomas with making lurid and degrading sexual overtures to her during her time as his assistant at both the Department of Education and the EEOC. She endured three days of grueling questioning by Thomas's Republican supporters, who attacked her credibility and motives. Throughout it all, she maintained a steely composure and was ultimately perceived as a damaging and compelling witness.

In response, Thomas, his confirmation clearly in jeopardy, characterized Hill's testimony and the efforts to discredit him as "a high-tech lynching for uppity blacks." He denied Hill's charges "categorically."

Despite Hill's allegations, Thomas went on the win Senate confirmation on October 15, 1991, by a narrow margin, 52 to 48, far short of the 69 to 11 vote endorsement the Senate had given the first Afro-American justice a quarter century earlier. He was sworn in eight days later.

Nevertheless, Hill had succeeded in refocusing the national debate. More was at issue after her testimony than partisan politics or the credibility of two articulate and persuasive individuals, a black man and a black woman pitted against each other. What began to matter more was who had the power to judge whether Anita Hill had told the truth or whether Clarence Thomas was fit to be only the second African American to serve on the Supreme Court. It seemed wholly out of balance that those judgments should be rendered by a Senate Judiciary Committee that was a wealthy, exclusive panel of all-white, all-male senators. On the day Clarence Thomas was confirmed, there were no blacks, and only one woman, serving in the U.S. Senate.

During the Court's 1991–92 term, his first as an associate justice, Thomas demonstrated himself to be exactly what his conservative proponents had hoped and his liberal opponents had dreaded. Most often, he aligned himself with the Court's two most conservative members, Rehnquist and Scalia. He has voted to restrict the constitutional protection accorded prison inmates; he has called for softening the wall that has traditionally separated church and state; and, dissenting from the Court's ruling in *Planned Parenthood of Southeastern Pennsylvania v. Casey*, decided on June 29, 1992, he has called for *Roe v. Wade* to be overturned outright.

Nevertheless, Thurgood Marshall's retirement may ultimately produce a farther-reaching social transformation than he could have brought about by remaining on the bench, given the Court's composition at the time. The reaction to Thomas as Marshall's replacement galvanized the women's movement; more women sought elective office in 1992 than ever in the nation's history. One result was the election of Carol Moseley Braun. Braun became the first black woman to serve in the U.S. Senate.

In his July 4, 1992, acceptance of the Liberty Medal, Thurgood Marshall warned America that the battle for equality was not over. His admonition raised the question of whether America's racial problems of the 1990s and the emerging twenty-first century can be solved with the tactics of the 1950s and 1960s as younger black Americans grow more distant from organizations like the NAACP.

Thirty years earlier, Thurgood Marshall had told NAACP executive secretary Roy Wilkins that his abiding ambition was to "put the NAACP and the Inc., Fund out of business." It was a lighthearted and optimistic remark meant to imply that one day racial intolerance would no longer be a part of the American landscape.

Decades later, in Philadelphia, Marshall said, "Unfortunately, much of the civil rights agenda has not changed, although Afro-Americans can eat and sleep in more places than they could decades ago."

But a lot of things have changed since Thurgood Marshall began his legal career more than a half century ago. The venerable civil rights lawyer and jurist, whose great-grandfather had been a slave, was responsible for many of those changes. In 1936, Senator "Cotton" Ed Smith stood on the steps of a South Carolina courthouse and derided the presence of black delegates at that year's Democratic National Convention in Philadelphia. In 1992, Ronald Brown, the first black chairman of the Democratic National Committee, rose to the podium in New York City's Madison Square Garden and gaveled the Democratic National Convention to order.

There were fewer than 500 black elected officials in 1965. In 1992, more than 7,400 blacks held elective office, including 26 members of the U.S. House of Representatives and Virginia governor L. Douglas Wilder, whose predecessor thirty-eight years earlier had launched an attack of "massive resistance" against school desegregation.

Moreover, white majorities have elected black mayors in Denver, Colorado; Seattle, Washington; Kansas City, Missouri; Rockford, Illinois; Dayton, Ohio; and Tallahassee, Florida. This is significant progress because it indicates that white America has begun to realize its moral obligation to assure fairness and equality for all citizens. Many of the civil rights problems formerly addressed by the NAACP and Marshall are now resolved by black elected officials or by the use of the ballot to make white elected officials responsive to the concerns of African Americans.

In addition, racial progress is reflected in the number of African Americans who hold positions on the boards of major corporations, anchor the evening television news, or have high-level positions in government, the military, in universities, and who sit on federal courts. In many ways, the NAACP has fallen victim to its own success as more African Americans enter the mainstream of the nation's life.

At the same time, income disparity between whites and blacks persists nationally. According to the *New York Times*'s analysis of 1990 census data, "[T]he 1989 median household income was $31,435 for whites and $19,758 for blacks. Put another way, a black household typically brought in 63 cents for every $1 that went to a white household. In 1979, it was 62 cents for every $1."

Moreover, the unemployment rate for blacks remains more than double that for whites. According to the U.S. Department of Labor, the annual average rate of unemployment for blacks in 1990 was 11.3 percent, compared with 4.7 percent for whites. In 1980, black unemployment was 14.3 percent, compared with 6.3 percent for whites.

Today the NAACP, which Thurgood Marshall so valiantly helped to lead, is faced with the dilemma that it is no longer relevant or in tune with a new generation of black Americans, many of whom have never been denied service at a lunch counter, refused admission to a school because of their race, turned away at the voting booth, or terrorized by the Ku Klux Klan. Benjamin C. Bradlee, former executive editor of the *Washington Post*, once asked retired NAACP executive director Benjamin Hooks, "Ben, I used to read about the NAACP all the time. What's happened to you?"

In a 1992 *Crisis* magazine article, Hooks acknowledged the organization's dilemma. "I know it's a problem," he wrote. "It's very upsetting."

Hooks went on to express his frustration. "My predecessor, Roy Wilkins, used to make the same complaint. Why can't the NAACP ever get credit? During his [Wilkins's] time it was the Student Non-Violent Coordinating Committee, the Southern Christian Leadership Conference, and the Congress of Racial Equality, and now its TransAfrica and the Black Congressional Caucus." Yet, Hooks pointed out, the NAACP's 1992 membership of nearly five hundred thousand in fifteen hundred adult branches is the largest it has ever been.

The change began in the early 1960s with the emergence of civil rights leaders like Martin Luther King Jr. and the civil rights protest by college students who challenged segregation in the streets instead of the courts. But it is clear that those protests could not have succeeded had it not been for Thurgood Marshall's unrelenting fight to win the cases that struck down legalized segregation in America.

The NAACP shares Thurgood Marshall's belief that there is still much to be accomplished. It is broadening its agenda beyond the traditional role of protecting civil rights through litigation. but the rapid gains made from the 1940s until the 1970s have slowed, and

Thurgood Marshall is among the first to recognize that the nation is far from realizing the ideals expressed by sociologist Gunnar Myrdal in his "American Creed" of the "essential dignity of the individual human being, of the fundamental equality of all men and of certain inalienable rights to freedom, justice, and a fair opportunity."

The NAACP is now turning its attention to black economic development, teenage pregnancy, infant mortality, substance abuse, and other problems that are endemic in black communities. These problems are heightened by the disintegration in black America of the traditional two-parent family and the fact that one of every four African-American men between the ages of twenty to twenty-nine is either in prison or on parole or on probation. Overt discrimination is masked in police brutality, unemployment, and inadequate health care, social problems that are latter-day extensions of segregation and discrimination.

The struggle for full equality continues, and America is far from becoming an egalitarian society. That goal remains elusive even though America champions the freedom of people the world over and the United States has frequently committed its military forces—white and black—to defend it.

But not everyone agrees that the NAACP should shift in emphasis as it attempts to address current social problems. Charles Tate, president of the Booker T. Washington Foundation, a research group based in Washington, D.C., said:

"There's been a lot of talk about the NAACP becoming involved in things like the drug problems, but I think it would be a serious error to push the group into other directions that detract from its abilities to handle civil rights. There are new civil rights challenges in areas such as environmental protection, since most toxic waste dumps are in black and Hispanic areas. It is misguided to suggest that the NAACP change its focus when we have people standing on the sidelines with no focus. If black people need to move in new directions, let's not change the direction of the NAACP. Let's build new institutions to move in new directions. The Congressional Black Caucus is an example of that."

No matter what direction the fight for equality now takes, it is clear all America has benefited from Thurgood Marshall's contribution to the nation's democracy, not just the country's 30 million black citizens. He used his legal talents to support the rights of the powerless and to make "equal protection of the laws" more than just an idealistic legal phrase. Thurgood Marshall did not write the Constitution, but no American can read it without recognizing his imprint on it.

Randall L. Kennedy, a professor at Harvard Law School, who was Marshall's law clerk in 1983, said, "It seems to me that Marshall worked as an advance guard. First, he was very much a disrupter and a rebel. Then others took over that position, and he became an advance guard at being a black American insider at very high levels of government. At each point, he has been a pioneer, opening doors that others have gone through behind him."

Thurgood Marshall, perhaps, offered the best assessment of his career on the day he retired from the Supreme Court. "I don't know what legacy I left. It's up to the people. I guess you could say, 'He did what he could with what he had.' I have given fifty years to it, and if that is not enough, God bless them."

EPILOGUE

Fanfare for the Common Man

> Inscribed above the front entrance to the Supreme Court building are the words "Equal justice under law." Surely no one individual did more to make those words a reality than Thurgood Marshall.
> —Chief Justice William H. Rehnquist

Retired Justice Thurgood Marshall looked forward to administering the oath of office to Vice President Albert Gore, but on Inauguration Day, Wednesday, January 20, 1993, he was too ill to make the twenty-two-mile trip from his Lake Barcroft home in Fairfax County, Virginia, to the West Front steps of the United States Capitol. His former colleague on the Supreme Court, Justice Byron R. White, substituted for him at the ceremonies installing only the second Democratic administration in a quarter century. On Sunday, January 24, at two P.M., just four days after William Jefferson Clinton became the nation's forty-second president, Thurgood Marshall died of congestive heart failure at Bethesda Naval Medical Center in Maryland. He was eighty-four.

Years earlier, when asked about the possibility of his retiring from the increasingly conservative Court, he jauntily replied, "Don't worry, I am going to outlive those bastards." It was probably fitting that if some of the "bastards" survived him, at least he refused to die on the watch of one of the Republican presidents whose appointments had propelled the Court from the liberal left Thurgood embraced to the conservative right he abhorred.

As news of his death spread across Washington, D.C., the nation, and the world, tributes to his life and achievements mounted. Newly elected President Clinton declared, "He was a giant in the quest for human rights and equal opportunity in the whole history of our country and every American should be grateful for his contributions." Senator Edward M. Kennedy of Massachusetts, whose brother had given Marshall his first appointment to the federal bench in 1961, called him "a living embodiment of our nation's highest ideals." Congressman Kweisi Mfume, chairman of the Congressional Black Caucus and a Maryland Democrat from the streets of Marshall's native Baltimore, said, "He gave the Constitution the power the Framers articulated but did not practice, that Lincoln affirmed but did not perfect."

Alluding to the fact that he had, as an advocate, already earned his place in history before ascending to the Court, Harvard law professor Laurence Tribe, a leading constitutional scholar, called him simply "the greatest lawyer in the twentieth century."

Civil rights leader Jesse Jackson spoke for millions of grateful people when he said, "For most of us who grew up under segregation, we have never known a day without Thurgood Marshall hovering over us to protect us."

Sherman A. Parks Jr., a forty-two-year-old black lawyer and president of the Topeka, Kansas, school board that was sued in *Brown*, reflected on how Marshall had changed his life in particular: "I am a black male, and now I am an attorney and the president of the school board that spawned the case."

Among past and present justices, even his ideological opposites voiced deep admiration. Retired chief justice Warren E. Burger recalled that, as a lawyer, Marshall "literally took his life in his hands" to try civil rights cases in the south. Justice Clarence Thomas, who replaced Marshall as the only African American on the Court, characterized him as "a great lawyer, a great jurist and a great man."

In a moving eulogy delivered from the pulpit of Washington's National Cathedral, where the nation's leaders gathered on January 28, 1993, Chief Justice William H. Rehnquist also heralded Marshall's personal bravery, which Marshall himself downplayed when he spun his entertaining yarns, his war stories.

"Some of these stories had a humorous twist to them," Rehnquist said, "but they also gave a sense of what he had been up against. His forays to represent his clients required not only diligence and legal skill but physical courage of a high order."

The sixteenth chief justice proceeded to make an extraordinary pronouncement: "Inscribed above the front entrance to the Supreme Court building are the words 'Equal justice under law.' Surely no one individual did more to make these words a reality than Thurgood Marshall." Thus, with the all-inclusive phrase "no one," Rehnquist ranked Marshall alongside Washington, Jefferson, and Lincoln. This statement was from the same man who, as a law clerk some thirty years earlier, had urged that *Plessy*'s separate-but-equal doctrine be upheld.

At five P.M. on the Sunday that Marshall died, Thomas Snyder of Washington, D.C.'s Gawler's Funeral Home dispatched a van to remove Marshall's body from the Naval Hospital's morgue and bring it to Gawler's, a stately, red brick mortuary on upper Wisconsin Avenue in the District of Columbia's affluent Friendship Heights subdivision.

Gawler's was one of Washington's oldest funeral parlors, established in 1850. Joseph Gawler, a cabinet-maker by trade, produced coffins as a side line in his small, three-story frame house on Pennsylvania Avenue, one block from the White House.

Over the years, Gawler's has handled the funerals of some of the nation's most prominent people, among them: presidents Woodrow Wilson, William Howard Taft, Franklin D. Roosevelt, Dwight D. Eisenhower, John F. Kennedy, and Supreme Court justices Oliver Wendell Holmes, Harlan Stone, Fred A. Vinson, Robert H. Jackson, Felix Frankfurter, Hugo Black, Earl Warren, Abe Fortas, Potter Stewart, and Arthur J. Goldberg.

Despite its reputation as the mortuary of the powerful and famous, some members of Washington's old-line black elite wondered about the Marshall family's decision to use Gawler's instead of McGuire's Funeral Home across town on Georgia Avenue. McGuire's, owned by a fourth-generation African-American Washington family, had traditionally buried the city's socially prominent black citizens since the turn of the century. "I guess they understood Thurgood was an integrationist to the very end," observed one of Thurgood's former law clerks.

Gawler's morticians prepared Marshall's body, draped his Supreme Court robe around him, and placed him in a pine coffin. "Justice Marshall's family said he wanted a simple pine casket," Thomas Snyder explained, "and we had one in our inventory." The coffin was taken to Gawler's Eisenhower room. "There was a brief, private viewing just for Mrs. Marshall, family members, and a few close friends," Snyder said.

At 9:30 A.M., Wednesday , January 27, Thurgood's pine coffin, covered with an American flag, was carried up the thirty-six steps of the Supreme Court through a somber phalanx of robed current and former justices and placed on a massive Vermont marble catafalque in the building's Great Hall outside the courtroom. Throughout the day and into the evening, some 18,000 people filed past the bier to pay their final respects to "Mr. Civil Rights." His sons, lawyer Thurgood Marshall, a member of Vice President Gore's staff, and John William Marshall, a Virginia state police officer, took turns standing vigil over their father's remains.

Early next morning, the grounds of the National Cathedral at the corner of Wisconsin and Massachusetts avenues, in the city's fashionable upper northwest quadrant, resembled a civil rights mass meeting of the 1960s. People—black and white, Jew and Gentile—who had been active in the civil rights movement and perhaps had not been together since the dark days of Montgomery, Selma, Atlanta, and Little Rock, a quarter century earlier, exchanged greetings in the unseasonably balmy, overcast January weather. The black war wagons of the U.S. Secret Service and uniformed officers from the Metropolitan Police force, the U.S. Park Service, the U.S. Capitol Police, and the Executive Protection Service appeared to stretch for miles, while uniformed policemen patrolled the area with dogs.

It might indeed have been a scene reminiscent of Birmingham, Alabama, decades before, when Police Chief Bull Connor's officers turned their vicious dogs and billy clubs on civil rights demonstrators. But on this day the law enforcement authorities were not concerned with the presence of people like Julian Bond, John Lewis, Jesse Jackson, Lonnie King, Marian Wright Edelman, and the scores of other veterans of the civil rights movement. The officers had not come to prevent black people from getting a meal at a lunch counter, attending classes at a southern school, or riding in the front seat of a Greyhound bus to Jackson, Mississippi. Instead, they were there to protect the President and Vice President of the United States and the leaders of Congress, including most of the members of the U.S. Senate and House of Representatives, along with every living current and former member of the Supreme Court. All were there to pay tribute to Thurgood Marshall.

Salutations were kept short because everyone seemed anxious to find seats in the crowded mahogany pews of the National Cathedral. The coffin, draped this time with the flag of the Episcopal Church, of which Marshall was a devoted member, was wheeled into the main chapel where it rested in front of 4,000 mourners, not all of whom were renowned. Among them were seventy-year-old Miriam Johnson and her sixty-seven-year-old friend Agnes Miles, who rode a bus all night from their homes in Birmingham, Alabama, to be there. "And we rode on the front seats," Mrs. Johnson said, knowing her comment was a testimony to Thurgood Marshall's career.

By 10:30 A.M., when Edward Madison Nassor began the prelude, "Land of Rest," on the fifty-three-bell Bessie J. Kibbey memorial carillon, it was clear to those in attendance that Thurgood Marshall's funeral would be more a celebration of his life than a mourning of his passing. He was described variously by those who eulogized him as a practical joker, a good-humored curmudgeon, and a champion of the weak and oppressed.

Ralph K. Winter, a judge on the United States Court of Appeals for the Second Circuit in New York, served as a law clerk in the early 1960s for Judge Marshall of the same court. He spoke of how, during the 1940s, Marshall would call travel agencies to uncover whether their booking practices were discriminatory and, if so, get them shut down. On one occasion, he was surprised when a travel agent reserved him a room in a Florida hotel. "Excuse me, is this hotel restricted?" Marshall asked.

"Oh, Mr. Marshall," replied the agent, "I didn't know you were Jewish!" Feigning black dialect, Marshall responded, "Ahh, sister, have I got news for you!"

Winter went on to relate that Marshall's favorite appellation for his law clerks was "knucklehead," concluding, "I'm prouder of the title 'knucklehead' than any other one I've ever had."

An old friend, William T. Coleman, the former transportation secretary who also worked on *Brown*, observed, "History will ultimately record that Mr. Justice Marshall gave the cloth and linen to the work that Lincoln's untimely death left undone." He went on to wonder aloud, as the justices looked on and listened, whether the civil rights cause would have suffered the same reversals at the hands of a more conservative court if Thurgood Marshall had been available to represent the NAACP, instead of thrust into the role of a dissenting, minority justice.

Coleman concluded with his gaze resting on the new President. He asked rhetorically, "Could a son of Arkansas be president if Marshall's efforts had not been successful? Please do not think us ungracious when we wonder if a son of Arkansas would be here today if Marshall, in that hot summer of 1958 had lost, not won, the Little Rock school case. Could there be a cabinet reflective of the American people if Marshall had lost *Brown v. Board of Education*?"

Vernon E. Jordan, former head of the National Urban League and a close adviser to President Clinton during the new administration's transition, delivered what was perhaps the most poignant appraisal of Marshall's life and work. His mission, said Jordan, was "to cleanse our tattered Constitution and our besmirched legal system of the filth of oppressive racism and to restore to all Americans a Constitution and a legal system newly alive to the requirement of justice."

He added, "He was a teacher who taught us to believe in the shield of justice and the sword of truth, a role model whose career made us dream large dreams and work to secure them, an agent of change who transformed the way an entire generation thought of itself, of its place in our society, and of the law itself. Farewell, Mr. Civil Rights. Farewell, Mr. Justice Marshall. We thank you for all you have done. Good night, sweet prince, and flights of angels sing thee to thy rest."

With that, the choir of Howard University raised their voices in "The Battle Hymn of the Republic," which Marshall often commented should be made the national anthem. Their exuberant rendition brought members of the audience to their feet to join in the singing. Soon the massive cathedral reverberated with the hymn's righteous indignation over slavery, injustice, and oppression, its solemn vow to trample the grapes of wrath. "Mine eyes have seen the glory of the coming of the Lord..."

The choir concluded the services with "Lift Every Voice and Sing," the James Weldon Johnson poem set to music that is known as the Negro National Anthem. The President and Mrs. Clinton joined in the singing without having to refer to the lyrics printed on the funeral program. Afterward, the cathedral's great organ burst forth with Aaron Copland's "Fanfare for the Common Man," and this most uncommon man's plain pine coffin was wheeled from the chapel and placed in a waiting hearse. Thurgood Marshall was buried the next day across the Potomac River, in Arlington National Cemetery, in the Supreme Court circle.

But his story was not yet over, for intrigue and controversy were to follow him even to his grave.

Within a month of his burial, Columbia University released to the general public transcripts of interviews that were taped during the 1970s for the university's oral history project. By agreement with the justice, the transcripts had been sealed until after his death. The transcripts contained extraordinarily candid, often intemperate, observations about some of the leading characters and personages Marshall had dealt with in his day. His comments, often critical, sometimes laudatory, always colorful, were hardly out of character. Yet they ignited a firestorm of controversy because of their potential for changing the favorable, long-standing perceptions accorded some of the leading figures in modern American history.

Marshall was especially biting in his criticism of Robert F. Kennedy, who, as attorney general, brokered the devil's pact with Mississippi senator James O. Eastland that had made Marshall a federal appeals court judge. His brother the President was, according to Marshall, "a very sweet man." By contrast, he said, "Bobby was like his father [Joseph P. Kennedy]. He was a cold, calculating character. 'What's in it for me?' I mean, not like his brother. He had no warm feelings. None at all."

He went on to say that the then attorney general "was primarily interested in getting the president reelected....He constantly pushed [President] Kennedy to push the dates back on which he would make these [civil rights] moves....It would have gone much faster but for that."

He was critical of black leaders, as well. Conceding that Dr. Martin Luther King Jr. was a "great" leader, he nonetheless maintained that King "wasn't worth diddly squat as an organizer." He complained, "All he [King] did was to dump all his legal work on us, including the bills. And that was all right with him. So long as he didn't have to pay the bills."

He reiterated his long-standing animus against Malcolm X, explaining, "I just don't believe that everything that's black is right and everything that's white is wrong. I think that anybody in their right mind knows it, and that's what they [the Black Muslims] were preaching."

He characterized Black Muslims generally as "the nicest, sweetest, most decent people you will ever run across." But he insisted, "I wouldn't agree with anything a Muslim ever said, any time, any place." He concluded with regard to Malcolm X, "In the end he kept wanting to talk to me, and I kept telling him to go to hell." The Black Muslim leader was slain in Harlem in 1965.

Some of his most vitriolic remarks were directed against President Dwight D. Eisenhower, whose conduct in the immediate wake of *Brown* he called "despicable." He also attacked General Douglas MacArthur's refusal to desegregate army units under his command.

"I questioned him about the continuation of segregation in the army," said the justice, recalling his visit to Korea in 1951, "and he said he was working on it. And I asked him how many years he'd been working on it. And he said he didn't really remember how many. He said he didn't find the Negroes qualified, and when he found them qualified they would be integrated. Well, we didn't part that friendly."

Again, his warmest praise was reserved for Lyndon Johnson, the president who appointed him to the Supreme Court and who, according to Marshall, was "a lovely guy" who "died of a broken heart." Marshall insisted, "If he'd been reelected, he'd have been still alive today."

Recalling the occasional phone calls he received from his old drinking buddy shortly after the former president left office, Marshall revealed, "He would call me for the express purpose of getting out of it. He would say, 'No moaning at the bar,' or something like that. And then he'd say, 'Okay, now, go have a drink.' I'd say, 'Providing you do.'"

As revealing as the Columbia University transcripts were, however, a far more explosive controversy erupted in May 1993 when the Library of Congress released the late justice's papers, including correspondence and case files, from his years on the

Court. The case files contain confidential notes and internal memoranda between Marshall, his law clerks, and the other justices, as well as draft opinions in various stages and other related materials. Taken as a whole, the papers, which consist of some 173,700 items and occupy roughly 231.6 linear feet of shelf space, provide a rare glimpse into the internal workings of the Court and the modus operandi of the various justices who jealously guard their privacy and the confidentiality of their deliberations.

Reaction to the documents' release was swift and strident. In a sharply worded letter to Librarian of Congress James H. Billington, dated May 25, 1993, Chief Justice Rehnquist accused the library of exercising "bad judgment" in making the papers available so soon after Marshall's death. Many of the issues the papers dealt with still confronted the justices, and many of the justices Marshall worked with, and whose thoughts and sentiments his papers reflected, still sat on the Court.

"Most members of the court recognize that after the passage of a certain amount of time, our papers should be available for historical research," Rehnquist conceded. "But to release Justice Marshall's papers dealing with deliberations which occurred as recently as two terms ago is something quite different."

Claiming to speak for a majority of the justices, who he said were "surprised and disappointed" by the opening of Marshall's files, Rehnquist warned, "Unless there is some presently unknown basis for the library's action, we think it is such that future donors of judicial papers will be inclined to look elsewhere for a repository."

The Marshall family protested the documents' release as well. On Friday, May 21, 1993, Cissy Marshall said through her attorney, William T. Coleman, "My husband had great respect for the court and its tradition of confidentiality. I am certain he never intended his papers to be released during the lifetime of the justices with whom he sat and I am surprised that the Library of Congress has chosen to release them at this time."

Coleman added, "All I can say is that we were shocked and utterly surprised at his [Billington's] attitude. We thought that he acted improperly, and that he was turning something that was a great contribution—namely the preservation of the papers—into an act destroying confidentiality, which certainly adversely af-

fected the Court and the way they do business." Convinced that
lawyers were somehow using the files to formulate strategies for
future cases, Coleman, who clerked for Justice Felix Frankfurter
during the Court's 1948–1949 term, complained, "I will say that
this is the worst thing I have seen happen in a long time around
this town."

Billington, for his part, insisted that he had merely carried out
the late justice's "exact intentions." He refused to restrict the
public's access to the collection. "The library must honor the
expressed wishes of one of our great jurists," he maintained. To do
otherwise, he contended, would be "a breach of contract and a
violation of the trust placed in the library" by Justice Marshall.
He concluded, "Open access to the papers, as called for in Justice
Marshall's instrument of gift, must be maintained."

The instrument of gift itself, signed by Justice Marshall on
October 24, 1991, provides, in relevant part:

> I hereby dedicate to the public all rights, including copyrights
> throughout the world, that I may possess in the Collection.
>   1. *Access.* With the exception that the entire Collection
> shall be at all times available to the staff of the Library for
> administrative purposes, access to the Collection during my
> lifetime is restricted to me and to others only with my written
> permission. Thereafter, the Collection shall be made avail-
> able to the public at the discretion of the Library.
>   2. *Use.* Use of the materials constituting this gift shall be
> limited to private study on the premises of the Library by
> researchers or scholars engaged in serious research.
>   3. *Reproduction.* Persons granted access to the Collection
> may obtain single-copy reproductions of the unpublished
> writing contained therein.

Aside from the question of how the files might be used by
lawyers to prepare cases for argument before the Court, there
seems to be little in the collection that is in the nature of a striking
revelation, or an embarrassment for the Court. In fact, the files
reflect a dignified and thoughtful collegiality among the justices,
who work hard and diligently, strive admirably to arrive at
consensus, and document even their most informal communications in order to avoid misunderstandings. The files appear to
contain few handwritten notes or vote tallies taken by Marshall

during conferences. Evidently, he was not a prodigious note-taker or, more often than not, chose not to include his notes in the collection.

The case files do reveal intensive jockeying back and forth among conservatives, liberals, and centrists over such volatile issues as abortion, civil rights, and sex discrimination. For example, in 1989, the Court apparently came within ten days of overturning *Roe v. Wade*, which established women's constitutional right to abortion. Late in the term, Rehnquist circulated the last of four drafts of a proposed majority opinion in *Webster v. Reproductive Health Services* that would have upheld a Missouri law imposing severe abortion limitations. Three justices, in proposed dissents, were prepared to pronounce "*Roe* no longer lives." In the end, however, Rehnquist failed to hold the majority he felt he had, and *Roe* was reaffirmed, if somewhat weakened. In *Webster*, Justice Harry Blackmun, *Roe*'s author, was able to declare, "For today, at least, the law of abortion stands undisturbed."

The files also reveal that during the 1988–1989 term, personal rancor surfaced between Justices William Brennan and Anthony Kennedy over the Court's commitment to racial equality. In *Patterson v. McLean Credit Union*, Brenda Patterson, an African-American woman who worked as a teller and file clerk for a credit union in Winston-Salem, North Carolina, sued her employers for racial harassment and the denial of a promotion. At issue was whether Patterson was entitled to unlimited monetary damages since the discrimination she complained of had occurred after, not before, she was actually hired.

Brennan said yes, that Patterson's claim to damages was valid. He prepared a majority opinion, but subsequently found himself in dissent. Bitter over the defeat he was about to suffer on what he regarded as a crucial civil rights issue, he prepared an angry opinion which charged, "The court's fine phrases about our commitment to the eradication of racial discrimination...seem to count for little in practice."

Incensed, Justice Anthony Kennedy prepared his own opinion that included a footnote rebuking Brennan, who, he wrote, "thinks it judicious to bolster his position by questioning the court's understanding of the necessity to eradicate racial discrimination." He concluded, "The commitment to equality, fairness, and compassion is not a treasured monopoly of our colleagues in dissent."

Ultimately, both Brennan's attack and Kennedy's rebuke were dropped from the final versions of their opinions.

The files show that Marshall found himself at odds with Justice Lewis Powell during the 1985–1986 term over a capital punishment case, *Vasquez v. Hillery*. Vasquez, who was black, was sentenced to death in 1962. He challenged his conviction on grounds that blacks had been systematically excluded from the grand jury that indicted him. Since Vasquez did not raise this particular issue in federal court until 1978, Powell wrote to Marshall on November 7, 1985, expressing concern over the timeliness of Vasquez's appeal. He asserted, "It could well be that the court's opinion in this case will encourage convicted persons with long sentences to defer seeking relief until retrial becomes difficult or impossible."

Marshall wrote back, "[I]t is hard for me to believe that any prisoner would voluntarily sit in jail for years, knowing he has a meritorious claim that could result in his freedom." He ended up writing the majority opinion, which held that a conviction could be reversed at any time after it is demonstrated that an indicting grand jury was improperly constituted. Powell and two others dissented.

What these and hundreds of other examples demonstrate is that liberal and conservative justices tend to disagree, which comes as no surprise. But if the Court is, more or less, what it appears to be, why then the desire on the part of the justices for secrecy?

Any outsider who has ever tried to probe the Court's internal workings or gain access to the justices knows that the Court is like what used to be said of the Kremlin: It is a closed society, an enigma wrapped inside a mystery locked up in a riddle. Critics have contended that the Court's denial of access to its deliberations is wholly inappropriate within the context of a democratic society.

While he was a federal appeals court judge, Warren E. Burger once said, "A court which is final and unreviewable needs more careful scrutiny than any other. Unreviewable power is the most likely to self-indulge itself and the least likely to engage in dispassionate self-analysis. In a country like ours, no public institution, or the people who operate it, can be above public debate." Yet when he became chief justice, Burger instituted a Draconian regime of secrecy.

He was not alone. Even justices who have been the most ardent defenders of First Amendment freedoms and the public's right to know have been xenophobic in their defense of the Court's secrecy. Hugo Black, an absolutist about free speech and press, burned many of his papers before his death so that their contents could never be revealed.

Thurgood Marshall contemplated destroying his papers as well. On July 24, 1980, Mrs. Anna T. James, law librarian at Texas Southern University's Thurgood Marshall School of Law, wrote to the justice, requesting that he deposit at least some of his papers at her institution. "The name of our law school implies that a collection of documents about your career is housed at our institution," she wrote. "To that end, we have begun to acquire materials which focus on three stages of your career: civil rights attorney, solicitor general, and jurist. To enhance this project, we would like to discuss the possibility of you donating a portion of your judicial papers and personal memorabilia to our library."

Marshall rejected her request out of hand. In a tersely worded reply dated July 31, 1980, he wrote, "I have your letter concerning the possibility of my placing a collection of documents about myself in your institution. I have very little to contribute because upon my death all of my personal records will be destroyed."

Obviously he changed his mind, which should have come as no surprise to anyone who knew him. As former National Security Adviser McGeorge Bundy wrote in a column for the *Washington Post*, "Are we not allowed to suspect that part of him really wanted his papers to be fully and promptly used? I myself suspect that he would have read [about this controversy] with some pleasure. He was never a stuffy man."

As to what the documents reveal about the Court as an institution and the individual justices as people, Charles Rodell's observation in his remarkable book *Nine Men: A Political History of the Supreme Court From 1790 to 1955*, is apt. "Supreme Court Justices," he wrote, "off the bench as well as on it—are deemed by the myth to be, properly, apolitical persons, unaffected by what goes on in the nation outside their marble temple, aloof and remote from the workaday world. Myths or no myths, solemn show or no solemn show, the Supreme Court is nothing other than nine sometimes wise, sometimes unwise, but always human, men." And, of course, these days, women. Thurgood Marshall was one of the wisest, and most human, of those who ever served there.

Index of Principal Cases Cited

U.S. SUPREME COURT DECISIONS

Ake v. Oklahoma, 470 U.S. 68 (1985)

Alexander v. Holmes County, Misssissippi, 396 U.S. 1218 (1969); 396 U.S. 19 (1969)

Beal v. Doe, 4321 U.S. 438 (1977)

Bolling v. Sharpe, 347 U.S. 497 (1954)

Brown v. Board of Education, 345 U.S. 972 (1953)

Brown v. Board of Education, 347 U.S. 483 (1954)

Brown v. Board of Education, 349 U.S. 294 (1955)

Chambers v. Florida, 309 U.S. 227 (1940)

Cooper v. Aaron, 358 U.S. 1 (1958)

Craig v. Boren, 429 U.S. 190 (1976)

Dandridge v. Williams, 397 U.S. 471 (1970)

Dred Scott v. Sandford, 60 U.S. (393)

Ford v. Wainwright, 477 U.S. 399 (1986)

Fullilove v. Klutznick, 488 U.S. 448 (1980)

Furman v. Georgia, 408 U.S. 238 (1972)

Gong Lum v. Rice, 275 U.S. 78 (1927)

Gregg v. Georgia, 428 U.S. 153 (1976)

H. L. v. Matheson, 450 U.S. 398 (1981)

Harris v. McRae, 448 U.S. 24 (1980)

Hodgson v. Minnesota, 110 S. Ct. 2926 (1990)

Hurd v. Hodge, 334 U.S. 24 (1948)

James v. Valtierra, 402 U.S. 137 (1971)

Johnson v. Committee of Admissions, 407 U.S. 915 (1972)

Kadrmas v. Dickinson public Schools, 487 U.S. 450 (1988)

Loving v. Vriginia, 388 U.S. 1 (1967)

McLaurin v. Oklahoma State Regents, 399 U.S. 637 (1950)

Milliken v. Bradley, 428 U.S. 717 (1974)

Mississippi University for Women v. Hogan, 458 U.S. 718 (1982)

Missouri ex rel. Gaines v. Canada, 337 (1938)

SECOND CIRCUIT APPEALS COURT DECISIONS

MISCELLANEOUS

Select Bibliography

BOOKS

Allen, Ivan, Jr., with Paul Hemphill. *Mayor: Notes on the Sixties.* New York: Simon and Schuster, 1971.

Ambrose, Stephen E. *Eisenhower: Soldier and President.* New York: Touchstone, 1990.

Ansbro, John J. *Martin Luther King, Jr.: The Making of a Mind.* Maryknoll, N.Y.:. Orbis Books, 1982.

Ashmore, Harry S. *Hearts and Minds: The Anatomy of Racism from Roosevelt to Reagan.* New York: McGraw-Hill, 1982.

———. *The Negro and the Schools.* Chapel Hill, N.C.: 1954.

Ball, Howard, and Cooper, Phillip J. *Of Power and Right: Hugo Black, William O. Douglas, and America's Constitutional Revolution.* (New York: Oxford University Press 1992.)

Birmingham, Stephen. *Certain People: America's Black Elite.* Boston: Little Brown, 1977.

Bland, Randall. *Private Pressure on Public Law: The Legal Career of Justice Thurgood Marshall.* Kennikat Press, 1973.

Blasi, Vincent, ed. *The Burger Court: The Counter-Revolution That Wasn't.* New Haven: Yale University Press, 1983.

Blaustein, Albert P., and Ferguson, Clarence C. *Desegregation and the Law: The Meaning and Effect of the School Desegregation Cases.* Littleton, Colo.: Rothman, 1985.

Califano, Joseph A., Jr. *The Triumph and Tragedy of Lyndon Johnson: The White House Years.* New York: Simon & Schuster, 1992.

Carmichael, Stokely, and Hamilton, Charles V. *Black Power: The Politics of Liberation in America.* New York: Vintage, 1967.

Carson, Clayborne. *In Struggle: SNCC and the Black Awakening of the 1960s.* Cambridge, Mass.: Harvard University Press, 1981.

Crouch, Stanley. *Notes of a Hanging Judge: Essays and Reviews, 1979–1989.* New York: Oxford University Press, 1990.

Davis, John P., ed. *The American Negro Reference Book.* Englewood Cliffs, N.J.: Prentice Hall, 1966.

Douglas, William O. *The Court Years, 1939–1975: The Autobiography of William O. Douglas*. New York: Random House, 1980.

———. *Points of Rebellion*. New York: Vintage, 1970.

Fitzpatrick, Sandra, and Goodwin, Maria R. *The Guide to Black Washington: Places and Events of Historical and Cultural Significance in the Nation's Capital*. New York: Hippocrene, 1990.

Franklin, John Hope. *From Slavery to Freedom, a History of American Negroes*, 4th ed. New York: Knopf, 1974.

Friedman, Leon, ed. *The Justices of the United States Supreme Court: Their Lives and Major Opinions*. New York: Chelsea House, 1978.

Friedman, Leon, ed. *Argument: The Oral Argument Before the Supreme Court in Brown v. Board of Education of Topeka, 1952–1955*. New York: Chelsea House, 1983.

Goodwin, Doris Kearns. *Lyndon Johnson and the American Dream*. New York: St. Martin's, 1976.

Harbaugh, William H. *Lawyer's Lawyer: The Life of John W. Davis*. New York: Oxford, 1973.

Isaacson, Walter, and Thomas, Evan. *The Wise Men: Six Friends and the World They Made*. New York: Simon & Schuster, 1986.

Kirby, John B. *Black Americans in the Roosevelt Era*. Knoxville, Tenn.: University of Tennessee Press, 1980.

Kluger, Richard. *Simple Justice*. New York: Vintage, 1977.

McCarthy, Abigail. *Private Faces/Public Places*. San Leandro, Calif.: Curtis, 1972.

McNeil, Genna Rae. *Groundwork: Charles Hamilton Houston and the Struggles for Civil Rights*. Philadelphia: University of Pennsylvania Press, 1983.

Myrdal, Gunnar. *An American Dilemma: The Negro Problem and Modern American Democracy*. New York: Pantheon, 1944.

Rampersad, Arnold. *The Life of Langston Hughes, Volume 1: 1902–1941 I. Too Sing America*. New York: Oxford University Press, 1986.

Rosenblatt, Roger. *Life Itself: Abortion in the American Mind*. New York: Random House, 1992.

Savage, David G. *Turning Right: The Making of the Rehnquist Supreme Court*. New York: Wiley, 1992.

Schlesinger, Arthur M., Jr. *A Thousand Days: John F. Kennedy in the White House*. New York: Fawcett, 1965.

Schlesinger, Arthur M., Jr. *Robert Kennedy and His Times*. New York: Ballantine, 1978.

Schwartz, Bernard, with Lesher, Steven. *Inside the Warren Court*. New York: Doubleday, 1983.

Schwartz, Herman, ed. *The Burger Years: Rights and Wrongs in the Supreme Court, 1969–1986*. New York: Penquin, 1987.

Sherrill, Herman. *Gothic Politics of the Deep South: Stars of the New Confederacy*. New York: Grossman, 1968.

Thomas, William R. *The Burger Court and Civil Liberties*. Brunswick, Ohio: King's Court, 1976.

Williams, Juan. *Eyes on the Prize: America's Civil Rights Years, 1954–1965*. New York: Penguin, 1987.

Woodward, Bob, and Armstrong, Scott. *The Brethren*. New York: Avon, 1981.

COLLECTIONS

Archives of the Afro-American Newspapers, Coppin State University
Archives of the Atlanta University Center's Woodruff Library
Archives of the United States Supreme Court
Ralph J. Bunche, unpublished letters and memorandums.
John P. Davis, unpublished papers and memorandums.
Moorland-Spingarn Research Center, Howard University, Washington, D.C.
Schomberg Center for Black Culture, New York Public Library.
Lincoln University (Pa.) Library
The New York Historical Society
Library of Congress, Manuscript Division
The White Law Library, Catholic University of America.
Lincoln University (Pa.) Library
The National Archives
New York Historical Society
The Vivian Harsh Collection at the Carter G. Woodson Regional Center of the Chicago Public Library
The National Association for the Advancement of Colored People, Baltimore, Maryland.
The Southern Christian Leadership Conference, Atlanta, Ga.

Index

MICHAEL D. DAVIS, a graduate of Morehouse College, was one of the leaders of the Atlanta sit-ins in the 1960s. In 1964 Davis became the first black reporter on the *Atlanta Constitution*. In 1967 he served as a war correspondent in Vietnam, winning a NAACP award for his coverage of black troops in Southeast Asia. He was a reporter for the Baltimore Sun Papers, and worked as a metropolitan editor for WRC-TV NBC Television News in Washington. Davis is the author of *Black American Women in Olympic Track and Field*. He lives in Washington, D.C.

HUNTER R. CLARK, an assistant professor of law at Drake University Law School, is a graduate of Harvard College cum laude and Harvard Law School. He met Justice Thurgood Marshall in high school while serving as chief page for the United States Supreme Court. Marshall wrote Clark's recommendation for admission to Harvard Law School. From 1981 to 1986 Clark wrote weekly articles for *Time* on subjects ranging from civil rights law and politics to science, religion, and the arts. Clark is the author of *The Camp David Agreements*. He lives in Des Moines, Iowa.